ACPL ITEM
DISCARD

D1553859

African Cherokees in Indian Ter

JUL 2 7 2009

**The John Hope
Franklin Series in
African American
History and Culture**

◆

*Waldo E. Martin
and Patricia Sullivan,
editors*

JUL 3 7 2003

African
Cherokees
in Indian
Territory

From
Chattel to
Citizens

CELIA E.
NAYLOR

The University of
North Carolina Press
Chapel Hill

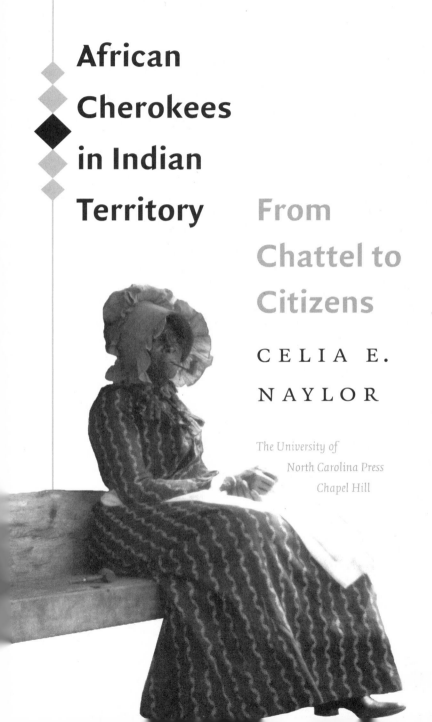

© 2008 The University of North Carolina Press
All rights reserved
Designed by Kimberly Bryant
Set in Quadraat and Quadraat Sans
by Keystone Typesetting, Inc.
Manufactured in the United States of America

The paper in this book meets the guidelines for permanence
and durability of the Committee on Production Guidelines for
Book Longevity of the Council on Library Resources.

The University of North Carolina Press has been a member
of the Green Press Initiative since 2003.

Library of Congress Cataloging-in-Publication Data
Naylor, Celia E.
    African Cherokees in Indian territory : from chattel to citizens / Celia E. Naylor.
    p. cm. — (The John Hope Franklin series in African American history and
culture)
    Includes bibliographical references and index.
ISBN 978-0-8078-3203-5 (cloth: alk. paper)
ISBN 978-0-8078-5883-7 (pbk.: alk paper)
    1. Cherokee Indians—History—19th century. 2. Cherokee Indians—Mixed
descent. 3. Cherokee Indians—Kinship. 4. Indian slaves—Oklahoma—History—
19th century. 5. African Americans—Oklahoma. 6. African Americans—
Oklahoma—Kinship. 7. Blacks—Oklahoma—Relations with Indians. I. Title.
E99.C5N39   2008   975.004'97557—dc22   2007048563

A portion of this work appeared earlier, in somewhat different form,
as " 'Born and Raised among These People, I Don't Want to Know Any
Other': Slaves' Acculturation in Nineteenth-Century Indian Territory,"
in Confounding the Color Line: The Indian-Black Experience in North America, ed.
James F. Brooks (Lincoln: University of Nebraska Press, 2002), and is
reprinted here with permission of the publisher.

cloth   12 11 10 09 08   5 4 3 2 1
paper   12 11 10 09 08   5 4 3 2 1

To my parents,
Cecil and Fay Naylor,
and my daughter,
Ayanbi

Contents

A section of illustrations and maps
follows page 110.

Acknowledgments

After worrying late one night about hurt feelings due to forgotten names, I dreamed that I simply included one line of acknowledgments —"Thanks to all who supported me and made this book possible." Although such a brief note to family and friends would have been efficient in a number of ways, I ultimately would not have been able to sleep (or dream) at night after the book appeared in print. And, so, I offer the thanks that follow as a very small token of my appreciation to all who have supported and encouraged me over the years.

So many have served as midwives to this book; so many have unselfishly offered their time and support as I made this journey. This journey would have been impossible without the stories of formerly enslaved people of color; it was their stories that captured me in the very beginning—their stories that demanded that I write this book. It is to those formerly enslaved and freedpeople, the most indispensable midwives of this book, that I owe the greatest debt; I only hope that in some small way I have been able to tell their stories—in a manner that they would have felt honored their lives.

Without the truly unconditional support and love of my parents, Cecil and Fay Naylor; my brother, Stuart; and my sister, Kathryn, this book simply would not have become a reality. There must have been many moments when the members of my family wondered why this book was taking so long; however, they never made me privy to such thoughts. Instead, as they have done so many times in the past, they offered words of encouragement over and over and over again. The love and spirit of my daughter, Ayanbi, enabled me not only to concentrate on the book but also to play when absolutely necessary; she, like no one else, demanded some degree of balance in our lives!

My research trips to Oklahoma—especially to Tahlequah, Oklahoma City, and Norman—always reinvigorated me and served as poignant reminders of the reasons why I needed to finish this book. With the guidance, generosity, and expertise of the staff members in the Archives and Manuscripts Division at the Oklahoma Historical Society, I made fruitful trips to Oklahoma City. I would like to thank especially a few past and current staff members at the society including Phyllis Adams, Joe Todd, Chester Cowen, Terry Zinn, and Delbart Amen. Thanks to the staff members at the Western History Collections at the University of Oklahoma in Norman, in particular John Lovett and Kristina Southwell, as well as a number of student staff members whose positive attitude made the long days in front of almost unreadable documents much shorter. Thanks to Tom Mooney, Cherokee National Society librarian at the Cherokee Heritage Center in Park Hill, and Delores Sumner, special collections librarian at Northeastern State University in Tahlequah, for taking time away from their busy schedules to offer help and assistance. Although my visit to the Gilcrease Museum in Tulsa was a brief one, I would like to thank the Gilcrease staff for being so helpful, especially Sarah Erwin.

I extend special thanks to the late Mrs. Bernice Riggs, Kathy Carter-White, Yvonne Davis, and Charles Gourd for speaking with me during visits to Tahlequah. In particular, I would like to thank Marilyn Vann and David Cornsilk for providing inspiration due to their commitment to the integrity of Cherokee laws for all Cherokee citizens in the present and future.

I owe a great deal to mentors who guided me early on—Cornell University professors Henry Louis Gates Jr., Carolyn "Biddy" Martin, and Mary Beth Norton, as well as Duke University professors Jan Ewald, David Barry Gaspar, Karla F. C. Holloway, Sydney Nathans, and Peter H. Wood. I have been honored and truly fortunate to have Peter H. Wood in my life; he has been an exceptional mentor and a source of constant support.

While working on this project, I have lived in several cities, and in every place I have developed incredible relationships with wonderful people. My thanks to the friends I met in Ames, Iowa, especially Liz Beck, Mary Ann Evans, Keecha Harris, Modupe Labode, Ed Lewis, Pat Miller, Mary Tandia, and Carlie and Gary Tartakov, who always offered words of encouragement over the years. For the friendships that began in Albuquerque, New Mexico, I would like to extend a special thank you to Yvonne Gillam, Roxanne Johnson, Asata Ratliff, and Kim Stanley. Women's Centers have been an important part of my life. I would still be working on this project had it not been for the support of staff members at the Margaret Sloss Women's Center in Ames, Iowa; the Duke University Women's Center; the Duke University Women's Resource Center; and the University of New Mexico Women's Resource Center. Thanks to my "old" friends who continue to honor me with their friendship, especially Astrid B. Gloade, Joseph Clark, Mariah Wilkins, Faith L. Smith, and Rodney Clare.

A number of colleagues in the field of Black Indian Studies have encouraged me along the way, especially Tiya A. Miles, Barbara Krauthamer, Claudio Saunt, and Circe Sturm. My colleagues at Dartmouth College in the History Department, African and African-American Studies Program, and Women's and Gender Studies Program have been instrumental in the "final push" for this book. Thanks to Colin Calloway for reviewing an earlier version of the book, as well as graciously sharing his expertise on Indian history. I must thank a few colleague-friends in particular for the depth of their support—Judith Byfield, Joseph Cullon, Deborah K. King, Annelise Orleck, Tanalís Padilla, and Craig S. Wilder. Special thanks go to Annelise Orleck for willingly reading and providing vital feedback on this book in the final stages.

Some of my research trips to Oklahoma would not have been possible without the support generously provided by the Walter and Constance Burke Research Awards for junior faculty at Dartmouth College. In addition, being awarded Dartmouth College's Arthur M. Wilson and Mary Tolford Wilson Faculty Research Fellowship and participating in the Nelson A. Rockefeller Research Scholars Program proved crucial to the completion of this book.

Special friends in the Dartmouth and Upper Valley community who must be commended include Savitri Beharry, Karen Fisher-Vanden, and Leah Prescott. To David N. M. Mbora, thank you for sharing your intellect, sense of humor, and life lessons, especially regarding "baboon politics." In addition to all the people at Dartmouth College who helped in numerous ways, one "body" that I must acknowledge is Occom Pond and the spirit of its namesake (and one of Dartmouth College's founders), Mohegan preacher Samson Occom; my walks—solo and with friends—around this pond on the Dartmouth campus worked wonders during difficult moments of this journey.

The drama that is publishing would have been painful had it not been for the unwavering support of my editor, Chuck Grench, assistant editor Katy V. O'Brien, Ron Maner, Brian MacDonald, and all the other staff members who worked diligently "behind the scenes" at the University of North Carolina Press. Though thanking one publishing house is usually appropriate, I would be remiss if I did not thank Alison Kalett at Cornell University Press for her advice and encouragement as I prepared this book for publication. Due to her support, there were many times when I wished I could have published one book with two presses.

No doubt when I read these words in print, I will wonder how I could possibly have forgotten so many significant names. To all whose names should have appeared here, please accept my thanks and apologies.

African Cherokees in Indian Territory

Introduction

It was a slow and steady movement of people, animals, and an array of property. Not a journey across the Atlantic Ocean, the route of this middle passage was outlined in the snow by a trail of blood and bodies. The Trail of Tears, *nv no hi du na tlo yi lv*, signifies the intense suffering experienced by those young and old who traveled in snow and mud, hungry and cold, without ample supplies of food or clothing. The journey by foot, and in some cases by steamboat, proved to be laborious; for a significant number of Cherokees who were forced to relocate during the dreadful winter of 1838–39, this would be their final trip. As a result of the horrendous conditions experienced by members of the Cherokee Nation forcibly removed from their homes in the late 1830s, one-third (4,000) of the 12,000 Cherokees who participated died. Some succumbed to death en route to Indian Territory (current-day northeastern Oklahoma); many died in the temporary encampments, which served essentially as nineteenth-century internment camps. Other southeastern Indians—the Creeks, Choctaws, and Chickasaws—also endured the horrors of this relocation process.

Yet those who traversed this passage were not solely of Indian descent. Accompanying Indians on this journey to a new home were also African-descended individuals, the majority enslaved by members of these Indian nations. Indeed, enslaved people represented a significant part of the inventory of property owned by these southeastern Indians. Even as scholars continue their efforts to assess the conditions and to enumerate the Indians who lost their lives in this mass relocation, it is unknown how many enslaved African-descended people perished along the trail. Their journey and the memories of those who survived or died during this passage remain a veiled and largely untold story. This exodus from the southeastern states to lands further west would have dire consequences for subsequent generations, creating various cultural, socioeconomic, and political realities for those, red and black, who survived the crossing.

Although attempts at estimating the actual number of enslaved blacks who participated in this middle passage may be fruitless, the presence and legacy of these enslaved individuals and families who survived this journey expose a very different perspective on the lived experiences of African-descended people in the nineteenth century. Copious accounts of the Trail of Tears have been fashioned by a range of scholars, some crossing the boundaries of historical commentaries and literary tales. Yet these narratives have offered truncated versions of the complete story, due to the ignored and silenced voices of those enslaved blacks who walked alongside and even carried Indians along the trail. If told in its entirety, the story of the Trail of Tears would recount how southeastern slaveholding Indians were among those relocated—Indians who demanded recognition of their rights as slave owners and transported enslaved blacks with them to the West. Many clearly comprehended the possible benefits of having slaves within their reach during the journey and beyond.

Accounts of the journey of enslaved blacks of Indians along the Trail of Tears strike an unfamiliar and unexpected chord. The story of enslaved people of African descent in the United States appears to be a very familiar story of enslavement, forced migration, and eventual emancipation. Most of the images of enslaved African Americans portray them as toiling on southern farms and plantations for European American enslavers. Yet the story is far more complicated, especially if we consider the lives of African-descended people who were enslaved not by European Americans but by Indians, and enslaved not in the southeastern states of Georgia, Virginia, and the Carolinas, but much further west in a place called Indian Territory.

The story of these people of African descent held in slavery by Indians begins in the familiar manner of enslavement and also ends ultimately with emancipation; nevertheless, accounts of enslaved blacks living within the confines of Indian Territory transform the contours of slavery on a very fundamental level by drawing attention to groups other than European Americans who enslaved people of African descent. They include small numbers of African Americans who enslaved other African Americans in the United States. Although they sometimes justified their actions as providing an avenue for liberating kin, this remains a troubling topic in African American and United States history and complicates our notions of what slavery was and who benefited from it.[1] Similarly, questions about the very nature of slavery emerge when examining bondage in Indian Territory. What transpired between Indian owners and enslaved blacks? Do the issues of enslavement, hegemony, and oppression still remain intrinsic to the whole notion of slavery if we interject Indian enslavers actively buying, selling, and enslaving blacks? The usual "white over black" construction of power and enslavement is one dilemma. The startling "black over black" question strikes many historians and lay readers as problematic. But the notion of "red over black" has, until very recently, seemed almost unimaginable. For that reason, the fabric of these enslaved people's lives in this seemingly implausible reality has remained behind the veil, awaiting a more meticulous and critical investigation.

This book lifts the veil by allowing readers to enter into the world of enslaved and free African-descended people in the nineteenth-century Cherokee Nation, Indian Territory.[2] This lost world is illuminated largely through interviews of former enslaved blacks and their children in Oklahoma, conducted in the 1930s (during the Depression) by the Works Progress Administration (WPA). These narratives allow us to see this history through the eyes of African-descended people who were enslaved by Indians in the Southeast and who were "removed" west with them, as well as those who were born and enslaved in Indian Territory within these exiled nations; their tales of bondage and freedom serve as the cornerstone for the story that follows.

In order to evaluate the changing nature of the experiences of enslaved and free blacks in the Cherokee Nation over time, I examine the period between the resettlement of Cherokee people in Indian Territory in the 1830s and the admission of the state of Oklahoma into the Union in 1907. The birth of the state of Oklahoma sounded the death knell for Indian Territory. Within that framework, this book traces the development of particular sociocultural and political dimensions of the lives of enslaved and freed African-descended people in the nineteenth-century Cherokee Nation—on a trajectory determined by the intricacies of bondage, resistance, and belonging.

Over the course of the nineteenth century, shifting notions of bondage and the multifaceted process of belonging shaped the layered paradoxes of black and Indian identities. In this book, I explore how these intersecting paradoxes emerge in the lives of enslaved African-descended people in a place called Indian Territory. Some of these enslaved people had great-grandparents, grandparents, and even parents who spoke of home far away in a continent called Africa—who remembered words in African languages like Ewe, Twi, Yoruba, Igbo, Hausa, Mende, Bambara, Soninke, Wolof, Umbundu, and Kikongo. Although their parents or grandparents might have recalled an African home far away, the central ideas of home for these enslaved African-descended individuals, having been born in the Americas, were primarily grounded in Indian-dominated spaces and nations. This book delves into the lives of African-descended people who became enslaved by Indians—Cherokee Indians. It is a difficult and often painful story that speaks of the horror of bondage, shatters ideas about "kind" Indian masters, ruptures conceptions of a monolithic enslaved black community, and challenges preconceived, popular beliefs of "black Indians" with mythical Indian kin. It is not a romanticized tale of black refuge in Indian country. The accounts of enslaved blacks being whipped, running away, and even murdering Indian owners disrupt any delusion of such a legend. What follows is an attempt to expose the nuances of identity, the contradictions of belonging, and the complexities of bondage for people of African descent in Indian country.

As enslaved people living in Indian Territory—not the United States—they cannot be defined as African Americans; they were neither enslaved within the United States nor owned by citizens of the United States. Once these people of African descent became enslaved in Indian Territory, they became denizens of Indian nations—outside the national boundaries of the United States. Beyond geography and national borders, some enslaved people of African descent—whom I describe as African Indian—developed sociocultural connections to Indian people, communities, and nations. When using this term "African Indian," I do not automatically imply biraciality or multiraciality; however, some African Indians in Indian Territory certainly were of African and Indian descent. When referring to such individuals in particular, I specifically state "biracial African Indians" or "biracial African Cherokees." Unlike enslaved African Americans owned by European Americans in the United States, enslaved African Cherokees in Indian Territory encountered a different world of bondage. This world shaped the contours of their day-to-day experiences, as well as their overall conceptions of themselves as individuals, members of their families, and integral parts of Cherokee communities.

The heart of this book focuses on the lives of enslaved and freed African Cherokees who were born and raised in the Cherokee Nation and who developed intimate relationships with Cherokees—on the basis of not only bondage but also sociocultural ties and a sense of belonging. Sociocultural identifiers of their Indianness represented crucial factors in their self- and group identification as members of the Five Tribes. Those with multigenerational associations with the Five Tribes, cemented in the old country east of the Mississippi before the Trail of Tears, shared life experiences grounded in Indian cultures and traditions. After arrival in Indian Territory, enslaved African Cherokees embarked on a new beginning in a new land, but within familiar Cherokee communities and structures.

Indian Territory, however, became the pathway of indoctrination to Indian people and mores for newly purchased enslaved people who had been owned previously by European Americans in the southeastern states. Indian Territory served as a site of a cultural and nationalistic transition for those who had never experienced living in Indian communities. No longer would the mores and rules of European American enslavers dictate the lives of these enslaved people of African descent. Instead, new Cherokee enslavers and their laws would now control their bodies and their progeny's future.

Whether newly enslaved by Cherokees or continuing an intergenerational legacy of bondage to Indian people, enslaved African Cherokees in the Cherokee Nation constructed several layers of connections and disconnections between themselves and Cherokees in nineteenth-century Indian Territory. Some enslaved African Indians perceived their cultural connections with the Five Tribes as immutable ties that bound them to Indian people, communities, and nations. Such cultural links to the Five Tribes illustrated their sense of belonging to and within Indian nations; "blood" and familial relationships with Indians reinforced and accentuated cultural ties to Indian communities. Due to the specific circumstances of their bondage—complicated by conceptions and realities of belonging and "blood" relations—those enslaved within the Five Tribes crafted a distinctive African Indian cultural milieu in antebellum Indian Territory.

The lives of the Cherokees and other southeastern Indian people who were relocated to Indian Territory also reflect the distinctive nature of these Indian communities. Though not the primary focus of this book, the shifting and paradoxical position of Cherokees (and other southeastern Indian nations generally) in relation to people of African descent suggests that European American belief systems permeated southeastern Indians' conceptions of themselves—as Indians, as "civilized Indians," as slave owners, and as people who often defined themselves as superior to those of African descent. During the eighteenth and nineteenth centuries, the national policies of the United States and the presence of European and European American men who had married Indian women also altered the sociocultural fabric of these communities. Unions between Indian women and European men created biracial European Indians like Principal Chief John Ross, a Cherokee who had three generations of Scottish men in his lineage, including his father Daniel Ross. Moreover, in the eighteenth and nineteenth centuries, a number of European and European American slave-owning men not only married Indian women but also became citizens of Indian nations—referred to as "intermarried whites" in the Five Tribes. Though they were only a minority of the population in Indian Territory, their views about people of African descent, often reflecting racialist southern sensibilities, impacted the slave-master interactions in Indian Territory.

Even as members of Indian nations—including Indians, enslaved African Indians, and intermarried whites—attempted to reestablish their lives after removal in a new land west of the Mississippi, the tribulations of the United States continued to shape their destinies. As the Civil War approached, the federal government of the United States and the Confederacy pulled the Five Tribes into the war. Due to the actions of the United States and the Confederate States of America, as well as sociocultural and historical connections to southerners, the Five Tribes created alliances with the Confederacy. These alliances would usher in a new era of change for the Five Tribes in the post-Reconstruction period, ending with the temporary dissolution of their sovereign nations and the creation of the segregated state of Oklahoma.

The ownership of human beings transcends both time and space. Although European and European American involvement in the transatlantic slave trade often dominates the standard narrative concerning the enslavement of Africans throughout the Americas, the participation of African societies was integral to the development of this slave trade from the fifteenth to the nineteenth century. However, to categorize the ownership of individuals as a fixed state and process is to misunderstand entirely the fluidity of slavery on the African continent and elsewhere.[3] Slavery within West African nations cannot be equated with bondage and servitude in European and European American colonies. In a similar vein, bondage within an array of Indian nations throughout North America did not simply duplicate impressions of ownership and property within European and European American worldviews.[4] Unlike plantation slavery in the Americas, bondage in African and indigenous Indian communities rarely involved hereditary enslavement; instead, captivity and debt primarily served as the rationale for conditions of servitude. Moreover, enslaved individuals often eventually became part of African and indigenous Indian communities by either marrying into these communities or being adopted into clans. Nonetheless, the concept of human beings as property, as belonging to another person or people, materialized within the social and political systems of some Indian societies long before the arrival of enslaved Africans in colonial North America.

Before contact with Europeans, the ownership of individuals existed within indigenous Cherokee society. The Cherokee term *a tsi na tla i* referred to an individual who had been captured during warfare. The word, *a tsi na tla i*, is the phonetic version of the Cherokee word for slave.[5] It was possible for such individuals to be adopted into one of the seven matrilineal Cherokee clans—the principal unit of social and political organization in indigenous Cherokee society. If a clan chose not to adopt a war captive, however, this person would remain outside the clans and thus without any formal or informal kinship connection. The Cherokees patently distinguished between those war captives who had been adopted within a clan and those without any clan affiliation. The Cherokees granted no rights to *di ge tsi na tla i*, who had no clan association.[6] Whereas the Cherokees conferred tribal membership to adopted captives, neither membership nor related liberties were extended to unadopted *di ge tsi na tla i*.[7] Due to the gendered division of labor among the Cherokees in which men hunted game and women cultivated crops, *di ge tsi na tla i* worked within the dictates of their specific gender roles. Such unfree individuals assisted their owners with tasks related to hunting and, to a limited extent, helped with some aspects of crop cultivation.[8] Although the labor of *di ge tsi na tla i* enhanced the productivity of aspects of indigenous Cherokee society, the Cherokees did not utilize *di ge tsi na tla i* to produce surpluses for sale in external markets. Rather, the Cherokees consumed the fruits of the labor of *di ge tsi na tla i* within familial and clan settings in indigenous Cherokee society. With the dearth of documentation concerning the position of the *a tsi na tla i* in indigenous Cherokee society, it is difficult to ascertain how and if the collective status of these unfree individuals changed prior to contact with Europeans; however, after such contact occurred, their "place" was irreversibly altered.

By the late seventeenth century, the "value" of Indian war captives in North America, including the *di ge tsi na tla i*, and the role of Indian warfare had been revolutionized due to complicated interactions, alliances as well as enmities, between Europeans and Indians. As a result of such developing relationships, by the last quarter of the seventeenth century, the capture and enslavement of Indians had "infected" the South. Indeed, in the vital port of Charles Town more Indians were exported than Africans were imported between 1670 and 1715.[9] The Indian slave trade expanded beyond the southern American colonies; enslaved Indians were sold to northern American colonies as well as to planters throughout the Caribbean. This transformation occurred throughout North America as Indian nations developed extensive relationships with private traders from Spain, France, and England. These interactions generated trading networks that integrated members of the southeastern nations, including the Cherokees. During the first half of the eighteenth century, the Cherokees and other Indian nations purchased a range of manufactured items from European and European American traders, especially those from Virginia and the Carolinas. Weaponry, guns, and knives, in particular, constituted the most attractive commodities.[10] Although the Cherokees and other southeastern Indian nations did not initially designate war captives as primary objects of exchange, these individuals became crucial currency in the thriving intercolonial Indian slave trade before the advent of the American Revolution.

The standard chronicle outlining the formation of North American colonies accentuates the desire for cheap labor—a desire that remained unsatiated with the importation of European indentured servants and convict laborers. In the late seventeenth century, the increasing European and European American fervor for cheap laborers to cultivate land in combination with Indian demand for European manufactured goods fueled the Indian slave trade. Indian involvement in the Indian slave trade, however, transpired not entirely as a result of Indian dependence on European goods. A range of sociocultural and geopolitical forces shaped Indian participation in the Indian slave trade.[11] As a result, an interdependent and intricate rapprochement existed between Indians, Europeans, and European Americans in the American colonies in the late seventeenth and early eighteenth centuries. Concurrently, the escalated value of enslaved Indians in southern colonies, particularly in South Carolina, exacerbated tensions between Indian nations. Warfare ultimately became a tangible avenue for supplying ample Indian captive-slaves in exchange for prized European goods. These circumstances were not exceptional; a similar dynamic occurred between several West African nations as a result of the transatlantic slave trade. The Indian slave trade in the American colonies served to some extent as a preface to the transatlantic slave trade, providing the transition from European and European American enslavement and exploitation of indigenous Indians to Africans. The early coexistence of both slave trades in the southeastern American colonies provided opportunities not only for European contact with Indians and Africans but also for a range of interactions between Indians and Africans.

Scholars can only speculate on how members of the southeastern Indian nations responded to initial contacts with Africans.[12] Some argue that the Cherokees did not initially distinguish between "races."[13] Yet, even if the Cherokees had no concrete conception of "race," it is difficult to believe that when they originally encountered Europeans and Africans, they did not recognize the difference in skin color between these two groups. Furthermore, just because the Cherokees may not have categorized this difference in skin color in racially grounded terms does not eliminate the possibility that they distinguished between Africans and Europeans based on the variation in skin coloration, facial features, hair texture, accents, and languages. Some Cherokees may even have expressed an early qualitative response to the differences between these groups and articulated what they might have considered appealing or repugnant. Regardless of indigenous Cherokee predilections, by the early eighteenth century the Cherokees and other Indian nations became cognizant of European racialist ideologies that categorized Africans as culturally inferior and well suited as manual laborers.

Although di ge tsi na tla i in indigenous Cherokee society certainly did not occupy a position equivalent to enslaved Africans and African Americans in the American colonies, particular dimensions of those defined as di ge tsi na tla i mirror elements of the system of enslavement

3 1833 05560 4661

of Africans and African Americans in the United States. The fact that Cherokee owners did not exploit *di ge tsi na tla i* in order to produce wealth for themselves or for Cherokee society in general does not alleviate the state of bondage of the *di ge tsi na tla i*. Enslavement cannot be defined only in relation to economic productivity linked to the procurement of wealth for slave owners. Just as European American enslavers refused to grant enslaved African Americans rights or privileges as citizens of the United States, so too did Cherokees forbid the *di ge tsi na tla i* from engaging and participating in various aspects of Cherokee society, particularly the political realm of Cherokee life. Although seen as human, *di ge tsi na tla i* were not perceived or treated as "equal" to clan members of the Cherokee Nation. The limited humanity granted to *di ge tsi na tla i* within the Cherokee Nation echoes the partial humanity granted to enslaved Africans and African Americans throughout the Americas. Early on, the founders of the United States appropriated the three-fifths percentage directive in the Constitution as one way of codifying this incomplete humanity. Although the Cherokees established no such percentage of humanity for the *di ge tsi na tla i*, in some ways no specified figure was necessary. The *di ge tsi na tla i* would have been wholly aware of their inferior and outsider position in Cherokee society. The sociocultural and political position of *di ge tsi na tla i*, outside the limits of Cherokee society, would have certainly paralleled the devalued state of enslaved Africans and African Americans in the slaveholding United States.

Because different conceptions of ownership existed within indigenous Cherokee society and the United States, the Cherokees did not simply emulate a European American version of slavery, even after decades of contact with Europeans and European Americans. Rather, the position of the *di ge tsi na tla i* may have been transformed to provide the context and foundation for the incorporation of enslaved blacks and the creation of *di ge tsi na tla i* of African descent. By the late seventeenth century, European tenets about the ownership of human beings certainly permeated the understanding of bondage in Cherokee society. Nonetheless, the Cherokees might have employed their own indigenous ideas of ownership, embodied in the *di ge tsi na tla i*, to position enslaved people of African descent within, while simultaneously outside of, the margins of their society. Rather than being provided the possibility of adoption into the nation, such individuals and their progeny could have been deemed perpetually clanless— without any kinship links whatsoever to the Cherokee Nation. As a result, enslaved blacks over time could have fulfilled the role of the di ge tsi na tla i in Cherokee society. Moreover, denying such enslaved people sociopolitical rights and equivalent humanity could be perceived not as an abrogation of Cherokee ways but as an extension of the traditional position of the di ge tsi na tla i in the Cherokee Nation. Scholars have yet to explore how the dynamic social construction of race and ideas regarding Africanness, and even "blackness," within European American and Cherokee societies affected the evolution of bondage and human property in the Cherokee Nation. Moreover, it is possible that enslaved African Cherokees capitalized on indigenous Cherokee ideas of ownership to reconfigure bondage in the Cherokee Nation in the wake of removal to Indian Territory.

Evolving Cherokee notions of blood, belonging, and blackness emerged well before removal to Indian Territory. Matrilineality had served as the cornerstone and principal channel for the perpetuation of legitimate clan members of indigenous Cherokee society. Indeed, "for much of Cherokee history, being Cherokee meant being born of a Cherokee woman."[14] Historically, Cherokee women served as the symbolic and literal creators of Cherokee life. Traditional conceptions about the life-giving blood of Cherokee women and clan-based bloodlines reflected core elements of Cherokee cosmology.[15]

Beginning in the colonial era, the role of Cherokee women as the sole creators of Cherokee life changed partially due to increasing interracial unions, particularly between Cherokee women and European men. Though some of these European men sought formal adoption within a Cherokee clan, others remained outside the limits of the Cherokee clan system and became "husbands of clan members."[16] With the integration of growing numbers of European and European American spouses of Cherokee women, in 1819 a new Cherokee statute protected Cherokee women's rights as property owners in Cherokee society and limited access of European and European American spouses to the property of their Cherokee wives.

Even as the Cherokee Nation reinforced Cherokee women's role and rights as property owners, the Nation began redefining the contours of Cherokee membership. In 1825 a new Cherokee law conferred citizenship to the children of Cherokee men and their European and European American wives.[17] Due to evolving race-based ideas about people of African descent in the Cherokee Nation, this law excluded children of Cherokee men and free women of African descent from being recognized as legitimate members of the Cherokee citizenry. In addition, due to the limitations of their status, enslaved women of African descent could not produce free Cherokee citizens, even if these children had been fathered by free Cherokee men. The Cherokee Nation's New Echota Constitution of 1827 delineated that the children of Cherokee men and free women, except women of African descent, would be granted citizenship. Children of Cherokee women and "all free men" remained citizens;[18] however, the progeny of marital unions between Cherokee women and free men of African descent would be granted incomplete and restricted Cherokee citizenship (they could not, for example, serve in the Cherokee National Council).[19] Early nineteenth-century Cherokee statutes concerning the legislation of interracial unions began highlighting not only the integration of a new racialized hierarchy in the Cherokee Nation that linked blackness with inferiority but also a set of codified rules that eventually conflated blackness with bondage.

By the dawn of the nineteenth century, slavery within the "Five Civilized Tribes"—the Cherokee, Creek, Chickasaw, Choctaw, and Seminole nations—had become an integral aspect of life in these southeastern Indian nations. What began as the trading of enslaved Indians primarily due to warfare evolved in the eighteenth century into the ideologically nationalized enslavement of people of African descent. Not only were some Indians enslaving people of African descent, but as plantations became more profitable, European American planters also became more sensitive to the possibility of a united front composed of Indians, Africans, and African Americans. The reality and rumors concerning runaway slaves of African descent seeking refuge within southeastern Indian nations only intensified European apprehension about collusion between these populations. In order to assuage this trepidation, in the eighteenth century European and European American planters offered significant rewards to Cherokees, Choctaws, and other Indian slave catchers.[20] Increasing contact and interaction between European traders and settlers and Indians in the Five Tribes also cultivated a growing population of "mixed bloods"—people of European and Indian descent.

Interracial contact between Indians and Europeans not only produced "mixed bloods" but also shifted alliances and concomitant power dynamics, particularly due to treaties between southeastern Indian nations and the British before and during the American Revolution. With the colonists' victory in the American Revolution, the new republic established a plan to "civilize" Indian people and assimilate them within the sociocultural fabric of the United States. The devastation of Cherokee towns by American forces, as well as Cherokee cession of considerable land during the American Revolution in negotiations with the British and Americans, forced the Cherokees to concede partially to tenets of this civilization agenda. One of its major elements, heralded by President George Washington, centered on the Cherokees' adoption of private property in lieu of their communal property system, whereby no member of Cherokee society individually owned land in Cherokee territory. In addition, European American advocates of this "Indian civilization" program believed that the Cherokees' gendered division of labor would also have to be significantly altered, so that Cherokee women would relinquish their traditional roles as farmers and adopt European American women's roles centered on a range of domestic activities, including spinning and weaving. The new plan also transformed Cherokee men's roles from hunters to cultivators of the land—the traditional role of Cherokee women. The increasing assimilation of European American belief systems in Cherokee society, as well as in other southeastern Indian communities, included the profitable use of enslaved blacks. European Americans encouraged the utilization and exploitation of enslaved African labor by southeastern Indians as a way to develop and "civilize" Indian societies, as well as to bolster their integration in the southern slave economy.

Even as some members of the Five Tribes began to incorporate aspects of European American mores and worldviews in their socio-political framework in the late eighteenth century, the U.S. federal government contrived more elaborate and comprehensive plans to limit the Indian presence within the boundaries of the United States. With the uncompromising demands of European American settlers for land occupied by southeastern Indian nations, government leaders and officials decided to remove these nations to a region west of the Mississippi River. Most members of these nations were unwilling to move to what would become Indian Territory. Furthermore, they recognized that other Indians, specifically the Siouan-speaking groups like the Quapaws, Osages, and Otos, already occupied the land in the eastern part of Indian Territory. Other Indians who lived in the western portion of Indian Territory were the Wichitas, the Caddos, and a variety of Plains Indians.

The vehement objections of Indian nations to removal did not deter the United States from its goal of Indian relocation. Although the U.S. government's interest in the removal of southeastern Indian nations actually began before 1800, a formal and methodical plan was not implemented until after 1817.[21] The U.S. government initially relocated groups of Cherokees, Chickasaws, Choctaws, and Creeks to Arkansas Territory. In 1817 Andrew Jackson, Governor Joseph McMinn of Tennessee, and General David Meriwether negotiated a treaty with the Cherokees; according to this agreement, the Cherokees ceded approximately one-third of their land east of the Mississippi River to the United States and in return obtained an equal acreage in the White and Arkansas valleys.[22] These emigrants joined smaller groups of Cherokees who had moved to Arkansas beginning in the 1790s to circumvent European American encroachment. The 1817 Cherokee emigrants, often referred to as "Old Settlers" or "Western Cherokees," were to be paid for real property improvements or to receive equal value in the Arkansas land. The U.S. government agreed to provide boats and any other provisions for the journey, and, as in the case of other removal treaties, intruders were not allowed to settle on the land ceded by the Indians until the government had made its decisions concerning the reoccupation of the land. On 6 May 1828 another treaty was signed between Cherokee representatives and Secretary of War James Barbour; the Cherokees agreed to relinquish their holdings in Arkansas and receive 7 million acres of land located west of Arkansas and north of the Arkansas River—the northeastern section of present-day Oklahoma.

In order to encourage and organize Indian removal, the United States crafted more treaties with representatives from Indian nations. President Andrew Jackson became one of the most prominent American supporters of the removal of southeastern Indians. During Jackson's administration, on 28 May 1830, Congress passed the Indian Removal Act, which authorized the president of the United States to negotiate removal treaties with Indian nations living in regions east of the Mississippi River. On 14 July 1832, in his fourth year in office, President Jackson appointed a special commission to report on conditions in Indian Territory—the Stokes Commission. The members of the Stokes Commission met with representatives from a number of Indian nations, including the Senecas, the Quapaws, and the Osages.[23] The commission cajoled these nations to remove their people to new areas assigned by the government. The Senecas and the Quapaws moved to northeastern Oklahoma; the Osages eventually moved to southern Kansas. Even with the construction of treaties in the 1820s for the cession of Creek, Choctaw, and Cherokee land, not to mention the passage of the Indian Removal Act in 1830, when the time came for removal, many of the members of these southeastern Indian nations were neither prepared nor willing to move.

Varied Cherokee responses to the U.S. government's removal of the Nation reflected a fissure within Cherokee society related to the question of slavery. As Cherokees could not own individual tracts of land in the Nation, enslaved blacks became an important source of property and wealth. Although most Cherokees did not enslave blacks, before removal a small group of property-owning Cherokees, whom Tiya

Miles describes as a burgeoning Cherokee "middle class," exhibited "qualities that set them apart from most Cherokee people."[24] Over time, plantation slavery in the Cherokee Nation contributed to the creation of "two distinct classes within Cherokee society not only in an economic sense but also in terms of values and world views."[25] Cherokees who supported removal often emulated southern, white slaveholding sensibilities and rejected the adherence to traditional Cherokee belief systems. Cherokees who opposed removal primarily believed in traditional Cherokee worldviews and questioned the legitimacy and relevance of European American mores. The dissension about plantation slavery and Cherokee belief systems, as well as the ramifications of slaveholding in Cherokee society, would continue to plague the Cherokee Nation even after removal to Indian Territory.

Estimates vary as to the number of southeastern Indians forcibly relocated to Indian Territory. Historians are equally uncertain about the preremoval population of enslaved blacks in the Cherokee, Creek, Choctaw, Chickasaw, and Seminole nations. A census of the Cherokee Nation, conducted in December 1835 by the U.S. War Department, indicated that the Cherokee Nation in the East included 16,542 Cherokee Indians, 1,592 enslaved blacks, and 201 intermarried whites in the states of North Carolina, Georgia, Alabama, and Tennessee.[26] Most scholars agree that prior to removal, there were at least 900–1,000 enslaved blacks in three of the five nations—the Cherokee, Creek, and Chickasaw nations. Yet, due to the smaller number of Indians in the Chickasaw Nation (between 5,000 and 6,000 in 1837), compared to the Cherokee Nation (at least 15,000 in 1835) and the Creek Nation (at least 20,000 in 1832), the percentage of enslaved blacks in the Chickasaw Nation was significantly higher than in the other nations. A census of the Choctaw Nation in 1831 reported 512 enslaved blacks in a population of more than 19,500. Yet some scholars have argued that the enslaved population in the Choctaw Nation could have been considerably smaller.[27]

Although the enslavement of African-descended people existed within all Five Tribes, the Seminoles absorbed enslaved people within their communities in a manner that scholars have described as far less rigid and constrained than the other four nations.[28] Possibly due to the particular nature of the Seminoles' relationship with blacks, the Seminole Nation refused to reveal the number of free or enslaved African Seminoles in the period before removal. The African Seminole population, enslaved and free, could have been as high as one-fifth or one-sixth of the total Seminole population of approximately 5,000.[29] Overall, only a small percentage of Indians in the Five Tribes enslaved blacks; the majority of these slave owners operated small farms with fewer than ten enslaved blacks before and after removal.

During and after the removal process, enslaved people in the Five Tribes assisted with the survival and reestablishment of these nations in Indian Territory. Enslaved African Cherokees who relocated with their Cherokee enslavers in the winter of 1838–39 performed duties that sustained the removal detachments overall. As they traveled, some slaves trekked ahead and cleared the way for the larger groups. Cherokee owners utilized enslaved people along the trail as they had before removal. Enslaved African Cherokees worked as watchmen, hunters, cooks, and nurses. By assisting their owners and others during the removal process, enslaved people helped to minimize the intensity of some aspects of this intolerable journey for all Indians, whether they owned slaves or not.[30] Experiencing the range of challenges along the trail perhaps cemented among some enslaved people a sense of mutual struggle and survival in relation to Indians. Others might have viewed their additional tasks and their different "place" within the removal detachments as simply a reinforcement of their outsider status in these Indian nations. However they might have construed their passage to Indian Territory, after arrival their duties as enslaved people underscored that journeying and suffering together would not engender equal status in the new land.

After removal, owners employed slave labor in a variety of ways. Enslaved African Cherokees worked in prescribed roles as domestics within their owners' homes and as agricultural laborers. Prior to removal, enslaved people had worked with a variety of crops in the southeastern states, including cotton, tobacco, potatoes, and indigo;

however, their new home's climate and soil quality restricted the range of crops harvested. Enslaved people principally cultivated wheat, corn, and other grains in Indian Territory. King Cotton could not be produced to the same extent in this new land; instead, it was primarily grown for use within the individual households of the new residents in Indian Territory. Land in the Cherokee Nation, though, offered a new product for exportation. Cherokee businessmen exploited the natural salt mines in the region as a fruitful business venture. Enslaved blacks also worked in other skilled areas, including blacksmithing, tannery, and midwifery.[31] Although alterations proved necessary after resettlement in Indian Territory, the desire for slave labor remained constant. By 1860 enslaved blacks composed 15 percent of the residents in the Cherokee Nation, 14 percent of the residents in the Choctaw Nation, 18 percent of the residents in the Chickasaw Nation, and 10 percent of the residents in the Creek Nation.[32] Their presence and status in these nations would irrevocably affect the very core of these societies by the turn of the twentieth century.

◈ Questions concerning interactions between Africans and Indians emerge in the pages of several articles and books on slavery within Indian nations. For the most part, though, scholars who have described Indian enslavers and enslaved people of African descent in nineteenth-century Indian Territory have attempted to compare and contrast respective treatment of enslaved blacks by Indian and European American slaveholders. This information has enlarged the historiography of slavery. Yet, outside of the usual descriptions regarding the conditions of servitude, there has been limited analysis of enslaved blacks' perspectives of their Indian enslavers or themselves.[33] Even though enslaved blacks figure in several texts regarding the presence of slavery within the Five Tribes, their particular stories have not been placed at the focal point of most of these studies. Rather, the inclusion of enslaved blacks' experiences in many of these works functions primarily as the backdrop against which the more "interesting" perspectives of Indians are brought to the forefront. As a result, there has not been a thorough examination of enslaved people's varied responses to their bondage and eventual freedom in Indian Territory, between the time of removal and the post-Reconstruction era.

I chart the journeys of enslaved African Cherokees beginning with their arrival in the Cherokee Nation, Indian Territory, in the 1830s at the conclusion of the Trail of Tears and ending with the challenges and complexities of their freedom in the decades following the Civil War. In the immediate resettlement period in the 1840s and 1850s, I investigate forms of African Indian acculturation in antebellum Indian Territory. After their forced relocation to this region west of the Mississippi River, African Indians and Indians alike attempted to begin anew in Indian Territory. As well as being instrumental to the reestablishment of the socioeconomic and national infrastructure of the Five Tribes, enslaved African Indians also engaged in Indian cultural activities. Even though I focus primarily on the Cherokee Nation, I present examples of enslaved African Indian perspectives among the Creeks, Choctaws, and Chickasaws to demonstrate instances of enslaved African Indians' shared cultural experiences and their sense of belonging within these Indian nations. I explore particular customs related to language, clothing, food, and medicinal practices. Their participation in and incorporation of such folkways in their lives distinguish them in tangible ways from African Americans who, though also enslaved, lived in predominantly European American communities in the southeastern United States.

Even as some enslaved African Indians developed considerable ties to Indians in Indian Territory through a variety of cultural practices, for others immersion in Indian traditions simply reflected their subservient position steeped in servitude and subjection. The entrenched nature of Indian cultures in their daily lives was a constant reminder of their second-class status within these communities. As a result, even as some enslaved African Cherokees developed relationships that joined them to Cherokee people, others grew demoralized by the enslaver-enslaved linkages that chained them to the Cherokee Nation. Their disdain for Cherokee slavery and enslavers motivated them to break the shackles that bound them in Indian Territory. Indeed, antebellum reward advertisements for runaway slaves in the Cherokee Nation remain one concrete form of evidence of resistance, often offering substantial information about the fugitive slaves and their experiences in Indian Territory. Enslaved African Cherokees in the Cherokee Nation employed various manifestations of resistance while living in nineteenth-century Indian Territory. Instead of reiterating a mythology presenting benign slavery in Indian nations, I break this cycle of silence and denial by recounting how some enslaved African Cherokees resisted the harsh and inhumane conditions of bondage on an individual and collective basis in the Cherokee Nation, Indian Territory.

The connections and exigencies between enslaved and free people within the boundaries of Indian Territory reached a crescendo with the coming of the Civil War. Although seemingly outside the geographical perimeters of the war between the North and the South, Indian Territory became a prime site of intense warfare and devastation as the Five Tribes chose sides in this national crisis. During Reconstruction, African Cherokees engaged in a new struggle to define their place as "free" members and citizens of the Cherokee Nation. In my examination of the Cherokee Nation in the wake of the Civil War, I concentrate on the challenges of Cherokee freedpeople (formerly enslaved African Cherokees) in the Reconstruction era to attain equal rights as Cherokee citizens—not as citizens of the United States. Although similar to the constitutional and legalistic challenges of African American freedpeople in the United States proper, African Cherokee freedpeople's struggle centered on their development, articulation, and preservation of their sense of a unique African Cherokee national identity. Their interactions with Cherokees, based on blood ties and cultural customs, shaped how they construed their "free" place in the Cherokee Nation. Having lived and survived bondage in the Cherokee Nation, Cherokee freedpeople strategically articulated how bondage and acculturation grounded them firmly within Cherokee communities and the Cherokee Nation itself. By so doing, they continued their transformation from a life in slavery to freedom, from bondage to belonging, from chattel to citizens of the Cherokee Nation.

As they adjusted to and disputed their place in Indian communities, many previously enslaved African Indians grappled with their multi-racial, cultural, and national identities within specific nations in Indian Territory after the Civil War. Even then, some previously enslaved biracial African Cherokees could not sever their ties to the Cherokee Nation. African Cherokee freedman Milton Starr, who was born and raised in the Cherokee Nation, remained on his Cherokee master-father Jerry Starr's plantation for some time after the Civil War, because the Starrs treated him like "family." Even some African Indian freedpeople, who did not declare a "blood" relationship to a specific Indian nation, claimed cultural connections with Indian people, communities, and nations in the post–Civil War era. As a result, the gradual "Indianization" of such African Indians engendered a sense of belonging—of common ground—for many African Indian freedpeople in Indian Territory. Indeed, this sense of belonging and the Cherokee freedpeople's struggle for recognition and equal rights that emerged in nineteenth-century Indian Territory continue even today in the Cherokee Nation in Oklahoma.

The lived experiences of enslaved and free people of color in Indian Territory raise questions about the usual rendering of bondage in the United States. By complicating the traditional accounts of enslavement, resistance, and freedom in the United States, these stories vividly demonstrate the multifaceted realities for enslaved and free people of African descent in the nineteenth century. Life in nineteenth-century Indian Territory also necessitates a reconceptualization of the enduring association between Indians and victimization, as well as romanticized notions of only cooperative and collusive relationships between African-descended people and Indians in United States historiography. Furthermore, the stories of enslaved African Indians in Indian Territory challenge the traditional portrayal of enslaved blacks and, indeed, a monolithic African American cultural identity in the United States, whether in the nineteenth century or in the present day. These stories call into question the seemingly inexorable and static conceptions of culture, identity, ethnicity, and even race in the United States and in Indian country. My analysis of enslaved and free African Cherokees distinctly challenges the racial binary and elucidates the complex interplay of racial, cultural, and national identities; examines the experiences of African-descended people in North America beyond the confines of U.S. society's reductionist ideas about race; broadens the comparative analysis of slave systems by including a critical examination of slavery within the Cherokee Nation; and posits how the contours of bondage within the Cherokee Nation shaped the self-constructed identities of enslaved and free African Cherokees. The stories of African Cherokees convey an alternative narrative about the enslaved and free lives of people of African descent in the nineteenth century and demand a more dynamic, synergetic, and organic understanding of racial categorizations, cultural subjectivities, and national politics of exclusion and sovereignty—then and now.

I ▶ On the Run in Antebellum Indian Territory

$50 REWARD

*Ranaway from the subscriber on the 15th inst. my yellow
boy Jacob—he is well known all over the Nation. I will give the
above reward for his apprehension and delivery to me unhurt,
at my residence or Fort Gibson.*

    JOHN W. WEST, *Fort Gibson, March 20th 1852*

    ◆ *Cherokee Advocate, 23 June 1852*

Resistance within Chaos

Having survived the Trail of Tears—the long, perilous passage to Indian Territory—enslaved African Cherokees quickly
discovered that the chains of bondage that linked them to
Cherokee owners and communities remained constant and
taut even in the new territory. Many who made this journey had
been forced to leave family members and friends behind. They
grieved about being separated and wondered if they would ever
reconnect with those living in the old country. Some had traveled to Indian Territory with expectations of gradual emancipation in a new land. Collective suffering of African Cherokees
and Cherokees along the trail, however, had not generated
enough of a sense of humanity, equality, and freedom; those
enslaved before removal, who had survived the horror of the
passage to the West, remained in bondage after arrival in Indian Territory. As the enslaved arrivals became more aware of
their duties in the new Indian country and their ongoing state
of bondage, some also detected the intensity of discord per-
meating the Cherokee Nation in their new territory. Differences between warring sociopolitical sects became intense.
Sensing this initial turmoil, enslaved African Cherokees living

in Cherokee communities sought to benefit from, and even contribute to, the unruly state of affairs after arrival. Unlike free Cherokee citizens who engaged in the sociopolitical mayhem as a way of demolishing old adversaries, resolving conflicts, and solidifying the Cherokee Nation itself, enslaved African Cherokees capitalized on the political tensions in order to amplify the discord in Cherokee domestic affairs and to achieve some distance from the boundaries of bondage. Maintaining the integrity of the Cherokee Nation was not their goal; instead, it was widening the fissure in the Cherokee polity through which they hoped to attain some sense of freedom.

Even though enslaved African Cherokees demonstrated their will to be free and resisted their enslavement in Indian Territory, most scholars have simply ignored these actions in order to project particular interpretations about the "mild" nature of bondage in Indian nations.[1] Yet the vulnerability of enslaved African Cherokees in the Cherokee Nation was underscored time and time again as they were hired out, sold, and auctioned off to satisfy the personal whims and business interests of their enslavers. Like European American enslavers in the southeastern states, Cherokee slave owners defined the position of bondsmen and bondswomen in the Cherokee Nation by their individual needs, as well as the overall laws of the Nation. As part of the rebuilding process in the postremoval period, the Cherokee Nation established more restrictive "slave codes" that controlled the lives of enslaved African Cherokees in the new territory. Cherokee statutes reinforced the position of enslaved African Cherokees as inferior to free Cherokee citizens. Even though the stigma of blackness may not have been featured within earlier Cherokee societies, by the time of resettlement in Indian Territory Cherokee laws embodied the intertwined codification of racial identification, status, and Cherokee citizenship. The word "slave" in these laws specifically related to a person of African descent.[2] Although there might have been a small number of enslaved people of Indian descent, who were not of African descent, within the confines of the Cherokee Nation, Indian Territory, such individuals would have been deemed exceptions to the rule in the postremoval period.

Soon after removal to the new territory, the Cherokee Nation re-established the place of race and bondage within the boundaries of Cherokee country. One of the first laws passed by the Cherokee National Council in Tahlequah—the new capital of the Cherokee Nation in Indian Territory—concerned the prevention of "amalgamation with colored persons."[3] Enacted on 19 September 1839, this act declared "that intermarriage shall not be lawful between a free male or female citizen with any slave or person of color not entitled to the rights of citizenship under the laws of this Nation." The punishment for committing said crime was not to "exceed fifty stripes for every such offence." This act included a more severe punishment for men of African descent, specifically stating that "any colored male who may be convicted under this act shall receive one hundred lashes."[4] The more severe punishment for men of African descent who committed this offense reflected concerns about legislating not only black male sexuality but also free Cherokee women's sexuality.[5] Such laws reveal the significant, though changing, position of women in the Cherokee Nation—an Indian nation grounded in a matrilineal clan system. As the primary source of Cherokee life, women's spousal choices not only disclosed their individual, personal desires but also had implications for the nature and color of Cherokee people—of the Cherokee race. Though individuals certainly crossed the racial lines, Cherokee laws concerning interracial marriage point to particular conceptions of racial inequality and separation linked to the legislation of intimate relationships and, more important, Cherokee marriage and lineage.

Another act passed on 19 September 1839, regarding the rape of Cherokee women, also stipulated a significantly different and more severe punishment for men of African descent. This act declared that "any person charged with the offense of having committed a rape on any female . . . shall be punished with one hundred lashes on the bare back; and upon the conviction of any negro for the aforesaid offence against any free female, not of negro blood, he shall suffer death by hanging."[6] These laws concerning the punishment for raping women in the Cherokee Nation not only reflect notions about the protection of free female sexuality from black male sexualized aggression but also reinforce the idea of enslaved women of African descent as undeserving recipients of the same protection granted to free women—whether of European or Indian descent.[7]

In addition to attempting to regulate interracial sexuality and unions, the Cherokee National Council also legislated the specific ways that a range of rights and liberties bestowed on free Cherokees would not be extended to free blacks, who were not of Cherokee descent, or enslaved people of African descent. The council specifically enacted a law on 7 November 1840, declaring it unlawful "for any free negro or mulatto, not of Cherokee blood, to hold or own any improvement within the limits of this Nation."[8] Traditional Cherokee customs forbade individual members of the Cherokee Nation from owning tracts of land within the Nation's limits; instead, communal land-ownership existed for all land within its boundaries. Cherokee citizens could certainly build houses on Cherokee land; the Nation defined such houses, as well as other structures including barns, as "improvements." Cherokee citizens owned such improvements, as well as the right to monetary compensation from the sale or transfer of such improvements to another citizen of the Cherokee Nation.[9] Because property could not own property, however, it was unlawful for enslaved people to own not only homes but also "horses, cattle, hogs, or fire arms."[10] Interestingly, in Indian Territory, free biracial African Cherokees could own property. Their "Cherokee blood"—not Cherokee status based on matrilineal clan association—granted them access to this particular right of free status within the Cherokee Nation.

This interjection of "Cherokee blood" in the new laws in antebellum Indian Territory reflected evolving ideas of belonging and status within the Cherokee Nation. Legal statutes in slaveholding regions of the United States did not differentiate between the status and limited rights of biracial free people of African and European descent and those of free people of African descent in the slaveholding republic. Rather, European American conceptions of race in "black and white" literally and figuratively dictated the rights and liberties of free people of color in the United States. One drop of "black blood" automatically restricted one's free status in the slaveholding regions of the

United States; whether one also possessed "white blood" did not erase the restrictions imposed by the legalized stigma of blackness. Although blackness certainly shaped one's enslaved and free status in the Cherokee Nation, "Cherokee blood" in conjunction with free status guaranteed limited rights to biracial African Cherokees—rights not granted to those free people of African descent with no "Cherokee blood" lineage. In the antebellum Cherokee Nation, clan association no longer dictated one's position and rights; instead, race, status, and "blood," often intersecting concepts, defined one's respective place and privileges.

As a slave-owning society, the Cherokee Nation enacted laws to restrict the literal "place" of enslaved people. Like slaveholding regions in the United States, the Cherokee Nation instituted surveillance mechanisms to supervise, intimidate, control, and punish enslaved African Cherokees in order to achieve acquiescence. To limit the mobility of enslaved people in the Cherokee Nation, on 19 October 1841 the Cherokee National Council authorized the lawful organization of "patrol companies in any neighborhood, where the people of such neighborhood shall deem it necessary; and such company, when organized, shall take up and bring to punishment any negro or negroes, that may be strolling about, not on their owner's or owners' premises, without a pass from their owner or owners."[11] The council further enacted on the same date a law that "any negro not entitled to Cherokee privileges, that may be found or seen carrying weapons of any kind, such as guns, pistols, Bowie-knives, butcher knifes [sic] or dirks, such patrol company may take, and inflict as many stripes as they think proper, not exceeding thirty-nine lashes."[12] On 21 October 1841, the council declared it unlawful "for any person or persons, citizens of this Nation, or others, to carry secret arms, such as Bowie-knives, spears, dirks or pistols of any kind."[13] It is not surprising that the council decided to enact an overall law regarding arms in the Nation. The disorderly nature of the times often involved murder with a variety of weapons. Although the establishment of patrol companies and the control of weaponry within the reach of those enslaved and free undeniably reflected a heightened sensitivity to the violence of the postremoval period, such laws also reinforced the link between the presence of Cherokee blood and related liberties within the Cherokee Nation.

Consistent with other laws enacted in the southeastern slaveholding states to make clear the privileges of the free versus the restrictions on the enslaved, on 22 October 1841 the Cherokee National Council passed an act "prohibiting the teaching of negroes to read and write." Although literacy and education were routinely viewed as important issues in the Cherokee Nation, enslaved African Cherokees might use the ability to read and write to abscond from their owners. In an effort to eliminate the literacy of enslaved people, the act stipulated that "it shall not be lawful for any person or persons whatever, to teach any free negro or negroes not of Cherokee blood, or any slave belonging to any citizen or citizens of the Nation, to read or write."[14]

An array of statutes enabled the Cherokees to reestablish and codify their societal rules after removal to Indian Territory. Cherokee blood granted free biracial African Cherokees access to certain Cherokee privileges. Those free African Cherokees without a Cherokee blood connection could enjoy only quasi freedom in the Nation. Free status could only guarantee some rights; in postremoval Indian Territory, the Cherokee Nation refused to extend additional rights and privileges to free people of African descent if they did not meet a Cherokee blood requirement. Cherokee statutes also clearly delineated those who would and would not be granted rights, liberties, and freedoms based on their racial identity, status, and citizenship. Relocation to Indian Territory could have been a transitional period during which the Cherokee Nation reevaluated and eradicated slavery within its boundaries. Instead, the Nation chose to retain and maintain the peculiar institution in the new territory.

During the turbulent period immediately following Cherokee removal, the free residents of the Cherokee Nation in Indian Territory not only focused on rebuilding the laws and policies that would define their slaveholding communities but also strove to reestablish their homes, government, schools, and collective identity.[15] But the task was difficult, and theft, murders, and other crimes occurred frequently during the early period in Indian Territory. Discord erupted soon after removal between the Old Settlers or Western Cherokees, who had moved west of the Mississippi before the Indian Removal Act, and the Eastern Cherokees, who had been forcibly relocated to Indian Territory after passage of the act. The formal resolution of tensions between the separate communities of Western Cherokees and the new arrivals of Eastern Cherokees occurred during a National Convention on 23 August 1839. At this gathering, both branches concurred about creating a written covenant to form "one body politic, under the style and title of the Cherokee Nation." Only two weeks after reaching agreement on the "Act of Union between the Eastern and Western Cherokees," the reunited Eastern and Western Cherokees established the Tahlequah Constitution of the Cherokee Nation on 6 September 1839.[16]

The creation of "one body politic" in August 1839 failed to resolve all tensions within the Cherokee Nation. Much of the ongoing bedlam was attributed to the incessant antagonism between various sociopolitical sects, specifically between the Ross Party and the Ridge-Boudinot or Treaty Party. The discord centered on different stances concerning the federal government's removal plan. Major proponents of removal—Major Ridge, John Ridge, Elias Boudinot, and Stand Watie—stressed the ways that removal would place the Cherokee Nation in a better strategic position for future agreements with the federal government. Though representing a minority view in the Cherokee Nation, approximately 200 advocates of Cherokee removal met with U.S. representatives on 29 December 1835 in New Echota and signed a treaty agreeing to Cherokee removal within a two-year period. Supporters of the Treaty of New Echota became known as the Treaty Party. Under the leadership of John Ross, principal chief of the Cherokee Nation, 15,000 Cherokee citizens signed and submitted a petition to the U.S. government protesting the deceptive and unlawful nature of the actions of the Treaty Party. The efforts of the Ross Party, however, fell on deaf ears; in May 1836, the U.S. Congress ratified the Treaty of New Echota.

After removal to Indian Territory, due to heightened tensions and animosity, these two factions established their own law enforcement in order to defend their respective parties, as well as to intimidate, harass, and murder sympathizers of their opposing parties. Between 1839 and 1846, confrontations between supporters of the two parties created violence and havoc in the Cherokee Nation. Enslaved African Cherokees, even children, became conscious of the feuding between the Ross Party and Treaty Party, including how slaveholding served as additional fodder for such tensions in the Nation. As Cherokee freedwoman Chaney Richardson recalled, "My master and all the rest of the folks was Cherokees, and they'd been killing each other off in the feud ever since long before I was borned, and jest because old Master have a big farm and three-four families of Negroes them other Cherokees keep on pestering his stuff all the time. Us children was always afeared to go any place less'n some of the grown folks was along. We didn't know what we was a-feared of, but we heard the Master and Mistress keep talking 'bout 'another Party killing' and we stuck close to the place."[17]

The mayhem infringed on the lives of enslaved African Cherokees in unforgettable ways. When she was ten years old, Richardson remembered how "that feud got so bad the Indians was always talking about getting their horses and cattle killed and their slaves harmed. I was too little to know how bad it was until one morning my own mammy went off somewhere down the road to git some stuff to dye cloth and she didn't come back." About a week later, Richardson recalled, "two Indian men rid up and ast old master wasn't his gal Ruth gone. He says yes, and they take one of the slaves along with a wagon to show where they seen her. They find her in some bushes where she'd been getting bark to set the dyes, and she been dead all the time. Somebody done hit her in the head with a club and shot her through and through with a bullet too. She was so swole up they couldn't lift her up and jest had to make a deep hole right along side of her and roll her in it she was so bad mortified . . . they never catch on to who done it."[18] Richardson's mother and other enslaved African Cherokees served as tangible targets for some Cherokees to attack in order to demonstrate their opposition to plantation slavery in the Nation. In addition, enslaved African Cherokees could also have been targeted in this way, as they duly symbolized a potent reminder of heightened class and status distinctions in postremoval Cherokee society.

Beginning in September 1844, the bloody discord was discussed in the pages of the first newspaper established in the Cherokee Nation, Indian Territory.[19] In its second month, the *Cherokee Advocate* ran an editorial on "Our Town" by editor William Potter Ross, nephew of Chief John Ross.[20] Editor Ross presented a brief description of Tahlequah—the new capital of the Cherokee Nation in Indian Territory—as well as details regarding the Cherokee government. In his article Ross proudly declared that "the great mass of our people render cheerful and voluntary obedience to the requirements of laws that have been enacted, from time to time, by legislators, who receive their authority directly from them." Ross cautioned the readers, "there are however, others, few in number it is true, with whom it is different. Like all communities, we have those who are impatient of even necessary restraint, who despise all law and who are ready to perpetrate any enormity." In dealing with these individuals, Ross insisted, "no considerations of moral obligation will have the slightest influence. It is therefore important that laws for the punishment of theft, murder and similar offenses should be enforced to the very letter. Nothing short of such steps can check and arrest the dishonesty and impudent rascality which have manifested themselves recently in our midst."[21] Ross had ample evidence for his concerns, because the same issue carried numerous notices of violence.[22]

A year and a half later, in March 1846, William Potter Ross raised similar concerns regarding the ruthless actions of renegades within the Nation. Recognizing that "the overwhelming mass of the people are sincerely desirous of peace," Ross seriously doubted whether this majority could enjoy tranquillity "in consequence of the infamous acts of a few debased and murderous wretches who manage to keep themselves beyond the reach of justice." Moreover, he vehemently questioned "how long must such continue to be the case? How long must not only our peace and prosperity, but our lives and property be left exposed to the same men? How long must we be compelled to witness the murdered and mangled bodies of esteemed and useful men, as they fall one by one beneath the cowardly attacks of the 'confederacy of fiends' who have preyed upon old and young, rich and poor, for years? How long must every honest man in the country, 'hold his life in his hand' and be under guard, both day and night, not only ready, but fortunate if he may have the opportunity to defend it from the secret assaults of these assassins?"[23] The bloodshed between the two parties "officially" ceased when leading party representatives John Ross and Stand Watie signed a peace treaty on 14 August 1846, terminating all hostilities between the two parties.[24]

"All Who Cannot Give a Good Account of Themselves"

Believing that their owners were otherwise occupied by the personal problems and political crises about which William Potter Ross ruminated, some enslaved African Cherokees took advantage of the situation and left their owners' farms and plantations to obtain their freedom.[25] The unrest of these early years presented a long-awaited window of opportunity for enslaved African Cherokees; in spite of serious risks, some chose to run away. Articles and advertisements in the Cherokee Advocate expose some sense of the desperation enslaved African Cherokees felt to escape the shackles of bondage in the Cherokee Nation. However preoccupied Cherokee slave owners may have seemed during the 1840s, most enslaved African Cherokees soon discovered that runaway slaves were definitely not overlooked. In early December 1846, four or five slave catchers had tracked several runaway slaves to their "place of concealment."[26] While the slave catchers were in the process of encircling the place, "one of the negroes hearing the noise, became suspicious, and attempted to escape. His pursuers however, soon overhauled him, demanding a surrender. Presenting a large knife in one hand and a club in the other, he refused—bidding them at the same time in language of defiance, to approach. With guns presented they insisted on his submitting. He then attempted to run. They fired—and he was killed."[27]

The defiance expressed by this unnamed runaway slave toward Cherokee slave catchers underscores the violent and sometimes fatal nature of the confrontations that occurred during the capture of runaways. Although the specific reasons for this enslaved person's acts remain unknown, the sequence of events in this episode seem strikingly similar to others that occurred time and time again in the southeastern states. The hope for freedom—of a temporary or permanent nature—certainly served to motivate this runaway attempt. His actions communicated his refusal to accept his enslaved position in the Cherokee Nation. Whether or not he had endured the atrocious conditions of the Trail of Tears, by striking out for his freedom in this way he expressed his refusal to live a life in bondage. Owners and slave catchers in the Cherokee Nation also hunted down runaway slaves from other nations. One notice in the *Cherokee Advocate* simply stated: "Two runaway negro men belonging to Mr. Willison of the Creek Nation were killed recently in an attempt to arrest them. We learn that they threatened the life of Mr. W., and when come upon, refused to submit, wherefore they were shot."[28] The murder of these unnamed enslaved people and others not only demonstrated the extent to which runaway slaves fought for their liberation but also reinforced, for those runaways who were not murdered, the limited value of their lives—at the very least that their lives could well be terminated before they attained freedom in Cherokee country.

Other "criminal" activities of African Cherokee runaways—acts of resistance against the peculiar institution—also added to the chaotic conditions in the early years of resettlement in the Cherokee Nation. While on the run, and often in preparation for such attempts, it was necessary for runaways to procure items that would improve the chances of a successful escape. Prior to the murder of the unnamed runaway in December 1846, Cherokees in the area had been losing "poultry, vegetables &c., which led to the belief that the offenders were runaways that have been committing depredations for an indefinite time, on the property of our citizens."[29] Cases of theft of animals and food attributed to runaways were not uncommon in Indian Territory and beyond. In his slave narrative, Henry Bibb, who was enslaved for a brief period in Indian Territory, explained that he "did not regard it as stealing." He believed he "had a just right to what I took, because it was the labor of my own hands."[30] It is easy to understand that the "theft" of such property would have generated a certain degree of satisfaction and a sense of retribution among those who had worked tirelessly on their Cherokee owners' farms and plantations; in the end, their labor had solely benefited their enslavers.

Disorderly actions of runaways, however, not only heightened the tumultuous state of affairs in the Cherokee Nation but also exposed an imbalance of power that had to be addressed within the Nation. Cherokee slave owners and, in some cases, those who did not own African Cherokees viewed runaways as troublesome emblems of the unruly times. Using the murder of the runaway in December 1846 as an opportunity to speak about the situation in the Cherokee Nation, editor William Potter Ross expressed a "few remarks, relative to negroes in our country."[31] At first his comments were of a general nature, later becoming more specific regarding the regulation of enslaved people by slave owners from inside and outside the Cherokee Nation. Ross explicitly stressed that he did not "advocate murder," warning young people "in particular, to be guarded, lest they wantonly use their weapons in taking of human life." However, while not openly condoning murder, he did believe "that it is time, high time that some thing be done toward regulating such property in the Cherokee country. It is not our place to discuss the right or wrong of Slavery. That it exists among us, is a matter of fact—and existing, they should know the relations they bear to free born citizens."[32] Ross recommended that "those who own negroes" should "be kind, yet strict in the enforcement of proper regulations—and as for others, it is but right that you use the utmost vigilence [sic] in ferreting out and arresting all who cannot give a good account of themselves. It is due to those who have lost such property. It is due also to the well disposed part of the black populace—and lastly it is realy [sic] essential to the mentainance [sic] of good order and quiet among some portions of the community."[33]

Ross's statements exemplify the complexities of the simultaneous existence of bondage and freedom in the Cherokee Nation. For order to be maintained free Cherokees had to fortify and demonstrate their place and position relative to enslaved African Cherokees. Although conveying a message of righteous slaveholding, Ross and others concurrently reiterated the significance of order and "place" within a slaveholding society. The penchant of enslaved African Cherokees for running away revealed not only the necessity of controlling the movements of enslaved people for the benefit of their owners but also the destabilizing effect of runaways on members of the Cherokee Nation and Cherokee society in general. Control over enslaved African Cherokees established some measure of order in the Cherokee Nation; conversely, disorderly "property" reflected and encouraged an unruly and "uncivilized" slaveholding society.

The actions of runaways countered the hopes of Cherokee slave owners for order, as well as the desire for the submission of their enslaved property. Runaway slave advertisements highlight the extent to which some enslaved African Cherokees demonstrated their abhorrence for bondage. Such advertisements, like those in southeastern newspapers, provide specific physical descriptions of runaways, including age, gender, build, clothing worn and taken, special talents, languages spoken and understood, occupations, physical disabilities, and particular scars and disfigurement often acquired as punishment due to previous attempts to escape. Enslaved people who absconded most frequently from their owners' farms and plantations were truants or absentees—who were "laying out" for several days or weeks, usually to visit relatives living in the general area, and who then returned on their own accord. Unlike truants or absentees, runaways absconded from their owners' residences with no intention of returning, at least not as a slave.[34]

Evidence of runaways' activities appears within the pages of the *Cherokee Advocate*, and frequently these references are embedded within other stories.[35] In the coverage regarding the 24 August 1844 explosion of the steamboat *Lucy Walker*, near New Albany, Indiana, on the Ohio River, there are ambiguous references to enslaved African Cherokees on the steamboat who were missing following the explosion. Cherokee Joseph Vann (1800?–1844), often referred to as "Rich Joe," was one of the wealthiest Cherokee slave owners in the Cherokee Nation.[36] In addition to his property holdings and slaves, he also owned a line of steamboats, which included the *Lucy Walker*. Joseph

Vann was among the fifty passengers who died, or were pronounced missing, as a result of the explosion.[37] Passengers reported as dead included twelve enslaved people and one deckhand. The list of missing persons included "four negro fireman [sic]." In addition, "five slaves belonging to Captain Vann" were on the uninjured list.[38] In the next issue of the *Cherokee Advocate*, however, a small article indicated that "the three negroes belonging to Captain Vann, who were saved from the 'Lucy Walker,' the *Louisville Courier* states, have been run off by two unknown white men."[39] It is not clear whether they voluntarily or involuntarily ran off with these unknown men. Undoubtedly, enslaved people on board would have considered the explosion of the *Lucy Walker* a prime opportunity for running away—such an opportunity was not to be wasted. Indeed, some enslaved African Cherokees who regularly worked on the *Lucy Walker* might have been preparing and strategizing for such a moment for days, weeks, even years—waiting for, planning, possibly instigating such a disruptive, emergency situation that would allow them to take their first steps toward freedom.

Few enslaved people traveled such long distances as those aboard the *Lucy Walker*; yet many enslaved African Cherokees accompanied their owners in the local vicinity, using these trips to gain a better understanding of the area in which they lived. Those who regularly traveled with their enslavers commonly served in this capacity due to their owners' level of trust and faith in them; often enslavers viewed such companions as their most loyal servants. As George Murrell's slave coachman, Spencer often accompanied Murrell on trips within the Cherokee Nation. Murrell—an intermarried white citizen of the Cherokee Nation—might have considered Spencer one of his most trusted enslaved African Cherokees.[40] Certainly, Murrell would not have anticipated that, on 29 April 1845, while visiting Captain John Benge at his residence in the Skin Bayou District of the Cherokee Nation, Spencer would take advantage of this trip to run away.[41] In his reward notice, Murrell described Spencer as a "*Dark Mulatto*, between 35 and 40 years of age, 5 feet 8 or 10 inches in height—weighs from 150 to 160 lbs—square built, tho' inclined ordinarily, to stoop a little when walking—usually wears half whiskers—when he left, however, they were shorn off; is very tidy in dress, quick spoken when speaking, but slow when spoken to. No scars remembered—prides himself much on his abilities as a Coachman and Barber. He was purchased in New Orleans, La., consequently when conversing with negroes, seldom fails to enumerate the pleasures, &c. of a city life."[42] The advertisement noted that Spencer, when last heard of, was still in the vicinity of his home. However, having resided among Creeks in Alabama and "acquired a limited knowledge of their language," it was possible that Spencer would abscond initially to the Creek Nation. George Murrell offered a reward of forty dollars if Spencer was delivered to his residence in Park Hill, Cherokee Nation, or fifty dollars to "any one who will arrest and safely deliver said slave to Scott, White, & Co., at Van Buren, Arkansas."[43]

From the details of the advertisement, Spencer seemed to have intimated his dissatisfaction or, at the very least, his frustration with his enslaved life on the Murrell plantation. As Murrell himself points out, Spencer quickly communicated his thoughts, though had trouble "when spoken to"—possibly when told to perform certain duties. Perhaps by the spring of 1845 Spencer had decided he would not answer to any more of his enslaver's orders. Spencer's repeated stories of New Orleans, and his love for a "city life," might have further triggered his desire to run away from Murrell's plantation in the small town of Park Hill. In order to create a partial facial disguise for himself, he had removed his whiskers, in preparation for the runaway attempt.

Where runaways like Spencer decided to go depended on a variety of factors, including the location of family members who would offer assistance, the possibility of blending into cities with a free black presence, and their own limited sense of direction or the directions from others who had previously escaped.[44] Spencer's familiarity with other towns and cities, due to his previous experiences as well as his position as Murrell's coachman, no doubt motivated him to believe his runaway attempt would be a successful one. While George Murrell prepared to visit John Benge, Spencer mapped out his strategy for this journey from slavery to freedom. As his owner visited with John Benge at his home, Spencer proceeded to implement his plan in the most effective way possible. As George Murrell slept, he felt assured that his trusted coachman would greet him the next morning and return him home safely. Instead, Spencer utilized the night to mask his movement and slip surreptitiously through the Cherokee Nation. As Murrell welcomed ideas of a warm greeting from Spencer in the morning, Spencer anticipated a new morning on his own—far from his owner's reach and power. Spencer's plan appeared to be a fruitful one. Two months after his escape, Spencer remained at large; perhaps he found his way to the Creek Nation, or to New Orleans, or north to freedom.

Spencer's escape from the Cherokee Nation no doubt surprised his master; indeed, a number of reward notices demonstrated that owners were seemingly unaware of any possible motive for their enslaved persons to run away. Murrell and others probably experienced depths of deception and depression when trusted enslaved African Cherokees they had relied on for years fled for their liberty. As a result, many advertisements offered no reason for these runaway attempts of slaves but simply descriptive information about runaways. When Allen absconded from the residence of Peter Hildebrand—German-born, intermarried white citizen of the Cherokee Nation—on 21 September 1845, Hildebrand's attempt to recapture Allen included a twenty-dollar reward for Allen's arrest and return to his residence. In his advertisement, Hildebrand offered no explanation for Allen's departure, only a brief description of Allen's physical characteristics, including a noticeable speech impairment. It may not have been Allen's initial attempt at running away. As Hildebrand explained defensively, Allen had "marks of the whip, inflicted before he came into my possession."[45] Hildebrand insinuated that he was not the kind of slave owner who would whip enslaved people. It is possible that Hildebrand did indeed make these marks on Allen. Nonetheless, it was important to him to describe himself in a certain way—as the kind of righteous slave owner William Potter Ross promoted in his *Cherokee Advocate* editorial. Although the treatment by one's enslaver could certainly affect decisions about running away, whether Hildebrand and other enslavers in the

Cherokee Nation chose to whip enslaved people or not, Allen and other runaways refused to be defined as chattel—as the property of other human beings. Instead, they sought freedom by fleeing their owners and the site of their bondage—the Cherokee Nation.

Even though many reward postings included no reasons for a runaway's escape, in Indian Territory, as in the southeastern states, some reward notices provide evidence that one of the reasons why enslaved people ran away from their owners involved a desire to see their family. Because enslaved people frequently ran away to be closer to relatives, owners often became knowledgeable as to the whereabouts of enslaved people's wives, husbands, parents, and children. Family members often harbored runaway relatives and provided a temporary refuge for kin on the run. Some owners predicted the probable destinations of runaways. Even with their owners' quasi understanding of their family networks, enslaved African Cherokees developed cunning ways of escaping recapture. Though some might be cautious about the repercussions of hiding kin, others welcomed fugitive kin and strategized about hiding maneuvers and processes to protect runaway family members and friends.

When twenty-eight-year-old Harvey escaped from his owner's residence in Beattie's Prairie, Delaware District, Cherokee Nation, in September 1848, one of his destinations was believed to be his father's home. Identifying Harvey in the reward advertisement specifically as the "Son of Abram on Caney," James A. Thompson, Harvey's owner, noted that Harvey would "be lurking either in the vicinity of Fort Gibson, the Bayou, Green Leaf, or at his fathers on Caney." Thompson offered a twenty-five-dollar reward for Harvey's apprehension and return or fifty dollars if Harvey were caught outside of the Cherokee Nation and delivered to his home at Beattie's Prairie.[46] Although there were individual runaways who made the journey to Indian Territory without any family members en route, others like Harvey might have considered themselves fortunate to have kin who had also been relocated to Indian Territory, especially within the boundaries of the Cherokee Nation. Harvey might have absconded so that he could visit with his father before he left the Cherokee Nation entirely; he might also have visited his father in an attempt to convince him, too, of running away in search of a free life.

Some absconded to visit husbands or wives in order to strengthen familial connections. The numerous runaway attempts of some husbands demonstrated their overwhelming need and desire to reunite with spouses.[47] When Isaac ran away in August 1849, owner George Murrell assumed that he had escaped to see not one wife but two wives. Because Isaac had previously belonged to Cherokee James Vann Sr. and later to James S. Vann, it was assumed that he was "either about James Vann's Senr., or the mouth of the Illinois River, as he has a wife at each place."[48] This escape was not Isaac's first attempt, for Isaac ran away from James S. Vann's residence around 1 February 1849. The persistence of George Murrell must be noted here; he continued to offer a reward eight months after Isaac's disappearance. Beginning in January 1850, Murrell increased his reward for Isaac's apprehension from twenty dollars to fifty dollars. Even with Murrell's determination, in April 1850, Isaac still remained at large.[49]

In addition to worrying about runaways who belonged to Cherokee owners, members of the Cherokee Nation also expressed concern that runaways from neighboring states were likely to find refuge in the Nation. Most enslavers were well aware of the attraction that Indian Territory held for runaways who were willing to pursue freedom outside of the states. Enslaved people who "lived close in proximity to free territory—near the Pennsylvania line, along the Ohio River, in the west or near the Indian nations, on the border with Florida, or in southern Texas—frequently tempted fate by striking out for freedom."[50] Reward notices for runaways from other southern states, including Arkansas and Louisiana, appeared in the *Cherokee Advocate*.[51] Although such runaways may have viewed the Cherokee Nation as a refuge, if caught, some runaways soon discovered that the Cherokee Nation was also a very dangerous and sometimes lethal place. In April 1848, for example, two runaways from the Creek Nation were killed in the Cherokee Nation during an attempt to arrest them.[52] Residents and authorities from the United States also posted notices for runaways from the Cherokee Nation whom they had captured in their own states.[53]

Isaac, Harvey, Spencer, and other runaways in the Cherokee Nation who avoided capture, as well as those named and unnamed who were murdered during the recapture process, indisputably demonstrated a conscious desire to escape from bondage, to forgo all dictates of their owners, and to navigate the perilous journey toward freedom. Some who had participated in the trek to Indian Territory in the late 1830s recognized that their enslavers would not be as knowledgeable of their new surroundings as they had been of their communities in the old Cherokee country in the Southeast. Their owners' initial unfamiliarity with the landscape and geography in Indian Territory could certainly be advantageous in their runaway attempts during the resettlement era of the 1840s. Although only becoming more aware of their new environs themselves in this period, enslaved African Cherokees grasped the remarkable convergence of opportunity and potential for escape in an unfamiliar place during a chaotic time. Taking advantage of the postremoval conditions in Indian Territory, runaways in the Cherokee Nation orchestrated their escape plans, routes, and processes. Expressing no sense of loyalty to their enslavers or the Cherokee Nation, runaways attempted by any means necessary to resist recapture. Some freed themselves in the process; others, who were unsuccessful in their runaway attempts, achieved freedom in death as they flouted recapture and reenslavement.

Collective Resistance

During the postremoval period, individual enslaved African Cherokees successfully absconded from their Cherokee enslavers; yet there is also evidence that groups of enslaved people attempted to escape collectively. Some runaways absconded with parents, siblings, children, and even friends from the same plantation or neighboring farms. Runaways who escaped with their offspring realized that they faced particular obstacles. Such runaway attempts proved even more hazardous for pregnant women and mothers who had young children.[54] Not all groups of enslaved people who ventured to escape together belonged to the same family. In an interview long after the Civil War, Betty Robertson, formerly enslaved by Cherokee Joseph Vann, recalled that "my pappy run away one time mammy tell me, and at that time a whole lot of Cherokee slaves run off at once. They got over in the Creek country and stood off the Cherokee officers that went to git them, but pretty soon they give up and come home." Her mother told her that "they was lots of excitement on old Master's place and all the negroes mighty scared, but he didn't sell my pappy off. He jest kept him and he was a good negro after that. He had to work on the boat [*Lucy Walker*] . . . and never got to come home but once in a long while."[55]

The runaway attempt that Robertson described began at approximately four o'clock in the morning on 15 November 1842, when at least twenty runaways, most of whom were enslaved by Cherokee Joseph Vann, congregated near Webbers Falls in the Canadian District of the Cherokee Nation. After being joined by a number of runaways from the Mackey, Tally, and other plantations, they stole "horses, mules, etc. [rifles and ammunition] to transport them off" and then they "started for the Mexican Country."[56] Once their escape had been discovered, "a group of about forty went in pursuit. The Cherokees trailed the slaves from near Webbers Falls, southwest into the Creek Nation, where they were apparently joined by slaves from the plantations of Creek Indians named Bruner and Marshall, bringing their number to about thirty-five."[57]

Once in the Creek Nation, a group of Creeks, joined by Cherokees, pursued the runaways and overtook them about ten miles beyond the Canadian River. However, "the Negroes, who making resistance, compelled the Creeks to abandon them."[58] Approximately fifteen miles from the encounter with the Cherokee and Creek party, the group of Cherokee and Creek runaways encountered James Edwards, a white man, and Billy Wilson, a Delaware, who had taken custody of eight runaways—one man, two women, and five children. These runaways had escaped from a man named Thompson, "a Choctaw or white man with a Choctaw family."[59] When the runaways encountered the group of captured African Choctaws, they "released the captives and killed Edwards and Wilson. The Choctaw Negroes then joined the runaway party and were in company when they were all overtaken and captured."[60]

Mention of this attempted exodus on 15 November 1842 appeared in the official records of the Cherokee Nation. Two days after the runaways' departure, the Cherokee National Council passed a resolution, approved by Chief John Ross, validating that the council had "been informed, by good authority, that certain Negroes, belonging to Joseph Vann of the Canadian District and other citizens of the Nation, have plundered their owners, bid defiance to the laws of the country, and absconded: thereby making their way to the Creek Nation." In order to recapture these runaways the council ordered that Captain John Drew be "appointed to command a company, which shall consist of *One Hundred* effective men, to pursue, arrest, and deliver over said negroes, to the commanding officer at Fort for safe keeping."[61] Captain John Drew, a prominent member of the Cherokee Nation, traveled to Indian Territory several times before the signing of the Treaty of New Echota in 1835 and served as the head of the removal detachment in which Chief John Ross emigrated in 1838–39. During the 1830s, he owned a mercantile business with Richard Fields at Bayou Menard and also owned the Drew Salt Works in Webbers Falls, Canadian District. He was a practicing lawyer in the Cherokee Nation in the 1850s. His legal training assisted in his active role in the slave trade in Indian Territory.[62] The council called on Drew in this particular case due to his position as Cherokee militia captain.

On 21 November Captain Drew and a company "consisting of about ninety men" left Webbers Falls to pursue the runaways.[63] Five days later, they reached the site of the battle between the runaways and the Cherokee and Creek party. "After going 12 or 15 miles further on the route," Drew's company found the bodies of Edwards and Wilson, whom they "supposed to have been killed 4 days [before]." They found the runaways on 28 November approximately seven miles from the Red River and "about 280 miles from Webbers Falls."[64] Thirty-one of the blacks, including the enslaved African Choctaws, surrendered "being in an almost starving condition"; two runaways were not captured as they had been out hunting at the time.[65]

Drew and his company escorted the runaways back to the Cherokee Nation. They arrived at Webbers Falls on 7 December "without any occurrence of note taking place."[66] The next day, Captain John Drew reported to the Cherokee National Council. The council instructed him to return "all the Cherokee Negroes to their respective owners," except for five Cherokee runaways, who were "turned over to the Commandant of Fort Gibson for safe keeping" until they could be brought to trial for the murder of Edwards and Wilson. Hardy, one of the enslaved African Choctaws, was also turned over to the commandant. "The other Choctaw Negroes, two women and five small children," remained in Drew's custody, until they could be returned to the Choctaw Nation.[67]

Extant records—the Cherokee National Council's official response to the situation, as well as Captain John Drew's summation of selected events—reveal some aspects of this collective runaway attempt; untold, however, are the specific experiences of the runaways, in particular, their stories of what motivated them to organize this runaway attempt in a cooperative manner. It is also challenging to discuss and assess the roles of enslaved women in relation to this collective runaway attempt. Gender often shaped and limited the opportunities for women who sought to run away. For pregnant women and mothers accompanied by children, attempts to escape proved to be extremely hazardous. Being on the run alone was difficult enough; for parents who took their children with them, it was particularly dangerous for them to provide food, clothing, and other basic necessities while simultaneously eluding capture and reenslavement. Although the enslaved African Choctaws involved in this escape are identified by gender, in the extant Cherokee records (especially the official statement of Captain John Drew regarding their recapture), this is not the case for the Cherokee and Creek runaways. Nonetheless, the escape of 1842 probably included both men and women from the Cherokee, Creek, and Choctaw nations.

No written records survive about the process by which enslaved

African Cherokees on several farms in the Cherokee Nation communicated, synchronized, and strategized with enslaved African Creeks in the Creek Nation in the days, weeks, and months leading up to their escape. Instead of focusing on family members and even friends on one plantation to organize the escape, enslaved people on multiple plantations in the Cherokee and Creek nations mobilized a strategic, intertribal operation. Though their enslavers belonged to various nations, these runaways recognized their common state of bondage and yearning for freedom. Moreover, they further demonstrated this sense of camaraderie when the group of enslaved African Indians from the Cherokee and Creek nations released and welcomed the eight captured African Choctaws; as a result, by the time Captain Drew and his company overpowered this group of runaways, they included enslaved African Indian women, men, and children from three nations in Indian Territory. The collective escape of 1842 not only illustrates enslaved African Cherokees' resistance to the peculiar institution but also represents how their interactions with enslaved people of other Indian nations might have engendered and reinforced new possibilities and dreams for a free life.[68]

Although other runaway attempts and uprisings of enslaved African Indians were rumored to have occurred within Indian Territory, substantial evidence for these occurrences is lacking within the extant documents. For example, the St. *Louis Argus* reported that a slave uprising involving enslaved African Cherokees and Choctaws occurred in the summer of 1841.[69] The newspaper claimed that "large numbers of Indian negroes, and mongrels from Florida have been placed upon the borders of Arkansas and Missouri. By a gentleman direct from Fort Leavenworth, we learn that some 600 negroes from Florida and runaways from the Choctaws and Cherokees and from the whites, united with a few Indians, and perhaps a few white men, have been gradually associated in the fastnesses west of Arkansas."[70] The St. *Louis Argus* noted that this group of runaways built a log fort along the Red River. It also specifically stated that "three companies of Dragoons," reinforced by "a fine company of infantry and a couple pieces of cannon," destroyed the fort.[71]

On 7 August 1841, Niles' *National Register* reprinted the St. *Louis Argus* article regarding this dramatic confrontation and the "carnage that ensued" between runaways and the dragoons.[72] However, as the next issue of Niles' *National Register* noted, "the supposed contemplated insurrection of slaves, which occasioned alarm in Mississippi—of which the last Register contained a notice—is likely to turn out to be a false alarm. Most of those that were arrested have been examined and acquitted."[73] There were no further articles in Niles' *National Register* regarding the occurrence or resolution of this insurrection.

Although no report of this violent encounter has been found in official documents, it is possible that some portion of this account could be historically accurate, especially because authorities responded with legislation the following year. On 2 December 1842 the Cherokee National Council passed an act specifically referring to the actions of "free Negroes" in the Cherokee Nation. An immediate cause for this legislation was most likely the runaway attempt of the previous month. Section 4 of this act stated "that should any free negro or negroes be found guilty of aiding, abetting or decoying any slave or slaves, to leave his or their owner or employer, such free negro or negroes, shall receive for each and every such offence, one hundred lashes on the bare back, and be immediately removed from this Nation."[74] This law omitted any reference to a different level of punishment or protection for "free Negroes" of Cherokee blood. Though Cherokee blood granted certain privileges to free biracial African Cherokees, it would not protect such individuals who engaged in transgressions that challenged the place of enslaved African Cherokees in the Cherokee Nation.

Even though no other references to enslaved people running away en masse are found within the extant documents, in a letter from H. L. Smith to Stand Watie dated 4 April 1846, Smith mentioned that "Lewis Rosses negroes had been collecting amunition [sic] & guns and a few days since he discovered it and found several fine guns & considerable quantity of powder & lead. He could not make them confess what they intended doing with these guns and ammunition."[75] As a result of the importance of deception and secrecy surrounding slave uprisings, it is impossible to know of other failed revolts or aborted schemes similar to the escape of 1842.[76] Certainly, if there was one instance of collective resistance on the part of enslaved African Cherokees, there were probably other unrecorded attempts of this nature.

Such attempts of collective action on the part of enslaved African Cherokees, whether on the same plantation or from surrounding farms, expose the chasm between enslaved African Cherokees and free Cherokees during the resettlement era in Indian Territory. Rather than seeking to cultivate relationships with their Cherokee enslavers and other Indian neighbors in Indian Territory after arrival, some enslaved African Cherokees equated relocation to the new land with the promise of freedom. Having survived the Trail of Tears, enslaved African Cherokees embraced the possibilities of the new land—not as a final destination with their Cherokee enslavers but as the initial step to a free life on their own terms. After arrival in the new territory, runaways focused on escaping bondage from their Cherokee enslavers, while slave owners simultaneously began reasserting their power over their bondsmen and bondswomen. The horrific journey itself to Indian Territory might have heightened enslaved African Cherokees' hopes of freedom, as well as magnified the distance between their lives and those of their enslavers. A new place stimulated new perspectives about one's bondage and one's sense of self grounded not in Cherokee society but in a life away from Cherokee country—a life devoid of the shackles of bondage and filled with even higher expectations of liberty.

Although some scholars have contended that Cherokee slave owners practiced a "benign" form of slavery, such a proposition would have failed to reflect or alter the reality of enslaved African Cherokees in the Cherokee Nation who fully recognized that they were enslaved human beings. Enslaved African Indians in the Cherokee Nation, and in Indian Territory in general, were always acutely aware that neither they nor their offspring were free. As a result, some enslaved African Cherokees chose to resist the peculiar institution, no matter how "mild" its incarnation in Indian Territory. As Creek freedwoman Lizzie Jackson contended, "even if the master was good the slaves was bad off."[77] Fully cognizant of their position and "place" within the boundaries of Cherokee laws and society, some enslaved African Cherokees in the Cherokee Nation challenged conceptions of their innate inferiority steeped in racialist ideologies of blackness, Cherokeeness, and status. The tumultuous aftermath of removal amplified divisions in the Cherokee Nation and provided opportunities for enslaved African Cherokees to test the chains of bondage. Some set out on foot determined to seize freedom at any cost; others carved out other strategies for demonstrating their resistance to being categorized as property—as chattel—in the Cherokee Nation, Indian Territory.

Day-to-Day Resistance to the Peculiar Institution and the Struggle to Remain Free in the Antebellum Cherokee Nation

Uncle expecting to go turkey hunting the next morning, had Smoot help him mould bullets to use. That day, Uncle had sold a good horse and had the money in the house. That night after they had gone to sleep, Smoot took an ax, killed Uncle Harry and pounded Aunt Cyntha until he thought she was dead. Then taking the money, a good horse, and an old rifle he left the place. ◆ Cherokee Grover Hanna

Slave resistance. The phrase has historically conjured up particular icons: Sojourner Truth, Frederick Douglass, Nat Turner, Harriet Tubman. It has also invoked certain spaces and images: the hold and deck of slave ships during the Middle Passage; the auction block; slave cabins; rice, sugarcane, cotton, and tobacco plantations throughout the South; the Big House; women, men, and children on the run; the very bodies of enslaved people engraved with marks of the whip and other instruments of torture. In the last half of the twentieth century, scholars have complicated and interrogated our understanding(s) of slave resistance—of the resisters and the various manifestations of resistance itself.[1] We no longer categorize resistance as solely centered around acts of collective rebellion grounded in slave uprisings. Scholarly discourse about slave resistance has evolved to incorporate the actions of enslaved women to manipulate their fertility and obstruct male access to their bodies. It also includes special languages created by enslaved people to communicate beyond the scope of their owners' comprehension. Everyday acts of slave resistance emerge, too, in clothing and other adornments, as well as the

51

geographical spaces of celebration marked out by the enslaved far from their owners' gaze.[2]

Yet, even with the expanding, critical discussions on this subject matter, the specific topic of African Indian slave resistance in Indian nations remains largely ignored, as if it were essentially nonexistent.[3] Thus, the commodification and vulnerability of enslaved African Indians in Indian nations have been veiled time and time again, buried by a particular construction of Indian spaces as solely sites of African American refuge. Shattering that notion of a safe haven, scattered documents reveal stories of the resistance of enslaved African Cherokees to daily indignities of bondage in the antebellum Cherokee Nation. For enslaved men and women, a range of disorderly acts fashioned their inner lives in an Indian country that, to them, represented not a sanctuary but a site of severe repression. Even though the actions of individual enslaved people did not terminate the presence of bondage in the new Cherokee territory, the opposition of enslaved and free African Cherokees to enslavement exposed the precious and meaningful substance of freedom to the free and unfree in the Cherokee Nation.

While reward advertisements for runaways provide evidence of this specific form of slave resistance, documentation of other rebellious behavior in Indian Territory remains more ambivalent and elusive. Some enslaved people, particularly women, employed acts of noncooperation, retaliation, and theft, as well as verbal and physical confrontation. Free blacks, too, in antebellum Cherokee country struggled to distance themselves from any form of bondage in order to retain their status as free persons of color in Indian Territory. Although passing as free people of color became a useful and effective disguise for some runaways, the plight of free people of color in Indian Territory and other slaveholding communities was not always a secure, safe, or even an enviable one. Some African Cherokee families in Indian Territory included individuals who were enslaved people, freedpeople, and freeborn persons of color, as well as those who vacillated along the continuum from slavery to freedom. Whether enslaved or free, people of African descent in the Cherokee Nation understood that bondage shaped their lives as well as the lives of their loved ones as radically as slavery impacted the lives of their counterparts in the Southeast.

Although the traditional story of collusion and cooperation between African Americans and Indians still dominates the narrative of black-Indian interaction in the United States, the actions of enslaved African Cherokees in the Cherokee Nation dispute such a generalization and identify it as a selective representation of the past. In fact, the specific pathways of resistance taken by enslaved African Cherokees in the Cherokee Nation illustrate some commonalities between slave resisters and acts of transgression in Indian Territory and the southeastern states. Although they did not decide to abscond permanently from Indian Territory, unruly enslaved African Cherokees who remained on their owners' farms and plantations subtly and overtly expressed their opposition to bondage on a daily basis. Even as they became more accustomed to life in Indian Territory in the antebellum era, enslaved African Cherokees tested the chains of bondage in the new Cherokee country west of the Mississippi.

Day-to-Day Slave Resistance

Even when enslaved people chose not to risk the copious repercussions of running away to procure their freedom, many still demonstrated their abhorrence for their enslaved state in actions ranging from unforeseen deeds to calculated strategies. Enslaved people often feigned illness, worked slowly, and even refused to work in order to rebel against their overseers and enslavers. Many simply curbed their productivity on their owners' farms or plantations, as a way of directly affecting the overall efficiency and output of their owners' businesses. Cherokee freedman Henry Henderson, formerly enslaved by Cherokee Martin Vann, remembered slave owners in the Cherokee Nation "always treated their slaves good, only whipped the mean ones who wouldn't work."[4] Some of the Cherokee slave owners "built log pens on their place for keeping a negro should he get mean or do something wrong. They called it the bull ring. . . . The master put that slave in the bull ring and lay on with the lash. When the whipping is over the master say: 'Now go do that again!' Most always the man didn't do it again."[5] As in the southeastern states, some Cherokee owners applied the lash as an appropriate punishment for uncooperative "property." Reasserting their position as enslaver might have been even more significant for Cherokee slave owners in the new territory. By reinforcing the rules of enslavement in various ways after removal, especially in response to disorderly conduct, Cherokee slave owners conveyed a crucial message—enslaved people should not imagine the new territory in the West as a site for renegotiating, and possibly eradicating, their enslaved status.

Even as owners attempted to buttress their authority over enslaved people, those enslaved tested and challenged the extent of their owners' influence in the new territory. One of the frequently practiced forms of slave resistance involved the theft of goods and property, including food, clothing, and animals. As was the case for enslaved people in the southeastern United States, enslaved African Cherokees stole an array of items from their owners. These acts served to protest vile treatment and harsh conditions, as well as to provide necessities for themselves and their families. Cherokee freedwoman Sarah Wilson recalled that her aunt "was always pestering around trying to get something for herself." However, one day while she was cleaning the yard, their master—Ben Johnson—saw "her pick up something and put it inside her apron. He flew at her and cussed her, and started like he was going to hit her but she just stood right up to him and never budged, and when he come close she just screamed out loud and run at him with her fingers stuck out straight and jabbed him in the belly. He had a soft belly, too, and it hurt him. He seen she wasn't going to be afraid, and he set out to sell her."[6]

Such actions contested owners' sweeping control over enslaved people's daily lives. Most owners expected obsequious behavior from enslaved people on their farms and those in surrounding Cherokee communities; instead of complying with her owner's expectations of submissiveness, Wilson's aunt communicated, through her words and actions, no such deference for her owner's authority. In response to her offenses, Ben Johnson utilized one of his primary privileges as enslaver and attempted to sell Wilson's aunt—a particular course to penalize those deemed "troublesome property." Like other enslavers in the Cherokee Nation and in the southeastern states, Ben Johnson recognized that such expressed misconduct not only served to defy his authority but also encouraged others along a similar path of rebelliousness. Just as the presence of runaways in the vicinity of plantations vexed Cherokee slave owners, so, too, did private and public acts of rebellion on their farms prove economically and emotionally taxing to owners in Indian Territory.

Whether or not the altercation between Wilson's aunt and Johnson specifically motivated others to question his authority, Johnson became involved in verbal and physical confrontations with other enslaved people during the antebellum period. In order to curtail misdemeanors on his plantation, he took some of the enslaved men to a hanging in Fort Smith, Arkansas. Johnson "tied them all in the wagon, and when they had seen the hanging he asked them if they was scared of them dead men hanging up there." All but one of these men said yes. Nick, Sarah Wilson's uncle, rebuffed " 'No, I ain't a-feared of them nor nothing else in this worl',' and old Master jumped on him while he was tied and beat him with a rope." As Wilson remembered, after they returned home, Johnson "tied old Nick to a tree and took his shirt off and poured the cat-o-nine tails to him until he fainted away and fell over like he was dead. I never forget seeing all that blood all over my uncle, and I could hate that old Indian any more I guess I would, but I hated him all I could already I reckon."[7]

It is interesting that Sarah Wilson refers to Ben Johnson here as an "old Indian." Ben Johnson, like other white men in the Cherokee Nation, had married a Cherokee woman (Annie Johnson) and thus become a member of the Nation through marriage. Though such men were not biologically "Indian," Sarah Wilson and others in the Cherokee Nation recognized many of these individuals as "Indian." Indeed, many enslaved African Cherokees may have become so accustomed to interacting with light-skinned, biracial European Cherokees in the Nation that intermarried white members of the Cherokee Nation may have more easily blended into some communities in the Nation due to the legacy of European and Cherokee interactions and relationships. Based on 1860 census data, Michael F. Doran estimated that 716 whites resided in the Cherokee Nation, constituting approximately 4 percent of the total population.[8] As stated earlier, an increasing number of white men married Cherokee women in the eighteenth century; such unions continued to occur into the nineteenth century. Ben Johnson's ideas of mastering reflected his individual personality; however, he and other white masters, who married into the Cherokee Nation, shared their mastering techniques with other members of the Nation. Even though brutal mastering techniques of Cherokee owners also emerged in the Nation, the presence of white slave-owning men in Indian Territory certainly shaped the overall tenor of enslaved-enslaver interactions in the new land. Cherokee and intermarried white slave owners in the Cherokee Nation habitually employed intimidation as a useful tactic to inhibit unruly activities of enslaved people. Even though this strategy regularly resulted in the desired responses, some enslaved people would not be swayed and continued to express their indignation toward their enslavers.

Other forms of punishment and torture could also be callously utilized on those who continued to resist in order to achieve acquiescence. Like Sarah Wilson, Cherokee freedwoman Charlotte Johnson White also recalled the harsh treatment her family experienced while enslaved by Ben and Annie Johnson. One day when her mother was too sick to get up, "de old master [Ben Johnson] come around to see about it, and he yelled, 'Get out of dere and get yourself in de fields.' She tried to go but was too sick to work. She got to the door alright; couldn't hurry fast enough for de old master though, so he pushed her in a little ditch dat was by the cabin and whipped her back wid the lash, den he reached down and rolled her over so's he could beat her face and neck." Charlotte Johnson White remembered that her mother "didn't live long after dat and I guess de whippin's helped to kill her, but she better off dead than jest livin' for the whip."[9]

Though enslaved people often feigned illness as a way to refuse regular duties, Charlotte Johnson White presented her mother's illness as all too real—so real, in fact, that death followed soon after this beating. Ben Johnson probably believed that White's mother was pretending to be ill in order to shirk her responsibilities, as others had attempted to do at various points before and after arrival in the new Cherokee territory. Even if he had recognized that White's mother was too sick to work, this actuality failed to persuade him to excuse her from fieldwork that day. Instead, he used this opportunity to emit a clear message in a public space about the demands of labor and the strict regimen on his farm. Certainly, the death of White's mother soon after this beating relayed a message to other enslaved people who witnessed (or heard about) this attack—a message louder than the sound of Johnson's orders or the whip against her skin.

As eyewitnesses of such beatings of parents and kin in general, enslaved children regularly observed a range of horrific acts of torture, and they quickly deciphered the meanings of such actions. Their responses to these episodes ranged from compliance to outright insolence. Having witnessed her mother's treatment at the hands of Ben Johnson, it is possible that Charlotte Johnson White vented her anger about her mother's death in acts of resistance cloaked as negligence. When she was about twelve years old, she "was tendin' the master's children like what dey tell me to do, and den one day somehow I drop one of dem right by where de old master was burning some brush in de yard. 'What you do that for?' he yelled, and while I was stoopin' to pick up de baby he grabbed me and shoved me into de fire! I sent into dat fire head first, but I never know how I got out. See this old drawn, scarred face? Dat's what I got from de fire, and inside my lips is burned off, and my back is scarred wid lashings dat'll be wid me when I meet my Jesus!"[10] White eventually got "sick of being treated mean by everybody," and after her mother died, she "slipped off in de woods to get away and wandered 'round 'til I come to a place folks said was Scullyville. . . . But de old master track me down and dere I is back at de ol' farm for more whippin's."[11] It is difficult to ascertain whether Charlotte Johnson White accidentally or intentionally dropped one of Ben and Annie Johnson's children. Because one duty of enslaved children often involved the care of their owners' children, enslaved children like Charlotte Johnson White recognized that interactions with their owners' children represented more than child's play. Indeed, some enslaved children and women entrusted with the care of their young masters and mistresses manipulated their access to these children to harm or even kill them.

Although White spoke of Ben Johnson's visceral response to her dropping one of his children, there is no indication of how her mistress, Cherokee Annie Johnson, responded. Some sense of how her mistress reacted to this "accident" might be gleaned from Annie Johnson's other interactions with enslaved people. As Sarah Wilson explicitly stated, Old Master (Ben Johnson) "wasn't the only hellion neither. Old Mistress [Annie Johnson] just as bad, and she took most of her wrath out hitting us children all the time." However, she was "afraid of the grown Negroes. Afraid of what they might do while old Master was away, but she beat us children all the time."[12] In response to the severe actions of her enslavers, Charlotte Johnson White might have decided to literally take matters into her own hands and dropped one of their children into the fire as an act of retribution for past deeds against herself and loved ones.

A great deal of attention has been focused on slave-owning men and their interactions with and control of enslaved people; yet, slave-owning women, like Cherokee Annie Johnson, also benefited from the peculiar institution in the Cherokee Nation, as they did in other slaveholding societies.[13] Due to the particular place of women in the matrilineally based Cherokee society, some Cherokee women enslaved African Cherokees before and after removal to Indian Territory. Indeed, the Cherokee Nation enacted several laws in the nineteenth century in order to protect the property, including enslaved people, of Cherokee women who had married non-Cherokee men.[14] With the creation of a Cherokee republic in the early nineteenth century, women's authority in the new Cherokee Nation had become truncated, partially due to the emulation of European American values. Their changing status in the Cherokee Nation affected Cherokee women's interactions with those they enslaved. As their position and roles continued to evolve, Cherokee women recognized that one signifier of their ongoing control and power after removal to Indian Territory rested with the enslaved members of their households. Cherokee women's power and control over enslaved people in their households remained constant and concentrated even as other aspects of their lives altered around them.

In the new nation west of the Mississippi it is hard not to imagine the struggles that transpired between enslaved and enslavers in slaveholding households. Where Cherokee women's authority had diminished due to the changing sociopolitical nature of the Cherokee Nation after removal from their homeland, enslaved African Cherokees attempted to thwart their enslavers' control over them. Even though Cherokee children represented particularly accessible and vulnerable targets in slaveholding households, enslaved African Cherokees primarily directed their aggression toward their adult enslavers, men and women, who were responsible for their state of bondage. Cherokee Grover C. Hanna, for example, recalled the surprising actions of one trusted enslaved individual called "Nigger Smoot." One night, Hanna's uncle, "expecting to go turkey hunting the next morning, had Smoot help him mould bullets to use. That day, Uncle had sold a good horse and had the money in the house. That night after they had gone to sleep, Smoot took an ax, killed Uncle Harry and pounded Aunt Cyntha until he thought she was dead. Then taking the money, a good horse, and an old rifle he left the place." One of Hanna's other uncles, Zeke Proctor, "trailed him from the Illinois River to Fredonia, Kansas."[15] Proctor located Smoot and forcibly returned him to the Cherokee Nation, where he was hung ten days after murdering his owner.[16]

Although it is unclear what specific conditions motivated Smoot, what is clear is that his murderous intentions were directed at not only his master but also his mistress. Undeniably, as Smoot brandished the ax, his master and mistress must have wondered how and why such a trusted slave could resort to such actions against them. Perhaps Smoot's owner recalled his final orders as he succumbed to the ax; as Smoot pounded his mistress with the ax, she (even more than her husband) might have been entirely perplexed and astonished by his actions. Even as Smoot presented himself as a trusted servant, or had been perceived by his owners and others as such, he had been waiting for this prime opportunity when he had access to weapons and money.

Smoot could have taken the money, horse, and rifle and simply ran away; however, his plan included the murder of his master and mistress. His use of the ax against both of them symbolizes his resignation not only to abscond from his site of enslavement but also to terminate the lives of those who enslaved him and perpetuated his state of bondage. Any affinity or loyalty he might have felt to either his master or mistress at an earlier point had been obliterated with his lethal handling of the ax.

Although Smoot and other enslaved African Cherokees sought to repossess their bodies and lives by murdering their enslavers, some employed self-mutilation as a means of publicly declaring ownership of their bodies and countering notions of their inhumanity. Acutely aware of the value of their labor and physical bodies, enslaved people vehemently displayed their refusal to be sold as chattel on the site that embodied the very essence of bondage. In one dramatic case, Cherokee freedwoman Nancy Rogers Bean described her aunt as a "mean, fighting woman. She was to be sold and when the bidding started she grabbed a hatchet, laid her hand on a log and chopped it off. Then she throwed the bleeding hand right in her master's face."[17] Enslaved African Cherokees, like Nancy Rogers Bean's aunt, understood how the commodification of their bodies shaped and secured the socioeconomic structures in the Cherokee Nation and other slaveholding communities. As a result, such actions of self-mutilation, though physically painful for those who committed them, simultaneously hindered the ongoing sale of enslaved African Cherokees and epitomized their reclamation of their own bodies in Indian Territory.

Even though some historians have contended that Cherokee slave owners practiced a "benign" form of slavery, such a proposition would have failed to reflect the thoughts of Smoot or Nancy Rogers Bean's aunt when she mounted that auction block. Enslaved African Cherokees in the Cherokee Nation, Indian Territory, fully recognized that they were enslaved human beings—the property of Cherokees. They were exceedingly aware that neither they nor their offspring were free. Some had family members and friends who ran away or challenged their enslavement via other avenues; in fact, multigenerational acts of resistance served as signposts of a family's legacy of rebellion. Others, like Charlotte Johnson White, had not only witnessed the beatings of mothers, fathers, sisters, brothers, aunts, and uncles but also experienced the whip for themselves. Such images, sensations, and scars remained firmly imprinted in their psyche as well as on their bodies for decades; the memories and marks would be with them, as Charlotte Johnson White uttered, even in the afterworld.

Stolen Property and Kidnapped Free African Cherokees

Theft of property, including enslaved African Cherokees, must also be seen as a form of resistance by enslaved people in Cherokee country. As a result of the significant incidence of thefts occurring in the Cherokee Nation during this time, the Cherokee National Council passed an act on 19 September 1839 to address this particular criminal activity. The act stated "that any person who shall be convicted of stealing a horse, mule, jack or jinny, shall be punished by not less than thirty-nine nor more than one hundred stripes on the bare back, and be compelled to make payment to the amount of damages or injury sustained, if such stolen property be not restored, for the benefit of the person so injured." In the case of "all other property which may be stolen, upon conviction of the party so offending, the punishment shall be in proportion to the magnitude of the offence, at the discretion of the court, and judgment against the offender for damages to the party injured."[18]

This act addressed theft of property without any specific reference to the theft of enslaved people. Due to the growing number of thefts of enslaved people during the 1840s, however, the Cherokee National Council passed an act on 17 October 1846, amending the 1839 act. In order to deter such criminal activities, the council authorized a harsher penalty for the theft of property. The punishment for stealing enslaved people was the gallows. The amended act stipulated "that any person or persons, who may be convicted of stealing a negro or negroes, shall suffer death by hanging. And any person or persons, who may be convicted of stealing a horse, mule, jack or jinny, for the first offence shall be punished with not less than one hundred stripes on the bare back, and compelled to make payment as is provided for in said act, and any person or persons, who upon conviction before any Court having jurisdiction of the same, of stealing a horse, jack, mule or jinny, for the third offence, shall suffer death by hanging."[19] Due to the frequency of theft of human property, the council revised the law in order to dissuade perpetrators of such crimes. The severity of the punishment for stealing enslaved people, compared to that for stealing other "property," underscored the socioeconomic importance of enslaved African Cherokees to Cherokee slave owners and the Cherokee Nation itself.

Although advertisements for missing enslaved people usually pertained to runaways, owners also offered rewards for enslaved people who were abducted or "stolen" from their masters or mistresses.[20] On 18 January 1846 Cherokee Jane Love discovered that Log, her fourteen-year-old slave, "had been taken," presumably "by some of the Cherokee outlaws." In the reward notice, Love expressed her belief that Log would "be conveyed probably to Rusk county, Texas, or to the Cherokee Village on the Brasos." Love must have considered Log particularly important, for she offered $100 for his recovery and delivery to her residence in Going Snake District, Cherokee Nation. Perhaps Log's ability to speak "Cherokee well" was a partial explanation of his worth to his mistress.[21] The theft of enslaved people was not particular to Indian Territory. In fact, slave stealing often occurred throughout the slaveholding United States. Kidnappers transported abducted enslaved and free people of color to "different parts of the South, then secretly took them before a magistrate and, for a price, secured false titles and other legal documents saying that they were the slave owners. If questioned, they could claim that they were bringing in a fugitive."[22]

Though reports often indicated the theft of an individual enslaved person, like Log, within the Cherokee Nation, kidnappers also sought to steal several enslaved people and other property. As the Cherokee newspaper noted on 17 March 1846, two months after Log was stolen, five or six "villains" crossed into the Cherokee Nation, "pushed themselves into the negro-houses of Mrs. Elizabeth Pack, and kidnapped a couple of negro children, and stole two mules." This group of men "went prepared to resist to the utmost, any attempt that might be made to frustrate their object; and committed the daring outrage within a few yards of the dwelling-house of Mrs. Pack." The men "were pursued a short distance and fired upon once, but without effect. One of the mules got loose and returned home; and a horse which one of the party was riding, dashed up against a stump and was crippled so badly that he had to be left." Residents found and recognized articles belonging to the robbers including a gun and a cap. They also identified the crippled horse as the property of "Madison Gerring, a white man, connected with the banditti."[23] Moreover, "Mrs. Pack's negroes recognized James Taylor, as being one of the party; and he has since been arrested."[24] This was the second time these men had stolen from Mrs. Pack; the first time they took two mules from her residence. The acts of Gerring and his Cherokee associates did not always occur in a random fashion. Instead, they demonstrated the rippling effects of the post-removal schism in the Cherokee Nation between treaty signers and opposers.[25] It is clear from the *Cherokee Advocate*'s description of events that not only did Cherokee authorities address kidnapping attempts in a timely manner, but Cherokee residents also became invested in the judicious resolution of such crimes within the boundaries of their communities.

The Cherokee newspaper not only reported the theft of enslaved people but also considered their return newsworthy. In November 1846 the *Cherokee Advocate* described the kidnapping of two boys enslaved by Johnson Whitmire (the wealthy Cherokee slave owner of Whitmire Plantation on Peavine Creek in the Flint District). The article named Mat Guering and Creek Starr as the kidnappers in this case.[26] These two boys were found two months after being stolen. The same $100 reward advertisement for these two boys appeared every week in the *Cherokee Advocate* (most times in Cherokee and English) beginning on 26 November 1846 and ending in January 1847 with the recovery of the boys.[27] In another kidnapping situation, a short article in the *Cherokee Advocate* simply stated: "kidnapping.—We understand that a negro boy belonging to Mr. Jas. M. Payne, was kidnapped on Tuesday the 10th inst. The boy has since returned home."[28] It is not clear whether the boy was actually kidnapped, escaped, and then returned home or if he ran away and returned.

With the prevalence of the kidnapping of enslaved people during the chaotic postremoval period, some enslaved African Cherokees used these circumstances to their advantage. They could, in fact, have been "lying out" for a couple of days, later claiming when they returned on their own accord that they had been stolen from their owners' residences. Other enslaved people surely seized upon such opportune moments to garner some time away from their owners' farms and plantations in order to enjoy a moment when they could be the masters of their own destiny. The existence of such acts of theft provided additional cover for enslaved people testing the viability of running away without dire consequences; if caught, they could attempt to explain their absence with a fabricated kidnapping story. Cherokee owners, on the other hand, would have to ascertain the veracity of a "missing" person's story based on the enslaved person's past history of loyalty or deceit, particular circumstances of departure, and current kidnapping cases in the Nation. An epidemic of "missing" enslaved people in an area could also encourage some to run away under the guise of being kidnapped. Just as Maroon communities throughout the Americas often countered slave owners' control of their human property, a rash of "kidnappings" and "missing" enslaved people in the Cherokee Nation could foster more disorderly activities of enslaved African Cherokees on Cherokee farms and plantations.

Even as enslaved African Cherokees sought freedom, on the other hand, free African Cherokees knew how fragile their status as free people was in the Cherokee Nation. Due to the profitable business of selling enslaved people of African descent, kidnappers calculated ways to abduct not only enslaved African Cherokees but also freedpeople and freeborn people of color. The kidnappings of African Cherokees illustrate not only the vulnerability of enslaved people but also the tenuous position held by freeborn people of color in Indian Territory.

One's position as an enslaved person, freedperson, or free person of color directly characterized and influenced one's status, one's rights, and the nature and conditions of freedom in the Cherokee

Nation. In the postremoval period, the Cherokee Nation differentiated enslaved people from freedpeople, as well as freedpeople from free Cherokee citizens. As previously stated, the Cherokee National Council distinctly delineated the status of emancipated slaves, usually referred to in the records as "free Negroes," within the Cherokee Nation and clearly correlated "Cherokee blood" with certain liberties. There was also a distinction in the laws between freedpeople in general and enslaved people who were freed by Cherokee citizens. On 2 December 1842 the council, possibly concerned with the undue influence of recently freed Seminoles on enslaved African Cherokees, required "the Sheriffs of the several Districts of this Nation to notify all free Negroes who may be in this Nation, excepting such as may have been freed by our citizens, that they must leave the limits of this Nation by the first day of January, eighteen hundred and forty-three; or as soon thereafter as may be practicable." For those "free Negroes" who refused to leave, the sheriffs were empowered "to report such negro or negroes to the United States' Agent for the Cherokees, for immediate expulsion from the Nation."[29]

Even as Cherokee laws demanded the expulsion of "free Negroes" not directly connected to Cherokees, the Cherokee National Council also curbed the activities of emancipated African Cherokees. The council mandated that Cherokee citizens who freed enslaved people would be "held responsible for the conduct of the negro or negroes so freed: and in case the citizen or citizens so freeing any negro or negroes, shall die or remove from the limits of this Nation, it shall be required of such negro or negroes, that he, she, or they give satisfactory security to any one of the Circuit Judges, for their conduct, or herein failing, he, she, or they shall be subject to removal as above specified."[30] Such laws restricting the activities and rights of free blacks often characterized quasi freedom in the United States.[31]

Cherokee freedpeople were cognizant of their precarious position and limited liberties as residents in the Cherokee Nation.[32] Articles in the Cherokee newspaper reflected their unpredictable conditions. Just as enslaved people were stolen from their owners in the Cherokee Nation and sold within Indian Territory and in surrounding states, freedpeople and freeborn people of color in the Cherokee Nation were kidnapped and sold as enslaved people in other areas. The *Cherokee Advocate* reported that on the night of 27 September 1847 "two mulatto children were kidnapped from their mother on Grand River, and run off into the State. The children are girls, both free, and of Cherokee mixture, and were taken by three men, two of whom were recognized as white men." The kidnappers "entered the house, enquired of the mother where her children were, tied them while in bed in her presence and took them off—one of them representing himself as the sheriff of Delaware District." Due to the "very gross and daring" nature of this "outrage," *Cherokee Advocate* editor William P. Ross demanded that "some measure should be adopted by those in authority to restore its unfortunate victims to freedom." It was believed that the "notorious villain, Mat. Gerring, and some of his associates were the perpetrators of the outrage."[33]

Sometime after their kidnapping, Charles Landrum, sheriff of Delaware District, Cherokee Nation, "received information as to the course they had taken, and set out in pursuit of them in company with a Cherokee and a white man." They found the two girls "about twelve miles beyond Warsaw, Missouri at a house at which they had been left for sale." Landrum subsequently "brought them back to the Nation and restored them to their freedom."[34] Editor Ross maintained that Landrum deserved "great credit for interesting himself in this affair and for recovering these two girls, who had been kidnapped and run off by that notorious wretch, Mat Guering, and one of the Starrs."[35] On 12 November 1847 the Cherokee National Council allocated twenty-three dollars out of the National Treasury "for the benefit of Charles Landrum and Pigeon Half-breed. That amount having been expended by them in pursuing into the State of Missouri, and recovering the two grand-daughters of Shoe Boot, deceased, who had been kidnapped on the night of the 27th of September last, from the residence of their mother in Delaware District, Cherokee Nation, for the purpose of being sold into slavery."[36]

The theft and sale of free people of African descent, whether or not they were also of Cherokee descent, occurred within Indian Territory and the United States. Free African Americans in the United States could be "cast back into bondage illegally, kidnapped in the North and taken to the plantations in the deep South or taken in the Upper South and transported with coffles of slaves to the lower states. . . . There were penalties for illegally selling free people of color, but the profits could be substantial, and it was difficult for reenslaved free blacks to bring their cases to court."[37] This type of activity was not exceptional by any means. However, the fact that Sheriff Charles Landrum traveled all the way to Warsaw, Missouri, in order to return the two girls to their home reveals some sense of the Cherokee Nation's accountability to free African Cherokees, especially those of Cherokee descent. It is also possible that Sheriff Landrum wanted to be part of the recovery effort because one of the kidnappers had misrepresented himself as Sheriff Landrum. If the girls had not been of Cherokee descent, in particular descendants of Captain Shoe Boots, it is uncertain that such an effort would have been made by the sheriff and others to return them to their home in the Cherokee Nation. As Tiya Miles posited, the "liberation of Shoe Boots and Doll's granddaughters bears out the contention that Cherokees and other slaveholding Indians made special allowances for kin of African descent. At the same time, this incident, as well as the Cherokee slave revolt, raises the disturbing question of what became of slaves whom Cherokees did not recognize as relatives."[38]

A year and a half after the kidnapping of Shoe Boots's granddaughters, on 19 February 1849, the *Cherokee Advocate* reported another case involving the kidnapping of Cherokee freedpeople from the Nation. A lengthy letter dated 16 January 1849 from J. T. Trezevant, mayor of South Memphis, addressed to the editor of the *Cherokee Advocate* provided detailed information regarding the status of two freedwomen who claimed they had been kidnapped from their home in the Cherokee Nation.[39] Mayor Trezevant's letter indicated that the "two Cherokees" were living at his residence. One of the women who had been kidnapped related her story to Cherokee John Brown during his visit to Trezevant's residence in July 1848.[40] Aiky explained that about 25 May 1848, "she and her daughter Nannie were stolen and carried away from Archibald Campbell's by a young man named Chisholm (A.F.) and a negro Spaniard—called Moses." She recalled "that she was knocked down and her hands tied, and she and her daughter put in a canoe— that Chisholm made her lie down in the canoe, whenever they were passing a settlement on the River—that they were brought to Ft. Smith or Little Rock . . . and then put on a Steam boat and brought to this place to be sold." Although Chisholm held a bill of sale for them it was "doubtless manufactured for the purpose."[41]

When Aiky and Nannie arrived in Memphis, members of the Memphis community requested Trezevant's intervention in their sale, as some citizens "thought there was foul play going on." Although he was uncertain about what actions to take, Trezevant was "convinced from observations, and from signs from the woman, that she was not an Indian Negress." In June 1848 Trezevant, a lawyer by profession, "commenced suit against Chisholm; and upon application, the Judge had her taken out of his custody by the Sheriff, with instructions to place her somewhere." Because "no one would take them," and not wanting them to "go to prison merely for safe keeping," Trezevant took them to his residence, "where, they have been ever since." In response to the actions of Trezevant, Chisholm left Memphis and promised "to return with evidence to prove her a slave . . . but he has not yet come."[42]

Trezevant estimated that the case would be presented in March 1849. Because he did not believe Chisholm would return for them, he thought that the women would be set free again. Trezevant's letter appealed to the Cherokee people to compensate him for the expenses he had incurred in providing for these women. He described the women as a "dead expense," as they did not "know how to do the business or duties of a house servant." Even though he had provided for these women for several months, he thought they were also "in a way—dirty and offensive." If he won the suit, Trezevant requested $500 from the Cherokee Nation to compensate him not only for expenses already paid to provide for the two women but also for their passage home.[43]

In February 1849 James S. Vann, editor of the *Cherokee Advocate*, highlighted the urgency of the freedwomen's situation in a lead article.

He supported the veracity of the women's story, emphasizing that the "statements therein made by the women, Aiky and Nannie, are substantially true, so far as we are able to ascertain the facts. Those women were given their freedom by their mistress at her death—of which fact there is indubitable proof in the country. The writer of the will is now living, and is at the present time the high Sheriff of Canadian District.—The witness to the same is also alive—Mr. John Leack of Canadian District. . . . He is well known by most of the citizens of this Nation to be strictly a man of truth."[44]

Vann recalled that two years earlier, in 1847, "there was a Cherokee prosecuted and tried by the authorities of the Nation, for the offence of selling these same free women. But the evidence not being sufficient to prove the fact, he was acquitted of the charge. In this trial and acquittal, *the question of their freedom was not at all involved.* That was an acknowledged fact, as well as proven on the day of trial. The question was not, were these persons free or not—but did the prisoner sell them? The evidence was not sufficient to convict, consequently he was liberated."[45] Having never considered Chisholm "an honorable man," Vann also expressed doubt as to "A. F. Chisholm being the owner, or in any way concerned in the concocting of the bill of sale." Vann believed "*it the duty of the nation to attend to the matter, and extend the same watchfull care to these unfortunate women, it has ever intended to their citizens, when placed in unfortunate circumstances.* The magnanimous and philanthropic conduct and aid which the generous Mayor of Memphis has extended to our suffering citizens, should not be passed by in silence. But the most prompt and efficient measures should be taken to aid him in bringing about an act of justice."[46] Vann clearly identified these two women as part of the Cherokee Nation, part of the Cherokee community, part of the Cherokee citizenry. This was not an issue of Cherokee "property" being stolen; it was a matter of two Cherokee citizens being in "unfortunate circumstances" and "suffering" as a result of their freed status being compromised.[47]

Aiky and her family had been plagued with kidnapping attempts. Even while Aiky and her daughter Nannie attempted to regain their freedom while retained in Memphis, Aiky's other two daughters engaged in a legal battle for their own freedom. In her story, Aiky stated that "she had two [other] daughters, Peggy and Betsy," who were stolen in 1847 and sold "by a man named Shore." After they were stolen, "she and Nannie ran in the woods and kept out of the way, until one of the Coodeys, who was a friend of hers got her to go to Arch Campbell's or his sons—to stay, until some suit about her freedom should be decided. While at Campbell's she [Aiky] was stolen, during his absence from home." Peggy and Betsy would finally have their say in court three years later. In October 1850, *Cherokee Advocate* editor David Carter included a notice indicating that the case of Peggy and Betsy, "claiming their freedom, as free-born Cherokees," would be addressed "in the Courts of Judicature, in the State of Mississippi."[48] At the time the notice appeared in the newspaper, those involved with this case were in the Cherokee Nation "procuring what testimony they may be able to gather in reference to the subject." Mr. Wair, "the innocent purchaser of Peggy and Betsy from the Shores,[49] certain negro-traders of the State of Arkansas, having been sued by Peggy and Betsy for their freedom, as well as for damages to the amount of several thousand dollars, is desirous of procuring all the testimony that can be got in the Cherokee country in reference to such fact."[50]

While investigating Peggy and Betsy's story, Wair had "learned that Peggy and Betsy were once owned as slaves by a Cherokee woman named Wut-ty, who set them free by a Will, at her death. Or, that Peggy and Betsy had failed to establish such Will by law, and were consequently held as estate property and sold as slaves." From Mr. Wair's statement, it appeared that he had "no wish whatever, to enslave the said Peggy and Betsy as freed negroes, and much less as free-born Cherokees. But that his sole object is to ascertain whether they are freed negroes or free-born Cherokees." This distinction was particularly important "as the damage in the later case will be a large amount. Whereas in the former it will be but trifling, perhaps only the purchase money and cost of suit."[51]

Editor Carter explained that "the report in this country, so far as we have been able to learn is, that Peggy and Betsy were set free, or intended so to be, by the old Lady Wut-ty, at her death." However, "the said Peggy and Betsy not understanding what would be necessary for them to do in the premises, and not knowing any thing of the formalities of law, and from the sinister motives of those who ought to have instructed them in this matter, they remained in ignorance of their true situation, until since they have been placed in the situation they are now in." Carter noted that "a Mr. Montgomery, a citizen of the State and neighborhood where Peggy and Betsy were sold, in connection with a Mr. Hildebrand, a citizen of this Nation, have undertaken to assist Peggy and Betsy to secure their freedom, by a suit at law in the State where they live." Carter expressed his hope "that those who may know any thing of the matter, will not hesitate to let it be known, in order that the truth may be ascertained." In addition, any person having information on this matter was asked to attend a meeting on 7 October 1850 to provide evidence that would restore Peggy's and Betsy's freedom.[52] Unfortunately, from the extant documents, it is uncertain if Aiky and her daughters ever regained their freedom.

The kidnapping attempts on Shoe Boots's two granddaughters, as well as Aiky and her three daughters—Nannie, Peggy, and Betsy—in the late 1840s underscore the fragility of freedom and vulnerability of Cherokee freedpeople and freeborn people of African and Cherokee descent in the Cherokee Nation. Nonetheless, the actions of individual Cherokees and the Cherokee National Council to resolve the perilous situation of these African Cherokees reflect the Nation's sense of duty concerning previously enslaved African Cherokees and freeborn biracial African Cherokee members of the Nation. Following each of these kidnapping episodes, members of the Cherokee citizenry and the council explicitly conveyed that they intended to maintain and protect the liberty of their recently freed and freeborn citizens of African descent. Even though slaveholding citizens of the Cherokee Nation supported the passage of the Fugitive Slave Act of 1850,[53] enacted only months after the kidnapping of Aiky and one of her daughters, the position of the Cherokee citizenry on freed and freeborn people of color in the Nation reflected a different kind of sensibility. For those defined as enslaved members of the Nation, attempts to subvert bondage and attain freedom would not be tolerated. However, if manumission had been granted by Cherokee citizens, the Nation recognized the rights, though limited, of African Cherokee freedpeople and sought, whenever possible, to sustain some semblance of their free life in the Nation. These kidnapping events demonstrate that even as the Cherokee Nation curtailed the liberties and privileges of African Cherokee freedpeople, it simultaneously reserved the right to combat external forces that compromised the "free" lives of such individuals beyond the boundaries of the Cherokee Nation. By extending a level of protection to Cherokee freedpeople and freeborn African Cherokees, the Nation proclaimed these individuals a valuable part of the Cherokee Nation—worthy of its attention, support, and resources.

As evidenced by the responses to the kidnapping of Shoe Boots's two biracial African Cherokee granddaughters, Cherokee blood ties and related notions of Cherokee rights certainly affected the magnitude of the Nation's actions and extent of its responsibility. The interjection of "Cherokee blood" within postremoval statutes of the Cherokee Nation highlighted separate rights and privileges of free people of African and Cherokee descent; such rights included the protection of one's status as a "blood" member of the Cherokee Nation. Bloodlines demarcated the connection of Shoe Boots's granddaughters to Cherokees and their place within the Cherokee Nation. In light of the Nation's response to their kidnapping, did Shoe Boots's granddaughters and other kin comprehend and possibly capitalize on their position in the antebellum Cherokee Nation? As a result of their blood connection to Shoe Boots, as well as their place within their Cherokee community in the Delaware District, did Shoe Boots's African Cherokee family members expect certain actions on their behalf? Were Shoe Boots's kin, African Cherokees and European Cherokees alike, surprised by the extent of the Nation's response to the kidnapping or had they merely assumed such actions would be taken on their family's behalf? Whether astonishing or expected, the aftereffects of the kidnapping of Shoe Boots's granddaughters unequivocally verified an understanding of free African Cherokees belonging to Cherokee communities. Possible expectations and claims of free biracial African Cherokees, including Shoe Boots's kin, establish some degree of consciousness about their identity as part of the Cherokee Nation—as legitimate members of Cherokee communities. Such claims reflected intertwined realities of bondage and freedom, as well as blood relations between red and black in the antebellum Cherokee Nation.

Though not granted the same rights as Shoe Boots's granddaughters, being neither of Cherokee ancestry nor freeborn Cherokee citizens, Aiky, her daughters, and other Cherokee freedpeople in the Nation may also have developed a similar kind of consciousness about their legitimate place in the Cherokee Nation and expected some degree of protection. Indeed, the Nation's responses to the kidnapping attempts of Aiky and her kin articulated a belief about freedpeople belonging to the Nation—not owned by the Nation. When Aiky and her daughters discovered the actions of free Cherokees to reinstate their freedom, did such dealings mirror their own conceptions of belonging to and being a part of the Cherokee Nation beyond the realm of bondage? While enslaved, they had certainly become familiar with the degrading aspects of bondage. Nevertheless, after their Cherokee mistress manumitted them, they remained within the boundaries of the Cherokee Nation. Their decision to stay after attaining freedom might not have simply occurred as a result of their familiarity with Cherokees; it could have reflected deeply embedded feelings about the Cherokees and the Cherokee Nation as home. Even without blood ties to the Cherokees, Aiky and some recently freed African Cherokees in antebellum Cherokee country believed that they belonged to Cherokee communities not merely because of their previously defined position as chattel owned by Cherokees.

If Aiky and her family considered the Cherokee Nation as home after manumission, how did they grapple with and delineate home and community while enslaved by Cherokees in Indian Territory? Bondage undeniably defined enslaved African Cherokees' lived experiences on a daily basis in the Cherokee Nation before and after removal; in response to enslavement some had strategically challenged and continually resisted their position as slaves—running away, refusing to work, stealing from their slaveholders, and even murdering their masters and mistresses. Cultural connections only accentuated the roots and conditions of their bondage. Instead of honoring Cherokee traditions, they sought to sever their relationships with their Cherokee owners and shatter the cycle of bondage that entrapped them in Indian Territory. Even as some slaves tested the chains of bondage and their subservient place within the antebellum Cherokee Nation, others simultaneously developed a sense of community grounded not only geographically in the new Cherokee country in Indian Territory but also culturally in Cherokee customs and traditions. Enslaved African Cherokees' development of such cultural connections with free Cherokees in Indian Territory did not assuage the atrocities of enslavement or erase the presence and necessity of resistance. Yet the array of cultural connections, often intensified by blood ties to the Cherokee Nation, complicated and problematized enslaved African Cherokees' notions of themselves, kin, community, and home in the antebellum Cherokee Nation.

Conceptualizing and Constructing
African Indian Racial and Cultural Identities
in Antebellum Indian Territory

3 ▶

I was born a slave, but was not treated like other slaves and my folks never told me anything about slavery. So there is very little I can tell of those days. My birthplace was in the old Flint District of the Cherokee Nation; the nearest town was Russellville, Arkansas, and the farm was owned by Jerry Starr, half-breed Cherokee, who was my master and father . . . my folks never told me about slavery; they never whipped me, always treat like I was one of the family, because I was. ◆ Cherokee freedman Milton Starr

My mammy was a Cherokee slave, and talked it good. My husband was a Cherokee born negro, too, and when he got mad he forgit all the English he knowed. ◆ Cherokee freedwoman Betty Robertson

Even as Shoe Boots's free African Cherokee kin grappled with notions concerning their Cherokee blood ties, sense of belonging, and meanings of birthright, especially during particularly perilous moments in the antebellum era, enslaved African Indians in the Five Tribes also developed a keen understanding of their rootedness to these Indian nations after removal to Indian Territory. The links between "blood," belonging, and racial identity—and, by extension, innate group characteristics—not only became entrenched within European American life beginning in the colonial period but also encroached on the worldviews of African Indians and Indians residing in nineteenth-century southern Indian communities to the east and west of the Mississippi River. Before removal to Indian Territory, the creation of a Cherokee republic in the early nineteenth century transformed various elements of Cherokee society and ushered in significant changes and contradictions in the social fabric of the Cherokee Nation.[1]

The development of the Cherokee republic in the first decades of the nineteenth century and the emergence of a plantation economy "brought new forms of inequality to Cherokee society, which suffered not only from changes in race and gender relations but from a growing class antagonism between slaveholding and non-slaveholding Cherokees." Some divisions in the new Cherokee state emerged "according to degree of Cherokee racial ancestry ('fuller blood' vs. 'lesser blood')."[2] Although the distinction between "mixed bloods" and "full bloods" among the Cherokees is often presented in terms of a "correlation between white racial ancestry, a higher class standing, and slave ownership," crucial exceptions existed within the Cherokee Nation, as well as in the other southeastern slaveholding Native nations.[3] As Choctaw freedman Edmond Flint explained, "slavery, as it existed in the Indian Territory was not different from slavery in the states. There were humane and inhumane masters and occasionally some of the cruel and brutal type." However, he noted, "as a rule the slave-owning Indians were of mixed blood, tho' there were also a few full bloods who owned slaves."[4]

While recognizing the complexity of attitudes within the Cherokee Nation—across, between, and beyond bloodlines—the politics of removal in the nineteenth century at times sparked tensions about southeastern Indians' interactions with European Americans and Indians' retention of traditional customs.[5] Although "full bloods" occupied a central place in Cherokee society before removal, after resettlement in Indian Territory a number of "mixed blood" Cherokees firmly ensconced themselves within the Cherokee polity in the new territory.[6] Even though it is important not to overgeneralize about divisions between progressive "mixed bloods" and traditional "full bloods" in the Five Tribes, the fact that these terms became woven into the landscape of nineteenth-century Indian Territory, particularly within the viewpoints of enslaved African Indians, underscores how notions of blood and racial identity permeated various strata of southern Indian nations in the new homeland west of the Mississippi.

Partially due to the articulation of racial identity along bloodlines in antebellum Indian Territory, enslaved African Indians perceived differences between "full bloods," "mixed bloods," and European Americans in their management styles on their farms and plantations in Indian Territory. These differences manifested in the way they identified and reared their livestock, planted their crops, and managed other relevant aspects of their household. In his account of his travels through Indian Territory in 1842, Ethan Allen Hitchcock conveyed this difference specifically in relation to Indian slaveholders, noting that "the full-blood Indian rarely works himself and but few of them make their slaves work. A slave among wild Indians is almost as free as his owner, who scarcely exercises the authority of a master, beyond requiring something like a tax paid in corn or other product of labor." As a result, "more service is required from the slave among the half-breeds and the whites who have married natives, they become slaves indeed in all manner of work."[7]

Enslaved African Indians' awareness of Indians not only was affected by what they witnessed Indians doing or not doing but was also shaped by the prevailing European and European American ethnocentric beliefs concerning differences among Indians. Reflecting the discourse about "mixed bloods" and "full bloods" in Indian communities in Indian Territory, enslaved African Indians differentiated between groups of Indians along bloodlines as well. As Creek freedman Ned Thompson described, "the only negroes who had to work hard were those who belonged to the half-breeds. As the Indian didn't do work he didn't expect his slaves to do much work."[8] For Thompson to remark on these supposed differences between "full bloods" and "mixed bloods" indicates that these distinctions may have been recognized and discussed among not only Indians but also enslaved African Indians in Indian Territory.[9]

Although it is plausible that enslaved African Indians recognized such differences without understanding the intricacies of the sociopolitical divide between "full bloods" and "mixed bloods," the fact that they presented Indians in these specific categories, using this particular terminology, reveals some cognizance of the diversity among Indians, as well as the prevailing association between "mixed bloods" and slave ownership. Enslaved African Indians who had lived in southeastern Indian communities and relocated with their Indian owners to Indian Territory could have been more sensitive to and aware of the escalating politics of "blood" compared to those who were born in Indian Territory in the postremoval period. It is unclear if enslaved African Indians' understanding of degrees of "Indian blood" and identity had already been embedded in their worldviews before removal and simply became more ingrained after resettlement in Indian Territory or if Indian Territory served as the place where such ideas became implanted in their consciousness. Some enslaved African Indians' ideas about "Indian blood" filtered into not only how they labeled and categorized a range of Indians—slaveholders and non-slaveholders alike—but also how they envisioned and defined the "Indian blood" that flowed through their enslaved bodies.

My Master and Father

The phrase "my master and father" echoes long and deep—divulging a legacy interwoven in the family stories of generations of African Americans in the United States. Master and father—these two words reflect different conceptions of ownership, possession, kin, and belonging. The historical discourse concerning enslaved individuals who understood that the person who owned them had also sired them has been rooted primarily in the stories of associations between European and European American slaveholding men and enslaved African and African American women. The dichotomy of enslaved black woman and free white owner overshadows and masks the stories of such intimate interactions, consensual and forced, between enslaved African Indians and free Indians. Like enslaved people of African descent in other parts of the Americas, enslaved African Indians in Indian Territory experienced various dimensions of servitude, including the remarkable and all too familiar intersection of blood ties and bondage. For enslaved people of African descent in Indian communities, such a blood connection might have embodied a familial as well as a sociopolitical relationship to Indian nations. Nevertheless, the existence of these blood ties served not to assuage the tenets of bondage for enslaved African Indians. Rather, it reinforced the denial and indifference of free Indian people to their darker, enslaved kin in Indian Territory.

In antebellum Indian Territory, enslaved people of combined African and Indian descent recognized their "mixed blood" and construed their "Indian blood" as a tangible connection to specific Indian families, communities, and nations in the postremoval era. When Cherokee freedman Milton Starr reminisced about his life in Indian Territory, he declared that he was born on 24 February 1858 "right in [his] master's house." Milton Starr was born and raised in the Flint District of the Cherokee Nation on the farm of his enslaver, Cherokee Jerry Starr, relative of renegade Tom Starr.[10] Living among the Cherokees during his childhood, Milton Starr remembered that though he was born a slave, he "was not treated like other slaves and my folks never told me anything about slavery." He inherited preferential treatment partly because, as he stated, "half-breed Cherokee" Jerry Starr "was my master and father."[11] After the Civil War, Starr did not leave the Cherokee Nation. Instead, young Milton Starr remained with Millie and Jerry Starr, his stepmother and father respectively, especially because they "never whipped me, always treat like I was one of the family, because I was."[12] Though he recollected that he had never been whipped in his master-father's home, were there other dynamics within Jerry Starr's slaveholding household that regularly demarcated Milton Starr's status as enslaved person and property? Still a child at the onset of the Civil War, his age might have protected him somewhat from some of the harsh realities of slavery. Perhaps he translated his limited duties not as those designated to an enslaved child but as linked to his position as a child of the master.

It is difficult to determine to what extent his young age, complemented by his blood relationship to his master-father, restricted his duties on Jerry Starr's plantation. Even if his enslaved and free kin sheltered him from some of the horrors of slavery, he still witnessed the ways his experiences differed from those of other enslaved people, perhaps partially due to his relationship. Like some enslaved biracial African Americans in other slaveholding communities, enslaved people of African and Indian descent endured bondage within their masters-fathers' homes. For Milton Starr and other enslaved biracial African Cherokees, no matter how much they were treated "like family," their biological connection to Cherokee fathers failed to eradicate their enslaved status on their fathers' farms and plantations, as well as within the Cherokee Nation itself.

Because he was born in the Cherokee Nation, Indian Territory, Milton Starr developed his understanding and perceptions of Cherokee society entirely west of the Mississippi, yet other enslaved African Cherokees in Indian Territory, who had experienced bondage before removal, approached life in the new land from a different vantage point. Although recognizing that he was treated differently due to his connection to Jerry Starr, Milton Starr did not indicate any special treatment toward his mother, Jane Coursey. Enslaved initially in Tennessee, she was "picked up by the Starrs when they left that country with the rest of the Cherokee Indians. My mother wasn't bought, just stole by them Indians."[13] Although Milton Starr described his master-father favorably, Coursey may not have embraced such positive feelings about Jerry Starr. As Milton Starr recalled, when his mother was freed after the Civil War, she returned to Tennessee. Like so many other recently freed people, Coursey may have been motivated to return to Tennessee by her desire to reconnect with kin from whom she had been separated due to removal to Indian Territory. Her interactions with Cherokees, and with Jerry Starr in particular, may also have influenced her decision to leave the Nation. Perhaps the Starrs did not treat her like family, or perhaps she did not desire to be part of their family.

Silences surrounding the interactions between Jane Coursey and her enslaver Cherokee Jerry Starr mirror those associated with intimate relations between African American women and their enslavers in other slaveholding communities. It is not always clear under what conditions these interactions between Indian slave owners and enslaved African Indian women occurred. One cannot necessarily conclude that sexual interactions always transpired in a consensual manner, as a result of emotional bonds between the parties involved. For enslaved women, moreover, such sexual interactions oftentimes proved complex in nature, involving a delicate balance between power and resistance.[14]

Though Jane Coursey left no extant written record of her personal views about Cherokee Jerry Starr, Choctaw freedwoman Peggy McKinney Brown hints at the complexities of such interactions and presents a very gendered perspective in her description of her father-master Choctaw Jesse McKinney. After the Civil War, while releasing his slaves from his ownership, Jesse McKinney simply told her that he was her father. Brown described her master-father as "a very hard master. He had no regard for himself or any of the slave women, especially if they were of pleasant looks. He did not hesitate to bring half-breed children into the world."[15] Although she provided no information specifically about her mother in her interview, Peggy McKinney Brown attempted to fill the apparent silence surrounding the sexual interactions between her mother (and potentially other enslaved women) and Jesse McKinney. It is possible that Brown uncovered what sort of interaction McKinney had with her mother, but decided she either did not want to or could not speak about it. Did she forget what she might have heard about the situation resulting in her birth? It would have been easier to believe that Brown had forgotten to mention her mother and the necessary events leading up to her birth, but with Brown's descriptions of her father-master as a man "who did not hesitate to bring half-breed children into the world," her silences may not be a result of the failing memory of an old woman. Nonetheless, Brown provided critical commentary on the actions of her father, Jesse McKinney. In her interview, she speaks for her mother and other enslaved women for whom she believed Jesse McKinney had no regard.

Did Cherokee Jerry Starr have no regard for Jane Coursey as well? In addition to being "stolen" by the Starr family during the removal process, Jane Coursey might have believed that Jerry Starr had stolen from her in multiple ways after resettlement in Indian Territory. For Coursey, the removal and resettlement processes could have represented a dreadful cycle beginning with the forced separation from kin in Tennessee and continuing with sexual victimization, by Jerry Starr and possibly others, in Indian Territory. Although the particular circumstances of the interactions between Jane Coursey and Jerry Starr remain unknown, Coursey's decision to leave the Starr household after the Civil War conveys her disconnection from, and possibly loathing of, the Starr family. The Civil War provided an opportunity for Coursey to disengage from the Starr family and attempt to live her life unfettered by Starr and his kin—even though that also meant separation from shared kin—her son. The longing Coursey must have experienced for her kin and friends left behind in Tennessee could not be replaced by the birth of her son, Milton Starr; simultaneously, Milton Starr's connection to the Starr family, as well as Indian Territory, extinguished any ideas about leaving Indian Territory and relocating to Tennessee with his mother.

Milton Starr's description of his mother, Jane Coursey, being "picked up" by the Starrs reinforced this crucial difference between Starr and his mother.[16] Neither born nor raised in Indian Territory, Jane Coursey was what enslaved African Indians in Indian Territory called a "crossland Negro," whereas Milton Starr was a "native" of Indian Territory.[17] Perhaps it was partially because of this difference that Jane Coursey decided to return to her "home" in Tennessee and her son decided to remain in his "home" in Indian Territory. The connection to Indian Territory held a special meaning for some enslaved African Cherokees and later Cherokee freedpeople. The fact that Cherokee freedpeople classified those who "crossed over" the Mississippi as "crossland Negroes," separate and apart from "natives," reflects the significance of birthright and belonging linked to Indian Territory. Jane Coursey's sense of home and belonging remained east of the Mississippi, whereas her son, Milton Starr, defined home and family decisively west of the Mississippi within the context of the Cherokee Nation, Indian Territory.

Just as generational positions often shaped enslaved people's connection to or disconnection from the Cherokee Nation, whether one was born in Indian Territory—before or after the Civil War—also affected one's perception of place and belonging. A "native" like Milton Starr, Cornelius Neely Nave was born and raised in the Cherokee Nation. Because he was born in 1868, after the Civil War, Nave clarified that what he "knows about slave times is what my pappa told me." As his mother died when he was only two years old, Nave based his early memories of Indian Territory primarily on his father's stories concerning life in the Cherokee Nation. Cherokee Henry Nave enslaved Cornelius Nave's father, Charley Nave.[18] After the Civil War, Cornelius Nave remembered "setting in the yard watching the river (Grand River) go by, and the Indians go by. All Indians lived around there, the real colored settlement was four mile [sic] from us."[19] Living mostly among Cherokees, Cornelius Nave "wasn't scared of them Indians for pappa always told me his master, Henry Nave, was his own father; that make me part Indian and the reason my hair is long, straight and black like a horse mane."[20] After his father revealed their family's Cherokee "blood" connection, this tempered Cornelius Nave's responses to Indians among whom they lived in Indian Territory. Knowing that his paternal grandfather, Henry Nave, was a Cherokee man mitigated fears Cornelius Nave might have developed about Indians. Though this connection minimized Nave's trepidation, his description of "them Indians" reflects the existence and retention of some cultural distance between himself and Cherokees.

Although emphasizing his physiognomic connection to Indians, Cornelius Nave, like Milton Starr, underscored the generational separation between enslaved African Cherokees and the descendants of Cherokee freedpeople. Even though Cornelius Nave recalled stories his father and others told him about slavery, his stories of slavery are not based on his own personal experiences. Partly because of this generational distance from slavery, Cornelius Nave is able to speak fondly of his childhood in the Cherokee Nation following the Civil War. Moreover, Nave's statement regarding his visible blood connection to the Cherokees reinforces an association that, for him, was not entirely based on bondage and exploitation.

Not all enslaved and free African Cherokees who claimed a blood connection to the Cherokee Nation experienced this relationship in only positive ways and in terms of preferential treatment. Some enslaved African Cherokees directly associated the negative treatment they received with the fact that they were related by blood to their

Cherokee owners. Sarah Wilson proudly proclaimed, "I was a Cherokee slave and now I am a Cherokee freedwoman, and besides that I am
a quarter Cherokee my own self. And this is the way it is." She was
born in 1850 on the Johnson farm, in the southeastern corner of the
Sequoyah District in the Cherokee Nation.[21] Sarah Wilson's owner,
Ben Johnson, a European American man who married Cherokee Annie
Johnson, had relocated his family, including Sarah Wilson's grandmother, from Tennessee to the Cherokee Nation during the 1830s.
One of Sarah Wilson's childhood memories revolved around the tension between her mother and Annie Johnson, her Cherokee mistress.
She specifically recalled disagreements over the name by which she
was supposed to be called. Her mother called her Sarah, but her mistress called her "Annie." Wilson explained that her mistress "would
call me 'Come here Annie!' and I wouldn't know what to do. If I went
when she called 'Annie' my mammy would beat me for answering to
that name, and if I didn't go old Mistress would beat me for that. That
made me hate both of them, and I got the devil in me and I wouldn't
come to either one." In order to escape from the consequences of not
responding to either her mother or her mistress, Wilson often sought
the protection of her maternal grandmother, who "wouldn't let anybody touch [her]."[22]

It was not until Cherokee Annie Johnson died that Wilson understood one of the reasons for the conflict between her mother and
her Cherokee mistress. When she was eight years old, her maternal
grandmother told her "why old Mistress picked on me so. She told
me about me being half Mister Ned's blood. Then I knowed why
Mister Ned would say, 'Let her along, she got big, big blood in her,'
and then laugh."[23] "Mister Ned" was Ben and Annie Johnson's son.
Sarah Wilson's father was also her young master. Thus, the tension
of which she spoke occurred between her mother and her paternal
grandmother. What Sarah Wilson's young Cherokee master-father
found humorous constituted a power struggle between three generations in a mixed-race family. The fact that Cherokee Annie Johnson
attempted to have Sarah called by her name ("Annie") perhaps reflects
Johnson's efforts to demonstrate her power and control as mistress in

her plantation household, as well as her warped connection to Sarah Wilson as her paternal grandmother. Sarah Wilson's mother might have used the name-calling situation as an opportunity to express her maternal rights over her daughter. Her position as enslaved mother, however, compromised and restricted the expression of maternal feelings, actions, and rights. For Sarah Wilson, this conflict between her mother and paternal grandmother illustrated the contentious aspects of her very existence, as well as the dissension in a Cherokee family that united blood and bondage.

Such tensions reverberated throughout slaveholding households in the antebellum Cherokee Nation; as a result, the contradictions of blood ties intermingled with bondage did not always foster a sense of belonging and stability for those enslaved by kin.[24] Cherokee freedman R. C. Smith's family history illustrates the precarious situation of many African Cherokee individuals, whose status changed from free to enslaved person due to the complexities associated with the enslavement of kin.[25] R. C. Smith's "father was half Cherokee Indian. His father was bought by an Indian woman and she took him for her husband. She died and my grandfather, father and Auntie were bought by John Ross." However, Principal Chief John Ross "later bought up a lot of land claims from some Indian people named Tibets and he paid for the claims with slaves. My father was in this trade. Ross kept my grandfather till he died and he gave my auntie to one of his sisters." Although Smith remembered his father's stories of pleasurable experiences during his "free" childhood, once his grandmother died and his father was sold by John Ross to another master, "it was purty hard for him to git used to being a slave."[26]

This transition in R. C. Smith's family status hinged on his relationship to a free Cherokee woman—Smith's paternal grandmother. Though a free Cherokee woman, her status as such neither protected nor maintained her progeny's freedom. By the time R. C. Smith's Cherokee grandmother died in antebellum Indian Territory, her altered position in Cherokee society could not protect her biracial African Cherokee children from being enslaved and sold. Their free status had been maintained while their Cherokee relative lived; however, her passing led to their conversion from free to enslaved people. The fact that their matrilineal connection to her, and to the Cherokee Nation, could be wholly disregarded reveals how the status and power of Cherokee women had been severely compromised after removal to Indian Territory.

Cherokee freedwoman Agnes Walker, like R. C. Smith, also articulated her Cherokee blood connection to a Cherokee woman; in her case, too, this blood link to a Cherokee woman did not guarantee freedom for her African Cherokee kin. Walker declared that her "maternal grandmother was a full blood Cherokee and my [maternal] grandfather was a negro. Their home was located on Spring Creek, twenty miles northwest of Tahlequah." Born during the Civil War in 1862, in Fort Gibson, Indian Territory, Walker explained that her father, "Houston Rogers, was born near Tahlequah, Indian Territory" and her mother, "Sidney Ross-Rogers, was born on the old Oliver Ross place on Grand River in the Indian Territory." Walker stated that her "parents were former slaves. Clem Rogers was my father's master and Oliver Ross was my mother's."[27] Walker's statement regarding her maternal grandmother being a "full blood Cherokee" and her mother being a slave on Oliver Ross's place is confusing. Walker's maternal grandmother might have been an enslaved person of Cherokee and African descent. In this case, it would have meant that Walker's maternal grandmother was an enslaved woman and thus her daughter would also have inherited the enslaved condition of her mother. Though Walker specifically stated that her parents and paternal grandparents were enslaved people, she did not indicate the status of her "full blood Cherokee" maternal grandmother. With her disclosure of other aspects of her family's lineage, if her maternal grandmother had been an enslaved woman, it seems plausible that Walker would have mentioned this fact. If Walker's grandmother had been a full blood Cherokee woman, her status as a free Cherokee woman, like that of R. C. Smith's paternal grandmother, did not protect or prevent her kin from being enslaved. The traditional matrilineal system of belonging in the Cherokee Nation had been undermined; socioeconomic changes in association with the peculiar institution resulted in a shift away from matrilineal clan identity to a patrilineal race- and "blood"-centered identity.

Unlike the African Cherokee family members of Cherokee Shoe Boots, families similar to those of R. C. Smith and Agnes Walker readily discovered that Cherokee bloodlines could not and did not erase entirely the stigma of enslavement associated with being of African descent. Had the kin of R. C. Smith and Agnes Walker been linked by their blood relationship to a Cherokee man, especially one of Shoe Boots's prominence in the Cherokee Nation, then their freedom might well have been assured and maintained in the antebellum period. Instead, their "black blood" eclipsed freedom and inextricably embedded their lives in bondage even with tangible, blood connections to Cherokee women. As a result, enslaved African Cherokees in Indian Territory endured bondage in the households of free Cherokee kin, some within the households of their slave-owning Cherokee fathers and mothers. Though hopeful that such blood ties might eradicate the chains of bondage, many painfully discovered that the presence of their "Indian blood" could not purge the blight of blackness in the antebellum Cherokee Nation.

It is difficult to ascertain how the presence of Cherokee bloodlines shaped the daily experiences of enslaved African Cherokees, owned by kin or not, in slaveholding communities on small farms and larger plantations in Indian Territory. Whether "treated like family" as Cherokee freedman Milton Starr remembered or simply sold off indiscriminately like R. C. Smith's kin, the intersection of blood ties and bondage affected the dynamics in slaveholding households. Though not specifically stating that she received preferential treatment due to her "Indian blood," Cherokee freedwoman Lucinda Vann discussed how being "part Indian and part colored" influenced her position on Joseph Vann's large plantation in Webbers Falls, Cherokee Nation.[28] Lucinda Vann explained that with "five hundred slaves on that plantation," the workers were divided into different classes.[29] Thus, "the slaves who worked in the big house was the first class. Next, came the carpenters, yard men, blacksmiths, race-horse men, steamboat men and like that. The low class work in the fields."[30] The kind of social stratification Lucinda Vann described was probably not widespread. It would have been deemed necessary only on significantly larger plantations, of which there were very few in Indian Territory. Although Joe Vann was a large Cherokee slaveholder, Lucinda Vann overestimated the slave population on his plantation. In 1835, before removal to Indian Territory, Joseph Vann enslaved 110 African Cherokees.[31] After removal he steadily increased the number of enslaved people on his plantation. He had approximately 300 enslaved people on his plantation at the time of his death in 1844.

Vann particularly stressed that her "mother, grandmother, aunt Maria and cousin Clara, all worked in the big house."[32] Vann's categorization of house slaves as "first class" and field slaves as the lowest class is certainly not a new idea in the history of slavery in the United States. Even though enslaved people who claimed Cherokee ancestry did not necessarily aver any correlation to class or status, Lucinda Vann implied a correlation between the fact that her people were "part Indian and part colored" and their position in the big house. Vann thus linked her "mixed blood" to her social status on the Vann plantation.

Even though being "part Indian" possibly engendered a certain degree of status—anticipated or realized—on larger plantations, for Lucinda Vann and others self-identifying as "part Indian" also accentuated the distance between being "part Indian" and entirely "Indian." Certainly, individuals like John Ross and other "mixed bloods" did not refer to themselves as "part Indian" or "part Cherokee." Such conceptions, "part Indian" or "part Cherokee," might have represented African Cherokees' beliefs about their Indianness—that is, as unfulfilled, incomplete, and unattainable within the confines of the antebellum Cherokee Nation.

It is feasible that by merely invoking their blood connection to Cherokees, enslaved and free people of African and Cherokee descent believed they were also claiming their association to a group of people whose "mixed blood" qualified them as individuals of a higher social status than enslaved people of African descent, who had no identifiable or alleged Cherokee ancestry. Some enslaved African Cherokees' conceptions of birthright and bloodlines underscored and intensified their ideas about their sense of belonging to the Cherokee Nation. Even as European Cherokees firmly established themselves within the Cherokee polity before and after removal, African Cherokees attempted to carve out their sense of Indianness, intermingled with an expression of their humanity, to counter their defined status as chattel. Though the Cherokeeness of European Cherokees remained intact and unquestioned, enslaved African Cherokees experienced a truncated sense of belonging to the Cherokee Nation due to the stigma of blackness overtly reinforced by the peculiar institution.

It remains unknown to what extent enslaved African Cherokees understood the layers of Cherokee factionalism and blood politics before or after removal, yet enslaved and free African Cherokees articulated their thoughts regarding overt differences they identified during the antebellum period between "full bloods" and "mixed bloods." By so doing, enslaved and free African Cherokees not only expressed their impressions about the range of Cherokee racial identities but also demonstrated how such thoughts informed their conceptualization of their own African and Cherokee racial attributes and identities during bondage and beyond. Their multifarious ideas of race influenced how they inscribed Indian "blood" on their consciousness and bodies as an indicator of their Indianness. Some African Cherokees' familial Cherokee connections shaped their perceptions of being part of Cherokee communities in the antebellum era, with the pervasive element of "blood" occupying a particular place in their understanding of their (mixed) racial identity. Did enslaved African Cherokees' understandings of their own Cherokee blood and blood quantum serve only to verify their Cherokee ancestry? Furthermore, did their self-identification as "mixed blood" or "part Indian" create a means of accessing potential avenues for preferential treatment and entitlement, especially within slaveholding households? By injecting "blood" into their cultural consciousness and racial identity, enslaved and free African Cherokees identified a peculiar sense of birthright buttressed and intensified by their "blood" relationship to Cherokees. Their blood served literally as the body of evidence for their connection to the

Cherokee Nation. Enslaved African Indians who could not proffer such Indian blood associations unearthed other elements of their lived experiences in antebellum Indian Territory to establish their socio-cultural linkages to the Five Tribes.

Clothing, Language, and Foodways as Emblems of Cultural Indianization

Was "blood" the only deciding factor that linked enslaved African Indians to the Five Tribes in antebellum Indian Territory? Although "blood" was most definitely an aspect of their association with these southeastern Indian nations, there were enslaved people born and raised in Indian Territory who lived among the Five Tribes for all or a significant part of their lives and who closely identified themselves with the Five Tribes and their customs who mentioned no "blood" connection whatsoever. How do we define African Indians with such associations with Indians, especially within the context of slavery?[33] Bondage certainly dictated the extent and mode of interactions between enslaved African Indians and their Indian owners; enslavement shaped and, to some degree, restricted enslaved African Indians' access to and connection with Indian traditions, customs, and institutions. Nevertheless, due to the multifarious dimensions of bondage and belonging in antebellum Indian Territory, race and various manifestations of Indian cultures and customs grounded the particular experiences of enslaved African Indians there. Some enslaved African Indians, particularly "natives," engendered unique multicultural identities through their association with Indians. As a result, blood relationships did not provide the sole avenue for Indianization processes for enslaved African Indians.[34] Even without conventional blood ties to the Five Tribes, some African-descended enslaved people became culturally "Indianized" in antebellum Indian Territory. Consequently, external, sociocultural signs of Indianness—unveiled and accentuated in their clothing, language, and foodways—symbolized crucial features in their self- and group identification with Indian communities and nations. Their cultural Indianness fortified their sense of belonging to and within the Five Tribes.

Clothing

Clothing represented one of the most visible signs of enslaved African Indians' cultural identification with Indians in antebellum Indian Territory. Even as wearing "Indian" clothing before removal might have demonstrated their position as slaves of the Five Tribes east of the Mississippi, after removal such garments not only served as reminders of the traditional attire of the Five Tribes but also patently expressed the transference of elements of Indian customs west of the Mississippi. As European American fashion continued to become absorbed within the Five Tribes in the postremoval era, Indian garb might well have signified one of the most visible signs of Indianness, especially for those who considered themselves traditionalists and balked at the influx of European American ideals within the southeastern Indian nations. Undeniably, not all enslaved African Indians viewed donning Indian clothing in a positive light; wearing the national attire of their Indian enslavers could have simply reinforced some African Indians' sense of their subservient position in a slaveholding society. For those who embraced Indian garb as their own, however, it became one of several signifiers of their association with the Five Tribes—rooted in a complex web of birthright, belonging, and bondage.

Enslaved African Indians in Indian Territory understood that clothing and material culture in general often represent several layers of cultural meaning and significance. Clothing is a form not only of basic protection and adornment but also of self- and group expression.[35] Viewed as historical documents, "clothes always signify more than they appear to, like the words of a language which need to be translated and explained."[36] In many cultures, including Indian cultures, clothing has historically revealed social status, group membership, as well as religious and spiritual connotations.[37] Among Indians, "clothing has always served a complex function that is at once practical and highly symbolic." Moreover, Indians "came to utilize clothing as one of their principal means of visually communicating information about the groups to which they belonged as well as about themselves as individuals."[38] Just as European Indian members of the Five Tribes associated certain forms of dress with particular nations, and often with traditional or progressive stances, enslaved African Indians, too, recognized differences in Indian attire and categorized such differences in terms of national association.

In antebellum Indian Territory, clothing served as one of the ways of differentiating between "Indianized" enslaved people of African descent and those enslaved who chose not to adopt Indian customs. Born and raised in North Carolina, Henry Clay was a "crossland slave," who crossed over (or more accurately was brought over) to Indian Territory when he was a teenager. Though born in North Carolina, Henry Clay was sold at the age of fifteen to Dyson Cheet. After hiring Henry Clay out for five years to work on a steamboat in Louisiana, Dyson Cheet gave Clay to his son, Tom Cheet. Clay explained that Tom Cheet brought him "to the Creek Nation because his wife come from Mississippi and she is just part Creek Indian, so they can get a big farm out here if they want it."[39] From Clay's description of Dyson Cheet and his Creek wife, it is probable that Cheet was white and that it was his wife's Creek connection that enabled them to obtain land in the Nation. Clay indicated that they settled "south of where Muskogee is now about two miles from the Honey Springs town."[40]

Clay lived in the Creek Nation, Indian Territory, for the majority of his adult life. Even so, he stated that he "never did get along good with these Creek slaves out here. . . . In fact I was afraid of these Creeks and always got off the road when I seen Creek negroes coming along." Clay explained that he could always identify them for "they would have red strings tied on their hats or something wild looking."[41] Henry Clay distinctly used clothing as a cultural marker that associated "Indianness" with "wildness." From Clay's perspective, close affiliation with Creek Indians made the Indianized enslaved African Indians in Creek country look and dress "wild." Clay's description of the "wild" nature of these enslaved African Indians was also perhaps a way of distinguishing himself as different from and possibly more "civilized" than those owned by and associated with Creeks and other southeastern Indian nations. In this instance, it is unclear what the red strings signified to the enslaved African Creeks who wore them. It is possible that some enslaved African Creeks employed these items as markers of their distinctive Creekness and as a way of expressing their group identification with Creeks.

The unique character of Indianized enslaved African Creeks' clothing allowed Henry Clay to identify them easily—enabling him to distance himself, literally and figuratively, from those he viewed as different due to their close association with Creeks and adoption of Creek culture. After his owner, Tom Cheet, insisted that he marry, however, Clay interacted with Indianized enslaved people even though "them Creek negroes was so funny to talk to."[42] Although Clay initially harbored negative feelings toward "them Creek negroes," he eventually overcame these feelings for he married enslaved African Creek Maggie Brooks.[43] It appears, from his union with Brooks, that he must have adjusted somewhat to the "funny" ways of those "Creek negroes."

Like Henry Clay, other visitors to the Creek Nation noticed the distinctive style of clothing worn by some enslaved African Creeks in Creek territory. While traveling through the Creek Nation, Indian Territory, in 1845, Lieutenant James W. Abert expressed his delight with the Creek style of dress. In his 15 October 1845 journal entry, Abert commented that "the Indians were dressed most tastefully. Handsome shawls were gracefully twisted around their heads. They also wore leggins and moccasins of buckskin, handsome calico shirts, and beautiful pouch, with broad belt ornamented with massive beadwork. These form the general costume of the Creek Indians." Abert also specifically remarked on the clothing worn by African Creeks living among the Creeks. In his 17 October 1845 journal entry, he noted that he and Lieutenant William Guy Peck "met several negroes on the road who were dressed in the picturesque costume of the Creek Indians, which certainly becomes them well." The following day, Abert noted in his journal that he and Peck "saw great numbers of blacks wearing shawl-turbans, which seem well suited to their pseudo-Moorish character."[44] This description conveys how the clothing draped on the bodies of African Creeks in Creek territory transformed the presence of these enslaved people themselves, and perhaps elevated them, in the eyes of this European American traveler. Dressing in such articles of clothing might have resulted in a personal kind of transformation of presence and status for Indianized enslaved African Creeks in the Creek Nation. What might have been a sign of "wildness" and otherness for Henry Clay and other crossland slaves could have translated into a symbol of eminence for those who dressed in Creek-style attire. Indianized enslaved African Creeks in the Creek Nation may not have dressed in the exact clothing worn by Creeks; they might have created their own "Indian fashion," which integrated and modified Creek styles.[45]

While Henry Clay used clothing to distinguish himself from Indianized enslaved African Creeks, Creek freedwoman Sweetie Ivery Wagoner used clothing to reinforce her connection with Creeks. When Wagoner claimed that her father was a Creek Indian enslaved by Cherokees and her mother was an enslaved woman of African descent, she emphasized, "my folks was part Indian alright; they wore blankets and breeches with fur around the bottoms."[46] Her father being Creek, and her people being "part Indian," verified her blood connection to the Creeks. For Wagoner, what her people wore served as the cultural manifestation of her claimed Creek connection. Though Wagoner clearly affirmed her Creek blood connection, the fact that her people wore Indian garb corroborated her people's Creekness. Blood served as one element of Indianness; however, cultural expressions and customs like Indian clothing authenticated being "part Indian." By adopting "Indian" clothing, enslaved African Indians selectively accentuated such visible markers and underscored the complexity of their identity as enslaved people in Indian country.

Although wearing Indian attire confirmed particular cultural connections between African Indians and Indians in Indian Territory, enslaved African Indians, due to their position as chattel, had certain duties and responsibilities regarding the preparation of wool and cotton clothing in slaveholding households. Cherokee freedwoman Eliza Whitmire, who was born on George Sanders's plantation in the old Cherokee Nation in Georgia and migrated to Indian Territory as a young girl, recalled enslaved women's work of spinning and weaving.[47] Whitmire described how enslaved African Indian women's position in antebellum Indian Territory translated into their role as conduits of some knowledge to Indian women, as well as recipients of culturally based information. "Every farm home," she remarked, "or most of them owned an old time spinning wheel and during slave times it was the duty of slave women to do the spinning and weaving, and many an old Indian woman, who was used to having slaves to do this work for them learned the art and did this for themselves and for their entire family, after we were set free."[48]

In addition to enslaved women's responsibility for and expertise at spinning and weaving, Whitmire specifically demonstrated her knowledge of dyeing cloth—a process currently referred to as tie dyeing. She remarked that the women on the farm "made excellent yellow dye from the inside bark of the oak tree. Indigo was bought to dye blue. Different shades were made, according to the dye used." Designs were made by "tying strings around the goods ever so often, and wherever the string was tied the goods would not dye, making a sort of pretty model design."[49] Although enslaved women primarily engaged in the cloth production and tie-dyeing processes, enslaved men also remembered the arduous and time-consuming process of enslaved women preparing and dyeing cloth. Like Whitmire, Cherokee freedman Johnson Thompson remembered his mother working "late in the night, and I hear the loom making noises while I try to sleep in the cabin. . . . [A]nd Aunt 'Tilda dyed the cloth with wild indigo, leaving her hands blue looking most of the time."[50] Preparing and dyeing this clothing with their own hands, often from late at night into the morning, certainly engendered a sense of pride in their handiwork.

Dyeing offers a good example of the complex, shifting, and adaptive nature of culture—in this case material culture. Can the cloth dyeing process that Eliza Whitmire described be viewed merely as knowledge enslaved African Indians obtained as a result of their "Indianization"? The use of dyes extracted and prepared from the flowers, bark, branches, berries, roots, and other parts of plants, as a way of coloring clothing, has historically occurred not only in Indian cultures but also in African and South Asian cultures. Though enslaved African Indians who had been born and raised in Indian Territory gained some knowledge about dyeing from Indian women before and after removal, these enslaved people of African descent would have possessed their own African-based knowledge of tie-dyeing essentials and techniques to pass on to Indian women.[51] The often tangible, fluid nature of various forms of material culture enabled and encouraged compound exchanges and sources for the development of African Indian and Indian cultural expressions in antebellum Indian Territory. Even as cross-cultural pollination between Indians and African Indians enhanced multicultural expressions, it did not alter basic understandings about the position of enslaved African Indians and their specific and primary function as chattel in Indian Territory.

While Indian owners restricted the quality, quantity, and range of clothing provided to enslaved people in Indian Territory, as did enslavers in slaveholding southeastern communities, enslaved African Indians regarded their clothing as an external and visible marker of cultural identity. For crossland slaves, like Henry Clay, the type of clothing worn by Indianized enslaved people represented one way of marking or identifying "natives" as different from himself and other crossland slaves. For Sweetie Ivery Wagoner and other native enslaved people born and raised in Indian Territory, the material representation of what they perceived and identified as "Indian" clothing was instrumental to their personal claim to Indian heritage and to their individual and familial acculturation within the Five Tribes in Indian Territory. Even though European Indians in the Five Tribes might have construed donning Indian attire in the postremoval era in ways different from enslaved African Indians, Indian attire as an indicator of Indian culture crossed the boundaries of bondage. Though wearing Indian clothing alone did not substantiate one's Indianness, for enslaved African Indians it became a determining factor in displaying their sense of belonging to Indian communities and nations in Indian Territory.

Language

In addition to recognizing their connection to Indians by the Indian garb they wore, enslaved African Indians also proclaimed their affiliation with the Five Tribes in antebellum Indian Territory by the particular languages they spoke to communicate their everyday thoughts and feelings. Scholars have long recognized that some enslaved people learned Indian languages and often served as interpreters for their southeastern Indian enslavers before removal to Indian Territory.[52] Even after removal, enslaving a bilingual or multilingual person of African descent would have been useful for an Indian owner who spoke or understood English in a limited manner.[53] However, slave bilingualism or multilingualism was not merely an issue of utility for Indian owners or enslaved African Indians in antebellum Indian Territory.[54] Representing another discernible marker of cultural identity, some enslaved African Indians in the antebellum period in Indian Territory learned and incorporated Indian languages within their daily lives not as a duty of bondage but as an element of their acculturation within the Five Tribes.

For Indianized enslaved people of African descent in Indian Territory, understanding and communicating in Indian languages demonstrated their facility with languages. They considered Indian language acquisition an aspect not only of their Indian owners' culture but also of their own cultural identity. Certainly, some enslaved African Indians decided to learn Indian languages in an attempt to manipulate their owners, especially as they planned runaway attempts, with the objective of achieving eventual and everlasting freedom. Nonetheless, learning Indian languages did not represent a strategy of resistance for all enslaved in Indian Territory. An Indian language, whether Cherokee, Creek, Chickasaw, Choctaw, or Seminole, became some African Indians' first language, their mother tongue—the language they believed accurately expressed who they were and what they thought.

Born in 1852 near Tahlequah, the capital of the Cherokee Nation, Cherokee freedwoman Chaney McNair, formerly enslaved by Cherokee William Penn Adair, mentioned that she was hired out to a European American family in Kansas during the Civil War. However, she had trouble understanding the people there, because she "didn't know white folks language."[55] Like other "native" slaves, having been born and raised among Indians who primarily spoke their own native language, Creek freedwoman Lucinda Davis could speak only Creek when she was a little girl. She belonged to "a full-blood Creek Indian and . . . didn't know nothing but Creek talk long after de Civil War." Even though her mistress was "part white and knowed English talk . . . she never did talk it because none of de people talked it." Davis heard English sometimes, "but it sound like whole lot of wild shoat in de cedar brake scared at something."[56] For Chaney McNair and other enslaved African Indians, English remained the language of strangers or foreigners in antebellum Indian Territory and beyond.[57]

Some enslaved African Indians who developed a facility for English and one or more Indian languages acted as mediators between European Americans and Indians not only before removal but also following resettlement in Indian Territory. In the winter of 1834, Cassandra Sawyer Lockwood witnessed the way a woman of African descent played such a role when Lockwood arrived in the Cherokee Nation to meet her husband, Rev. Jesse Lockwood, who served as a missionary at Dwight Mission for the American Board of Commissioners for Foreign Missions (ABCFM) from 25 January 1834 until his untimely death on 11 July 1834.[58] On the day of her arrival in the Cherokee Nation, Indian Territory, in January 1834, Cassandra Sawyer Lockwood recalled how "for the first time, I beheld Cherokees, the shore being lined with Indians & negroes. The negroes were the slaves of the Indians. . . . They were much interested in viewing the boat & its passengers, & were constantly talking in Cherokee, & of course, unintelligible to us." After she landed she was quickly "introduced to a black woman, who was the only person among them, who could talk English."[59] After removal to Indian Territory, missionaries (like Cassandra Sawyer Lockwood's husband) utilized enslaved African Indians in order to spread Christianity within the Five Tribes, particularly among those who did not or chose not to speak English.[60]

It is uncertain what speaking Cherokee meant to the unnamed African Cherokee woman with whom Cassandra Lockwood communicated at Dwight Mission; however, as a result of the particular conditions of bondage in Indian Territory, bilingualism expressed a degree of acculturation and belonging for some enslaved African Indians. Thus, there were enslaved African Indians whose primary language

was not English, but Cherokee, Creek, Chickasaw, or Choctaw. Cherokee freedwoman Betty Robertson asserted that her "mammy was a
Cherokee slave, and talked it good." She also remarked that "her
husband was a Cherokee born negro, too, and when he got mad he
forgit all the English he knowed."[61] On the other hand, Robertson's
father, who "come from across the water when he was a little boy, and
was grown when old Master Joseph Vann bought him . . . never did
learn to talk much Cherokee."[62] Robertson clearly described how her
mother's and her husband's connection to the Cherokees and the
Cherokee language, specifically being native enslaved African Cherokees, differed from the disconnection from the Cherokee language
experienced by her father, having been a crossland slave who had
previously been enslaved by European Americans. The fact that Robertson's mother and husband spoke the Cherokee language illustrated
her family's acculturation in the Cherokee Nation. Furthermore, Robertson's specific point about when her husband "got mad he forgit all
the English he knowed" reveals a profound level of Cherokee language
usage. The Cherokee language for him and other Indianized, multilingual enslaved African Cherokees functioned not only as an avenue
for basic communication but also as the vehicle through which core,
passionate sentiments could be articulated in the most authentic manner. Basic ideas as well as concentrated feelings could be conveyed
only through their mother tongue—Cherokee.

Due to their conceptions of their position and place in Indian communities, some experienced a deep appreciation for Cherokee and
other Indian languages and took pride in their bilingual abilities as
a way of underscoring their cultural connections to Indians and their
sense of belonging to Indian communities. Cherokee freedwoman
Patsy Taylor Perryman, born and raised in the Cherokee Nation, mentioned that her mother had "always been with Mistress Judy Taylor."
She maintained that her mother "was raised by the Indians and could
talk Cherokee."[63] Perryman recalled "nobody around the place but
Indians and negroes; I was a full grown girl before I ever saw a
white man." Perryman's brother, Lewis, "married a full-blood Indian
woman and they got lots of Indian children on their farm in the old

Cherokee country around Caney Creek. He's just like an Indian, been with them so much, talks the Cherokee language and don't notice us negroes any more." Her brother decided to associate with Cherokees exclusively because as he told his sister he was "darn tired looking at negroes!"[64] Perryman relayed how consumed her brother became with Cherokee culture when she indicated that his children were not "mixed" in any way, but simply and wholly "Indian children."

Though siblings, Patsy Taylor Perryman and her brother developed connections to the Cherokee language, culture, and people based on different premises. When Perryman discussed her affiliation with the Cherokees, she did so as a matter of fact—noting how her exposure to Cherokees, as well as limited contact with European Americans, explained the connection she and her mother had to Cherokees. Even after the war, she expressed a longing for the simplicity of her childhood days on Judy Taylor's plantation. Though she identified with her brother in some ways, her explanation of her brother's relationship to the Cherokee language and people illustrates a different kind of reasoning. For Perryman's brother, his desire to disassociate from the stigma of blackness partially grounded his need to speak Cherokee and to identify closely with Cherokee people. His marriage and children strengthened his link to Cherokee culture and distanced him from the bane of blackness and bondage.

The experiences of Perryman and her brother should not be viewed as exceptional in Indian Territory. Indeed, the acculturation of enslaved African Indians west of the Mississippi cannot be understood as a singular, linear process either forced on or voluntarily adopted by enslaved people. Enslaved African Indians in Indian Territory would have identified themselves in relation to Indians in multiple ways depending on a variety of factors, including their relationship with Indian slaveholders and nonslaveholders, as well as the scope and depth of their understanding, acceptance, or rejection of Indian customs and cultures. During the antebellum period, enslaved African Indians' conceptions of their cultural identities cannot be defined as a neutral way of being or thinking. Their social construction of their cultural identities would have been influenced significantly by their conditions of bondage, power dynamics between themselves and their enslavers, and their sense of belonging to or disassociation from Indian and African Indian people and communities. Moreover, their cultural identities could have changed over time and place—from living east of the Mississippi before removal to resettlement after relocation to Indian Territory.

The resettlement process itself in antebellum Indian Territory might have expanded African Indian integration of Indian languages within their daily lives, as well as developed new ways of utilizing and altering these Indian languages. Just as enslaved African Indians could have created their own "Indian fashion" by donning Indian garb in distinctive ways, so too might they have formulated a creole or patois based on mixtures of Indian languages and English. When Henry Clay recalled that "them Creek negroes was so funny to talk to," he may have been commenting on not only the manner in which Indianized enslaved African Creeks spoke but also the language they used to express themselves. It is possible that some enslaved African Creeks in the Creek Nation, as well as enslaved people of the Cherokees, Seminoles, Choctaws, and Chickasaws, developed not only a facility for these Indian languages but also particular dialects that integrated, but did not entirely reproduce, aspects of southeastern Indian languages. Whether enslaved people of African descent became proficient in Indian languages or created a patois or creole infused with Indian words, they used the spoken word as another means of expressing their cultural connection to Indians and their inclusion within Indian nations.

The use of language is not limited to communication; language also embodies other aspects of culture, namely mores, values, oral history, and tradition. Enslaved African Indians' abilities to communicate in Indian languages in antebellum Indian Territory symbolize an additional dimension of acculturation and Indianization. Certainly, bondage influenced enslaved African Indians' understanding of their bilingualism or multilingualism in Indian Territory. Such knowledge of English and Cherokee, for example, might not have represented a particular cultural affinity for Cherokee custom and language on the part of enslaved African Cherokees but could have occurred simply as a result of a long-term association with European Americans and Cherokees east of the Mississippi. Some enslaved African Indians serving as translators in the Five Tribes might have viewed this particular role as merely one of their duties as enslaved people—no different from the litany of tasks related to their enslaved position. Other enslaved African Indians could have manipulated their role as cultural mediators in order to attain heightened status in slaveholding communities in Indian Territory. Perhaps some had employed their bilingualism as a kind of currency when their Indian owners discussed possibly selling them or their kin to settle a debt or to purchase more commodities. Indeed, the intricacies of bondage and belonging could have allowed enslaved African Indians in the Five Tribes to simultaneously recognize Indian languages as their mother tongue as well as a tool of negotiation, resistance, and acculturation.

Foodways

Preparing and eating Indian food, like speaking Indian languages, represented another human expression embodying interconnected cultural dimensions of identity for enslaved African Indians in antebellum Indian Territory. The study of food and culture, commonly referred to within some academic circles as foodways, has expanded our understanding of the cultural, historical, and traditional meanings surrounding food and food-centered activities.[65] Eating food certainly represents more than physical sustenance; it involves a complex "eating culture."[66] What people eat, who prepares meals, how meals are prepared, and how people take in their food are all aspects of a group's cultural identity. Within many traditions, including Indian cultures, food has represented one of the symbolic markers of cultural and national identity. Responsible for preparing meals before and after removal to Indian Territory, enslaved people of the Five Tribes developed an understanding of Indian cuisine. Their creation of such meals illustrates their knowledge of a variety of Indian foods but also reveals their connection to another significant aspect of Indian cultures and customs.

As a result of being born and raised in antebellum Indian Territory, enslaved and free African Indians learned to prepare a range of dishes particular to the Indian societies in which they lived. Enslaved children recalled the food their mothers prepared. Cherokee freedwoman Patsy Taylor Perryman remembered that "mostly we had bean bread and bean dumplings with corn bread. Making corn bread was a big job. First the corn had to be soaked, then put in a mortar and pounded to meal with a pessel—'beating the meal' is what my mammy called it."[67] Due to their familiarity with Indian cuisine before and after removal to Indian Territory, some enslaved African Indians deemed Indian meals as their own—as part of their personal and familial culture and custom. When Kiziah Love, a former slave of "full blood" Choctaw Frank Colbert, briefly explained the preparation of certain Chickasaw and Choctaw meals, she noted "one of *our* choicest dishes was 'Tom Pashofa,' an Indian dish. We'd take corn and beat it in a mortar with a pestle. They took out the husks with a riddle and a fanner. The riddle was a kind of a sifter. When it was beat fine enough to go through the riddle we'd put it in a pot and cook it with fresh pork or beef. We cooked *our* bread in a Dutch oven or in the ashes."[68] Even as Love specifically defined these meals as "Indian," her repeated use of the word "our" in describing these dishes expressed her relationship to them as not only Indian but also her own. Such meals did not serve as basic nourishment alone for enslaved African Indians; instead, many claimed these Indian dishes as part of their essential personal and cultural diet.

Like Kiziah Love, Choctaw freedwoman Polly Colbert also recalled "cooking all sorts of Indian dishes: Tom-fuller, pashofa, hickory-nut grot, Tom-budha, ash-cakes, and pound cakes besides vegetables and meat dishes.[69] Corn or corn meal was used in all de Indian dishes. We made hominy out'a de whole grains." Colbert vividly described the preparation of particular meals. "Tom-fuller," she explained, "was made from beaten corn and tasted sort of like hominy. We would take corn and beat it like in a wooden mortar wid a wooden pestle. We would husk it by fanning it and we would den put it on to cook in a big pot. While it was cooking we'd pick out a lot of hickory-nuts, tie 'em up in a cloth and beat 'em a little and drop 'em in and cook for a long time. We call dis dish hickory-nut grot." In order to make "pashofa we beat de corn and cook for a while and den we add fresh pork and cook until de meat was done. Tom-budha was green corn and fresh meat cooked together and seasoned wid tongue or pepper-grass."[70]

Colbert also explained that they "cooked on de fire place wid de pots hanging over de fire on racks and den we baked bread and cakes in a oven-skillet. We didn't use soda and baking powder. We'd put salt in de meal and scald it wid boiling water and make it into pones and bake it. We'd roll de ash cakes in wet cabbage leaves and put 'em in de hot ashes and bake 'em. We cooked potatoes, and roasting ears dat way also. We sweetened our cakes wid molasses, and dey was plenty sweet too."[71] Kiziah Love and Polly Colbert accurately described the preparation of the Chickasaw dish *pashofa* as well as several Choctaw meals. In addition to explaining the fundamental purpose of the mortar and pestle, they mentioned how baskets, specifically called the riddle and fanner, were used for sifting and cleaning ground corn.

Whereas enslaved women like Kiziah Love and Polly Colbert prepared meals for slaveholding Indian households, enslaved men engaged in the hunting of animals for such meals. Jefferson L. Cole, who was born and raised among the Choctaws, remembered that in the antebellum era "there was lots of game; deer and turkey, and I don't know what all. Everyone hunted some; some of the Indians made their living that way. After I got older I hunted now and then myself." Cole especially recalled "a way of hunting deer called 'fire huntin.'" This type of hunting occurred "at night. You took a pan with a long handle and set pieces of rich pine afire in the pan. You'd go where deer were thick; the light blinded them, and you could shoot them as they stood looking into the light." In order to prepare beef, they would "cut it up into slices and put [it] on top of the house to dry. Now and then we would turn the meat over so it would dry evenly. Then we'd build a fire under the scaffold and dry the meat some more. We would barbecue the chunks of meat that clung to the bones."[72] Though enslaved men's position as chattel certainly dictated their roles in hunting activities, some embraced such modes of hunting as part of their cultural identity in Indian Territory. Their understanding of hunting—a traditional feature of Indian men's roles—reinforced their connection to Indian customs and communities in antebellum Indian Territory.

Complementing their experience with meal preparation and hunting, enslaved African Indians also became knowledgeable at doctoring people through the use of herbal medicine—a talent revered within their respective communities. Enslaved African Indian children often heard about or witnessed older enslaved members in Indian Territory preparing concoctions to cure a range of illnesses. As Cherokee freedwoman Rachel Aldrich Ward admitted, persons of her own generation "didn't know what doctoring was." However, "some of the older men and women used to dig roots and get different herbs for medicine; them medicines cure the chill fever and such."[73] R. C. Smith, who was of Cherokee and African descent, recalled how he "used to get a weed called hoarhound, it grows everywhere wild. I'd make a tea and drink it and it would cure the worst kind of kidney ailment. Peach tree leaves tea and sumac seed tea also were good kidney medicines. These were Indian remedies."[74] Smith specifically described these tonics as "Indian remedies" that he had become adept at preparing and applying for his personal use. Being of Cherokee descent no doubt reinforced his cultural access to such medications; however, other African Indians who claimed no Indian ancestry also became experienced at creating and dispensing herbal remedies steeped in Indian cultural and medicinal beliefs.

Some enslaved African Indians became so knowledgeable about herbal remedies that they were deemed "medicine men," "herb doctors," or "Indian doctors." Cherokee E. F. Vann explained that "in every community there were one or more Medicine Men or Mid-wives. Many remedies prepared by the Medicine Men were held as profound secrets by them," but others in the community were aware of some remedies.[75] Choctaw freedwoman Irena Blocker described her aunt, Penny Brashiers, "as an 'herb doctor' whose practice it was to use a 'horn cup' in the cure of certain 'miseries' which would not yield to treatment through the virtues of herb concoctions, such as rheumatism or neuralgia. In some instances she would use a piece of glass to make an abrasion in the skin over the seat of the 'misery,' then place the horn cup over the abrasion and suck until a vacuum was formed, thus bringing about profuse bleeding of the affected parts and the elimination of the poison which had caused the pain."[76] The horn cup itself "was made from the small end of a cow's horn. The large end would be trimmed until it was made smooth and straight so as to fit snugly and encompass the abrasion, while a small hole would be made in the other and through which air would be extracted and a powerful vacuum created." This particular treatment with the horn cup in addition to "her herb remedies brought ailing people of all races to the door of Aunt Penny, many to die after their arrival and many more through the ministrations of the good old doctor were cured of their ills and enabled to return to their homes to sing the praises of this colored medicine woman."[77]

The cupping procedure, highlighted by Irena Blocker, did not occur solely in the Choctaw Nation. The Chickasaws used a similar procedure, referred to as "medicine horn," with the horn of a steer. Cherokee Tom Foster also recalled how "cupping or bleeding was resorted to in some sickness, rheumatism was one. The doctor would puncture a place where the pain was most severe, twist some paper, light it, place it in the cup, and attach the cup to the ailing part. This would draw out a quantity of blood. This was repeated until the sick man got relief." In addition to observing this practice in the Cherokee Nation, Foster personally remembered "being in Muskogee [Creek Nation] one day where two men were brought in, suffering with spinal meningitis. I was asked to help the doctor treat them, which he did by bleeding. He took his knife and punctured the skin at the base of the skull until it bled freely. Then he attached his cup with the burning paper in it and drew two cups of blood each, from the sick man. They, I know, got well."[78]

In addition to remembering this procedure, Cherokee Tom Foster described how one enslaved woman, owned by his Cherokee grandfather, fashioned cures for illnesses and delivered a specific "service" in his community. Of the people enslaved by his family, Tom Foster "especially remember[ed] Aunt Martha. She was quite a doctor in her young and middle life, acting as mid-wife to most all families in that community. She was present at my birth, so she told me."[79] Foster expressed no ambivalence in his recollection of the healing powers of this enslaved woman. Other slave-owning and non-slave-owning families throughout Indian Territory benefited from the midwifery and related doctoring skills of enslaved African Indian women. As in other southern states, enslaved women performed a range of duties and their healing skills often sustained the families of enslaved African Indians and Indian owners alike.[80]

Though enslaved women exclusively served as midwives, general doctoring was not limited to them alone.[81] A person's gender did not dictate her or his healing abilities; rather, knowledge of medicinal herbs and healing processes and, of course, healing successes confirmed one's expertise in this area. Cherokee freedwoman Victoria Taylor Thompson remembered that "for sickness daddy give us tea and herbs. He was a herb doctor, that's how come he have the name 'Doc.' He made us wear charms. Made out of shiny buttons and Indian rock beads. They cured lots of things and the misery too."[82] Choctaw freedman Jack Campbell, who was of Choctaw and African descent, proudly claimed his position as an "Indian doctor" among the Choctaws in Indian Territory. Campbell pronounced that he "was an Indian doctor when I was grown and when an Indian would get sick he would send for me. I would always go and see the sick Indian, if this sick Indian was a real sick fellow. The Choctaw tribe in those days called their sick spells after some of the animals that roamed the woods and some of the fowls."[83] The fact that Choctaws would see Campbell to treat various illnesses strongly suggests a level of trust and connection between Campbell and the Choctaws who sought his help.

Campbell indicated how serious he considered being an Indian doctor was as he declared that he "never would tell the names of the roots and herbs that I dug up and cooked down for the sick." Interviewer Bradley Bolinger noted that Campbell "refused to tell [him] yesterday when [he] was talking to him. He said it was against his belief."[84] Campbell's resolve to withhold information about the herbs and roots he used as medicine suggests the significance he associated with the particular knowledge he possessed.[85] By refusing to speak openly about his knowledge of sacred herbs and roots, Campbell also expressed his allegiance to the culture out of which he, and other enslaved African Indians, gained such knowledge. Transferring this knowledge to Bolinger undeniably symbolized a breach of faith in Campbell's position as an Indian doctor to the Choctaw people—as a person responsible for the healing and continuity of the Choctaw Nation.

◆ In nineteenth-century Indian Territory, enslaved African Indians' interactions with slaveholding and nonslaveholding Indians shaped their lives on a daily basis. Some enslaved African Indians recognized their cultural ties to specific Indian nations in terms of particular cultural markers. Henry Clay at first distanced himself from those "Creek negroes" because they had a "funny" way of speaking and whenever he saw them along the road wearing their strange attire he was afraid and thus kept out of their way. On the other hand, it is precisely because her folks wore "blankets and breeches with fur around the bottoms" that Sweetie Ivery Wagoner claimed her association with Creek culture. "Indian" clothing represented one of the most palpable signs of African Indians' cultural identification with Indians in nineteenth-century Indian Territory. We learn from Kiziah Love, Polly Colbert, and Jefferson Cole that their preparation of basic meals and the hunting of animals were grounded inextricably in Indian cultural traditions—Indian ways of cooking and hunting. As a result of their interactions with Indians, some African Indians, like the relatives of Patsy Taylor Perryman and Betty Robertson, communicated in an Indian language. Utilizing Indian herbal treatments to cure diseases was important to R. C. Smith; however, in the cases of Victoria Taylor Thompson's father, Irena Blocker's Aunt Penny, and Jack Campbell himself, to actually become, or to be known as, an "herb doctor" or "medicine woman" represented an entirely different cultural position within Indian communities. Moreover, by engaging in and remembering specific processes of meal preparation and doctoring in Indian Territory, enslaved African Indians also served as cultural agents through which Indian traditions were remembered and passed on.

No one cultural dimension—clothing, language, or food—established one's cultural affinity to Indian customs or sense of belonging to Indian communities in antebellum Indian Territory; instead, a combination of cultural elements—sometimes heightened by blood ties—demonstrated aspects of Indianness and positioned individuals, free and enslaved, African Indian and European Indian, within the fabric of southeastern Indian nations in antebellum Indian Territory. Yet, no matter the depth or intensity of that sense of belonging, the peculiar institution of slavery restricted freedom for enslaved African Indians and free people of color alike in antebellum Indian Territory. Though firmly ensconced in antebellum Indian communities in Indian Territory, both would have to wait for a civil war to finally attain perpetual emancipation.

Mrs. Benson, Cherokee freedwoman, circa 1930s.
Courtesy of the Oklahoma Historical Society, photo no. 14855

Morris Sheppard, Cherokee freedman, circa 1930s, Grant Foreman Collection.
Courtesy of the Oklahoma Historical Society, photo no. 10753

Payment at Hayden on Big Creek in Cooweescoowee District, Cherokee Nation, Indian
Territory, in 1897, after federal suit in which Cherokee freedpeople won the right to share
in distribution of Cherokee funds, T. L. Ballenger Collection. Courtesy of the Western
History Collections, University of Oklahoma, photo no. 19

Captain Archibald S. McKennon interviewing freedmen as part of the Dawes Commission's process for enrolling members of the Cherokee Nation at Fort Gibson, Indian Territory, circa 1899–1901, Aylesworth Album Collection. Courtesy of the Oklahoma Historical Society, photo no. 15813

Camp of freedpeople during enrollment before the Dawes Commission, circa 1899–1901, Aylesworth Album Collection. Courtesy of the Oklahoma Historical Society, photo no. 15797

Store run by freedpeople at Fort Gibson, Indian Territory, during enrollment before the Dawes Commission, circa 1899–1901, Aylesworth Album Collection. Courtesy of the Oklahoma Historical Society, photo no. 15805

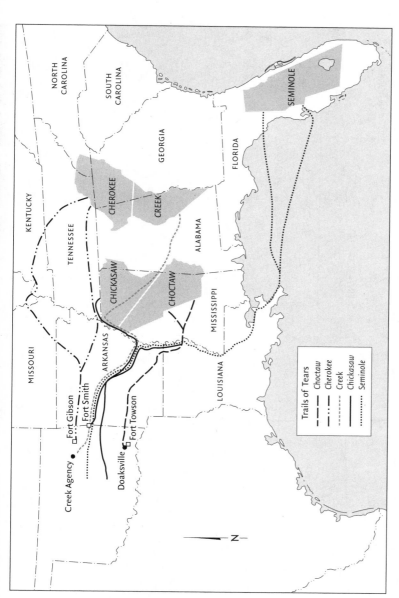

Removal of the Five Tribes (Historical Atlas of Oklahoma, 3rd ed., map no. 20)

All maps adapted from *Historical Atlas of Oklahoma*, 3rd ed., by John W. Morris, Charles R. Goins, and Edwin C. McReynolds. Copyright © 1965, 1976, 1986 by the University of Oklahoma Press, Norman. Reprinted by permission of publisher. All rights reserved.

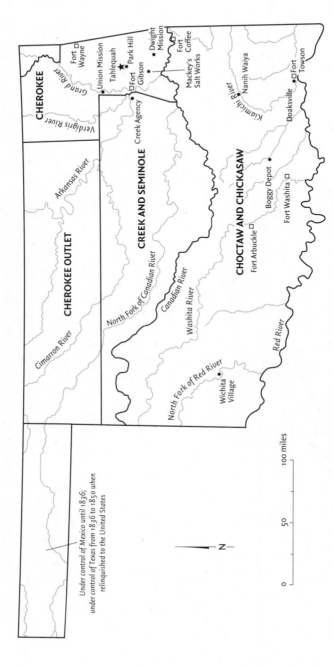

Indian Territory, 1830–55 (Historical Atlas of Oklahoma, 3rd ed., map no. 23)

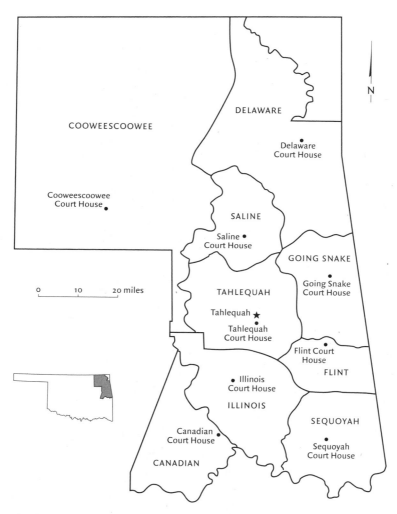

COOWEESCOOWEE

DELAWARE

Delaware
Court House

Cooweescoowee
Court House

SALINE

Saline
Court House

GOING SNAKE

Going Snake
Court House

0   10   20 miles

TAHLEQUAH

Tahlequah ★
Tahlequah
Court House

Flint Court
House

FLINT

Illinois
Court House

ILLINOIS

SEQUOYAH

Canadian
Court House

Sequoyah
Court House

CANADIAN

N

Cherokee Nation: Political Divisions (Historical Atlas of Oklahoma, 3rd ed., map no. 35)

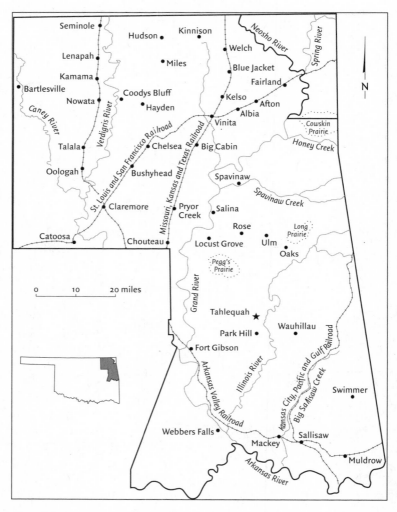

Cherokee Nation: *Important Places* (Historical Atlas of Oklahoma, 3rd ed., map no. 36)

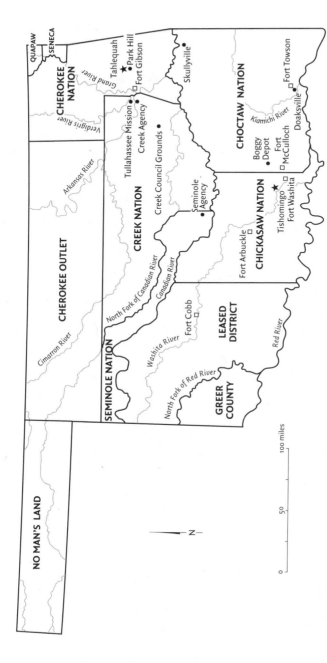

Indian Territory, 1855–66 (*Historical Atlas of Oklahoma*, 3rd ed., map no. 26)

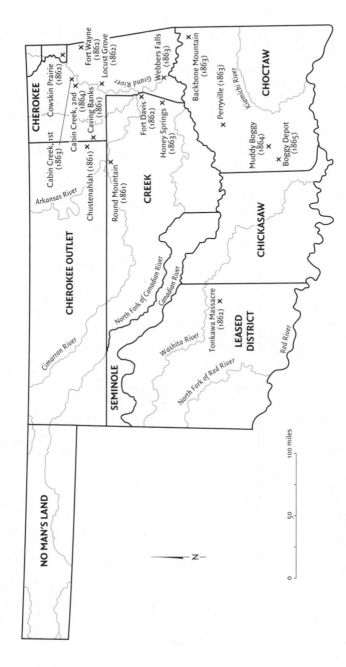

Civil War Battle Sites (Historical Atlas of Oklahoma, 3rd ed., map no. 28)

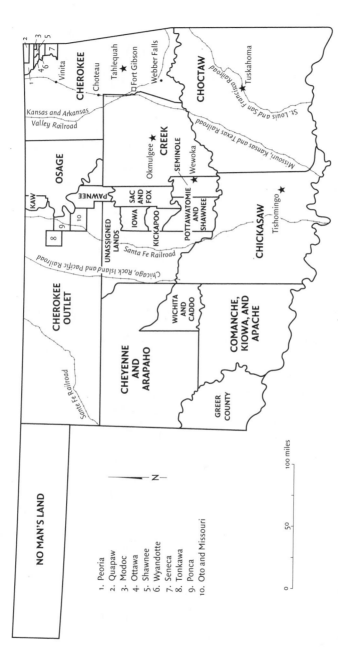

Indian Territory, 1866–89 (*Historical Atlas of Oklahoma*, 3rd ed., map no. 33)

NO MAN'S LAND

1. Peoria
2. Quapaw
3. Modoc
4. Ottawa
5. Shawnee
6. Wyandotte
7. Seneca
8. Tonkawa
9. Ponca
10. Oto and Missouri

—N—

0   50   100 miles

CHEROKEE OUTLET

Santa Fe Railroad

CHEYENNE AND ARAPAHO

GREER COUNTY

COMANCHE, KIOWA, AND APACHE

WICHITA AND CADDO

Chicago, Rock Island and Pacific Railroad

CHICKASAW

Tishomingo

Santa Fe Railroad

UNASSIGNED LANDS

OSAGE

KAW

PAWNEE

IOWA

SAC AND FOX

KICKAPOO

POTTAWATOMIE AND SHAWNEE

Kansas and Arkansas Valley Railroad

CHEROKEE

Vinita
Choteau
Tahlequah
Fort Gibson
Webber Falls

CREEK

Okmulgee

SEMINOLE

Wewoka

CHOCTAW

Tuskahoma

St. Louis and San Francisco Railroad

Missouri, Kansas and Texas Railroad

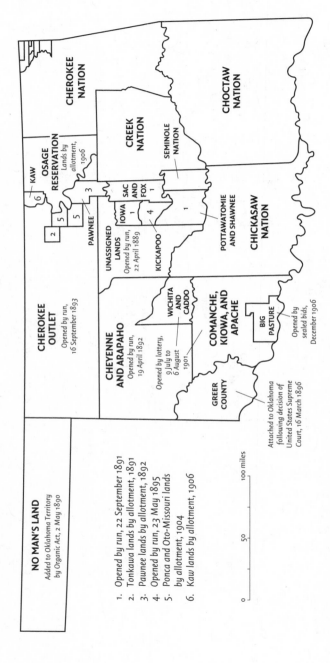

NO MAN'S LAND

Added to Oklahoma Territory
by Organic Act, 2 May 1890

CHEROKEE OUTLET

Opened by run,
16 September 1893

CHEROKEE NATION

KAW 6

OSAGE RESERVATION

Lands by allotment, 1906

2 5 5 5 PAWNEE 3

PAWNEE

CREEK NATION

CHOCTAW NATION

UNASSIGNED LANDS

Opened by run, 22 April 1889

IOWA 1 **SAC AND FOX** 1

4 **KICKAPOO**

1

SEMINOLE NATION

POTTAWATOMIE AND SHAWNEE

CHICKASAW NATION

CHEYENNE AND ARAPAHO

Opened by run, 19 April 1892

WICHITA AND CADDO

Opened by lottery, 9 July to 6 August 1901

COMANCHE, KIOWA, AND APACHE

BIG PASTURE

Opened by sealed bids, December 1906

GREER COUNTY

Attached to Oklahoma following decision of United States Supreme Court, 16 March 1896

1. Opened by run, 22 September 1891
2. Tonkawa lands by allotment, 1891
3. Pawnee lands by allotment, 1892
4. Opened by run, 23 May 1895
5. Ponca and Oto-Missouri lands by allotment, 1904
6. Kaw lands by allotment, 1906

0   50   100 miles

Land Openings (Historical Atlas of Oklahoma, 3rd ed., map no. 48)

Trapped in the Turmoil
A Divided Cherokee Nation and the Plight of Enslaved African Cherokees during the Civil War Era

We camped around the garrison place at Fort Gibson and there was no buildings there like there is now. The soldiers was all camped there in tents. They was all Confederate soldiers and I mean there was lots of soldiers camped in the tents. The negroes piled in there from everywheres, and I mean there was lots of them, too. Cooking in the open, sleeping most anywhere, making shelter places out of cloth scraps and brush, digging caves along the river bank to live in. There was no way to keep the place clean for there was too many folks living all in one place, and if you walk around in the nighttime most likely you stumble over some negro rolled up in a dirty blanket and sleeping under a bush.

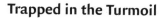 Cherokee freedwoman Rochelle Allred (Rachel Aldrich) Ward

All Negro and other slaves within the limits of the Cherokee Nation, be, and they are hereby Emancipated from Slavery. And any person or persons who may have been held in slavery, are hereby declared to be forever free.

◆ Act of the Cherokee National Council, 21 February 1863 (effective 25 June 1863)

Although multiple processes of acculturation and acts of resistance had not resulted in mass emancipation, enslaved African Cherokees in the antebellum Cherokee Nation had, by the late 1850s, become seasoned residents grounded in Cherokee communities. Rumors of an impending war between the North and South triggered fresh hopes of life beyond bondage. The Civil War served as a monumental opportunity for those enslaved in the Cherokee Nation to grasp the seemingly unattainable prospect of freedom. Discussions about the existence and maintenance of slavery in the United States and international movements to abolish slavery also permeated the consciousness of free Cherokee citizens in Indian Territory—from private discussions in slaveholding Cherokee households to public statements in the *Cherokee Advocate*.

National and international debates on slavery did not serve as the sole catalyst for discussion of the topic; a point of contention before removal, slavery remained a controversial issue that intensified clashes in the Cherokee Nation after resettlement in Indian Territory. However, the convergence of external and internal forces concerning the existence of slavery, as well as the Civil War itself, reignited intense debates on abolition in the Cherokee Nation and other southeastern Indian nations in Indian Territory. Some families within the Cherokee Nation had enslaved African Cherokees for generations and relied on enslaved labor to sustain their quality of life. Many had opposed the institution before removal and continued to challenge the presence of human property in the new territory. Others had changed their views of enslavement as a result of convincing arguments about the necessity or inhumanity of slavery. Due to the differing positions on slavery, abolition, and the looming Civil War, the Cherokee Nation experienced a rekindling of preremoval and postremoval factionalism. Just as the Civil War created monumental divisions in families and communities in the United States, it also opened up wide rifts within the Cherokee Nation. The Civil War brought irrevocable changes and signaled a time of devastation, destitution, and displacement for Cherokee slaves and owners alike.

Slavery and Factionalism in a Fragmented Cherokee Nation

Before the onset of the Civil War, national and international arguments concerning slavery and Christianity had already fueled the debates over slavery between various constituents within the Cherokee Nation itself. The moral, religious, and political beliefs of European American missionaries on slavery proved to be especially problematic in Indian Territory.[1] In the postremoval period, the views of missionaries working for the American Board of Commissioners for Foreign Missions (ABCFM), in particular, spawned disputes over the presence of slavery in antebellum Indian Territory.[2] Founded in 1810, the ABCFM operated under the auspices of the Boston-based Prudential Committee. Although aware of the existence of slavery in the Cherokee Nation from the establishment of its missions there, the ABCFM chose not to challenge directly its missionaries' role in relation to slavery in Indian Territory until the board's annual meeting in 1844.[3] The ABCFM's annual report related that one of three memorials presented at the annual meeting that year addressed slavery within ABCFM missionary communities in Indian Territory.[4] The memorial described slavery as a "system of oppression . . . a system whose unhappy subjects are as ignorant and degraded as many heathen in foreign lands." As a result of the oppressive nature of slavery, the memorialists expressed disappointment over being "informed that slavery is actually tolerated in the churches under the patronage of the Board among the Choctaws and other Indian tribes, by the admission of slaveholding members, and has most evidently interposed an obstacle to the missionary cause."[5] Moreover, "for these and other reasons, many liberal and devoted Christians have withheld their contributions from the Board, and many more have given with great reluctance, and, without a redress of grievances, the funds of the Board, will be seriously diminished, or a large increase prevented."[6]

In light of the volatility of this situation, the memorialists requested that the board "take this subject into serious and prayerful consideration. . . . We ask the Board earnestly to entreat all the missionaries and agents under its patronage to bear a decided testimony against the sin of oppression, wherever and in whatever form it exists; and most especially to declare . . . that American slavery is a sin against God." Furthermore, the memorialists implored the board to "immediately take measures to ascertain to what extent slavery or oppression exists in the churches under its patronage, and especially among the Choctaws and other Indian tribes; and take such action at this meeting as shall speedily remove the evil, or exonerate them and their missionaries from all the responsibility and guilt of its continuance or toleration."[7] In response to this request, the committee charged with reviewing the subject reported that "so far as they are at present informed, they see no reason to charge the missionaries among the Choctaws, or any where else, with either a violation or neglect of duty." However, the committee "requested that they may have time to make a thorough inquiry into the state of the churches in our various missionary stations in regard to slavery" and to present a more detailed report at the next annual meeting.[8]

At the 1845 annual meeting in Brooklyn, board members discussed several memorials and formal reports regarding slavery in Indian Territory, specifically within the Cherokee and Choctaw nations.[9] Although the committee presented a more extensive report on slavery, the board decided that a visit to Indian Territory had become imperative to the understanding of the role of ABCFM missionaries among the slaveholding Cherokee and Choctaw nations. As a result, at the 1847 annual meeting in Buffalo, the board directed Secretary Selah B. Treat to travel to the Cherokee and Choctaw nations in Indian Territory.[10] The Prudential Committee instructed Treat "to ascertain, as fully and accurately as practicable, the present state and prospects of the missions, for the information of the Committee, and for the assistance of himself in his correspondence hereafter with the missions." Moreover, the Prudential Committee requested that Treat embark on "a full and fraternal examination of the relations of the missions, and the churches under their care, to the subject of slavery."[11]

Secretary Treat left Boston on 30 November 1847 and arrived at Dwight Mission, located in the Sequoyah District of the Cherokee Nation, Indian Territory, on 4 January 1848. Treat spent eight weeks within the Cherokee and Choctaw nations. He returned to Boston on 1 April 1848. During his time in Indian Territory, Treat met with all the missionaries and assistant missionaries under the board's patronage within the Cherokee and Choctaw nations.[12]

Soon after Treat left Indian Territory, ABCFM missionaries working in the Cherokee Nation wrote a letter to Treat, and by extension to the Prudential Committee, expressing their predicament on the issue of slavery. On behalf of all four primary ABCFM missionaries working among the Cherokees, Dr. Elizur Butler and Samuel A. Worcester composed a letter, dated 21 March 1848, to Secretary Treat in response to his visit and outlined their views on the subject of slavery.[13] The missionaries poignantly voiced their opinion regarding any attempts to enforce their own views about slavery upon the members of their mission, as well as the related topic concerning the rejection of slaveholders as members of their mission churches. Emphasizing the congregational nature of their churches, they reiterated that, although the churches are in some ways subject to their dictation, they in fact "govern themselves." Even though the missionaries "mourn the existence of slavery, and long for the coming of the day when neither in our churches nor in the world shall a slaveholder or a slave be found," they "cannot doubt that the course which many would urge us to pursue in relation to our churches would only tend to retard, and not to hasten, the coming of that happy day."[14]

Just as the missionaries believed it would be fruitless to express their views regarding slavery, they also agreed that rejecting slaveholders from their churches for the mere fact of their being slaveholders would be impracticable. The missionaries argued that they could not in good conscience "make the adoption of all our views respecting it [slavery], and a corresponding course of action, a test of piety and a condition of fellowship in our churches."[15] Recognizing that their stance on this issue could lead to the ABCFM's termination of their work among the Cherokees, the missionaries professed that, "if support be withdrawn from us on account of views which we have expressed in this communication, it will of necessity be, so far as the board is concerned, an entire withholding of the word of God from the Cherokee people." Indeed, "to recall us on this ground, and send others who would pursue an opposite course," they contended, "would be manifestly preposterous and vain."[16]

On 15 June 1848 Treat submitted to the board his formal report regarding his visit to the Cherokee and Choctaw nations.[17] Treat's letter in response to ABCFM missionaries in the Cherokee and Choctaw nations described the Prudential Committee's overall sense of slavery as "at war with the rights of man, and opposed to the principles of the Gospel."[18] In their letter dated 14 September 1848, the missionaries serving the Cherokee Mission responded to Treat's letter of 30 June 1848. In this letter they reiterated the views they had expressed in their previous letter to Treat, especially in regard to the inclusion of slaveholding members of their church and their position on overtly voicing any antislavery ideas in the Cherokee Nation.[19] Though the tensions remained between the Prudential Committee and their ABCFM missions, the board did not vote to terminate its support of the Cherokee Mission until its 1860 annual meeting. The board emphasized that the closing of the mission was "not owing to the relations of our work among these Indians to the system of slavery." Rather, the board declared that "the Cherokee people have been Christianized, through the divine favor, and what remains for building up and sustaining the institutions of the Gospel—which is every where a work never brought to a close—must be left to others; for the reason that our appropriate work is no longer there."[20]

During their time in the Cherokee Nation, it is possible that some missionaries' views about slavery affected their interactions with enslaved African Cherokees; missionaries who were advocates of abolition could have created opportunities for runaways to escape the shackles of bondage. One of the issues Butler and Worcester addressed in their 1848 letter to Treat concerned the employment of enslaved people by missionaries. They firmly declared "that no slave has ever been purchased by any missionary of the Board in this nation, except with a view to emancipation; none who has not actually been emancipated; consequently, that none of us now holds a slave on any terms whatever." Moreover, they pledged that "no apprehension need be entertained that any slave will be held by any member of the mission hereafter."[21]

Although they expressed their agreement on the employment of enslaved people, they indicated their difference of opinion on the hiring of enslaved African Cherokees from their owners. Some missionaries viewed this hiring practice, "especially at the earnest desire, of the slave himself," as an "act of kindness." Other missionaries believed hiring enslaved people tended "to uphold and encourage the system of slavery, and is, therefore, an evil to be avoided as far as possible."[22] One of the later ABCFM missionaries, Rev. Charles Cutler

Torrey, utilized enslaved labor while stationed in the Cherokee Nation. Arriving in the Cherokee Nation in the autumn of 1855, in his autobiography he stated that "we were obliged to hire slaves from their owners, if we wished extra help, and always gave them some money for themselves in addition to what we paid their masters."[23]

What enslaved people thought of this arrangement remains unclear. Due to bilingual abilities, some enslaved African Cherokees might have served as interpreters and mediators between European American missionaries and non-English-speaking Cherokees in Indian Territory. Those who demonstrated a deep interest in Christianity might have been well positioned to participate in services offered by the missionaries in the Cherokee Nation. However, the extent of such involvement would have been curtailed by statutes forbidding slave literacy in the Nation. Indeed, as Cherokee freedwoman Nancy Rogers Bean recalled, "us slaves didn't know much about Sunday in a religious way. The Master had a brother who used to preach to the Negroes on the sly. One time he was caught and the Master whipped him something awful."[24]

Cherokee freedman Morris Sheppard explained how enslaved African Cherokees "had to have a pass to go any place to have singing or praying, and den they was always a bunch of patrollers around to watch everything we done. Dey would come up in a bunch of about nine men on horses and look at all our passes, and if a negro didn't have no pass dey wore him out good and made him go home. Dey didn't let us have much enjoyment."[25] Cherokee freedwoman Chaney Richardson also recalled the surreptitious nature of religiosity for some enslaved African Cherokees: "we had a church made out of brush arbor and we would sing good songs in Cherokee sometimes. . . . I still understand and talk Cherokee language and love to hear songs and parts of the Bible in it because it make me think about the time I was a little girl before my mammy and pappy leave me."[26] Sheppard and Richardson certainly echoed the beliefs of enslaved African Americans in the United States who utilized the "brush arbor" as a space to express their spirituality outside the gaze of their slave owners.[27]

Enslaved African Cherokees could have viewed missions in the

Cherokee Nation as potentially effective spaces for religiosity and resistance. Working primarily at the Fairfield Mission, Cherokee Nation, in July 1856, Torrey reported that he had in his "employ a slave named David, a member of our church, and a good man, and a good servant." When David discovered that he would be hired out elsewhere, he ran away. He was later captured and returned to his master.[28] In his notes, Torrey did not present his personal view of this runaway attempt. Certainly, David and other enslaved African Cherokees might have welcomed being hired out to a mission and viewed this as a possible way to accumulate funds in order to procure their freedom. Though Torrey described David as a "good servant," it is unknown what David's motivations were for good service. David could have been genuinely interested in being a member of the church and welcomed spiritual edification or he could have been a "good servant" as a cover while he strategized about running away to freedom. Hearing that he would be "hired out elsewhere," David might have conceived of a new plan for freedom or revisited a previous strategy for running away. Even if Torrey had not assisted David as he prepared to run away, other antislavery missionaries in the Cherokee Nation might have offered some level of assistance to enslaved people as they attempted to attain freedom in this way.

The dictates of the ABCFM and the Prudential Committee on the issue of slavery often placed the missionaries in a difficult position in terms of their interactions with Cherokee slaveholders and enslaved African Cherokees in antebellum Indian Territory. The annual meetings and reports of the ABCFM underscored the conflicts between the beliefs of the Boston-based Prudential Committee and those of ABCFM missionaries who lived and worked in Cherokee slaveholding communities before and after removal to Indian Territory. Although working under the auspices of the ABCFM and the Prudential Committee, some ABCFM missionaries who had worked closely with the Cherokees before and after removal expressed their allegiance to the Cherokee people above and beyond any duty to the ABCFM itself. Their decision reflected their unwillingness to compromise their beliefs on the slavery issue and their reluctance to defer to the demands of the

ABCFM's Prudential Committee, especially when doing so might well
have jeopardized their relationships with slaveholders within the Cherokee Nation. Having lived and worked within Cherokee communities,
ABCFM missionaries had developed their own sense of belonging in
the Cherokee Nation and may have prioritized their work in these
communities above the orders of the Prudential Committee.

Even after the board withdrew its support of the Cherokee missions
in 1860, a few of the missionaries remained in Indian Territory expressing their devotion to the people to whom they had dedicated a
significant part of their lives.[29] Certainly the physical distance between
Boston and Indian Territory facilitated the independent activities of
the ABCFM missionaries in the Cherokee Nation; however, this ideological and geographical separation would not endure for long. In the
end, the gradual external movement toward abolition would traverse
the boundaries of Indian Territory.

Just as the Prudential Committee in Boston attempted to dictate the
views of its missionaries and congregations in Indian Territory on the
issue of slavery, actions of the U.S. government and the Confederacy
stoked dissension within the Cherokee Nation concerning the war
between the North and the South. Having been grounded physically
and socially in southeastern communities before removal, some Cherokees supported the southern cause and the Confederacy. Simultaneously, due to previous treaties with the federal government and an
attempt to refrain from participating in the war, other Cherokees believed neutrality would best serve the interests of the Cherokee Nation.
Though a neutral position seemed possible at the beginning of the
conflict, it could not be maintained for the duration of the war. By May
1861, in order to strengthen their forces in the states, the U.S. War
Department had withdrawn from all existing federal forts in Indian
Territory. Before the evacuation, the federal government had provided
the Cherokees, Creeks, Choctaws, Chickasaws, and Seminoles with
various supplies, as well as military protection. As a result of the War
Department's decision to pull its troops from Indian Territory, the
Confederates effectively reoccupied the federal forts and began negotiations with each of the Indian nations in Indian Territory for its

support of the Confederacy. On 5 March 1861 the Confederate Congress appointed Albert Pike special Indian commissioner for the Confederate government. Commissioner Pike's duties included the creation of treaties with the various Indian nations in Indian Territory in order to garner their support for the Confederate States of America.

Though pressured at the onset of the war by internal and external forces, Cherokee Principal Chief John Ross initially supported a neutral position for the Cherokee Nation in the Civil War. In May 1861 Ross expressed that his "wish, advice and hope is that we shall be allowed to remain strictly neutral. . . . We do not wish our soil to become the battle ground between the states and our homes to be rendered desolate and miserable by the horrors of a civil war. If such war should not be averted yet by some unforseen [sic] agency but shall occur my own position will be to take no part in it whatever and to urge the like course upon the Cherokee people by whom in my opinion it will be adopted."[30] A month later, on 17 June 1861, in a letter to Brigadier General Benjamin McCulloch, Confederate commander at Fort Smith, Arkansas, Ross reiterated this position. He declared that "in regard to the pending conflict between the United States and Confederate States, I have already signified my purpose to take no part in it whatever. . . . We have done nothing to bring about the conflict in which you are engaged with your own people, and I am unwilling that my people shall become its victims. I am determined to do no act that shall furnish any pretext to either of the contending parties to overrun our country and destroy our rights."[31]

Chief John Ross attempted to maintain the Cherokee Nation's neutrality in the Civil War; however, as a result of the withdrawal of federal troops from Indian Territory, preparations by Confederate forces to invade the area, and increasing pressure from pro-Confederate sects within the Cherokee Nation to take a more active position in the war, he agreed to form an alliance with the Confederate States in August 1861.[32] The Cherokee Nation did unfortunately become the battleground that Chief Ross feared, and the Nation was indeed overrun by both Confederate and Union forces. A total of sixteen battles occurred in Indian Territory during the Civil War: seven in the Cherokee Nation, one in the Cherokee Outlet, four in the Choctaw Nation, three in the Creek Nation, and one in the Leased District. No major battles were fought within the limits of the Seminole or Chickasaw nations.[33]

The strategic plans of the federal government and the Confederacy heightened tensions within the Cherokee Nation about slavery and the Cherokee Nation's involvement in the Civil War. During the war, the Nation experienced a painful renewal of the internal divisiveness and violence that had emerged during the chaotic postremoval period. Both Union- and Confederate-supporting Cherokees created havoc by engendering a sense of fear, apprehension, and suspicion throughout the Cherokee Nation. Cherokee "full blood" Elizabeth Watts recalled that "years passed, and the bad feeling between the two factions seemed to get worse over the question of Slavery. Ross opposed it. Stand Watie, relative of Boudinot, was for it. Missionaries came along the 'Trail of Tears' and opposed it. Some Indian Agents were for it. The Indians did not want to fight. They had enough trouble, but they had to take one side or another and that caused much trouble at times."

In the Cherokee Nation, she explained, "not many full-bloods owned slaves and they had a secret society called 'Kee-Too-Wah.' They wore two common pins crossed on their coats for their emblem. Most all full-bloods belonged and wanted nothing to do with the white man's ways, but wanted to stay with tribal laws and customs. Most of them were [with] the Ross Faction and opposed slavery. Those who endorsed slavery had a society and it was made up of half-breeds and they owned most of the slaves."[34] While Watts underscored some of the complicated and interconnected forces present in the Cherokee Nation during the war, the position of enslaved people themselves is absent from her summation of the times. Though the debate over slavery necessarily invoked enslaved African Cherokees, their invisibility in Watts's observations reflected their exploited and second-class status in the Cherokee Nation and beyond.

Years later, Cherokee William Penn Adair recalled how, "during the four years of the war the contending armies, directly and indirectly, plundered our country and what one army did not take the other did so that between their depredations and the general effect of the war, the

Cherokees, Creeks, and Seminoles lost all their property of every description and had their houses destroyed or so wrecked as to render them of little value." Adair, a Cherokee slave owner and Confederate sympathizer, was well aware that loss of "property" included enslaved African Cherokees, and he may have had this in mind when discussing the drastic population decline associated with the disruptions of the war. He explained that "a remarkable circumstance connected with the loss of the Cherokees is that the war destroyed about one-half of their people for at the beginning of the war they had a population of about 25,000, whereas at the close of the Rebellion, their census rolls showed their population to be only 13,000."[35]

The debate over slavery in the Cherokee Nation, as well as throughout the United States, did not customarily include the viewpoints of enslaved people; rather, free citizens who supported or opposed slavery often served as the seemingly major actors in the unfolding drama of the Civil War.[36] In the Cherokee Nation, two specific factions took center stage—the Keetoowah Society and the Knights of the Golden Circle. As Elizabeth Watts explicated, during the Civil War Cherokees who opposed slavery often aligned themselves with the Keetoowah Society. Though founded on traditional notions of Cherokee polity, the Keetoowah Society received support not only from Cherokee residents in Indian Territory but also from European American missionaries who had worked within the Cherokee Nation before removal and continued to do so after resettlement in Indian Territory.

James W. Duncan, a longtime member of the Keetoowah Society, stated that "the Society was organized years before the civil war and was originally composed entirely of fullbloods. . . . In its early existence it was a strictly secret organization." He explained that "the original object of the Society was to maintain and assert the rights of all the Cherokee people or the Cherokee Nation under the laws and treaties with the government of the United States, and in fact that principle has been fundamental and carried out all along down the years since its organization."[37] In 1866 Albert Pike, special commissioner to the Indians of Indian Territory for the Confederate government, expressed his impression of the organization in 1861 in a letter to D. N. Cooley, commissioner of Indian affairs. In his letter, he mentioned the connection between the Keetoowahs and missionaries in the Cherokee Nation. He specifically stated that the Pins, "established by Evan Jones, a missionary, and at the service of Mr. John Ross," served the "purpose of abolitionizing the Cherokees and putting out of the way all who sympathized with the Southern State."[38] Just as other missionaries from a range of denominations played pivotal roles before and after removal to Indian Territory, Baptist missionaries Evan Jones and his son John Jones figured prominently as European American residents in the Cherokee Nation. They frequently voiced their abolitionist views to the members of their ministry and other members of the Cherokee Nation, especially in the years leading up to the Civil War.[39]

Though some Cherokees, as well as European American residents like Evan and John Jones, championed the Keetoowah Society during the war, others supported the tenets of the Knights of the Golden Circle—a secret society founded in 1854 in Cincinnati that supported slavery in the United States and other regions in the Americas.[40] Free Cherokee citizens in Indian Territory who espoused slavery in the Cherokee Nation created a version of this organization composed of Cherokees who supported the Confederacy during the Civil War.[41] The Constitution of the Knights of the Golden Circle in the Cherokee Nation declared in Article 1, Section 3, that "[n]o person shall be a member of the Knights of the Golden Circle in the Cherokee Nation who is not a proslavery man." Article 6, Section 1, instructed that the "Captain or in case of his refusal, then the Lieutenant has power to compel each and every member of their Encampment to turn out and assist in capturing and punishing any and all abolitionist in their minds who are interfering with slavery."[42]

Stand Watie and other Cherokee Confederate supporters established the Knights of the Golden Circle (later known as the Southern Rights Party), in opposition to the Keetoowah Society, in order to create support for their proslavery positions in the Cherokee Nation, as well as to promote the Confederate States of America.[43] By creating a branch of a national proslavery society in the Cherokee Nation,

Watie and other Cherokees reinforced their connection to southern slaveholding sensibilities about the existence and necessity of slavery. The establishment of this group reflected the movement of deeply ingrained views about the intersection of bondage and blackness over time and space—from preremoval Cherokee society east of the Mississippi to postremoval Cherokee communities in Indian Territory.

The conflicts between the Keetoowah Society and the Knights of the Golden Circle impacted the lives of not only free Cherokee citizens but also enslaved denizens of the Cherokee Nation. Enslaved African Cherokees witnessed the heightened hostility between these factions during the Civil War, and, in some cases, their position as enslaved people influenced the treatment they received from various sects in the Nation. Cherokee freedman Morris Sheppard, enslaved by Cherokee Joe Sheppard, was a young man in 1861 and could "remember it good as anybody." When the Civil War began, his Uncle Joe told them "to lay low and work hard and nobody bother us, and he would look after us." Morris Sheppard recalled that the other Cherokees "that lived around close to us . . . dey all had slaves. Dey was all wid the South, but dey was a lot of dem Pin Indians all up on de Illinois River and dey was wid de North and dey taken it out on de slave owners a lot before de War and during it too."[44] Morris Sheppard remembered how the Pins continually harassed his owner, Cherokee Joe Sheppard. Sheppard stated that the "Pins was after Master all de time for a while at de first of de War, and he was afraid to ride into Fort Smith much. Dey come to de house one time when he was gone to Fort Smith and us children told dem he was at Honey Springs, but they knowed better and when he got home he said somebody shot at him and bushwhacked him all the way from Wilson's Rock to dem Wildhorse Mountains, but he run his horse like de devil was setting on his tail and dey never did hit him."[45] Though his owner narrowly escaped, he recollected, the Pins "would come in de night and hamstring de horses and maybe set fire to de barn, and two of 'em named Joab Scarrel and Tom Starr killed my pappy [slave Caesar Sheppard] one night."[46] Although the exact circumstances of Caesar Sheppard's murder are unclear, his association with Joe Sheppard certainly triggered his fatal end. Though the Keetoowahs and Pins attacked Joe Sheppard and other Cherokee slave owners, they often intensified the degree of harassment of the enslaved. While Cherokee enslavers and enslaved people felt the wrath of the Keetoowahs and Pins, enslaved African Cherokees like Caesar Sheppard represented a tangible symbol of slavery that could be targeted and even physically eliminated for a more profound effect.

The rationale for acts of violence during the Civil War did not solely involve one's status as an enslaved person or slave owner; instead, at times it seemed to invoke a sociocultural and political divide between those deemed progressive "mixed bloods" and traditional "full bloods" within the Cherokee Nation. Throughout his private journal, Rev. Stephen Foreman, a slave-owning Cherokee minister at the ABCFM Park Hill Mission, documented the terror created in the Cherokee Nation during the Civil War, especially the Pins' contribution to this situation.[47] On 16 July 1862 Foreman explained his opposition to the Pins due to the fact that he "was a Watie man. I never had denied that I was, in some *particulars*, and the Pins knew it; the fact was, the *Pins made me so.*" The Pins, he stated, "had drawn a line of distinction between themselves and the half-breeds, and being a half-breed, I naturally fell on the Watie side. And not only so, but I had from the beginning opposed the Pin organization, and said much against it publicly."[48] Foreman viewed the Pins not only as advocates of abolition but also as opponents of "half-breed" Cherokees.

In contrast to Foreman's position on the Pins, Rev. Worcester Willey, ABCFM missionary at the Dwight Mission, Cherokee Nation, presented a different perspective on the attacks steeped in blood politics. Willey recounted how "the Indians killed each other at sight, whoever they met. The rebels took no prisoners. It was their declared purpose to blot out the full Cherokees." "It was fearful," Willey explained, "to hear of raids so frequently rushing through the country just to kill every body they could find, & steal whatever they could carry away, & when they got back to their own company boast of what they had done, & be applauded for their bravery and success."[49] The factionalism in the Cherokee Nation during the Civil War underscored the blood politics in the Nation. The potent tensions due to complicated sociopolitical stances only amplified the already volatile state of the Cherokee Nation during the war.

Though enslaved people and enslavers became vulnerable targets for harassment and abuse by factions in the Cherokee Nation, enslaved African Cherokees utilized the tumultuous and "unprotected" state of the Nation during the war to interject their own expressions of resistance to slavery. In his 11 July 1862 journal entry, Stephen Foreman described how during the war "every body seemed to be afraid to go out from home any distance. Women were afraid to venture out on account of the negroes, and men were afraid of each other, not knowing who was a friend or an enemy."[50] Foreman's reference to women's trepidation "on account of the negroes" hints at the kind of activities some enslaved African Cherokees might have engaged in during this time of panic. What had been deemed as avenues of slave resistance in the years and decades before the Civil War—stealing, killing, and running away—continued to be useful expressions of enslaved African Cherokees' opposition to bondage and exploitation. The fear surrounding enslaved people's actions during the Civil War, though, could also reflect some degree of Cherokee integration of European American stereotypical conceptions of African Americans and violence, especially stereotypical ideas of men of African descent as innately aggressive and oversexualized brutes.

Unruly behavior of slaves not only augmented the degree of fear throughout the Cherokee Nation but also, for enslaved African Cherokees, served to demonstrate a level of empowerment during this tumultuous time. Just as verbal and physical confrontations occurred between enslaved and enslavers in the Cherokee Nation in the era before the Civil War, so too did such altercations transpire as news of the war's progress reverberated throughout the Cherokee Nation. In his 15 July 1862 journal entry, only a few days after he noted the fear engendered "on account of the negroes," Stephen Foreman expressed that they "had a specimen today of what the Pins who have joined the Feds will do, and what they have been doing since they went north. . . . Two Pins piloted by one of Chief Ross's negroes came to my house, they rode up to the yard fence and looked as if they were hunting something. I called to them in Cherokee and asked what the matter was. They made no reply but looked at each other, talked a few minutes and then rode around my cornfield."[51] After some time, "[my] black boys, Jake and Charles came, bringing their horses and saying they were ordered into camps and ordered to take my mule. I could neither say nor do anything, knowing that the whole place was surrounded by Pins. I simply told the negroes I supposed they would have to obey orders." An hour later, "Charles returned saying that he was sent after my horse, that the officer said if he, Charles, did not come, he would come himself. . . . I told him to take the horse if he was ordered to do so. It was hard to see my negroes taken off, and harder still to see my own negroes take off my horses. But I thought there was policy in it, they thought I would refuse to let my own negroes take my horses and that would give them a pretext to come for them and kill me."[52]

As Foreman expressed, his "orders" and authority over his property —both enslaved people and horses—had been thwarted by the local and national dynamics of the war. Before the war he believed in his absolute control over his household. Like many other slave owners in the Cherokee Nation, during the Civil War he was forced to relinquish a great deal of that power to other Cherokees—in this case to Keetoo-wahs and Pins—as well as to enslaved African Cherokees. Foreman believed what his slaves had confessed—that Pins had ordered them to take his horses. However, it is possible that these enslaved African Cherokees, recognizing their owner's vulnerability, manipulated the situation to their own advantage. They might have conspired with the Pins or simply could have suggested this was the case to relieve Foreman of a couple of his horses. Deeming their enslaver's orders, needs, and wishes ineffectual, these African Cherokees enslaved by Foreman essentially subverted the master-slave dynamics and refuted Foreman's claims on his property—in human and animal form.

Enslaved African Cherokees in the Cherokee Nation not only took advantage of their enslavers' compromised position but also sought ways to exploit the particularly "alone and unprotected" state of their European Cherokee and European American mistresses who remained behind in the Nation. Slave-owning women in the Cherokee Nation, and in the United States, relied on enslaved people for some sense of protection, camaraderie, and even loyalty during the war. In her diary, Hannah Worcester Hicks explicitly related the overwhelming anxiety and fear experienced by European Cherokee and European American women who remained in the Cherokee Nation during the Civil War.[53] Though women like Hicks were not engaged in any military battles, their strength and tenacity enabled them to fight for food and other basic necessities in order to support their families during the Civil War. Although predictably Hannah Hicks recounted numerous acts of illness, death, and devastation, her diary also presented the particular life experiences of women residents in the Cherokee Nation during the war. Edith Hicks, one of Hannah Hicks's daughters, remembered that "it would take three days to go after supplies" at Fort Gibson. As a result, Edith Hicks related that the children "would have to stay alone while Mother and Percy, my twelve year old brother," made the trip to the fort. "Some Secesh would come in the night after they learned Mother had been to Fort Gibson . . . and they would make her cook their supper. I have seen her stand over the stove and cook the last bit of bacon and we would have to go without."[54] Emma Hicks, another daughter of Hannah Hicks, expressed that "the more I think about her, as the years go by, the more I feel that we did not realize what a brave and good woman she was, and how much sorrow and grief she was called upon to bear."

In her diary, Hannah Hicks recounted the numerous cases of theft, arson, torture, and murder occurring as a result of the actions of Stand Watie's supporters, who championed the Confederacy's cause, as well as the Union-supporting Pins.[55] On 8 November 1862 Hicks heard that "Watie's men declared their intention to come back and rob every woman whose husband has gone to the Federals, and every woman who has Northern principles, which would include us of course."[56] Hicks herself personally experienced the wrath of Watie's supporters. Just nine days after she had written of rumors concerning Watie's men, some of them arrived at her house and "took many valuable things, and overhauled every closet, trunk, box & drawer they could find. The leaders were Cherokees, those who have often eaten in my house, some of them."[57]

Her feeling of betrayal did not end there. In her entry on 4 January 1863, Hicks also mentioned the treacherous actions of a couple of enslaved African Cherokees in her household. She remarked that "the black women both started and left us without any help, but 'Aunt Edie' lost her horse, & had to come back—which I consider as specially ordered by a kind Providence."[58] Like Stephen Foreman, who witnessed two enslaved African Cherokees on his farm departing with his horses, Hicks also observed enslaved African Cherokees she had counted on absconding with her property. Experiencing what she perceived as treachery on the part of these enslaved people, she could not refrain from feeling gratified at the supposed act of divine retribution concerning Aunt Edie's lost horse.

Though forced to acknowledge disloyal enslaved people, Hicks and other free citizens of the Cherokee Nation continued to count on enslaved African Cherokees, hopeful that some would remain loyal and trusted servants. Hemmed in by the dangers of the war, Hannah Hicks and other slave mistresses relied on enslaved people to acquire and share some sense of the major events of the war. During the war, enslaved people throughout Indian Territory and the United States navigated long stretches of the country disseminating news about battles won and lost, as well as the current movements of Union and Confederate troops and supporters. With no mail service, residents in the Cherokee Nation depended on rumors in order to get any news of the activities of Union-supporting and Confederate-supporting Cherokee groups, significant battles between the Confederate and Union armies, and other important developments in Indian Territory. On 4 January 1863 Hicks shared that they had "heard nothing the past week except by Capt. Gunter's black man, Dred, who made his escape fr. the Southerners, & was about here a day or two."[59] Dred and other enslaved African Cherokees circulated news as they carefully navigated routes throughout the war-torn territory. Before the war, some enslaved African Cherokees had served as translators for some Cherokee enslavers; being messengers during the war represented a partial extension of their roles and duties in slave-owning households.

Though providing some information to their mistresses and others in the Cherokee Nation, some enslaved African Cherokees undeniably manipulated the stories they conveyed—sharing some details and withholding others for their own personal use. They still considered ways to circumvent their enslavers; some carefully controlled the information they disclosed about the war, especially if they could benefit from restrained disclosure. Having been enslaved in the Cherokee Nation for years, even generations, enslaved African Cherokees wholly recognized that ostensibly insignificant bits of information might make the difference between bondage and slavery. While some enslaved African Cherokees remained in the Cherokee Nation, circulating reports of the war, waiting for news of freedom, and even fomenting wartime chaos, others contemplated leaving Indian Territory in order to grasp the promise of liberty beyond the boundaries of the Cherokee Nation.

Displacement and Armed Service of Enslaved African Cherokees

Increasing acts of theft, arson, and murder committed within the Cherokee Nation, as well as devastating battles, forced some Cherokee citizens and enslaved people to abandon their homes and search for refuge elsewhere. Though enslaved people's mobility in the southern United States, and also in Indian Territory, was limited in the antebellum era, during the Civil War they found new opportunities to leave their owners' farms or plantations. Of their own volition, many enslaved people, including Hannah Hicks's two enslaved women, deserted the homesteads where they had been obliged to work for years. Frequently, they joined a nearby Union camp, in search of refuge and food as well as to serve in the war effort. Others, in contrast, left their familiar surroundings as a result of their enslavers' orders. During the Civil War, many enslavers in the South, as well as in Indian Territory, forced enslaved people to leave with them to flee actual warfare or the threat of warfare. Some Cherokee slave owners left their homes and belongings and temporarily moved their households—including enslaved African Cherokees—to Kansas, Arkansas, and Texas. Other Cherokee slave owners wanted to remain within the limits of Indian Territory and thus chose to relocate to areas in the Choctaw and Chickasaw nations, which had not suffered extensive war-related damage compared to the Cherokee, Creek, and Seminole nations.

This journey to surrounding areas—whether a voluntary escape or a commanded relocation—signified the first time many enslaved people, especially those born and raised in Indian Territory, traveled away from the only home they had known. One of the most vivid memories for Cherokee freedwoman Sarah Wilson concerned her Civil War journey, as a child, from the Cherokee Nation to an area "way down across the Red [R]iver in Texas . . . close to Shawneetown of the Choctaw Nation but just across the river on the other side in Texas bottoms." Her master, Ben Johnson, an intermarried white member of the Cherokee Nation, moved them "in covered wagons when the Yankee soldiers got too close by in the first part of the War."[60] Once in Texas, Ben Johnson and other owners who relocated from the Cherokee Nation continued to profit from the labor of enslaved African Cherokees. Johnson obliged his workers to live in camps during this time, and he "hired the slaves out to Texas people because he didn't make any crops down there."[61]

The disruptions related to war and relocating created new possibilities for freedom. Just before the Civil War, Cherokee freedman R. C. Smith recalled that "they had a heap of trouble with the Underground Railroaders. Nearly every body lost one or two slaves. Old Judge West had a sight of vexation about that time. I remember he lost one of his men who got clean away to the north and he couldn't git him back." Another enslaved person "decided he would try his hand at gitting away so he stole a horse and a suit of clothes and away he went. He got away to free territory and if the fool had had sense enough to a sold the horse they never would a done nothing about it but he strutted around with a fine horse and a fine broadcloth suit and his master told them that he'd stole the horse so they had to let him go back with his master. Judge West was purty hard on his slaves."[62] Cherokee freedwoman Rachel Aldrich Ward discussed various ways in which enslaved workers sought to procure their freedom. Ward recalled how "some of the slaves work around and get money and pay this money to their master for freedom, so there was some freed before the close of the war. Some others try to run away after the war start, and maybe they get caught."[63]

Getting caught by enslavers always positioned runaways in a precarious place; however, the intersections of bondage and blood proved particularly perilous for some. When Cherokee freedwoman Martha Phillips's father-owner died, her half brother, Cherokee William Thompson, inherited her and her other two brothers. During the war, William Thompson decided to sell them. When Phillips's mother discovered his plan, she ran away with all three of her children. At one point, she "attempted to swim the Grand River with the two small children on her back but was forced to turn back when Martha was caught by the current and pulled away from her down the river." Due to the assistance from an "Indian man," the family hid in the attic of a cousin's house for many days while Phillips's "brother and other relatives hunted for them."[64] Having evaded their relatives, Phillips's family finally sought refuge at Fort Gibson. While some enslaved people attempted to reunite with family members during the war, Phillips's mother sought to elude these family members, due to the complex web of bondage, ownership, and kin. Though connected to Cherokee William Thompson by blood, bondage compromised and severed notions of kin and belonging for Martha Phillips's enslaved family members. Whether they stole, bartered, or fought for their freedom, Phillips and other enslaved African Cherokees recognized wartime as a potential and tangible avenue for attaining their independence. Like their ancestors decades before who had seized upon the language, rhetoric, and reality of the American Revolution to delineate their rights, during the Civil War enslaved African Cherokees in the Cherokee Nation sought to fulfill generations of dreams of life beyond bondage.

As an escalating number of enslaved people took advantage of the tumultuous state of Indian Territory and ran away to attain their freedom, enslavers and patrollers intensified their efforts to recapture such fugitives in the territory. Some were enslaved within the Five

Nations; others had crossed state lines in search of freedom. Choctaw citizen T. D. Moore recalled how his father served as a patroller during the war. Serving in this capacity, his father "caught the slaves who had run off from their masters in Texas and were hiding out in the Territory. One day he traced fourteen negroes to the limekiln. . . . These negroes had their camping outfit and one young negro had gone out to kill game for food and Father waited at the entrance of the cave and when the negro came back with the young deer which he had killed Father ordered them all out of the cave and marched them back to Texas." Moore's father received fifty dollars for each negro caught.[65] Those who were not recaptured during the war, though, did not always escape punishment for such actions. Cherokee freedman Morris Sheppard described how his cousins Sam and Parsh ran away during the war and joined the Union army. When the war ended, "and the slaves were set free, they came back. It was not long until they were shot and killed. No one ever knew who killed them, but the ones who did it."[66]

Some slaves who did not run away were required to escort their owners away from the most war-torn areas in Indian Territory. Cherokee freedwoman Rachel Aldrich Ward mentioned that during the war she had been moved away from her owner Joe Beck's mill to live "around the garrison place at Fort Gibson." Ward remembered how many Cherokee enslavers, who supported the Confederate cause, relocated their enslaved African Cherokees to Fort Gibson for safety. Even though her enslaver mandated this relocation, her mistress "cried terrible when all the slaves leave in the night for the fort." Ward distinctly recalled that the "soldiers was all camped there in tents. They was all Confederate soldiers and I mean there was lots of soldiers camped in the tents."[67] Confederate troops controlled Fort Gibson during 1862 when Ward and other enslaved African Cherokees of Cherokee Confederate sympathizers would have been relocated to this fort. By the next year, however, Union troops regained control of this area. Forts in the region were ill-equipped to serve as refugee camps. As a result, Rachel Ward was not alone in experiencing a range of difficulties, including limited shelter, shortage of food, and sparse medical attention. Upon reaching Fort Gibson, she found "the negroes piled in there from everywheres, and I mean there was lots of them, too. Cooking in the open, sleeping most everywhere, making shelter places out of cloth scraps and brush, digging caves along the river bank to live in." Because of the unwieldy number of people living in these refugee camps, "there was no way to keep the place clean for there was too many folks living all in one place, and if you walk around in the nighttime most likely you stumble over some negro rolled up in a dirty blanket and sleeping under a bush."[68]

With the disastrous conditions at the farms and forts throughout Indian Territory, especially in the Cherokee and Creek nations, some enslaved African Cherokees sought to leave the territory itself. Whereas many enslaved people in the southeastern United States often followed the North Star as part of their strategy for escaping to northern states and even to Canada, enslaved people in Indian Territory cast their eyes in a southerly direction, much as those in colonial South Carolina had done during the eighteenth century.[69] Lucinda Vann, formerly enslaved by Cherokee Jim and Jennie Vann, explained that during the Civil War she and other enslaved people in the area who were "part Indian and part colored" got their "bed clothes together, some hams and a lot of coffee and flour and started to Mexico. We had seven horses and a little buffalo we'd raised from when it's little."[70] The idea of Mexico representing a haven was not new; it had also resonated for enslaved African Cherokees who attempted to run away from their Cherokee enslavers during the antebellum period. Not only did this group make it to Mexico during the Civil War, but Vann reported making a couple of trips between Mexico and the Cherokee Nation, before eventually reestablishing her home in the Cherokee Nation.

Other enslaved African Cherokees ran away from their enslavers with a specific mission—to join in the war effort. A few served in companies commanded by Cherokee Confederate supporters like Brigadier General Stand Watie; many more joined the Union in a Colored Infantry.[71] Cherokee freedman Henry Henderson explained that he was "a fighting man and a strong Southern soldier, until the Yanks captured me and made me fight with them. I don't know what year it was, but there was some Southern Indians took in the same battle and they fought with the North too. There was whole regiments deserted from the South, but I was captured; never figured on running away from my own people."[72] It is unclear why Henry Henderson expressed his support for the South during the Civil War. He may have felt compelled by his enslaver, Martin Vann, to join the Confederate army, or perhaps he was led to believe that an alliance with the Confederate States would prove to be more beneficial.

As was the case in the United States, the majority of enslaved people of African descent in the Cherokee Nation supported the Union. Cherokee freedwoman Chaney McNair remembered the service of slaves in the Union army: "when we reached Kansas most all the negro men folks joined the Northern Army, and the women were put to work in the fields just whereever [sic] we could find work. It was much different from what we expected."[73] Cherokee freedman R. C. Smith described how his father and other men "had slipped away and joined the northern army in Kansas. They belonged to the first and second Kansas regiment. They heard that if they would join up with the Yankees they would be free so that's what they done."[74] After his father fought for the Union army, he "died in Lawrence, Kansas at the close of the War. He and Mother never saw each other again after he enlisted. He died with pneumonia. Never got to enjoy his freedom after he fought so hard for it."[75]

The "northern army in Kansas" to which R. C. Smith referred included two units composed of African American and African Indian men, namely the Kansas 1st Colored Volunteers Infantry Regiment, later renamed the 79th U.S. Colored Troops, and the Kansas 2nd Colored Volunteers Infantry Regiment, later renamed the 83rd U.S. Colored Troops. The recruitment of men of African descent for Kansas's infantry regiments began on 22 July 1862, organized by James Henry Lane, recruiting agent in the Union Department of Kansas. On 13 January 1863 six of the ten companies for the Kansas 1st Colored Volunteers Infantry Regiment prepared to be mustered in. The other four companies of this regiment were mustered in by 2 May 1863, under white commander Colonel James M. Williams. In June 1863 the War Department authorized the creation of a second "colored" regiment. The entire Kansas 2nd Colored Volunteers Infantry Regiment was completed in November 1863.[76] During the last two years of the Civil War, the Kansas 1st Colored Volunteers Infantry Regiment participated in several major battles and military engagements in Indian Territory, particularly the First Battle of Cabin Creek on 2 July 1863, the Battle of Honey Springs or Elk Creek on 17 July 1863, and the Second Battle of Cabin Creek on 18–20 September 1864.[77]

Although recognizing the valiant effort of his entire command, a week after the Battle of Honey Springs, Major General Blunt specifically highlighted the actions of the Kansas 1st Colored Volunteers Infantry Regiment in his report from the field to Major General John M. Schofield. He remarked that the regiment had "particularly distinguished itself; they fought like veterans, and preserved their line unbroken throughout the engagement. Their coolness and bravery I have never seen surpassed; they were in the hottest of the fight, and opposed to Texas troops twice their number, whom they completely routed. One Texas regiment (the Twentieth Cavalry) that fought against them went into the fight with 300 men and came out with only 60."[78] Lieutenant Colonel John Bowles, acting commander of the 1st Kansas Colored Infantry, also applauded the efforts of this regiment in his report on 20 July 1863 from the field to Colonel William R. Judson. Bowles believed "it but justice and my duty to state that the officers and men throughout the entire regiment behaved nobly, and with the coolness of veterans. Each seemed to vie with the other in the performance of his duty, and it was with the greatest gratification that I witnessed their gallant and determined resistance under the most galling fire."[79]

The heroic efforts of the 1st Colored Infantry Regiment at the Battle of Honey Springs, which included African Indian soldiers, "marked the twilight of the Southern dominance in Indian Territory." Indeed, the "valor and fighting ability" of the men in the 1st Colored Infantry Regiment "greatly helped in pushing and containing the Confederate forces below the Arkansas River. For the remainder of the war in Indian Territory these black units would again meet Southern Indians on the field of battle and prove to all doubters their victory at Honey Springs was not chance."[80]

Although the courage and fighting abilities demonstrated by African American and African Indian troops in the Civil War assisted the Union in its successful encounters in Indian Territory, soldiers of African descent also benefited personally from their involvement in these battles. While serving in the Union army, these soldiers had "learned how to accept the reins of authority and how to properly serve in positions of responsibility and leadership within their regiments, usually as non-commissioned officers." Moreover, many soldiers of African descent "had their first opportunity to learn to read and write while in the Federal armed services. It was not unusual for a white company commander to drill his black recruits in the manual of arms during the work day and drill these same men in their letters at night while off duty."[81] Though literacy became an unexpected benefit for men of African descent who served in the Union army, the primary act of fighting in the war itself proved to be particularly gratifying. Serving as soldiers in the Union army represented the final campaign of enslaved African Cherokees' ongoing physical, sociocultural, and psychological battle against slavery, an institution under which they had long suffered peculiar hardships. Undeniably, some enslaved African Cherokees had challenged their bondage in physical acts of resistance in the antebellum Cherokee Nation; however, being a part of the Union army symbolized their collective, successful engagement in the war against slavery in Indian Territory and elsewhere.

The Emancipation of Enslaved African Cherokees and the Treaty of 1866

As the fighting persisted in the opening years of the Civil War, rumors spread throughout farms and plantations in the United States of President Lincoln's proclamation abolishing slavery. Issued on 22 September 1862 the Emancipation Proclamation declared freedom for enslaved people in the Confederate States of America, effective as of 1 January 1863. As news of the Emancipation Proclamation filtered into Indian Territory, it was unclear how this presidential proclamation would affect the lives of enslaved people of the Five Tribes. Although the Cherokee Nation had joined forces with the Confederacy, the Cherokee Nation had not seceded from the United States and was, indeed, a separate sociopolitical entity. Would the Emancipation Proclamation apply to enslaved African Indians in Indian Territory? Some enslaved people in the Cherokee Nation, and in Indian Territory in general, recognized that the Emancipation Proclamation did not automatically change their enslaved status. Though some had already run away from the Cherokee Nation long before the Emancipation Proclamation had been crafted, others remained apprehensive about the legality and boundaries of their enslavement and freedom. Having been held in bondage in Indian Territory, they questioned whether their Indian enslavers and the respective Indian national governments dictated the future course of their lives—as enslaved or free people of color.

Enslaved African Cherokees in the Cherokee Nation looked to the Nation—the nation in which many had belonged in multifarious ways for generations—for acceptance or rejection of the sentiments expressed in the Emancipation Proclamation. The Cherokee Nation unequivocally addressed this query in February 1863. Thomas Pegg, serving as acting principal chief, convened the Cherokee National Council for an unexpected session to discuss the status of its treaty with the Confederacy, as well as the status of slaves in the Cherokee Nation.[82] On 21 February 1863 the council passed an act declaring that "all Negro and other slaves within the limits of the Cherokee Nation, be, and they are hereby Emancipated from Slavery. And any person or persons who may have been held in slavery, are hereby declared to be forever free." The act would take effect on 25 June 1863.[83] As a result of this act, enslaved African Cherokees in the Cherokee Nation attained free status well before legal abolition of slavery occurred in the United States with the ratification of the Thirteenth Amendment on 6 December 1865.

As the end of the Civil War approached, the status of the Cherokee Nation and its free and previously enslaved residents had to be renegotiated with the federal government. Yet, the conflicting views of Union-supporting Cherokees and Confederate-supporting Cherokees continued to divide the Cherokee Nation. With the war over, the federal government of the United States scheduled a meeting at Fort Smith, Arkansas, in September 1865, in order to negotiate treaties of peace and reconciliation with Indian nations that had signed treaties with the Confederate States during the Civil War.[84] Recognizing the importance of coming to terms with the federal government, both factions in the Cherokee Nation prepared to present their position in an effort to generate support for their respective constituents. As a result, two separate Cherokee delegations attended the Fort Smith meeting in September 1865—the Southern Cherokee delegation and the Northern or Loyal Cherokee delegation.[85] The proceedings at the Fort Smith council made the differences between the two delegations of the Cherokee Nation even more apparent to the federal representatives. As a result, the Fort Smith council merely served as the beginning of treaty negotiations between the Cherokees and the federal government regarding the position of a post–Civil War Cherokee Nation.

After the Fort Smith council, members of the Loyal and Southern Cherokee parties continued the process of promoting their specific concerns and neutralizing the views of the opposing party. Because the Fort Smith council had failed to address all the pertinent terms of agreement within the Five Tribes, it was necessary to schedule additional meetings to resolve the future status of these nations. With the Cherokee Nation still divided over the particular terms of its treaty with the federal government, the Loyal Cherokees and the Southern Cherokees again appointed two separate delegations to treat with the federal government in Washington, D.C.[86] The Loyal and Southern Cherokee delegations worked diligently beginning in January 1866 to convince United States representatives of their particular positions regarding the future of the Cherokee Nation.

Due to differing views between Confederate- and Union-supporting Cherokees, the status of freedpeople within the Cherokee Nation was not decided until the final negotiations between the United States and the Cherokee Nation concluded on 19 July 1866. Although the act of the Cherokee National Council in February 1863 declared the emancipation of all slaves in the Cherokee Nation, it did not address the incorporation of freedpeople within the Nation. Proclaimed on 11 August 1866, the Treaty of 1866 specifically approved the Cherokee freed-people's inclusion as citizens of the Cherokee Nation (for the full treaty, see the appendix). Article 9 of the Treaty of 1866 reiterated that the Cherokee Nation had "voluntarily, in February, eighteen hundred and sixty-three, by an act of the national council, forever abolished slavery, hereby covenant and agree that never hereafter shall either slavery or involuntary servitude exist in their nation." Although both free Cherokee citizens and enslaved African Cherokees experienced the devastating effects of the war, for African Cherokees the question of slavery within the Cherokee Nation was finally laid to rest by the Treaty of 1866.

In the Treaty of 1866, the Cherokee Nation agreed that "all freed-men who have been liberated by voluntary act of their former owners or by law, as well as all free colored persons who were in the country at the commencement of the rebellion, and are now residents, therein, or who may return within six months, and their descendants, shall have all the rights of native Cherokees: *Provided*, That owners of slaves so emancipated in the Cherokee Nation shall never receive any compensation or pay for the slaves so emancipated."[87] This treaty not only reinforced the abolition of slavery in the Cherokee Nation but also guaranteed formerly enslaved people of the Cherokee Nation and their descendants all the rights, privileges, and liberties conferred to "native" Cherokee citizens. Though Cherokee bloodlines, specifically the language of "Cherokee blood" in some of the Nation's postremoval statutes, had granted free biracial African Cherokees some of these liberties, the Treaty of 1866 extended every right and all privileges to Cherokee freedpeople and their descendants, regardless of the presence or absence of "Cherokee blood" in their lineage. This treaty, however, engendered new questions during Reconstruction related to the status, rights, and citizenship of Cherokee freedpeople. No matter what the Cherokee freedpeople might have construed as their connection to the Cherokee Nation, their right to claim the Cherokee Nation as their home, and even the Cherokees as their people, would remain debatable within the Nation for several decades and still continues today.

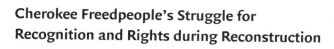

5 Cherokee Freedpeople's Struggle for Recognition and Rights during Reconstruction

Born and raised among these people, I don't want to know any other. . . .
I look around and I see Cherokees who in the early days of my life were my
playmates in youth and early manhood, my companions, and now as the
decrepitude of age steals upon me, will you not let me lie down and die,
your fellow citizen? ◆ Joseph Rogers, Cherokee freedman

Journey Back Home

Although, during the war, many enslaved African Cherokees left their enslavers' farms and plantations, either of their own volition or as a result of their enslavers' orders, once the war ended many formerly enslaved people in the Cherokee Nation were intent on returning to their homes in Indian Territory. Like freedpeople throughout the United States, formerly enslaved people of the Cherokees began searching for close kin after the Civil War. The separation of family members during slavery continued throughout the Reconstruction era. With few records of where anyone had moved during the war, families had to pursue any slim clues to the whereabouts of lost or sold family members. Many of the Cherokee freedpeople who had been relocated outside Indian Territory also made their way back in an effort to find long-lost relatives. Others returned because Indian Territory represented the only home they knew—the only place they identified as home. When reflecting on the immediate aftermath of the Civil War and the Reconstruction era, formerly enslaved African Cherokees articulated notions of nationalism, as well as a multifaceted connection to their homes and communities in Indian Territory. Furthermore, Cherokee freedpeople expressed their connection to the Cherokee Nation within their discourse of a Cherokee national identity.

155

The desire to return home resonated for formerly enslaved people in the Nation. Cultural connections between enslaved African Cherokees and free Cherokee citizens that had solidified before and after removal to Indian Territory only intensified in the antebellum era. By the end of the Civil War, Cherokee freedpeople conceived of only one home for their life beyond bondage—the Cherokee Nation. Interviewed more than seventy years later, Cornelius Nave recalled his father's need to return to Indian Territory after the Civil War. Nave identified the Cherokee Nation, the place where he and his father were born and raised, as "home." It was "that home after the war [that] brought my pappa back home."[1]

After completing his service in the U.S. Army's 10th Cavalry at Fort Sill, Nave explained that his father "took all the family and moved to Fort Scott, Kansas, but I guess he feel more at home with the Indians for pretty soon we all move back, this time to a farm near Fort Gibson," within the boundaries of the Cherokee Nation.[2] Cherokee freedwoman Eliza Hardrick also recalled how her "father said there was no end to the hardships the slaves went through in Kansas after they were set free." Hardrick stated that her father and other freedpeople who had been relocated to Kansas during the war "were glad when they could get back to the territory."[3] Cherokee freedwoman Chaney McNair voiced similar sentiments. Although her family had been relocated to Kansas during the war, she willingly returned to Indian Territory. She explained that she was "born down here, here's where I belong. You know how it is, when you go away from where you first belong, seems like something call you back."[4] Though undeniably complicated by the legacy of bondage, the familiarity of the Cherokee Nation and an enduring sense of belonging to that nation, its language and culture, engendered an unrelenting attraction—a call that could not be denied or ignored by many formerly enslaved African Cherokees.

Although Charley Nave, Cornelius Nave's father, successfully returned his family to the Cherokee Nation, other freedpeople were not as fortunate and were forced to rely on the generosity of their previous owners for their return to the Nation. Freedwoman Patsy Taylor Perryman and her mother had been relocated to Texas with their mistress, Cherokee Judy Taylor. After the war, however, their mistress decided that she "wasn't going to take [them] with her." Patsy Taylor Perryman distinctly remembered how, upon hearing of their mistress's decision to leave them behind, her mother "cried so hard she [her mistress] couldn't stand it and told us to get ready."[5] As a result of her mother's pleas, they did in fact return to the Cherokee Nation with their former mistress. For Perryman's family, and other displaced Cherokee freedpeople, the expressed angst emerged not only from a longing to return home to the Cherokee Nation but also from an apprehension about remaining in Texas or any other strong Confederate site in the United States. Possibly deemed by Cherokee freedpeople as representative of life in the United States, the particular racial and sociocultural realities in Texas during the post–Civil War era could have been viewed as utterly undesirable by Cherokee freedpeople. Moreover, Cherokee freedpeople's preconceived notions of life for enslaved and free African Americans in the United States certainly shaped their desires and demands to return to the Cherokee Nation. Cherokee freedpeople who had been relocated to Texas and other southern strongholds during the Civil War opted for the life they knew in Indian Territory over the range of uncertainties in Texas and other regions in the United States.

Even though there were owners who were willing to aid in their formerly enslaved people's return to Indian Territory, not all freedpeople accepted their previous enslavers' assistance. Ben Johnson had relocated his family and enslaved African Cherokees, including Sarah Wilson and her mother, to Texas during the Civil War. Sometime after the war ended, Ben Johnson offered to help those whom he had formerly enslaved "all get back home" if they "wanted to come." In response to his offer, Sarah Wilson's mother told Johnson that "she could bear her own expenses."[6] Determined to be independent, Sarah Wilson's mother also had specific reasons for refusing support from Ben and Annie Johnson. As previously mentioned, her enslavers' son, Ned Johnson, was the father of her daughter Sarah.[7]

It is unclear if Wilson knew exactly what happened between her mother and Cherokee Ned Johnson. What is clear is that her mother did not want to be indebted to the Johnson family in any way. Instead of creating a new life for herself and her daughter in Texas or even in another state, Sarah Wilson's mother was determined to make the journey back to the Cherokee Nation no matter what the cost. Because her mother refused Johnson's offer, Wilson and her mother had to "straggle back the best way we could, and me and mammy just got along one way and another till we got to a ferry over the Red River and into Arkansas. Then we got some rides and walked some until we got to Fort Smith."[8] They rested for some time in refugee camps along the way and then headed for Fort Gibson. Wilson recalled that the "trip was hell on earth. Nobody let us ride and it took us nearly two weeks to walk all that ways, and we nearly starved all the time. We was skin and bones and feet all bloody when we got to the Fort."[9] Though she might not have held familial feelings for her former enslaver's family, Sarah Wilson's mother still identified the Cherokee Nation as home—as the place where she and her family belonged.

It was no small feat to make the trip Sarah Wilson described from Texas to Indian Territory. Even if Sarah Wilson and her mother were able to take a ferry along the Red River into Arkansas, the distance from the area where the Red River crosses into Arkansas to Fort Smith, Arkansas, is approximately 120 miles. From Fort Smith to Fort Gibson, Cherokee Nation, would have been another 60 miles, possibly more, depending on the route they took. Recognizing what a laborious journey lay ahead of her, it is significant that Sarah Wilson's mother rejected Ben Johnson's assistance and made a point of making the trip on her own. Her mother may have believed that because she was free, she no longer would rely on her previous enslaver, even if that meant that she would die making the journey home. Although she did make the journey back, soon after arriving at Four Mile Branch in Tahlequah District, Cherokee Nation, Sarah Wilson's mother died of unknown causes.[10]

Like Sarah Wilson and her mother, many of the Cherokee freedpeople returning from Texas initially settled in the camps at Fort Gibson in the Illinois District. Cherokee freedpeople's resettlement patterns were in large part dictated by the places from which they had started their return journey.[11] For the most part, freedpeople in the refugee camps at Fort Gibson settled in the Illinois District or in the neighboring Tahlequah District. Freedpeople returning from Kansas resettled in the Cooweescoowee District, a large district in the northwestern section of the Nation just south of the Kansas line. The Sequoyah District in the southeastern area of the Cherokee Nation became a point of entry for those freedpeople returning from Arkansas.[12]

As formerly enslaved people of the Cherokee Nation made their way back to Indian Territory, they returned with hopes for a new life. It is hard to imagine that these freedpeople would have made the long journey back from Arkansas, Kansas, and Texas without good reason. It could have been the need to reunite with family members that compelled many to make the journey—a need enhanced by a significant cultural connection to the Cherokees. Their return signaled their personal recognition that the Cherokee Nation was indeed their homeland. Having developed multifaceted sociocultural (and oftentimes blood) connections to Cherokees before and after removal, formerly enslaved African Cherokees sought to attain what had eluded them in the antebellum era—freedom in Indian Territory. Freedom meant that their previous position among the Cherokees, that is as enslaved people, had been changed forever. Their transition from slavery to freedom, however, did not erase their significant connections to other Cherokee citizens. Now, they believed they were free to, and had a right to, rebuild their lives in the Cherokee Nation.

Rebuilding Free Lives as Cherokee Citizens

After the Civil War, residents in the United States and Indian Territory started the business of rebuilding and reconstructing their lives. It was a challenge even to think about rebuilding in some areas given the extensive devastation, the human losses, and the persistent animosities. In parts of Indian Territory, the range of destruction included the burning of homes and other buildings, the theft of property, and the damaging repercussions of the battles fought during the war. According to one report, the war had "thrown them back, so that in a great measure they [had] to do over again the work of years in building up their homes and fortunes."[13] J. W. Dunn, U.S. Indian agent for the Creeks, described 1867 as "a time of severe and necessary labor—a struggle for existence—and every energy of the people was directed to the cultivation of crops and the building of houses."[14] The Cherokee Nation also suffered in the summer of 1867 due to an epidemic of cholera.[15] Though all residents in the Nation experienced the range of severe aftereffects of the war, Cherokee freedpeople had the additional burden of carving a free life out of the rubble and despair with no material resources at all.

The first step toward rebuilding for Cherokee freedpeople was to locate an available area to build homes and plant crops. At the end of the war, many freedpeople initially worked, like freedpeople in the southern United States, as tenant farmers or sharecroppers. "Lacking any land or the provisions necessary to remove elsewhere," most freedpeople of the Five Tribes "chose to stay the first few years and work for their former owners. As in the South, the system which came to predominate the agricultural sector of the Indian Territory economy immediately after the Civil War was share wages."[16] Once the Treaty of 1866 had been ratified and, as delineated in the treaty, Cherokee freedpeople had been adopted into the Nation, "not surprisingly, the freedmen quickly withdrew their labor from Native American landholders to concentrate on cultivating their own fields."[17] Depending on the region in which they settled, the majority of freedpeople planted crops that were suitable for that section. Moreover, they also chose crops they were familiar with harvesting and useful in nourishing their families, particularly wheat, corn, and various fruits and vegetables. As far as the freedpeople were concerned, they had a right to make improvements upon land in the Cherokee Nation by virtue of Cherokee notions and laws regarding the "public domain."[18]

Only three months after the Treaty of 1866 had been approved and adopted, the Cherokee freedpeople's claims to Cherokee citizenship including land settlement became severely limited by the Cherokee Nation. In November 1866 articles of the Treaty of 1866 specifically related to Cherokee citizenship were included in the Cherokee Constitution as amendments. One of the significant changes to the Cherokee

Constitution pertained to the delineation of who would be considered part of the Cherokee citizenry. One amendment specified a time limit within which freedpeople of the Cherokee Nation who had left the Nation during the war had to return if they wanted to claim Cherokee citizenship. The amendment to Article 3, Section 5, of the Cherokee Constitution stated: "All native born Cherokees, all Indians, and whites legally members of the Nation by adoption, and all freedmen who have been liberated by voluntary action of their former owners or by law, as well as free colored persons who were in the country at the commencement of the rebellion, and are now residents therein, or who may return within six months from the 19th day of July, 1866, and their descendants, who reside within the limits of the Cherokee Nation, shall be taken, and deemed to be, citizens of the Cherokee Nation."[19] This and other related amendments were presented, approved, and adopted at a general convention of the people of the Cherokee Nation in Tahlequah on 28 November 1866; the following day, the Cherokee National Council ratified these amendments.[20]

In the first months following the Civil War, many Cherokee freedpeople returned to the Cherokee Nation; however, the return of some African Cherokees took several years. There were others who never made the journey back home at all due to limited resources, illness, and other circumstances. Not all Cherokee freedpeople had heard of the six-month limitation for their return to the Cherokee Nation stipulated by the amendment to the Cherokee Constitution. As Cherokee freedpeople from Saline District, Cherokee Nation, explained in their 1872 petition to President Ulysses S. Grant: "Some of us had fled North to get away from slavery, or to take our families away from the horror and sufferings of the War, while we ourselves enlisted in the Union army. Some of us, had been dragged by our owners, to the South to keep us from being freed by the Union army so that we were a long way off from the Cherokee Country when the Treaty was made. We were so far, that we had no way of getting back to our old homes so that we could not possibly have reached there in time, even if we had known what provision was made for us in the Treaty."[21] Those who returned after the six-month deadline, oftentimes referred to as the "too lates," became involved in a lengthy legal process not only with the Cherokee Nation but also with the U.S. government. Beginning immediately following the Civil War and continuing into the next century, this time requirement would become a point of contention in determining which Cherokee freedpeople would be recognized officially by the Cherokee government as Cherokee citizens.

The Right to Read and Write

Although reestablishing their lives in the Cherokee Nation after the Civil War signified a certain tangible connection to the Nation, Cherokee freedpeople also desired to maintain and expand sociocultural links to the Cherokees. Cherokee freedpeople, unlike freedpeople in the southern United States, did not, however, benefit from the variety of services offered by the Bureau of Refugees, Freedmen and Abandoned Lands, more commonly referred to as the Freedmen's Bureau.[22] Created in 1865, the Freedmen's Bureau provided medical assistance for freedpeople, helped with relocation to areas with more opportunities (particularly in the agricultural sector), funded freedmen's schools, and created opportunities for freedpeople to lease and even to purchase abandoned lands. One of the pertinent issues for freedpeople after the war concerned education, particularly the establishment of educational institutions for their children's edification. Though the Freedmen's Bureau proved instrumental in establishing schools for newly emancipated African Americans in other southern states, no such support existed for Cherokee freedpeople.[23] Instead, Cherokee freedpeople relied on the resources and support of the Cherokee Nation for the creation of their schools. Because it had been illegal to teach enslaved people to read and write in the Cherokee Nation during slavery, Cherokee freedpeople were eager to create opportunities for their children to receive education in schools created by the Cherokee Nation. Even in their Works Progress Administration (WPA) interviews conducted in the 1930s, Cherokee freedpeople still recalled their exclusion from formal education in the Cherokee Nation during slavery and the limited access they had to schools during Reconstruction.[24]

Following the model created in the South but at a slower pace, the

Cherokee Nation established separate schools for Cherokee freed-people. It was not until 1869 that the Cherokee Nation established 2 segregated primary schools for Cherokee freedpeople, and a third was established two years later. Compared to these 3 schools for Cherokee freedpeople, there were 56 schools in operation for the Cherokees exclusively in 1871.[25] Of the 71 day schools in the Cherokee Nation in 1876, 6 segregated schools were specifically for Cherokee freedpeople.[26] In 1879, only 10 of the 102 schools in the Nation were for freedpeople.[27] In 1887 the number of public schools for Cherokee freedpeople had increased to 12 but for Cherokees had decreased to 88.[28] By 1892, of the 100 primary public schools in the Cherokee Nation, 14 had been designated for Cherokee freedpeople.[29] Freedpeople would have to wait until 1889 before the Cherokee Nation agreed to build a high school specifically for Cherokee freedmen. The Colored High School in Tahlequah opened on 1 January 1890.[30] Unlike the steady growth of freedmen's schools in other southern states during this period, the Cherokee Nation provided only limited opportunities for freedpeople to educate their children.[31]

Established by the Cherokee Nation, freedmen's schools were forced to abide by the rules governing all schools in the Nation. Although the Nation provided teachers and books for the schools, the local communities were responsible for actually constructing the schools and maintaining the buildings. In order to remain in operation, every Cherokee school had to maintain a minimum enrollment of twenty-five students. Although seemingly a low minimum requirement, it was often difficult for Cherokee freedpeople to satisfy the minimum enrollment requirement in schools. The reason for low enrollment in Cherokee freedmen's schools during the 1870s, and thus the limited number of schools in operation, was not a lack of desire to become educated on the part of the freedpeople; it was the sparsely settled region. Freedpeople recognized that education represented one feasible way of gaining access to previously denied opportunities. "It is our extreme ignorance now," one freedman asserted in an article in the *Cherokee Advocate* specifically about Cherokee freedmen, "that is the barrier to social and political consequence to-day, and if we sit still and do nothing, our children will, when they grow up, labor under the same disadvantage."[32]

Although the desire for education existed, freedpeople in Indian Territory lived in areas not always within close proximity to their schools. With the limited number of freedmen's schools in the Cherokee Nation, freedpeople traveled long distances to attend these schools. Moreover, children working on their parents' farms helped to provide for the subsistence of families. Because of the time required to travel to and from school, many families decided it was inefficient and impractical to send their children to school. Although they acknowledged the importance of education, they were severely limited by the need to produce food and other basic necessities. Even if they lived within a reasonable distance from a school, oftentimes the Cherokee Nation did not recognize the families as citizens and thus denied them access to freedmen's schools.[33]

When the Cherokee Nation refused to build more schools, freedpeople decided to build and establish their own. Freedman Arthur Bean demanded that freedpeople demonstrate their commitment to their children's education. "Complaints are made that we do not get a free school, suppose we do not? Must our children go neglected if we cannot get a free school. Let us have a subscription school, by all means let us have some sort of a school. I say that he is no man at all who cannot pay one dollar a month to have his children educated."[34] Members of the local community organized subscription schools with families paying for teachers' salaries, books, and other supplies. Rarely able to donate adequate funds for the construction of a new building, freedpeople often created subscription schools by conducting classes in church buildings.[35] Because of the limited resources available to support them, subscription schools often proved inadequate compared to the schools established by the Cherokee Nation, especially in terms of the quality of the facilities and the limited resources for school supplies. After the Civil War, Cherokee freedman Johnson Thompson recalled that he "went to a subscription school for a little while, but didn't get much learning. Lots of the slave children didn't ever learn to read or write."[36] It is commendable that Cherokee freedpeople mobilized their resources to provide instruction for their children. Yet the fact that Cherokees restricted the number of freedmen's schools, by their refusal to recognize some freedpeople as citizens of the Nation, speaks directly to Cherokee leaders' unwillingness to accept freedpeople as citizens with legitimate rights to the same services provided to other Cherokees.

The Cherokee freedpeople's struggle to educate their children within the Cherokee Nation reflected freedpeople's understanding of their position as integral members of that nation. Enslaved no more, they demanded that the Cherokee Nation acknowledge their new status as free citizens and act accordingly in extending all the rights and privileges of Cherokee citizenship to them and their descendants. Cherokee freedpeople achieved some success in claiming their rights as Cherokee citizens during Reconstruction. However, they were soon involved in a litany of legal and governmental processes as they sought full recognition as Cherokee citizens. They understood that their official inclusion within the Cherokee Nation would not be instantaneous. Still, hopeful Cherokee freedpeople could not have predicted that the process would continue well into the twenty-first century.

In Search of Recognition

Cherokee freedpeople's struggle to achieve equal rights as Cherokee citizens involved continually proving that they had a viable and tangible connection to the Cherokee Nation. The fight to be recognized as Cherokee citizens represented a continuation of freedpeople's struggle to resist the system of slavery that had not recognized them as full human beings or as full citizens. Cherokee freedpeople's fight for equal rights after the Civil War included the battle for the right not only to own land in the Cherokee Nation but also to receive a percentage of the annuities made by the U.S. government to the Cherokee Nation. As a result, the Cherokee government was not the only entity making decisions regarding the status of Cherokee freedpeople. The U.S. government became actively involved in the negotiations between freedpeople and the Cherokee government. That intrusion of the U.S. government in the affairs of the Cherokee Nation during Reconstruction exacerbated tensions between the Cherokee Nation and Cherokee freedpeople.

Although Cherokee freedmen participated in local and national elections in the Cherokee Nation after the Civil War, they were rarely elected to the Cherokee National Council or other significant offices.[37] Nevertheless, they affected the political process by learning to navigate institutional systems of both the Cherokee Nation and the United States in pursuit of their rights as Cherokee citizens. This sparked ongoing resistance from the Cherokee political leadership, resulting in numerous appeals by the freedpeople to the Cherokee Nation and the United States.

One of the most telling aspects of the Cherokee freedpeople's struggle for recognition in the Cherokee Nation revolved around the controversial lists, more accurately called rolls, that were compiled to distinguish systematically and "objectively" those Cherokees who were rightful citizens of the Cherokee Nation from those classified as intruders or noncitizens.[38] European American encroachment on Indian land that had begun east of the Mississippi continued after the Civil War, when European American "intruders" or squatters from the United States attempted to claim illegally land in the territory. Although the Cherokee Nation had compiled information on some Cherokee freedpeople in the Cherokee census of 1880, census reports of the Cherokee Nation were generally questioned not only by Cherokee freedpeople but also by U.S. government officials.

One of the compelling reasons for a complete list of recognized citizens of the Cherokee Nation centered on economic interests.[39] In January 1883 the Cherokee Nation requested the remaining balance of funds for western lands sold to the United States that had been used to relocate various Indian nations, specifically the Pawnees, Poncas, Osages, Nez Perce, Otoes, and Missouris. Responding to this request, in March 1883 the U.S. Congress appropriated $300,000 to the Cherokee Nation. These funds were to be distributed as deemed appropriate by the Cherokee National Council. In order to handle the distribution of these funds, the council passed an act stipulating that the funds would be divided only among Cherokees by blood.[40] As a result of this act, Cherokee freedpeople, as well as adopted Shawnees and Delawares, would be considered ineligible to receive any portion of these funds. However, Principal Chief Dennis Wolf Bushyhead vetoed this act. He believed that the Cherokee National Council had overstepped its authority by excluding freedpeople and adopted citizens of the Cherokee Nation from their rightful claim to these funds. Chief Bushyhead contended that the Treaty of 1866 had guaranteed freedpeople and adopted citizens of the Cherokee Nation the same rights as "native-born Cherokees." Disagreeing with Chief Bushyhead's position, on 19 May 1883 the council passed an act providing for the creation of a roll of "citizens of the Cherokee Nation by blood," who would receive payments from the funds appropriated by Congress in March 1883.[41]

Even as members of the Cherokee National Council were debating this act, Cherokee freedpeople had begun organizing in various areas of the Cherokee Nation. On 19 May 1883, the day the act was passed by the council, Berry Mayes—a Cherokee freedman from Fort Gibson and one of the spokespersons for a group of Cherokee freedpeople— petitioned Secretary of the Interior Henry M. Teller on behalf of Cherokee freedpeople. The petition, signed primarily by fifty residents of Four Mile Branch and the Tahlequah District, "protested the act, asked the secretary to delay action on the per-capita money, and called for an investigation. The freedmen also proposed to send a delegation to Washington."[42] In addition to sending this petition, groups of Cherokee freedpeople also organized freedmen conventions in the Cherokee Nation. In 1883 Cherokee freedpeople held conventions in the Tahlequah and Cooweescoowee districts. At a meeting on 29 May 1883 in the Cooweescoowee District, a group of Cherokee freedpeople "drafted a protest against the violation of their rights under the Treaty of 1866, charging that their status had never been determined and that the Cherokees recognized them only as they wished, even though the Department of the Interior had denied the Indians' exclusive authority in this matter."[43]

In the years following the passage of the 1883 act by the Cherokee National Council, Cherokee freedpeople not only challenged the tenets of this act within the Cherokee Nation's political and electoral arena but continued to seek the assistance of the U.S. government in rectifying what they believed to be legislated injustice on the part of the Cherokee Nation. Recognizing the necessity of mobilizing their forces, they held another freedmen convention on 6 December 1883 at the Lightning Creek School in the Cooweescoowee District. At this meeting, James Milton Turner, an African American lawyer from St. Louis who had heard about the Cherokee freedpeople's petitions, addressed the freedpeople's concerns about their rights.[44] In response to the meeting in the Cooweescoowee District, another meeting of freedpeople was held at the African Methodist Episcopal church in Fort Gibson on 11 December. Freedpeople representing the Illinois, Tahlequah, Canadian, and Sequoyah districts attended this meeting. The freedpeople at the Fort Gibson meeting accepted the resolutions passed at the Cooweescoowee meeting. In addition, the Fort Gibson group selected five delegates to join the Cooweescoowee delegates on its behalf.[45] A joint convention to address specific concerns and to clarify their objectives was held on 21 December 1883, bringing together Cherokee freedmen representing the Cooweescoowee, Illinois, Canadian, Tahlequah, and Sequoyah districts. At this meeting, the group chose J. Milton Turner as its attorney and also selected Moses Whitmire and William Thompson to go to Washington to present the freedpeople's concerns.[46]

In addition to the assistance from attorney J. Milton Turner, the Cherokee freedpeople's claim to the Cherokee funds was supported by one government official—Commissioner of Indian Affairs J. D. C. Atkins. In March 1886 Atkins drafted a bill requesting that Congress allocate $75,000 for per capita payments (of $20 per adult) to Cherokee freedpeople and adopted Delaware and Shawnee citizens of the Cherokee Nation. Furthermore, he suggested that this allocation be held as a lien on any future payments to the Cherokee Nation for their unassigned western lands.[47]

Only a month after Commissioner Atkins's bill was presented to Congress, in a special session of the Cherokee National Council on 28 April 1886, the Cherokee Nation passed legislation further limiting the rights of Cherokee freedpeople. Once again the reason for this new legislation revolved around the issue of funds paid to the Cherokee Nation. This time the funds had been paid to the Cherokee Nation from the Cherokee Strip Livestock Association for grazing rights in the Cherokee Strip. Although the special session was called to decide on the per capita distribution of the $300,000 for grazing rights, the Cherokee National Council proposed and approved a "Construction of the Rights of Cherokee Citizenship as Designed to be Conferred upon Freedmen and Friendly Indians in the 9th and 15th Articles of the Treaty of 1866."[48] In this act regarding the "construction of rights" of Cherokee citizenship, the council reiterated the notion that freedmen had all the rights of native Cherokees. The council, however, specified that these rights did not include the right to Cherokee land or to the funds received from the sale of Cherokee lands. In response to this new act, attorney J. Milton Turner requested once again that Congress intervene on behalf of the Cherokee freedpeople.

Two years after the April 1886 act was passed by the Cherokee National Council, the U.S. Congress revisited the $75,000 appropriation bill proposed by Atkins, and this bill was declared law on 19 October 1888. As Atkins had proposed, Congress proclaimed that the $75,000 be distributed to Cherokee freedpeople, as well as adopted Delawares and Shawnees of the Cherokee Nation. Members of these three groups were to receive a per capita payment equal to what was paid to Cherokees by blood, as stipulated in the act passed on 19 May 1883 by the Cherokee National Council.[49] After a five-year battle to be recognized as citizens of the Cherokee Nation, with the same rights as other members of the Cherokee Nation, the Cherokee freedpeople had triumphed over what they believed was an injustice perpetrated by the Cherokee Nation.

Due to ongoing complaints by Cherokee freedpeople and the Nation's incessant refusal to consider freedpeople citizens as recipients of per capita payments, the U.S. government decided to oversee the enrollment of, and payment distribution to, Cherokee freedpeople, as well as adopted Shawnee and Delaware citizens of the Cherokee Nation. Government officials believed that they were well situated to distribute the per capita payments to rightful Cherokee citizens. In July 1889 John W. Wallace was appointed enrollment commissioner and was charged with creating the list of Cherokee freedpeople and adopted Shawnee and Delaware citizens of the Cherokee Nation. Arriving in Tahlequah in August 1889, Wallace began working on the first roll of Cherokee freedpeople authorized by the U.S. government. As word spread of Wallace's presence and mission in the Cherokee Nation, crowds of Cherokee freedpeople converged on his office (which moved to various locations throughout the Cherokee Nation), offering verbal and written testimonies that they should be recognized as rightful citizens of the Cherokee Nation. Some Cherokee freedpeople traveled long distances to Wallace's location in order to provide their personal testimonies. Although many freedpeople were residing in the Cherokee Nation during Wallace's time in the Nation, some traveled to the Nation from other states, including Texas, Arkansas, Kansas, and New Mexico.[50] However, not all freedpeople were able to make the trip, primarily due to health-related problems and insufficient resources, and thus were never listed on Wallace's roll.

Even though there were attempts to obstruct his work, Wallace completed his report in June 1890. He listed 1,998 freedpeople whose names also appeared on the Cherokee authenticated roll of 1880 and their descendants and an additional 1,243 freedpeople who he believed had provided satisfactory evidence of their claim to Cherokee citizenship. After reviewing and verifying almost 7,000 applications in 1890, Wallace included 3,216 freedpeople on the authenticated roll and 130 freedpeople on the doubtful roll.[51] Due to inconsistencies with Wallace's initial list, it was not until the summer of 1893 that Wallace's roll was finally closed. There were 3,524 freedpeople on this final roll.[52]

With all the time and effort expended on the Wallace Roll, ongoing controversy over this roll within the Cherokee Nation (including appeals from the Cherokee freedpeople and the Cherokee Nation to the Supreme Court) resulted in a compromise initially presented to the Cherokee Nation by the Cherokee freedpeople in December 1895. The freedpeople's compromise proposed that each freedperson receive $295.65, the same per capita amount that other Cherokee citizens had received, and that instead of the Wallace Roll, the Cherokee Roll of 1880 be considered the authentic and definitive roll.[53] In addition, the Cherokee Nation and freedpeople agreed that a commission would be created to update the Cherokee Roll of 1880. On 3 February 1896 attorney Robert H. Kern from St. Louis, representing the freedpeople, and E. C. Boudinot, representing the Cherokee Nation, submitted an amended decree to the U.S. Court of Claims for final approval.[54] The amendment to the decree stipulated that each freedperson would be able to receive only a maximum of $256.34. Both the Cherokee National Council and the Cherokee freedpeople agreed upon this decree. For the Cherokee Nation, the decree represented a victory because it nullified the results of the Wallace Roll.[55] However, the Cherokee freedpeople also believed that they too had been victorious. Not only were they to receive their rightful per capita payments, but the Nation would also finally recognize them as bona fide citizens who would be granted equal rights with other Cherokee citizens.

Soon after the decree was approved, Secretary of the Interior Hoke Smith requested that Commissioner of Indian Affairs Daniel M. Browning prepare guidelines to assist the commissioners who would be creating the roll. Browning suggested several questions be directed toward the applicants to verify and document their position within the Cherokee Nation. These questions included the applicants' place of birth, the names of their parents, the name of their owner if they were previously enslaved, the name of their parents' owner(s) if their parents were previously enslaved, and their maiden name and married name(s) if they were married women. Because of the six-month limitation issue, particular attention was devoted to the applicants' movements into and out of the Cherokee Nation since the time of the Civil War, ending with their residence at the time of their application to the new commission.[56] Although the initial decree had specifically included Cherokee freedpeople, the court of claims decided that free blacks who were residents of the Cherokee Nation at the time of the Treaty of 1866 or who had returned within the six-month period would also be included in the roll.[57] The secretary of the interior decided that the commission would be chaired by William Clifton of Georgia. The other two members of the commission were Robert H. Kern (attorney for the Cherokee freedpeople) and William P. Thompson (representing the Cherokee Nation).[58] The commissioners began working in April 1896 and were to submit a final report by 10 August 1896.[59]

As the commissioners heard and reviewed the testimonies of the applicants, they realized that there were inconsistencies in the Cherokee Roll of 1880. Although many of the applicants were listed on the Cherokee Roll of 1880, not all of the applicants' children were, and some Cherokee freedpeople's spouses remained unlisted, too. Moreover, some of the freedpeople had made several extended trips out of the Cherokee Nation, and this often complicated the determination of whether they had been residents before the six-month rule had expired. Thompson's questioning of the applicants often complicated matters further, due to the specificity he required from the freedpeople applicants in their responses.[60]

As was the case in compiling the Wallace Roll, the process moved slowly, often due to Thompson's detailed cross-examinations. Nevertheless, the commissioners finished taking testimonies on 8 August 1896, only two days before the deadline for submitting their final report. After several extensions, the final report of the Kern-Clifton Commission was submitted on 13 December 1896.[61] The report included 2,569 authenticated names and 1,902 unauthenticated names. After reviewing the testimonies, however, Commissioner D. M. Browning and other officials made adjustments to the two lists, many of which benefited the freedpeople. The reviewed and adjusted final Kern-Clifton Roll included the adjusted authenticated roll of 2,530 freedpeople, the adjusted unauthenticated roll of 1,878 freedpeople, and a new supplemental authenticated roll which included 144 freedpeople—a total of 4,552 freedpeople claiming Cherokee citizenship.[62] Soon after the rolls were finalized, Commissioner Hoke Smith appointed James G. Dickson as paymaster. Dickson was charged with disbursing the per capita payments to the Cherokee freedpeople listed on the Kern-Clifton

Roll. Commissioner Smith also scheduled the initial distribution for 15 February 1897 in Hayden, Oklahoma.[63]

When Cherokee freedpeople learned that Hayden, Oklahoma, would be the site for the first distribution of funds, several hundred freedpeople submitted petitions requesting that another venue be selected, particularly one in the Illinois District. In their petitions, Cherokee freedpeople noted that the majority of them resided in the Illinois District, while Hayden was located in the heart of the Cooweescoowee District, approximately seventy miles northwest of Fort Gibson, Illinois District. Their requests for a change of venue were denied. Even though Cherokee freedpeople from the Illinois District and other districts in the Cherokee Nation traveled to Hayden for their payments, many became ill while they waited due to the harsh winter weather conditions at the time. One freedman, Arthur Williams, was reported to have died as he camped waiting for his payment.[64]

Conflict and controversy plagued the Kern-Clifton Roll. There were charges of bribery, fraud, and overall corruption directed toward almost every individual involved in its creation and the subsequent dissemination of payments to the Cherokee freedpeople.[65] As a result of the shadow of corruption, the attention of many in the Cherokee Nation was directed toward proving or disproving these charges. Thus, the Cherokee freedpeople became pawns in a web of bureaucracy tinged with corruption. Even though many Cherokee freedpeople received their per capita payments as a result of the Kern-Clifton Roll, the ensuing corruption negatively affected not only the Cherokees' views of Cherokee freedpeople but also Cherokees' attitudes about their own nation's officials.

Though per capita payments signaled some recognition of their status within the Cherokee Nation, such payments did not entirely satisfy the needs and desires of Cherokee freedpeople who still believed the Cherokee Nation continued to regard them as second-class citizens. Though they were legally free citizens, elements of their enslaved status of the past haunted their daily lives in the Cherokee Nation and permeated the thoughts and actions of other Cherokee citizens in Indian Territory. Freedom could not be defined solely in monetary terms; instead, freedom—like bondage—blended psychological, cultural, racial, socioeconomic, and political dimensions of life in Indian Territory.

The Meaning(s) of Freedom

Although the changed "status" from enslaved to free denoted one dimension of emancipation, in order to comprehend the breadth of emancipation and its aftermath it is important to consider the economic, social, and psychological aspects of the meaning of freedom for the previously enslaved people of African descent and those defined as free people of color. What experiences during Reconstruction and beyond positively or negatively influenced the freedpeople's overall sense of themselves as citizens—free citizens? Is it possible to equate Cherokee freedpeople's ambivalent status within the Cherokee Nation with that of freedpeople living in one of the southern states? Extant documentation on some aspects of freedpeople's lives during Reconstruction offers one method of evaluating their lives. However, how do we capture other facets of their lives that are not readily accessible or comprehendible from merely reviewing archival documents?

Even though it is possible to compare specific existing programs or services for freedpeople in the Cherokee Nation with those in the United States, how do we compare their quality of life? Even though segregation de jure existed in the southern states and segregation de facto existed in the Cherokee Nation in relation to education, freedpeople in the southern states actually had greater access to educational opportunities, in the decades following the Civil War, compared to Cherokee freedpeople. Although the Freedmen's Bureau assisted freedpeople in the southern states by providing access to educational institutions and other social agencies and services, Cherokee freedpeople were unable to utilize the services of the bureau fully to assist them in their educational pursuits.

At the same time, however, during the Reconstruction era, freedpeople in southern states regularly encountered heightened violence in various forms, organized by newly formed white supremacist groups. Such groups developed secret societies in southern states as a way of regaining control of the South and especially newly emancipated African Americans. Throughout the southern states, many societies founded on white supremacist ideology were organized, including the Ku Klux Klan, the Knights of the White Camellia, and the White Brotherhood. Individual states also created local secret societies with similar objectives. Members of these organizations inflicted violence upon African Americans in a variety of heinous forms, including physical harassment, psychological intimidation, beatings, and mob lynchings.[66]

Although intense divisions over the status and rights of Cherokee freedpeople emerged in the period after emancipation, these divisions did not escalate to the same degree of violence targeted toward freedpeople in the South. That is not to say that Cherokee freedpeople were never harassed or abused because of their insistence on being a recognizable segment of the Cherokee citizenry.[67] As a child during the post–Civil War period, Morris Sheppard remembered that "[r]ight after de War de Cherokees that had been wid the South kind of pestered the freedmen some, but I was so small dey never bothered me; jest de grown ones." Sheppard's former enslavers "kept on asking [him] did de night riders persecute me any but dey never did. Dey told me some of dem was bad on negroes but I never did see none of dem night riding like some say dey did."[68] Though Sheppard and other freedpeople might not have referred to these "night riders" as part of the Ku Klux Klan, the activities of such individuals "pestering" freedpeople certainly mirrored the behavior and objectives of Klan members in southeastern states. Having been born and raised in the Cherokee Nation, and identifying themselves as part of the Nation, freedpeople resented the racial prejudice and violence expressed by some Cherokees, for it represented a formidable challenge to their sense of belonging.

Even though Cherokee freedpeople in Indian Territory did not confront exactly the same challenges as those faced by African American freedpeople in the United States, both experienced a socioeconomic and political transition from enslaved to free persons of color. T meaning of freedom cannot be equated with merely one aspect of society, namely educational opportunities, legal rights, or political and electoral representation.[69] The meaning of freedom for freedpeople in Indian Territory and the United States during the late nineteenth and early twentieth centuries was deeply embedded within the core of their sense of themselves as members, as citizens, of their respective nations.

On 24 August 1876 in Delaware District, Cherokee Nation, a group of Cherokee freedpeople organized an annual celebration in recognition and remembrance of emancipation and freedom.[70] At this event, freedpeople participated in a variety of activities, including a grand horseback parade, followed by presentations and a barbecue. The speakers addressed a number of issues during this celebration. They focused primarily on the importance of education, their ongoing concerns with the citizenship requirements within the Cherokee Constitution, their legal struggle to be recognized as rightful citizens of the Cherokee Nation, and the necessity of participating in Cherokee national electoral politics. One speaker, Joseph Rogers, focused on how the six-month time requirement had prevented him from being rightfully recognized as part of the Cherokee citizenry. As one of the "too tes," he discussed his frustration at not being officially acknowl-ɂed by the Cherokee Nation as a Cherokee freedman: "Born and ʾd among these people, I don't want to know any other. The green ʾnd blooming prairies of this Nation look like home to me. The ʒ of its pebbly bottom brooks made a music that delighted my and in my ear it has not lost its sweetness. I look around and I ʾkees who in the early days of my life were my playmates in ʾarly manhood, my companions, and now as the decrepi-ʾteals upon me, will you not let me lie down and die, your ʾ"[71] As Joseph Rogers passionately articulated, freedpeo-ʾen born and raised among Cherokees had developed a ʾling of their rootedness to the Cherokee Nation. Al-ʾation with Cherokees, specifically their position as ʾad been previously assumed, their construction of ʾerokees had resulted in tangible and appreciable blood-familial, cultural, and national connections with Cherokees. For them, the Cherokee Nation did not simply represent a place where they had been enslaved; it represented a place where they belonged. Cherokee freedpeople experienced a dual sense of belonging; they were previously enslaved by, and belonged to, Cherokees, but they were also persons who believed that they were part of, and belonged to, Cherokee communities in Indian Territory.

Contested Common Ground
Landownership, Race Politics, and Segregation on the Eve of Statehood

After the war was over we colored folks all had to go back to prove up; tell where you come from, who you belong to, you know, so we get our share of land. The government made a treaty with the Cherokees, if all the slaves come back they give 'em Cherokee citizenship, but we had to be back by '66.

◆ Cherokee freedwoman Chaney McNair

Let every colored man who wants 160 acres of land get ready to occupy some of the best lands in "Oklahoma," and should it be opened up, there is no reason why at least 100,000 colored men and women should not settle on 160 acres of land each, and thus establish themselves so firmly [sic], in that territory that they will be able to hold their own from the start.

◆ American Citizen (Topeka, Kansas), 1 March 1888

Rebuilding Free Lives on Forty Acres and More

While attention was directed toward the Wallace and Kern-Clifton rolls and the resulting consequences to the Cherokee Nation, legislation passed concurrently by the U.S. government would prove to be even more devastating to the integrity of the Cherokee Nation, as well as to the other nations of the Five Tribes. Following the Civil War, the federal government attempted to dismantle the Indian nations in Indian Territory, and thus to open the land in Indian Territory for white settlement. The General Allotment Act of 8 February 1887, also known as the Dawes Act, provided the president of the United States with discretionary powers to divide Indian reservations into allotments of land in severalty.[1] Although the Five Tribes were initially excluded from the provisions of the Dawes Act, on 3 March 1893 the U.S. Congress approved the establishment of a commission, the Dawes Commission, to negotiate agreements with the Five Tribes that would involve the termination of their national governments and the allotment of their lands to individual citizens—red, black, and white—of their respective nations.[2]

Even though the Cherokees, Chickasaws, Choctaws, Creeks, and Seminoles refused to negotiate with the Dawes Commission, the U.S. government continued exerting pressure on these nations. In 1895 Congress endorsed a survey of the lands in Indian Territory owned by the Five Tribes. On 10 June 1896 Congress passed an act authorizing the Dawes Commission to ascertain which individuals had a rightful claim to citizenship within the Five Tribes and to create what was to be the definitive roll of citizens of each of these nations.[3] Even as members of the Five Tribes continued to resist the dissolution of their nations, the U.S. Congress maintained its resolve to abrogate their sovereignty. On 28 June 1898 Congress passed the Curtis Act, which, without Indians' compliance, eliminated tribal rule and endorsed the allotment of lands in severalty.[4] By the spring of 1900, the Dawes Commission began the process of enrolling citizens of the Cherokee Nation. The citizens of the Five Tribes were to be classified in three categories: Indians by blood, freedmen, and intermarried whites. Within each of these major categories were three subcategories of newborns, minors, and adults.

Even as the Dawes Commission interviewed applicants for Cherokee citizenry, Cherokee freedmen continued to hold conventions in order to address their particular concerns regarding the creation of new citizenship rolls. At a Cherokee freedmen's convention held at Fort Gibson, Indian Territory, on 18 December 1900, Cherokee freedpeople drafted a list of resolutions, outlining a few of their concerns, which was sent to the secretary of the interior. One of their resolutions requested that the secretary of the interior "adopt and authenticate what is known as the Wallace Roll in said decree, as the basis of citizenship of the Cherokee Freedmen, this in our opinion being the most correct rolls of the Cherokee Freedmen." They further resolved that they "be allowed to choose one of the members of said Commission who are to enroll the Cherokee Freedmen in order that justice may be done us."[5]

One of the significant differences in the classification of enrolled citizens by the Dawes Commission, compared to the other rolls of the Five Tribes, was the indication of degree or quantum of Indian blood of its citizens. None of the Five Tribes had included this description of blood quanta in any previous census rolls. Distinctions between "mixed bloods" and "full bloods" were not new, "but every member of the tribe was entitled to equal rights and there had been no reason to keep track of degree of blood."[6] Although blood quanta were indicated for "visibly" Indian applicants, there was no such provision for applicants who were identified, or identified themselves, as persons of African and Indian descent. In these instances, the Dawes Commission enrolled the applicants as freedmen with zero degree of Indian blood. Indeed, all freedmen were automatically noted in the rolls as having zero degree of Indian blood, whether or not this was the case. This simple act of the Dawes Commission would have significant enduring ramifications for Cherokee freedpeople and their descendants in their struggle to maintain their status as Cherokee citizens and be accorded all the rights extended to other Cherokee citizens.[7]

As a result of the political agenda of the Dawes Commission, landownership would become a dimension of citizenship for recognized members of the Five Tribes—including Cherokee freedpeople. The mythical promise of "forty acres and a mule" popularized during Reconstruction still reverberates throughout scholarly analyses of the Reconstruction era in the United States; however, landownership for Cherokee freedpeople was not a myth.[8] After being enrolled by the Dawes Commission, by proving they were indeed Cherokee citizens, a significant number of Cherokee freedpeople received land allotments in the Cherokee Nation. On 4 March 1907, the date the Dawes Rolls were closed, 53,724 applications had been received for enrollment in the Cherokee Nation. In the end there were 41,798 enrolled citizens, of whom 4,924 were freedpeople.[9] By the end of June 1907, 4,208 Cherokee freedpeople had received land allotments totaling 409,500.26 acres and 749 Cherokee freedmen minors or newborn children had received tentative allotments.[10] Owning land in the Cherokee Nation represented the only way some African Cherokees declared their rightful position as Cherokee citizens. But landownership signified only part of the African Cherokees' struggle to be recognized as legitimate members of the Cherokee Nation; in addition to land, sociocultural dimensions confirmed their sense of legitimately belonging to Cherokee communities.

As a result of the work of the Dawes Commission, Cherokee freedpeople who were recognized as citizens were allotted land in the Cherokee Nation.[11] One Cherokee freedwoman who received a land allotment was Sarah Wilson. Although her mother died shortly after their long trek back to the Cherokee Nation after the Civil War, Wilson resettled in Four Mile Branch in the Tahlequah District and married Oliver Wilson, a Cherokee freedman. Wilson explained that she and her husband participated in the Cherokee enrollment process, claiming that they "both got [their] land on [their] Cherokee freedman blood."[12] Sarah Wilson indicated that she received her allotment not only because of her position as formerly enslaved by Cherokee Annie Johnson and Ben Johnson but also because of her "blood" connection to the Cherokee Nation by virtue of the fact that her father was Cherokee Ned Johnson. Wilson clearly expressed her belief that her connection to the Cherokee Nation, and indeed the reason why she received a land allotment, was due to what she called her "Cherokee freedman blood." Wilson's reference to blood serves to heighten her identity as Cherokee. Moreover, her phrase blends two separate yet often interrelated identities—the first identity being a Cherokee freedwoman and the second being a person of mixed racial heritage, specifically a person of African and Cherokee descent. Wilson's blended notion perhaps represents the creation of a distinct identity separate from the Cherokees generally and from Cherokee freedpeople who were not of Cherokee descent. It is possible that Sarah Wilson and other "mixed" Cherokee freedpeople conceived of their identity in these terms—a blended identity comprising status, blood, and nation.

Even though Sarah Wilson emphasized the role of her Cherokee "blood" in her enrollment as a Cherokee citizen and her acquisition of land in the Cherokee Nation, the Treaty of 1866 and the subsequent amendment to the Cherokee Constitution did not require freedpeople to prove a direct "blood" connection to the Cherokees in order to be enrolled. The requirement centered around freedpeople proving that they had been owned by Cherokee citizens residing in the Cherokee Nation, Indian Territory, and that they had fulfilled the six-month restriction previously discussed. As a result, Betty Robertson, who did not identify any "blood" connection to the Cherokee Nation, stated that she "got [her] allotment as a Cherokee Freedman, and so did Cal [her husband]."[13] Betty Robertson's claim as formerly enslaved by Cherokee Joe Vann satisfied the initial requirement for enrollment. The six-month limitation requirement did not restrict her because she and her family remained within the limits of the Cherokee Nation during the Civil War. Her owner at the time, Young Joe Vann, did not relocate them to another surrounding state like so many other Cherokee enslavers. Because she was able to prove her status as formerly enslaved by Joe Vann and her continued residence in the Cherokee Nation, Betty Robertson was readily enrolled as a Cherokee freedwoman and received a land allotment. Cherokee freedwoman Chaney McNair described the understanding of applying for citizenship and landownership widely held among freedpeople: "after the war was over we colored folks all had to go back to prove up; tell where you come from, who you belong to, you know, so we get our share of land. The government made a treaty with the Cherokees, if all the slaves come back they give 'em Cherokee citizenship, but we had to be back by '66."[14]

The enrollment process became more complicated than many Cherokee freedpeople could have ever imagined. Although familiar with the time-consuming and arduous elements of citizenship-associated issues, some experienced a great deal of frustration. Cherokee freedwoman Patsy Taylor Perryman described the cumbersome and arduous application process, which included the presentation of several detailed written testimonies.[15] At her home in Muskogee, Oklahoma, Patsy Taylor Perryman recalled that as a result of her writing skills, "all the writing about allotments had to be done by me." She had "written many letters to Washington when they gave the Indian lands to the native Indians and their negroes."[16] Even after she wrote letters regarding her family's right to land allotments, no evidence exists indicating that Perryman received land in the Cherokee Nation. Because her owner, Cherokee Judy Taylor, relocated Perryman and other members of her family to Texas during the Civil War, it is possible that they returned too late to claim a right to Cherokee citizenship and thus to any land in the Cherokee Nation.[17]

Victoria Taylor Thompson, Patsy Taylor Perryman's sister, stated that she was about eighty years old—at least "so they say down at the Indian Agency where my name is on the Cherokee Rolls since all the land was give to the Indian families a long time ago."[18] It is possible that Victoria Taylor Thompson and her sister, Patsy Taylor Perryman, were on one of the preliminary rolls conducted by the U.S. government. Even though they had been born and raised in the Cherokee Nation, their connection to the Nation was denied and as a result their names were not listed on the final Dawes Rolls of Cherokee freedmen.

Like Patsy Taylor Perryman and her sister Victoria Taylor Thompson, Morris Sheppard had been relocated outside of his home in Illinois District, Cherokee Nation, during the Civil War, by his enslaver, Joe Sheppard. They moved to "a place in de Red River bottoms close to Shawneetown [Choctaw Nation] and not far from de place where all de wagons crossed over to go into Texas. We was at dat place two years and made two little crops."[19] Even though Sheppard and his family returned to the Cherokee Nation after the six-month deadline, he stated that he "got a freedman's allotment up in dat part close to Coffeyville [Kansas]" in the Cooweescoowee District. However, as was the case for many Cherokee freedpeople, he "lost [his] land trying to live honest and pay [his] debts."[20]

Cherokee freedman Moses Lonian discussed his family's inability to be recognized as Cherokee freedpeople due to technicalities related to displacement during the Civil War. Like many other freedpeople, his family had been relocated to Kansas during the war. Although his family had been previously enslaved by Cherokee Lewis Ross, Moses Lonian stated that "the Kansas negroes did not like the idea of the slaves keeping the names of the Indian Masters." Even though Oklahoma freedpeople of African and Indian ancestry did not express any stereotypic ideas of the "wild" Indian in their interviews, there are references to a particularly high-spirited disposition of Indians by former slaves who were neither directly enslaved by Indians nor living in Indian Territory.[21] Like Henry Clay's response to the disturbing "wildness" of Creek slaves when he began to interact with them in Indian Territory, African American freedpeople in Kansas might have responded to the proclaimed connection of Moses Lonian's father and that of other African Indians as quite disconcerting. As a result of this reaction of African American freedpeople in Kansas, after the Civil War his father "decided to take the name of Lonian. This man was his white master, who owned him at Bentonville, Arkansas. This cost his children their rights in the Territory, as we were classed as doubtful when we came back, because we bore the name of a white master."[22] Their situation was not exceptional; more than 1,400 Cherokee freedpeople's enrollment applications were rejected by the Dawes Commission.

Certain formerly enslaved people who were not Cherokee freedpeople benefited from their familial association to someone who was recognized as a Cherokee freedperson. Although enslaved in Arkansas, Katie Rowe married Billy Rowe, a Cherokee freedman, in Little Rock, Arkansas. After they got married, they moved to an area near Tahlequah because Katie Rowe claimed that her husband "had land in de Cherokee Nation."[23] After Billy Rowe died, Katie Rowe continued to reside in the area and later moved in with one of her daughters, Lula, who lived in Tulsa, Oklahoma.[24] For Katie Rowe and other African Americans who had been raised on plantations in other southern states, the Cherokee Nation and Indian Territory in general represented a place of new beginnings, without the prevalence and intensity of racial violence common in the Southeast. For others, the Cherokee Nation represented the only home they knew and, for many, the only home they would ever know. For Cherokee freedpeople in the Cherokee Nation, like recently freed Americans in the South, the reality of owning land became one of the important symbols of a "free" life.

Due to recurring European American demands for land in Indian country, only a few years after receiving their land allotment certificates, landownership for African Cherokees and other citizens of the

Cherokee Nation became a fleeting reality. After formal enrollment by the Dawes Commission, each citizen "was to receive an allotment of land equal to 110 acres of the average allottable lands of the Cherokee Nation." The citizen then had to designate part of the land as a homestead—usually forty acres of this allotment. The homestead land was "nontaxable and inalienable during the lifetime of the allottee, not to exceed twenty-one years from the date of the allotment certificate." However, the remaining "surplus" land remained "inalienable for five years from the date of the allotment certificate."[25] Although the Curtis Act of 1898 had specifically decreed that all land allotments in Indian Territory were to be inalienable for set time periods, a congressional act in April 1904 lifted the restrictions on some categories of allottees. Another law, enacted on 27 May 1908, "divided the allottees into three classes: whites, freedmen, and mixed bloods of less than one-half Indian blood were released from all restrictions; mixed bloods of one-half or more and less than three-fourths Indian blood were free to sell their surplus, but their homesteads remained inalienable; and Indians of three-fourths or more Indian blood were restricted in all their holdings."[26] Indians, especially "full blood" Indians, challenged the federal government's plan for lifting these restrictions based on degrees of Indian "blood." Though European American advocates of the policy stressed how it served to "protect" Indians from land speculators, this policy and others reflected European American stereotypical notions of "backward" and "uncivilized" Indians being unable to govern themselves on an individual or collective basis.

Once restrictions had been removed, European American land speculators and grafters from the United States manipulated and deceived citizens of the Cherokee Nation—both African Cherokee and European Cherokee—into leasing their land for ridiculously modest amounts of money and even selling significant tracts of their land outright. The effects of Cherokee slave codes that outlawed literacy continued to plague the lives of African Cherokee freedpeople during this time.[27] Though some Cherokee freedpeople had become quasi literate in the decades following the Civil War, many of these individuals had unknowingly signed away their land to fraudulent land speculators. Not only had a number of African Cherokee citizens been swindled, but other Cherokee citizens had also fallen prey to the chicanery of grafters. As Angie Debo acknowledged, "In their poverty and bewilderment it is not strange that the Indians were glad to earn a few dollars by the simple process of making their mark on a paper. Usually they had no idea of the commitments they made. In other cases they realized they had leased or sold their land, but they had no use for it, they knew nothing of real estate values, and the pittance they received seemed like a great windfall. Since they did not understand the rules of the new economic society, they had no incentive to be thrifty as they had formerly been with the few dollars they had earned, and the money was spent as quickly as it came."[28]

African Cherokee freedpeople viewed their land allotments as a tangible sign of one of their rights as equal citizens in the Cherokee Nation. Yet, the land allotment policy instituted by the United States and the devious tactics of land speculators had resulted in the loss of millions of acres of land in Cherokee country. The freedpeople's participation—coerced and hoaxed in most cases—in the sale of vast tracts of Cherokee land contributed to the decreasing land base of the Nation, as well as the inexorable destruction of the Cherokee Nation itself. European American land speculators represented only one dimension of this invasion on tribal land; indeed, African Americans from east of the Mississippi also contributed to the American encroachment on Indian land as they sought to make a claim in a new promised land called Oklahoma.

Black Exodus to Oklahoma

Following the Reconstruction era, the status, rights, and position of freedpeople within Indian Territory and the United States generated a great deal of controversy and speculation. One particularly pressing question involved the possible separation or relocation of tribal freedpeople to the United States' recently acquired Oklahoma District or Unassigned Lands. Located west of Indian Territory, the boundaries of the Unassigned Lands were the South Canadian River on the south, the Indian Meridian and the Pawnee reservation on the east, the Cherokee

Outlet on the north, and the Cimarron River and the ninety-eighth meridian on the west. In terms of current Oklahoma cities, the Unassigned Lands ranged from Stillwater to Norman and from Choctaw to El Reno. Viewed initially as a site for the resettlement of tribal freedpeople and possibly for other Indian nations, the Unassigned Lands attracted the attention of white homesteaders, as well as African American nationalists and separatists in the United States. What began as the migration of black exodusters to Kansas and Arkansas in 1879 finally led to the conception and creation of all-black towns in Oklahoma. The new citizens who settled on "surplus" lands of Indian nations in Oklahoma territory changed the sociopolitical landscape of this area forever. Even as citizens of the Five Tribes continued to challenge the federal government's attempts to compromise the sociopolitical integrity of their respective nations in the late nineteenth century, they also struggled with the changing demographics of the region as successive waves of European Americans and African Americans migrated to the area with dreams of a new life.

In the South, the postwar economic depression, exacerbated by a heightened level of social discontent and mayhem, served as a key motivating factor for the search for a new home outside the limits of the southern United States. As Mozell C. Hill argues, "while the westward trek of Negroes in search of freedom, which culminated in the establishment of all-Negro communities in Oklahoma came later, it was, nevertheless, closely related to the great westward march of whites." Indeed, Hill maintains that "Negroes and whites who left the South had several things in common. First, both racial groups, dissatisfied with the Old South, were yearning for a better place to live. Secondly, both had an abounding faith in the frontier where land was free and opportunities unlimited. And finally, both groups were racially intolerant toward each other, believing that separation of the races was not only expedient and desirable, but, indeed, absolutely essential."[29]

Some African Americans' westward migration from the South to Oklahoma Territory occurred in two or more stages. During the 1870s and 1880s, African Americans from the South participated in the "Great

Negro Exodus" to Kansas and Arkansas—two states that served as promising black homelands.[30] Articles in African American news-papers throughout the country actively encouraged black migration from the South to the West. "For colored men to stay in the rebel-ridden South," one article stated, "and be treated like brutes is a disgrace to themselves and to the race to which they belong. The only way then that lies open to our people is to leave the South and come to the West. While we don't favor the colony idea very much, believing that the best course is to get as near other people as you can, yet, we would prefer that to being cheated and abused by the whites."[31]

Influential African American supporters of migration persuaded their people to move to Kansas in order to take advantage of poten-tial social and economic opportunities. Benjamin "Pap" Singleton, "Moses of the Exodus" to Kansas, linked his ideas regarding the ne-cessity of black separatism to African American migration to Kansas. Singleton believed that "the negroes must be segregated from the whites. In the South, after the failure to acquire land, the situation of the race was, he thought, precarious. The only remedy, he decided, was for the blacks to quit the South and go to a new country where they would not have to compete with whites."[32] Bishop Henry M. Turner of the African Methodist Episcopal Church, one of the major champions of African American mass migration to Arkansas, Kansas, and later Liberia, lured African Americans with his description of Arkansas. Turner believed that Arkansas was "destined to be the great Negro state of the Country. The rich lands, the healthy regions, the meager prejudice compared to some states and the opportunities to acquire wealth, all conspire to make it inviting to the Colored man. The Col-ored people now have a better start [there] than in any other state in the Union."[33] Although African Americans were lured by Arkansas's promising economic and political opportunities, the rising tide of segregation in the state in the early 1890s caused many to look else-where for the realization of a black homeland.[34]

Just as black newspapers served as a conduit for encouraging mi-gration to Kansas and Arkansas in the 1870s and 1880s, when condi-tions and opportunities changed in these two states, they continued their endorsement of western migration with their eyes directed toward a new black homeland—Oklahoma Territory. "Let every colored man who wants 160 acres of land," one article proposed, "get ready to occupy some of the best lands in 'Oklahoma,' and should it be opened up, there is no reason why at least 100,000 colored men and women should not settle on 160 acres of land each, and thus establish themselves so firmly [sic], in that territory that they will be able to hold their own from the start." The article claimed that even the "discontented and oppressed Europeans have heard of the intended opening of this country and are now falling over each other, so to speak, to reach America in time, to enter the best of these lands." African Americans could not allow this opportunity to pass them by. Instead, the article encouraged every African American to "keep his eye on 'Oklahoma,' and when the opening alarm shall have been sounded, move forward and take it."[35] Another black newspaper in Kansas claimed that "an immigration society which has been recently established here [Topeka] to provide for an exodus to Oklahoma has received letters from Tennessee, Georgia, Alabama, Louisiana and the Carolinas saying there would be 20,000 immigrants from those states as soon as they could gather their crops and get ready to leave."[36] Freedpeople who migrated from the South to Oklahoma Territory expressed their hopes for a new life in what they believed would be their promised land.

Even as African American individuals and groups attempted to persuade the federal government to open up the Oklahoma District for their settlement, cattlemen and ranchmen had been using this area in the 1870s and 1880s for their ranching business.[37] During the 1880s, many European Americans had made unsuccessful, illegal forays to carve out a portion of the "Unassigned Lands" for their own use. With the increasing demand and pressure for white settlement of "unoccupied" land in the Oklahoma District, on 23 March 1889 President Benjamin Harrison issued a special proclamation opening the Unassigned Lands to settlement by citizens of the United States.[38] As a result of this proclamation, at high noon on 22 April 1889, more than 50,000 persons participated in a literal run for land. As a result of the heightened anticipation and overwhelming desire for this land, many arrived early to strategically position themselves to claim the best piece of the 2 million acres of Unassigned Lands. By sunset on 22 April 1889, Oklahoma City and Guthrie had become established cities of more than 10,000 new residents. Only two years after the first run, "surplus" lands of the Iowa, Sac and Fox, and Shawnee-Pottawatomie nations were opened for settlement on 22 September 1891. More than 20,000 people participated in the second run for the 7,000 quarter sections, approximately 1,120,000 acres. The third run, on 19 April 1892, involved the settlement of 3 million acres of Cheyenne-Arapaho "surplus" lands.[39]

The initial group of white homesteaders who supported land openings in Oklahoma called themselves "boomers." They "were going to come 'booming' into the new lands, they said. Once they were there, they would bring about the creation of a new state."[40] After the opening of the Unassigned Lands in Oklahoma, "the *Boomers* no longer called themselves by that name. Instead they began to be called the *Sooners*, because they had come into Oklahoma *sooner* than anybody else, and because they would *sooner* be there than anywhere else. The name *Sooner* had a third meaning. It was also applied to the people who entered the Territory before the settlement date in the presidential proclamation. . . . These Sooners were first to reach the land offices and file on desirable quarter-sections of land in the new country." The initial group of boomers had attempted to claim land in Oklahoma based on their idea of "squatter's rights." However, the "new *Boomers*, who waited for the artillery cannon along the lines of the Unassigned Lands to *boom* out the signal to go forward, were law-abiding citizens. They waited for the government's permission to homestead, and they obeyed the homestead laws to the letter."[41] Whether in wagons, on horseback, or on foot, such land runs of thousands of boomers and sooners for "surplus" Indian land would lead to a significant migration of citizens of the United States to Oklahoma Territory.

The particular migration of African American boomers and sooners to Oklahoma Territory occurred not only as a result of black discontent with discrimination and racial violence in the South, but also because of the concerted efforts of boosters like William L. Eagleson, who encouraged black colonization in Oklahoma Territory.[42] Primarily due to the work of Eagleson and other prominent black leaders, by 1890 there were 3,008 African Americans living in Oklahoma Territory.[43] The majority of African American homesteaders settled in Kingfisher, Logan, Oklahoma, Canadian, and Payne counties, with only a few residing in Cleveland and Greer counties. The African American exodus to the territory facilitated the creation and development of all-black towns in Oklahoma. Although the major runs for land focused on Oklahoma Territory, the majority of all-black towns were established in Indian Territory, not Oklahoma Territory.[44] Although significantly motivated by the segregation and racial violence in the South, African American exodusters demonstrated their separatist motives in their voluntary relocation, and their establishment of all-black towns in Oklahoma. All-black towns promoted racial pride and unity within these communities. The degradation and oppression experienced during slavery had been replaced with self-determination and self-government—at least for a short time.

The Rise of Segregation, Discrimination, and Racial Violence in Oklahoma

With the increasing number of African Americans relocating to Oklahoma, European American residents in the Twin Territories— Oklahoma Territory and Indian Territory—became more concerned about the rumored propositions of Oklahoma's future as a black state. In an effort to reduce the black migration into the territory, within a year after the first run in Oklahoma Territory in 1889, local white newspapers circulated news downplaying the successes and achievements of African American migrants in the area.[45] By the end of the nineteenth century, the threat of "Negro domination" loomed large in the minds of European American settlers in Oklahoma. In order to limit the rights and opportunities of African Americans in Oklahoma, white Democrats promoted the passage of segregation laws in order to secure white rights and black subordination. The intensified interracial tensions between the residents in Oklahoma engendered individual and group acts of violence directed toward African Americans in the territory.[46] As the Twin Territories gradually moved toward statehood, the position and status of blacks in the new state echoed discriminatory practices that African American migrants had previously experienced in their old communities in southeastern states.

Although the development of all-black towns in Oklahoma contributed to a heightened sense of self-confidence and racial pride among residents in these towns, "life in black Boley and in similar Oklahoma towns did not offer total seclusion from mainstream society nor a solution to race problems. . . . The advantages of self-government, freedom of movement and association, distance from white racists, and a feeling of strength in numbers commended Boley and other all-black towns to those who desired isolation; but these communities never really escaped dependence upon an economic society controlled essentially by whites."[47] At a time when the Democratic Party wielded its political authority in the South, African Americans actively participated in Oklahoma Territory's political arena, primarily due to the dominant role of the Republican Party in the territory's early years. However, as the status of African Americans attracted more attention in the territory, the racist rhetoric of white Democrats in Oklahoma gained increasing support from white settlers in the area. As a result of the relentless efforts of Democratic Party supporters, "customs associated with the Deep South had had time to be transplanted by that region's native sons, and near the end of the nineteenth century they were being institutionalized in law."[48]

In order to endorse the separation of the races, white Democrats in Oklahoma espoused the importance of segregation within social institutions. As a result, the public school system became one of the primary targets for Democrat-supported segregation. In 1890 white Democrats, with some support from white Republicans, presented the first school bill sanctioned by the territorial legislature that allowed for the "local option of segregation" within the public school system. In the period between 1890 and 1901, "the tone of the school laws became more rigid, changing from separate schools 'may' be established in 1890, to 'should' be established in 1897, to 'must' be established in

1901."[49] With the fight for school segregation won in 1901, white Democrats directed their attention to segregation in public transportation. In 1903 the territorial legislature discussed a Separate Coach Bill to separate the races on railway coaches. Although this bill was not enacted at that time, de facto segregation on coaches occurred due to the predominant social pressures of the day.[50]

The injurious reaction of some white residents to black migration and settlement in Oklahoma Territory increased the occurrences of racial violence inflicted upon African American residents. The harassment of African Americans by racist white Oklahomans served as one strategy for demonstrating white intolerance to black settlement in the Territory. In September 1896, a report of the *Indian Chieftain* newspaper described how "whitecappers are expelling negroes from the southern part of this territory. Not a colored resident remains in Norman. Last night whitecappers whipped an old Lincoln county Negro and his two sons, and ordered the three out of the country." Moreover, white residents were also alerted to the importance of their racial loyalty when the "same aggregation of whitecappers numbering about a dozen, warned a white man named Scott with many negro tenants that all the latter must leave. The same work is going on extensively."[51] The violence inflicted on people of African descent in the Twin Territories at the turn of the century served only as a sign of the times ahead, due to the changing social and political climate of the area, which mirrored the southern climate on the race issue.[52]

As Republican control of national politics in the United States subsided, the "Redeemer" Democrats—white planters and businessmen of the South—dominated the political scene in the southern states. Intent on controlling and limiting the rights of African Americans in the United States, the "Redeemers" supported black disenfranchisement campaigns throughout the South. States utilized various methods to limit the voting power of African Americans, while maintaining the voting rights of white citizens.[53] In addition to limiting the voting rights of African Americans, Democrat-controlled southern states also strengthened segregation in public areas, including railway coaches, waiting rooms at railroad stations, streetcars, hospitals, hotels, and restaurants.[54] As the debates over Oklahoma statehood ensued, the Democratic Party looked to the segregation movements in the southern states and maintained that the future of Oklahoma could be secured only if segregation and white supremacy became the law of the proposed new state of Oklahoma.

While European Americans sought statehood for Oklahoma Territory, representatives of the Five Tribes attempted to secure statehood for Indian Territory. This movement began with a convention in Eufaula in 1902, followed by a constitutional convention in 1903. The name of the proposed state was Sequoyah—in honor of the noted Cherokee statesman and inventor of the Cherokee syllabary. The Sequoyah Constitutional Convention met in Muskogee (capital of the Creek Nation) on 21 August 1905. Those in attendance selected General Pleasant Porter, principal chief of the Creek Nation, as president of the convention. The vice presidents of the convention were William C. Rogers, principal chief of the Cherokees; William H. Murray, appointed by Chickasaw governor Douglas H. Johnston to represent the Chickasaw Nation; John Brown, chief of the Seminole Nation; Green McCurtain, chief of the Choctaw Nation; and Charles N. Haskell, selected as the representative of the Creek Nation. The convention drafted a constitution, an organizing plan for the government, and a map of proposed counties, and elected delegates to go to Congress to petition for statehood. The convention's proposals were endorsed and approved by referendum in Indian Territory.[55] Although residents in the Twin Territories proposed four separate plans on the question of Oklahoma statehood, on 16 June 1906 President Theodore Roosevelt signed the Oklahoma Enabling Act, which stipulated that Oklahoma statehood would be achieved by the joining of Indian Territory and Oklahoma Territory into one state.[56]

The Enabling Act also authorized a constitutional convention to be held in Guthrie, Oklahoma Territory (named as the temporary state capital until 1913), which would include 112 delegates—55 delegates from Indian Territory, 55 delegates from Oklahoma Territory, and 2 delegates from the Osage Nation. Indian Territory was divided into 55 districts. Oklahoma Territory was divided into 56 districts, with

1 district specifically for the Osage Reservation. By August 1906 the 112 constitutional convention districts had been established in the Twin Territories. The election of delegates for the constitutional convention was held on 4 November 1906. Although the Republicans had long controlled politics in Oklahoma Territory, the Democrats won 100 of the 112 seats in the constitutional convention, thus organizing and controlling the convention.[57]

The constitutional convention commenced in Guthrie on 20 November 1906. The Democrat-controlled convention elected William H. "Alfalfa Bill" Murray of Tishomingo, Chickasaw Nation, as convention president; Pete Hanraty of McAlester, Choctaw Nation as vice president; and Charles N. Haskell of Muskogee, Creek Nation, as majority floor leader.[58] Murray, an intermarried white citizen of the Chickasaw Nation, was a strong supporter of segregation. He immediately set the tone for the convention in his acceptance speech grounded in racialist language. Murray declared that "we should adopt a provision prohibiting the mixed marriages of negroes with other races in this State, and provide for separate schools and give the Legislature power to separate them in waiting rooms and on passenger coaches, and all other institutions in the State." Murray explained that "as a rule," African Americans "are failures as lawyers, doctors and in other professions. He must be taught in the line of his own sphere, as porters, bootblacks and barbers and many lines of agriculture, horticulture and mechanics." It is "an entirely false notion," Murray claimed, "that the negro can rise to the equal of a white man in the professions or become an equal citizen to grapple with public questions."[59]

Although the inclusion of segregation in the new state's constitution occupied the interests of the Democratic delegates, some were concerned that addressing segregation within the new constitution might provide a reason for its rejection by Republican president Theodore Roosevelt. Delegate Charles N. Haskell from Muskogee explained that "there is no necessity of antagonizing the president on this subject and giving him an opportunity to make a grandstand play, which he surely would do, for the sole purpose of rehabilitating himself with the negroes at the expense of the democrats."[60] In order to ensure that

President Roosevelt approved Oklahoma's constitution, many of the Democratic delegates agreed to exclude any segregation clause in their new state's constitution. Instead, they deferred their intentions until the first session of the state's legislature.

Cognizant of the Democratic delegates' strategy, African American residents held meetings and organized campaigns in order to defeat the ratification of the new constitution. African Americans also attempted to gather support for their cause by soliciting the support of black residents in other states. In 1907, a delegation of African American residents from the Twin Territories even traveled to Washington and presented their concerns to President Roosevelt to no avail.[61]

Although receiving some support from African Americans from other states, black residents in Oklahoma Territory oftentimes could not count on the support of freedpeople of the Five Tribes in Indian Territory. Indian freedpeople often distinguished between themselves and "state Negroes" as they called those who came to Indian Territory from the United States.[62] "Initially there was tremendous resentment," because freedpeople of the Five Tribes ("native" freedpeople) believed that "the new settlers showed too much subservience to whites. No doubt, 'native' freedmen were cognizant that it was the fear of a massive influx of 'state negroes' that lay behind the movement to restrict African-American civil rights."[63] The migration of African Americans from other parts of the United States to this area had transformed the lives of formerly enslaved people of Indian nations in Indian Territory; as a result many attempted to differentiate themselves from the "other" blacks in order to protect their peculiar place in an increasingly tripartite state.

African American residents also lacked substantial support from Indians in Indian Territory. With the dissolution of the sovereignty of the Cherokee, Creek, Choctaw, Chickasaw, and Seminole nations, and the sale and division of substantial portions of their land to freedpeople, most members of these nations chose not to support any movement by African American migrants or their freedpeople that would further jeopardize their position within the territory. Moreover, in order to appease Indians, "the Democrats provided that Native Americans be classified as 'white' for the purposes of enforcing the segregation law. In effect, in return for supporting the Democratic Party, Indians were granted honorary membership in the dominant race in a society which increasingly only recognized whites and blacks."[64] Granting Indians honorary white status not only served to placate Indians' concern for their sociopolitical position within the new state but also reflected the binary U.S. racial categorization that would be instituted in Oklahoma even if that meant transforming Indians into whites. The U.S. "civilization program" for the Five Tribes had attempted to do just that; by conceding honorary white status to Indians of the Five Tribes, the "civilization" process had concluded with the legal whitening of Indians in the new state of Oklahoma.

The proposed constitution was submitted to the Twin Territories' residents on 17 September 1907. It was ratified by a vote of 180,333 to 73,059. On that same day, residents also voted to elect a governor and other state officials. In the end, Charles N. Haskell, the Democratic candidate, won the governorship by receiving 137,559 votes. Republican candidate Frank Frantz, governor of Oklahoma Territory, received 110,292 votes. Socialist Party candidate C. C. Ross received almost 10,000 votes.[65] When the first session of the new Oklahoma legislature assembled on 2 December 1907, Democratic supporters of segregation quickly and successfully endorsed Jim Crow statutes. On 18 December 1907 Governor Haskell approved Senate Bill Number One, which required separate railway coaches and waiting rooms for African Americans.[66] The passage of this bill set the stage for subsequent laws requiring the separation of races. Even as African Americans continued to express their adamant disapproval of the first Jim Crow law in the state of Oklahoma, the state's first legislature passed a miscegenation law on 22 May 1908.[67] With the passage of such Jim Crow laws, segregation and white supremacy had indeed become the law of the land in the new state of Oklahoma.

The late-nineteenth-century migration of citizens from the United States to Indian Territory, which resulted in the annihilation of Indian Territory and the establishment of the state of Oklahoma, had significantly contributed to the gradual demise of Cherokee sovereignty and independence in Indian Territory. The influx of African American citizens to the region had complicated Cherokee freedpeople's hopes of maintaining a unique African Cherokee sociocultural and national identity in the Cherokee Nation. Generations of interactions and relationships between Cherokees and people of African descent before and after removal had engendered families and communities of African Cherokees who identified in multifaceted ways with Cherokees and considered themselves to be part of the Cherokee Nation. Following Reconstruction, Cherokee freedpeople attempted to preserve their exceptional place within the boundaries of the Cherokee Nation. However, their motivations for sustaining this separate and distinct identity in relation to the Cherokees, and in opposition to African American freedpeople from the United States, did not solely reflect their recognition of layered connections with the Cherokees and various disconnections with freedpeople from the United States—those they deemed "state negroes." Cherokee freedpeople, like other residents in Indian Territory and beyond, had become especially cognizant of the blight of blackness during the nineteenth century; they realized that the particular stigma associated with previously enslaved African Americans in the United States was to be avoided at all costs. With the creation of the state of Oklahoma, some of the categories of belonging and difference in the Cherokee Nation had been usurped by the heightened black-white racial divide in the United States. As a result of the evolving racial and sociopolitical landscape in Oklahoma, Cherokee freedpeople and their descendants soon discovered that an immense challenge lay ahead of them as they attempted to sustain their status as rightful citizens of the Cherokee Nation.

Afterword

Looking Back

The peculiar institution of slavery permeates the historical narrative of people of African descent in the Americas; bondage configured the everyday experiences of enslaved people and often directed their thoughts, words, and actions. Enslaved people of African descent of the Cherokee Nation in Indian Territory constructed their lives not only as enslaved human beings but also as people with evolving sociocultural identities about what and who they were in relation to Cherokees. Their story is neither static nor lifeless. Like many African American family sagas, theirs does not have a definite, concrete, and carefully documented beginning. Instead, the experiences of enslaved African Cherokees in the Cherokee Nation are primarily re-created from bits of newspaper articles, travelers' accounts, slave auction flyers, runaway slave advertisements, bills of sale, journal entries, missionary reports, and slave codes. Although these materials create one avenue for comprehending slavery in Indian Territory, they establish a limited understanding of the lives of enslaved African Cherokees in this region. They often emerge from the pages as property—chattel—and their conceptions of themselves are often extrapolated from the lines written about them, not by them. Indeed, until the last half of the twentieth century, U.S. history texts presented enslaved Africans and African Americans primarily as objects that were acted upon, rather than subjects who acted in their own right.

The resurrected slave narratives and WPA ex-slave interviews have provided an opportunity for historians, literary critics, and other scholars to reconstruct the lives of enslaved people of African descent from their own words and thoughts. These narratives and interviews have been instructive in a range of disciplines, enabling readers to imagine what it meant to be enslaved by another individual. Such narratives and interviews remain invaluable disclosures of the intricate and nuanced lives of enslaved people. Moreover, the interviews of formerly enslaved African Indians in the Five Tribes question the often simplistic rendering of the experiences of enslaved people of African descent in direct relation to European American individuals and communities alone. The recollections of previously enslaved African Indians in Indian Territory broaden the parameters of African American racial, cultural, and national identities by reframing and challenging the very constitution of African American lived experiences in North America. The ongoing unveiling of their history requires scholars to expand the traditional borders of African American history, Indian history, and southern history. The experiences of enslaved and free African Indians living within Indian nations, east and west of the Mississippi River, disrupt the usual tale of African American sociocultural legacies in the United States. Their stories weave yet another layer into the cultural quilt that is African American history.

One vital thread of African American history centers on the contested connections of African Americans to "Americanness" and to the United States itself. Even though formerly enslaved African Cherokees in Indian Territory oftentimes referred to their biological and sociocultural relationships with Cherokees in their WPA interviews, these connections became increasingly tenuous for such freedpeople after the Civil War. Indeed, many recently freed African Indians of the Five Tribes engaged in an ongoing struggle to prove their affiliation to the nations in which they had been born and raised. W. E. B. Du Bois noted one similar, though not equivalent, ambivalent connection at the beginning of the twentieth century. Du Bois described a particular "two-ness" experienced by Americans of African descent:

> The Negro is born with a veil, and gifted with second-sight in
> this American world,—a world which yields him no true self-
> consciousness, but only lets him see himself through the revela-
> tion of the other world. It is a peculiar sensation, this double-
> consciousness, this sense of always looking at one's self through
> the eyes of others, of measuring one's soul by the tape of a world
> that looks on in amused contempt and pity. One ever feels his two-

ness,—an American, a Negro; two souls, two thoughts, two unreconciled strivings; two warring ideals in one dark body, whose
dogged strength alone keeps it from being torn asunder.[1]

This experience of African Americans about which Du Bois ruminated
concerned a "two-ness" formed by the warring union of "American"
and "Negro." Could this notion also reflect a "two-ness" experienced
by the slaves and later freedpeople of the Five Tribes in Indian
Territory?

Certainly many enslaved African Indians living in Indian Territory
did not necessarily conjure up an image of an unreconciled division
between "red" and "black." Some formerly enslaved African Cherokees who had been born and raised in the Cherokee Nation described
themselves as close to, rather than separate from, Cherokees. Having
been born and raised among the Cherokees, Creeks, Chickasaws,
Choctaws, and Seminoles, some formerly enslaved African Indians
identified areas in Indian Territory among Indians as the familiar
places of their birth, and Indian cultural ways as their own. For freedpeople who remembered living within Indian communities in Indian
Territory, who recalled the Indian blood that gave them life, who
proudly spoke of their bilingual abilities, who carefully prepared Indian meals and herbal medicines, their experiences do not reflect a
divided "two-ness." Instead, their recollections portray a reality without such stark divisions. The extent of their cultural interactions, oftentimes intensified by their blood relations, established a group of
persons of African descent whose cultural and social ties were with
Indians. Without disregarding or discrediting the fact that these persons of African descent were indeed enslaved by Indians, one can still
talk about the strong cultural identification between some enslaved
people of African descent and the Indians with whom they interacted
in Indian Territory.

It is possible that some enslaved and free African Indians in Indian Territory used specific cultural manifestations of "Indianness"
(namely, clothing, language, and food) as a way of declaring their
bloodlines or establishing their blood claim to Indians. Perhaps by ex-

hibiting Indian cultural characteristics, some enslaved and free African Indians accentuated elements of Indian cultures in order to compensate for unsubstantiated blood connections to Indians. At the same time, other enslaved African Indians could have invoked their blood ties to Indians in order to confirm their cultural connection to Indian people. Identifying their racial and cultural connections to Indians also potentially served as a strategic way of claiming an Indian national identity. By so doing, some African Indian freedpeople attempted to gain due recognition as citizens of Indian nations, as well as access to tangible benefits in the late nineteenth century.

It is not surprising that many African Cherokee freedpeople decided to remain in the Cherokee Nation, Indian Territory, following the Civil War and wanted to be recognized as legitimate citizens of the Cherokee Nation. In their reflections on the post–Civil War period, Cherokee freedpeople asserted that they had received their land allotments and recalled the importance that landownership assumed in Indian Territory. Even those who had been forced by their escaping enslavers to leave Indian Territory during the Civil War chose to return to Indian Territory after the war had ended. Their connection to Indian Territory had not been eliminated with their emancipation. Rather, some Cherokee freedpeople felt a renewed affinity to the particular places of their birth and to the Cherokee people with whom they had interacted from their early years. They became committed to the only home they knew, to the only communities they knew. To some freedpeople of the Cherokee, Creek, Chickasaw, Choctaw, and Seminole nations, it was necessary that they begin their "free" life at home—in Indian Territory.

Yet, for other enslaved African Cherokees, who were not "more at home with the Indians," Du Bois's "two-ness" duly reflected their lives in bondage in nineteenth-century Indian Territory. The daily distinctions between themselves and their enslavers confirmed that they were not deemed equal participants in Cherokee communities; instead, they remained property—objects that could be bought and sold at an owner's whim. Some enslaved African Cherokees refused to identify with Cherokees with whom they resided in Indian Territory. Although living in predominantly Cherokee communities, they renounced thoughts of a collective identity with Cherokee people. Instead, they demonstrated their resistance to such notions of collectivity by committing a range of "crimes" from "talking back" to their enslavers to murdering them in the antebellum period. Running away from their Cherokee enslavers' farms and plantations represented the most effective course for pursuing their freedom. Rather than embracing Cherokee customs, some enslaved African Cherokees sought to rupture, by any means necessary, the forces that daily denied their personhood and humanity. No matter how much enslavers in the Cherokee Nation suggested that they deemed enslaved people as part of their "family," enslaved African Cherokees understood that slavery compromised family ties. Even as an enslaver extended some degree of kindness one day, he or she possessed the power to sell one's parent, spouse, sibling, or child the very next day. For many enslaved African Cherokees who were kin to their Cherokee enslavers, the denial of this blood connection only verified the corrupting force of bondage.

Exploring slave resistance in Indian Territory provides a useful way to assess the supposed and often-discussed "benign" nature of the enslavement of people of African descent by Indians. Perhaps like no other single topic in this area of study, the reality of slave resistance challenges romantic, essentialist, and one-dimensional notions of Indians and the contestation of power during the antebellum period. For those who ran away from their Indian owners, the desire for freedom surpassed any identification with Indians and any sense of "loyalty." To believe that Indian cultures made bondage more tenable to African Indians or somehow countered the denigrating process of enslavement is to deny the insidious nature of a system based on the ownership of human beings. Just as conceptions of African American slave resistance in the Americas evolved in the past century, with heightened attention and emphasis on the agency of enslaved women and men living within the confines of the peculiar institution, a similar transformation has become necessary in the exploration of enslavement in Indian nations. Indeed, the interactions between enslaved African Indians and Indian enslavers might provide evidence for a reconceptualization of slave resistance that speaks to the complicated power relations between enslaved and enslaver that are informed and problematized by notions of race, gender, ethnicity, culture, and nation.

Looking Forward

Understanding the forged relationships between African Indians and Indians in nineteenth-century Indian Territory provides one avenue for assessing the historical and cultural connections to Indians claimed by African Americans and black Indians today. The question of how people of African and Indian descent identified and intermingled in nineteenth-century Indian Territory has implications that reach down to the present. Past interactions give rise to broader contemporary questions concerning the identification and acceptance of black Indian people within current-day Indian nations. Just as black Indians continue to be rejected within some Indian communities, the struggle for recognition by descendants of freedpeople who were affiliated with the Five Tribes continues even today.

During the summer of 1997, Mrs. Bernice Rogers Riggs, a petite, brown skinned woman who was a descendant of Cherokee freedpeople and of Cherokee descent, submitted a petition to the Judicial Appeals Tribunal of the Cherokee Nation in Tahlequah, Oklahoma.[2] Mrs. Riggs, longtime resident of Tahlequah, had formally applied for membership in the Cherokee Nation, but her application had been rejected. Although her petition to the Cherokee Nation represented the individual plea of one woman in 1997, it was, in fact, one request in a long line of appeals from formerly enslaved people and their descendants who sought recognition as legitimate members of the Cherokee Nation. Mrs. Riggs's case not only provides some sense of her claim—her place—in the Cherokee Nation but also mirrors the complicated position of many from her generation and of several previous generations. The wPA recollections of formerly enslaved African Cherokees encompassed the story of Mrs. Bernice Rogers Riggs and her ancestors. Riggs's case is not simply the story of one individual or one family. Rather, Riggs's family story reflects the composite story of a group of people of African descent, some of whom were also of Indian descent, who shared common experiences and over time made and remade their identities and themselves within the sociocultural framework of Indian communities.

Mrs. Riggs's application for membership in the Cherokee Nation was deemed incomplete because she had not submitted roll numbers for "ancestors who are listed with a blood degree."[3] This blood ancestor requirement is not included in the 1975 Cherokee Constitution. Rather, the requirement was issued by the Cherokee Nation Tribal Council in 1983 in 11 Cherokee Nation Code Annotated (CNCA) § 12, which states: "Tribal membership is derived only through proof of Cherokee blood based on the Final Rolls."[4] Furthermore, this code notes that the "Registrar will issue tribal membership to a person who can prove that he or she is an original enrollee listed on the Final Rolls by blood or who can prove to have at least one direct ancestor listed by blood on the Final Rolls."[5]

A number of Riggs's ancestors (including her father, mother, paternal grandfather, paternal grandmother, and maternal grandmother) are listed on the Dawes Rolls, specifically the Cherokee Freedmen Roll. Furthermore, in her affidavit Bernice Rogers Riggs stated that her paternal grandfather, Joseph Rogers, "was part black and Cherokee Indian. He was the slave of Will Rogers, a Cherokee Indian. Will Rogers was his owner and his father. That is where we get our Indian blood."[6] She explained that her father, Gabe Rogers, "was at least half Cherokee Indian. He always said he was an Indian, but because he was colored, the government wouldn't let him prove it up."[7] Riggs's paternal great-grandfather, Will Rogers, is not listed on the Dawes Roll as he died before these rolls were created. Riggs also claimed that her mother, Malinda Bean Rogers, "had Indian blood too, but I can't remember where it came from. She was also part black."[8] In her affidavit, Bernice Riggs accurately deduced that her ancestors "*would have been* on the Dawes Roll of Cherokees by Blood if they had been Cherokee-White mixedbloods. But because they were Cherokee-Black mixedbloods, they were left off the main list."[9]

On 12 June 1998 the Judicial Appeals Tribunal of the Cherokee Nation heard Mrs. Riggs's case, *Bernice Riggs v. Lela Ummerteskee*. The primary argument in Riggs's case concerns the rights granted to Cherokee freedpeople and their descendants in the Cherokee Treaty of 1866, as well as citizenship rights outlined in the amendments to the Cherokee Constitution in November 1866. Moreover, Riggs's case also affirms that the 1975 Cherokee Constitution validates her membership in the Cherokee Nation. Article 3, Section 1 of the 1975 Cherokee Constitution states: "All members of the Cherokee Nation must be citizens as proven by reference to the Dawes Commission Rolls, including the Delaware Cherokees . . . and the Shawnee Cherokees . . . and/or their descendants."[10] The 1975 Constitution clearly states Dawes Rolls, which would therefore refer to all the Dawes Rolls, including the Freedmen Rolls. If this were not the case, the 1975 Constitution would have included a clause that specifically excluded people listed on the Dawes Freedmen Rolls from consideration for membership in the Cherokee Nation. Because a number of her ancestors are listed on the Dawes Rolls, specifically the Freedmen Rolls, Riggs believed she should be granted Cherokee membership.[11]

The Judicial Appeals Tribunal of the Cherokee Nation declared its decision on the *Riggs* case on 15 August 2001. The court determined that

> 11 CNCA § 12 as passed by the Council of the Cherokee Nation is consistent with and permitted by Article III of the Constitution of the Cherokee Nation of Oklahoma as adopted in 1975. The Cherokee Nation is a Sovereign Nation with the absolute right to determine it's [sic] citizenship. The Cherokee Nation need not go beyond it's [sic] Constitution to determine citizenship.
>
> IT IS THE ORDER of the Judicial Appeals Tribunal that Petitioner's prayed for relief be denied.
>
> IT IS THE FURTHER ORDER of the Judicial Appeals Tribunal that each appeal concerning an application for citizenship will be considered on a case by case basis consistent with the opinion entered herein.[12]

As a result of this ruling by the Judicial Appeals Tribunal of the Cherokee Nation, the position and status of Bernice Riggs and other descendants of Cherokee freedpeople appeared as if it would remain an unresolved one within the Cherokee Nation indefinitely.

However, as their ancestors had done before them, descendants of freedpeople of the Five Tribes in Oklahoma decided to challenge the court's decision via collective resistance. Not long after the ruling on the *Riggs* case, a number of individuals (including Marilyn Vann, Gail Jackson, and Ron Graham) established a new organization—Descendants of Freedmen of the Five Civilized Tribes Association.[13] Association members "are of mixed Black and Native American Indian heritage and are descendants of ancestors designated as Freedmen by the Dawes Commission."[14] The association's mission is to (1) "educate members, supporters and the general public regarding the history, culture and political rights of those particular to the Dawes Freedmen Enrollment"; (2) "plan, implement and administer, operate, and evaluate programs to carry out the objectives and purposes of the Association to assist in and promote, restore and preserve the rights of those descendants of the 5 Civilized Tribes (Cherokee, Chickasaw, Choctaw, Creek and Seminole Nations) particular to the Dawes Freedmen Enrollment"; (3) "promote, collect, and preserve Oklahoma Freedmen Genealogy, History and Artifacts and study the unique cultural diversity of Freedmen Descendants for the general benefit and good of the individual and collective Tribes and Representative Communities, in the State and Nation, and to improve the quality of life, to reinvigorate and promote cultural awareness and events relating to our heritage"; (4) "assist members in gaining knowledge of genealogy techniques and family contacts for the purpose of tying [sic] to our ancestors particular to the 5 Civilized Tribes"; and (5) "acquire political standing to regain status as tribal citizens through the Tribal or Federal Courts through revision of Bureau of Indian Affairs policies or regulations, or through congressional legislation."[15]

The educational dimension of this association has provided descendants of freedpeople of the Five Tribes with a more comprehensive understanding of their long history within the Five Tribes; in addition, heightened recognition by these descendants has engendered a movement to challenge the exclusionary policies of the Five

Tribes regarding their black Indian citizens. One individual in particular, who had become increasingly infuriated by the actions of the Cherokee Nation, vehemently believed that the *Riggs* decision had to be revisited. In September 2004, Lucy Allen, a longtime resident of Oklahoma with multigenerational connections to the Cherokee Nation, decided that the time had come to challenge the ruling in the *Riggs* case. On 24 September 2004, lay advocate Cherokee David Cornsilk filed a lawsuit on behalf of Lucy Allen in the Judicial Appeals Tribunal of the Cherokee Nation.[16] The core of the lawsuit concerned the inclusive language of the Cherokee Constitution in relation to tribal membership and the unconstitutional nature of 11 CNCA § 12. Allen and Cornsilk argued that the "blood" requirement included in 11 CNCA § 12 placed an undue, illegal burden on descendants of freedpeople of the Cherokee Nation.

On 7 March 2006, almost a decade after Bernice Riggs had initiated her case, the Cherokee justices on the Judicial Appeals Tribunal ruled 11 CNCA § 12 unconstitutional.[17] The majority opinion, written by Justice Stacy L. Leeds, delineated that the language in Article 3 of the Cherokee Constitution of 1975, that states that " 'all members of the Cherokee Nation must be *citizens* as proven by reference to the Dawes Commission Rolls' . . . expressly included both the Cherokees by blood and the Cherokee Freedmen."[18] The ruling also reinforced that "in the present case, there is no express 'by blood' requirement for citizenship in the Constitution."[19] Due to the court's thorough and critical reading of the 1975 Cherokee Constitution, it reversed the *Riggs* decision.[20]

As word of the monumental decision traveled through the Cherokee Nation and beyond, descendants of freedpeople of the Cherokee Nation celebrated the end of a struggle to be recognized as part of the legitimate citizenry of the Cherokee Nation. Soon after, the Cherokee Nation created a separate registration form for descendants of Cherokee freedpeople, and families began the registration process that had been denied to them since the 1980s. Throughout the Cherokee Nation there were expressions of jubilation and despair concerning the decision. Descendants of Cherokee freedpeople and their supporters waited to hear how this decision of the highest court in the Cherokee Nation could be overturned.[21] On 13 March 2006, only a week after the court's ruling on the *Allen* case, Principal Chief Chad Smith presented his viewpoints on the issue: "The process to decide the issue of Freedmen citizenship is a constitutional amendment at the polls. The constitutional question to determine citizenship—and especially whether to exclude Freedmen and intermarried whites—may be placed on the next general election ballot by a referendum petition or by a constitutional question authorized by resolution of the Council."[22] Principal Chief Smith also began traveling throughout Oklahoma speaking on the importance of a vote of the Cherokee people on this issue. At the Cherokee National Council meeting on 12 June 2006, the majority of the council voted to put the freedmen question before the Cherokee people in June 2007—the scheduled time of the Cherokee tribal elections.

Following the June 2006 council meeting, some Cherokee citizens proceeded with another plan to eliminate the vote of descendants of Cherokee freedpeople before the June tribal election. Article 15, Section 3, of the 1999/2003 Constitution of the Cherokee Nation states: "The first power reserved by the People of the Cherokee Nation is the initiative, and ten percent (10%) of the registered voters shall have the right to propose any legislative measures by petition and fifteen percent (15%) of the registered voters shall have the right to propose amendments to the Constitution by petition, and every such petition shall include the full text of the measure so proposed."[23] Such a petition circulated throughout the Cherokee Nation with the proposed measure:

> This measure amends the Cherokee Nation Constitution section which deals with who can be a citizen of the Cherokee Nation. A vote "yes" for this amendment would mean that citizenship would be limited to those who are original enrollees or descendants of Cherokees by blood, Delawares by blood, or Shawnees by blood as listed on the Final Rolls of the Cherokee Nation commonly referred to as the Dawes Commission Rolls closed in 1906. This

amendment would take away citizenship of current citizens and deny citizenship to future applicants who are solely descendants of those on either the Dawes Commission Intermarried Whites or Freedmen Rolls. A vote "no" would mean that Intermarried Whites and Freedmen original enrollees and their descendants would continue to be eligible for citizenship. Neither a "yes" nor a "no" vote will affect the citizenship rights of those individuals who are original enrollees or descendants of Cherokees by blood, Delawares by blood, or Shawnees by blood as listed on the Final Rolls of the Dawes Commission Rolls closed in 1906.[24]

Material circulated in the Cherokee Nation concerning the reasons for this petition often erroneously described all Cherokee freedpeople as being "non-Indian"—without any "Cherokee blood" whatsoever. In addition, supporters of the petition highlighted the enfranchisement of descendants of Cherokee freedpeople as synonymous with a financially compromised Cherokee Nation. Indeed, there would be some descendants of Cherokee freedpeople who, as citizens of the Cherokee Nation, would have a right to the particular services offered by the Nation to all its citizens, including the right to health services and, to those residing in the nation, the possibility of funding support through undergraduate and graduate school scholarships. It is worth noting that such racialist ideas of a correlation between blackness and welfare in the Cherokee Nation mirror similar preconceived and mistaken notions in the United States. Yet, many of the leading African Cherokees involved in this controversy personally and professionally challenge such conceptions of blackness and dependency.

The petition, eventually endorsed by 2,000 Cherokee tribal voters, resulted in a special election of the Cherokee Nation on 3 March 2007. There are approximately 280,000 enrolled members in the Cherokee Nation. Of 8,743 votes cast, 6,702 were for the measure and 2,041 against it.[25] Thus, the majority of voters decided to change the requirements for Cherokee citizenship, so that descendants of Cherokee freedpeople listed on the Dawes Rolls could be legitimate citizens of the Nation only if they proved a direct descendant on the "Cherokee by

Blood" Dawes Roll. Thus, the ruling of the Judicial Appeals Tribunal (now the Cherokee Supreme Court) on 7 March 2006 was essentially overridden in the special election.

Following the special election, descendants of Cherokee freed-people and their supporters began to work even more fervently on channels to counter this amendment to the Cherokee Constitution. They worked through the judicial branch of the Cherokee Nation in order to challenge the special election. On behalf of 250 descendants of Cherokee freedpeople, Nathan Young III—a court-appointed local lawyer—filed an application for a temporary order and temporary injunction with the District Court of the Cherokee Nation. Young asked the District Court "to issue a Temporary Order and Preliminary Injunction against Defendant, Lela Ummerteskee, from enforcing the Constitutional amendment adopted March 3, 2007." He requested "reinstatement of citizenship of Plaintiffs and those similarly situated former Cherokee citizens referred to as the Cherokee Freedmen. The Attorney General for the Cherokee Nation, A. Diane Hammons, representing Defendant Lela Ummerteskee, in her position as Cherokee Nation Registrar, has informed the Court that she has no objection to this Order."[26]

The plaintiffs—descendants of Cherokee freedpeople—asserted "that a temporary injunction should lie, reinstating their citizenship, during the pendency of this action, so that they will not be deprived of those essential rights that they previously held as citizens, including the right to vote in the upcoming Cherokee national election."[27] The plaintiffs' "underlying claims assert that Defendant has wrongfully removed their status as Cherokee citizens, and that the March 3rd Constitutional Amendment changing citizenship requirements for the Cherokee Nation was flawed and cannot be enforced. Should Plaintiffs ultimately prevail, and no injunction were to be entered, they will have been improperly expatriated from the Cherokee Nation for a period of time, and will have been denied one of the most fundamental rights of a citizen—the right to vote for governmental leaders."[28]

On 14 May 2007 Judge John Cripps, one of the Cherokee Nation District Court judges, ruled that "Defendant, Lela Ummerteskee, shall immediately reinstate to full citizenship with the Cherokee Nation the Plaintiffs and all similarly situated persons commonly known as 'Cherokee Freedmen.' This order shall remain in effect until the Court reaches a decision on the merits of Plaintiffs' claims in these actions, or until further order."[29] Attorney General of the Cherokee Nation A. Diane Hammons released a statement on 14 May 2007 confirming that she "agreed to an injunction staying the effect of the March 3rd Constitutional Amendment until our Cherokee courts make a determination as to the validity of that Amendment. . . . The stay will remain in place until the Court rules on the challenges filed by, at present, over 250 individuals who have exercised their rights under Cherokee law to have their Cherokee registration denials reviewed in court. Those challenges are still coming in, pursuant to a notice sent to individuals giving them ninety (90) days in which to appeal their adverse citizenship actions."[30] In her statement, Attorney General Hammons posited that she agreed to the injunction because she believed that "although the Cherokee citizens who voted to change the citizenship requirements on March 3rd have a right to have their determination implemented, those individuals who lost their citizenship status as a result of that election also have the right to have our Cherokee Nation courts consider the legality of the Amendment. In the interest of fairness and as a legitimate exercise of a reasoned democratic government, I believe that an injunction staying the effect of the March 3rd election, is proper from the Cherokee Nation court until the tribunal has the opportunity to fully review and decide the plaintiffs' claims."[31]

With this temporary reenfranchisement of descendants of Cherokee freedpeople, attention shifted to the possibility of change in the tribal election on 23 June 2007. As expected, Principal Chief Smith had extended his support to the group of petitioners for the constitutional amendment. He continued to express his position publicly for restrictions on Cherokee citizenship. Because of his concerted efforts opposing Cherokee citizenship for descendants of those listed on the Dawes Roll of Cherokee freedmen, Smith understood that most—if not all—descendants of Cherokee freedpeople would vote against him. Moreover, with Stacy Leeds as his challenger for principal chief of the

Cherokee Nation, Smith had even more cause for concern regarding his reelection. An associate professor of law at the University of Kansas, Leeds's experience and expertise as a justice on the Cherokee Judicial Appeals Tribunal/Supreme Court (2002–6)—the first and only woman to serve in this capacity—as well as her knowledge and work regarding tribal law cases, contributed to the potency of her challenge. In addition, because Leeds had written the majority position in the Cherokee Supreme Court's ruling on 7 March 2006, she could expect the support of descendants of Cherokee freedpeople and their supporters in the tribal election.

Even after the District Court's ruling in May 2007, descendants of Cherokee freedpeople continued to work tirelessly to generate support for their rights in the Cherokee Nation not only within the boundaries of the Nation but also from individuals and organizations outside the Nation's limits. News of the special election on 3 March 2007, and events leading up to it, had stirred action beyond the Cherokee Nation. As in the past, the rights of descendants of Cherokee freedpeople became an issue for the government and citizenry of the United States. In addition to national news coverage of the predicament of the descendants of Cherokee freedpeople, members of Congress, particularly the Congressional Black Caucus, had joined the movement in support of the Cherokee freedpeople.[32] In March 2007, after publication of results of the special election, twenty-six members of the Congressional Black Caucus sent a letter to Carl Artman—the assistant secretary of the Bureau of Indian Affairs—protesting the vote of the Cherokee Nation to disenfranchise descendants of Cherokee freedpeople.

In addition, only a few days before the election, on 21 June 2007, Representative Diane E. Watson of California—a member of the Congressional Black Caucus—introduced a bill in the House of Representatives (HR 2824) to "sever United States' government relations with the Cherokee Nation of Oklahoma until such time as the Cherokee Nation of Oklahoma restores full tribal citizenship to the Cherokee Freedmen disenfranchised in the March 3, 2007, Cherokee Nation vote and fulfills all its treaty obligations with the Government of the United

States, and for other purposes."[33] This legislation would essentially halt the approximately $300 million in federal funds that the Cherokee Nation receives annually, as well as suspend its authority to conduct gaming operations, until the Cherokee Nation permanently restores the full citizenship rights of descendants of Cherokee freedpeople. This bill has been referred to the House Committee on Natural Resources and the Committee on the Judiciary.

As election day approached, tensions escalated in the Cherokee Nation about the future direction of the Nation, including the tenuous position of descendants of Cherokee freedpeople. On 23 June 2007, Cherokee voters reelected Principal Chief Chad Smith. He received 8,035 votes and Leeds received 5,675 votes.[34] Descendants of Cherokee freedpeople, and many other Cherokee citizens, could only consider Smith's reelection a blow to the Cherokee freedpeople's fight for full citizenship rights. For now, all will have to wait for the Cherokee Supreme Court to weigh in on the legitimacy of the 3 March 2007 special election, as well as the future status of Cherokee freedpeople. No matter what the ruling of the Cherokee Supreme Court, the position and rights of descendants of Cherokee freedpeople will continue to be a controversial issue in the Cherokee Nation.

Even as people of combined African and Indian descent, like the late Bernice Riggs and Lucy Allen, explore the historical record and contemporary ramifications of their position within Indian communities, one major obstacle to their inclusion within many Indian communities and nations (especially federally recognized tribes) continues to be the qualification of Indianness by virtue of blood quantum. The idea of "blood" has shaped the lived experiences and histories of people of African, Indian, and European descent in the United States. Some scholars have criticized historical and current-day correlations between "blood" and racial identity as mere extensions of Eurocentric racialist categorizations established during the colonial era. The "one drop" cultural and legal convention in the United States historically served as the guiding principle for the racial divide between white and black.[35] The concept of blood was part and parcel of an entire ideological system that hierarchically categorized people of various cultures, ethnicities, and races in direct correlation to different levels of social, economic, and political potential.

This social construction of "blood" has been utilized not only to classify and separate races but also to determine access to socio-economic and political entitlements. Writer Adrian Piper explicates the rationale for the various criteria for the classification of Indians and African Americans. She posits economic reasons as the basis for the "asymmetry of treatment" between blacks and Indians: "A legally certifiable Native American is entitled to financial benefits from the government, so obtaining this certification is difficult. A legally certifiable black person is *disentitled* to financial, social, and inheritance benefits . . . so obtaining this certification is not just easy but automatic." Thus, racial classification in this country "functions to restrict the distribution of goods, entitlements, and status as narrowly as possible to those whose power is already entrenched."[36]

Present-day Indian tribal membership often revolves around the question of blood quantum—the amount of Indian genetic ancestry expressed in fractions.[37] The U.S. government currently acknowledges Indians who are members of the 561 federally recognized tribal governments, some of which still use blood quantum while others use descendancy as a tribal membership requirement. Some tribes require one-quarter or less blood quantum for tribal membership. A few demand one-half or more blood quantum for their tribal membership requirement. Some tribes allow you to "add together" blood quantum from all Indian blood. Others count only blood quantum from their specific tribe for tribal membership. Currently, a number of Indian nations are reducing the degree of blood quantum for membership or beginning to use a descendancy requirement, rather than blood quantum, for tribal membership.

Blood quanta have become inextricably linked to degrees of acculturation, assimilation, and Indian "authenticity." If blood quantum remains a predominant determining factor of Indianness, with continuing interethnic and interracial marriage, Patricia Nelson Limerick asserts that "eventually Indians will be defined out of existence." Limerick maintains that the federal government's association of Indianness with blood quantum carries the "added threat of making Indian-ness a racial definition rather than a category of political nationality."[38] With this possibility, Scott B. Vickers argues, "the criterion of blood quantum must be reconsidered and eventually disavowed as a mean-ingful marker of Indian identity." Yet, he contends, "the fact remains that without a certain quantity of Indian blood, such human beings will in scientific fact cease to belong to the racial group presently called 'Indian.' Thus the blood quantum argument is a major conun-drum that vexes Indian identity at its very core."[39] As a result, the "criteria by which both Indians and non-Indians are forced into or out of 'authenticity' becomes a quagmire of legitimacy and ethics bound to blood quantum, itself a highly controversial and ham-fisted method of establishing identity." With many Indians having "regained the power to 'write' their own histories and identities, it seems indeed tragic that some should seek to do so under the same 'aegis of a single principle' (genetic racial identification) that has degraded and divided them since contact."[40]

The mythology and reality of "Indian blood" emerge not only within Indian sociopolitical contexts but also in European American literary and historical landscapes. When European Americans claim "drops of 'Indian blood'—and especially in tracing it to Pocahontas or another 'Indian princess'—the victors naturalize themselves and legiti-mize their occupation of the land." On the other hand, "the van-quished are required to naturalize and legitimize themselves in terms of 'blood quantum'—an imposition of the victor's essentialized reck-oning of identity that becomes an integral, often taken-for-granted aspect of Native subjectivity."[41] Over time "Indian blood" has been transformed into a precious currency and possession sought after by individuals and groups as a way of authenticating access to oftentimes essentialized notions of "Indianness." The appropriation of "Indian-ness" and "Indian blood" by individuals deemed outside the bounda-ries of Indian communities creates a heightened level of suspicion of all who claim to be "part Indian." However, skepticism surrounding claims of "Indianness" has been dictated in part by the color not of "Indian blood" but of mixed "other" blood.

Although the place of "Indian blood" remains a controversial aspect of membership requirements for some Indian nations in the United States, one ignored dimension of this development in Indian nations is the seemingly problematic presence of "black blood." Pauline Turner Strong and Barrik Van Winkle posit that "the power of a drop of 'Indian blood'—if not more than a drop—is to enhance, ennoble, naturalize, and legitimate."[42] Conversely, "black blood" becomes a contaminating force that delegitimizes the claims of black Indian individuals and families to Indian communities and nations. A revamped "one drop" rule has permeated some discourses regarding Indian sovereignty. As a result, the historical stigma of "one drop" of "black blood" serves to erase any imagined or real drops of "Indian blood" and, by extension, any claims to "Indianness."

The growing attention focused on interactions between African Indians and European Indians, particularly the appropriate "place" and identity of black Indians in Indian communities, challenges the process of describing and defining Indians and indeed "Indianness." At the same time, the reaffirmation of the color line in the twenty-first century, complicated by notions of identity politics, has served as a means of erecting obstacles and establishing uncommon ground between African Indians, African Americans, and Indians. Just as descendants of African American freedpeople continue to fight for their rightful place within American society, the descendants of African Indian freedpeople of the Five Tribes of Oklahoma struggle for recognition as citizens of their respective tribal nations.

Appendix
Treaty with the Cherokee Nation, 1866

Articles of agreement and convention at the city of Washington on the nineteenth day of July, in the year of our Lord one thousand eight hundred and sixty-six, between the United States, represented by Dennis N. Cooley, Commissioner of Indian Affairs, [and] Elijah Sells, superintendent of Indian affairs for the southern superintendency, and the Cherokee Nation of Indians, represented by its delegates, James McDaniel, Smith Christie, White Catcher, S. H. Benge, J. B. Jones, and Daniel H. Ross—John Ross, principal chief of the Cherokees, being too unwell to join in these negotiations.

Preamble

Whereas existing treaties between the United States and the Cherokee Nation are deemed to be insufficient, the said contracting parties agree as follows, viz:

Article 1

The pretended treaty made with the so-called Confederate States by the Cherokee Nation on the seventh day of October, eighteen hundred and sixty-one, and repudiated by the national council of the Cherokee Nation on the eighteenth day of February, eighteen hundred and sixty-three, is hereby declared to be void.

Article 2

Amnesty is hereby declared by the United States and the Cherokee Nation for all crimes and misdemeanors committed by one Cherokee on the person or property of another Cherokee, or of a citizen of the United States, prior to the fourth day of July, eighteen hundred and

Reprinted from Charles J. Kappler, comp. and ed., *Indian Affairs: Laws and Treaties* (Washington, D.C.: Government Printing Office, 1904), 2:942–50.

sixty-six; and no right of action arising out of wrongs committed in aid or in the suppression of the rebellion shall be prosecuted or maintained in the courts of the United States or in the courts of the Cherokee Nation.

But the Cherokee Nation stipulate and agree to deliver up to the United States, or their duly authorized agent, any or all public property, particularly ordnance, ordnance stores, arms of all kinds, and quartermaster's stores, in their possession or control, which belonged to the United States or the so-called Confederate States, without any reservation.

Article 3

The confiscation laws of the Cherokee Nation shall be repealed, and the same, and all sales of farms, and improvements on real estate, made or pretended to be made in pursuance thereof, are hereby agreed and declared to be null and void, and the former owners of such property so sold, their heirs or assigns, shall have the right peaceably to re-occupy their homes, and the purchaser under the confiscation laws, or his heirs or assigns, shall be repaid by the treasurer of the Cherokee Nation from the national funds, the money paid for said property and the cost of permanent improvements on such real estate, made thereon since the confiscation sale; the cost of such improvements to be fixed by a commission, to be composed of one person designated by the Secretary of the Interior and one by the principal chief of the nation, which two may appoint a third in cases of disagreement, which cost so fixed shall be refunded to the national treasurer by the returning Cherokees within three years from the ratification hereof.

Article 4

All the Cherokees and freed persons who were formerly slaves to any Cherokee, and all free negroes not having been such slaves, who resided in the Cherokee Nation prior to June first, eighteen hundred and sixty-one, who may within two years elect not to reside northeast of the Arkansas River and southeast of Grand River, shall have the right to settle in and occupy the Canadian district southwest of the Arkansas River, and also all that tract of country lying northwest of Grand River, and bounded on the southeast by Grand River and west by the Creek reservation to the northeast corner thereof; from thence west on the north line of the Creek reservation to the ninety-sixth degree of west longitude; and thence north on said line of longitude so far that a line due east to Grand River will include a quantity of land equal to one hundred and sixty acres for each person who may so elect to reside in the territory above-described in this article: *Provided*, That that part of said district north of the Arkansas River shall not be set apart until it shall be found that the Canadian district is not sufficiently large to allow one hundred and sixty acres to each person desiring to obtain settlement under the provisions of this article.

Article 5

The inhabitants electing to reside in the district described in the preceding article shall have the right to elect all their local officers and judges, and the number of delegates to which by their numbers they may be entitled in any general council to be established in the Indian Territory under the provisions of this treaty, as stated in Article XII, and to control all their local affairs, and to establish all necessary police regulations and rules for the administration of justice in said district, not inconsistent with the constitution of the Cherokee Nation or the laws of the United States; *Provided*, The Cherokees residing in said district shall enjoy all the rights and privileges of other Cherokees who may elect to settle in said district as hereinbefore provided, and shall hold the same rights and privileges and be subject to the same liabilities as those who elect to settle in said district under the provisions of this treaty; *Provided also*, That if any such police regulations or rules be adopted which, in the opinion of the President, bear oppressively on any citizen of the nation, he may suspend the same. And all rules or regulations in said district, or in any other district of the nation, discriminating against the citizens of other districts, are prohibited, and shall be void.

Article 6

The inhabitants of the said district hereinbefore described shall be entitled to representation according to numbers in the national council, and all laws of the Cherokee Nation shall be uniform throughout said nation. And should any such law, either in its provisions or in the manner of its enforcement, in the opinion of the President of the United States, operate unjustly or injuriously in said district, he is hereby authorized and empowered to correct such evil, and to adopt the means necessary to secure the impartial administration of justice, as well as a fair and equitable application and expenditure of the national funds as between the people of this and of every other district in said nation.

Article 7

The United States court to be created in the Indian Territory; and until such court is created therein, the United States district court, the nearest to the Cherokee Nation, shall have exclusive original jurisdiction of all causes, civil and criminal, wherein an inhabitant of the district hereinbefore described shall be a party, and where an inhabitant outside of said district, in the Cherokee Nation, shall be the other party, as plaintiff or defendant in a civil cause, or shall be defendant or prosecutor in a criminal case, and all process issued in said district by any officer of the Cherokee Nation, to be executed on an inhabitant residing outside of said district, and all process issued by any officer of the Cherokee Nation outside of said district, to be executed on an inhabitant residing in said district, shall be to all intents and purposes null and void, unless indorsed by the district judge for the district where such process is to be served, and said person, so arrested, shall be held in custody by the officer so arresting him, until he shall be delivered over to the United States marshal, or consent to be tried by the Cherokee court: *Provided*, That any or all the provisions of this treaty, which make any distinction in rights and remedies between the citizens of any district and the citizens of the rest of the nation, shall be abrogated whenever the President shall have ascertained, by an election duly ordered by him, that a majority of the voters of such district desire them to be abrogated, and he shall have declared such abrogation: *And provided further*, That no law or regulation, to be hereafter enacted within said Cherokee Nation or any district thereof, prescribing a penalty for its violation, shall take effect or be enforced until after ninety days from the date of its promulgation, either by publication in one or more newspapers of general circulation in said Cherokee Nation, or by posting up copies thereof in the Cherokee and English languages in each district where the same is to take effect, at the usual place of holding district courts.

Article 8

No license to trade in goods, wares, or merchandise shall be granted by the United States to trade in the Cherokee Nation, unless approved by the Cherokee national council, except in the Canadian district, and such other district north of Arkansas River and west of Grand River occupied by the so-called southern Cherokees, as provided in Article 4 of this treaty.

Article 9

The Cherokee Nation having, voluntarily, in February, eighteen hundred and sixty-three, by an act of the national council, forever abolished slavery, hereby covenant and agree that never hereafter shall either slavery or involuntary servitude exist in their nation otherwise than in the punishment of crime, whereof the party shall have been duly convicted, in accordance with laws applicable to all the members of said tribe alike. They further agree that all freedmen who have been liberated by voluntary act of their former owners or by law, as well as all free colored persons who were in the country at the commencement of the rebellion, and are now residents therein, or who may return within six months, and their descendants, shall have all the rights of native Cherokees: *Provided*, That owners of slaves so emancipated in the Cherokee Nation shall never receive any compensation or pay for the slaves so emancipated.

Article 10

Every Cherokee and freed person resident in the Cherokee Nation shall have the right to sell any products of his farm, including his or her live stock, or any merchandise or manufactured products, and to ship and drive the same to market without restraint, paying any tax thereon which is now or may be levied by the United States on the quantity sold outside of the Indian Territory.

Article 11

The Cherokee Nation hereby grant a right of way not exceeding two hundred feet wide, except at stations, switches, waterstations, or crossing of rivers, where more may be indispensable to the full enjoyment of the franchise herein granted, and then only two hundred additional feet shall be taken, and only for such length as may be absolutely necessary, through all their lands, to any company or corporation which shall be duly authorized by Congress to construct a railroad from any point north to any point south, and from any point east to any point west of, and which may pass through, the Cherokee Nation. Said company or corporation, and their employés the laborers, while constructing and repairing the same, and in operating said road or roads, including all necessary agents on the line, at stations, switches, water tanks, and all others necessary to the successful operation of a railroad, shall be protected in the discharge of their duties, and at all times subject to the Indian intercourse laws, now or which may hereafter be enacted and be in force in the Cherokee Nation.

Article 12

The Cherokees agree that a general council, consisting of delegates elected by each nation or tribe lawfully residing within the Indian Territory, may be annually convened in said Territory, which council shall be organized in such manner and possess such powers as hereinafter prescribed.

First. After the ratification of this treaty, and as soon as may be deemed practicable by the Secretary of the Interior, and prior to the first session of said council, a census or enumeration of each tribe lawfully resident in said Territory shall be taken under the direction of the Commissioner of Indian Affairs, who for that purpose is hereby authorized to designate and appoint competent persons, whose compensation shall be fixed by the Secretary of the Interior, and paid by the United States.

Second. The first general council shall consist of one member from each tribe, and an additional member for each one thousand Indians, or each fraction of a thousand greater than five hundred, being members of any tribe lawfully resident in said Territory, and shall be selected by said tribes respectively, who may assent to the establishment of said general council; and if none should be thus formally selected by any nation or tribe so assenting, the said nation or tribe shall be represented in said general council by the chief or chiefs and headmen of said tribes, to be taken in the order of their rank as recognized in tribal usage, in the same number and proportion as above indicated. After the said census shall have been taken and completed, the superintendent of Indian affairs shall publish and declare to each tribe assenting to the establishment of such council the number of members of such council to which they shall be entitled under the provisions of this article, and the persons entitled to represent said tribes shall meet at such time and place as he shall approve; but thereafter the time and place of the sessions of said council shall be determined by its action: *Provided*, That no session in any one year shall exceed the term of thirty days: *And provided*, That special sessions of said council may be called by the Secretary of the Interior whenever in his judgment the interest of said tribes shall require such special session.

Third. Said general council shall have power to legislate upon matters pertaining to the intercourse and relations of the Indian tribes and nations and colonies of freedmen resident in said Territory; the arrest and extradition of criminals and offenders escaping from one tribe to another, or into any community of freedmen; the administration of justice between members of different tribes of said Territory and persons other than Indians and members of said tribes or nations; and the common defence and safety of the nations of said Territory.

All laws enacted by such council shall take effect at such time as may therein be provided, unless suspended by direction of the President of the United States. No law shall be enacted inconsistent with the Constitution of the United States, or laws of Congress, or existing treaty stipulations with the United States. Nor shall said council legislate upon matters other than those above indicated: *Provided, however,* That the legislative power of such general council may be enlarged by the consent of the national council of each nation or tribe assenting to its establishment, with the approval of the President of the United States.

Fourth. Said council shall be presided over by such person as may be designated by the Secretary of the Interior.

Fifth. The council shall elect a secretary, whose duty it shall be to keep an accurate record of all the proceedings of said council, and who shall transmit a true copy of all such proceedings, duly certified by the presiding officer of such council, to the Secretary of the Interior, and to each tribe or nation represented in said council, immediately after the sessions of said council shall terminate. He shall be paid out of the Treasury of the United States an annual salary of five hundred dollars.

Sixth. The members of said council shall be paid by the United States the sum of four dollars per diem during the term actually in attendance on the sessions of said council, and at the rate of four dollars for every twenty miles necessarily traveled by them in going from and returning to their homes, respectively, from said council, to be certified by the secretary and president of the said council.

Article 13

The Cherokees also agree that a court or courts may be established by the United States in said Territory, with such jurisdiction and organized in such manner as may be prescribed by law: *Provided,* That the judicial tribunals of the nation shall be allowed to retain exclusive jurisdiction in all civil and criminal cases arising within their country in which members of the nation, by nativity or adoption, shall be the only parties, or where the cause of action shall arise in the Cherokee Nation, except as otherwise provided in this treaty.

Article 14

The right to the use and occupancy of a quantity of land not exceeding one hundred and sixty acres, to be selected according to legal subdivisions in one body, and to include their improvements, and not including the improvements of any member of the Cherokee Nation, is hereby granted to every society or denomination which has erected, or which with the consent of the national council may hereafter erect, buildings within the Cherokee country for missionary or educational purposes. But no land thus granted, nor buildings which have been or may be erected thereon, shall ever be sold or [o]therwise disposed of except with the consent and approval of the Cherokee national council and the Secretary of the Interior. And whenever any such lands or buildings shall be sold or disposed of, the proceeds thereof shall be applied by said society or societies for like purposes within said nation, subject to the approval of the Secretary of the Interior.

Article 15

The United States may settle any civilized Indians, friendly with the Cherokees and adjacent tribes, within the Cherokee country, on unoccupied lands east of 96°, on such terms as may be agreed upon by any such tribe and the Cherokees, subject to the approval of the President of the United States, which shall be consistent with the following provisions, viz: Should any such tribe or band of Indians settling in said country abandon their tribal organization, there being first paid into the Cherokee national fund a sum of money which shall sustain the same proportion to the then existing national fund that the number of Indians sustain to the whole number of Cherokees then residing in the Cherokee country, they shall be incorporated into and ever after remain a part of the Cherokee Nation, on equal terms in every respect with native citizens. And should any such tribe, thus settling in said country, decide to preserve their tribal organizations, and to maintain their tribal laws, customs, and usages, not inconsistent with the constitution and laws of the Cherokee Nation, they shall have a district of country set off for their use by metes and bounds equal to one hundred and sixty acres, if they should so decide, for each man, woman, and child of said tribe, and shall pay for the same into the national fund such price as may be agreed on by them and the Cherokee Nation, subject to the approval of the President of the United States, and in cases of disagreement the price to be fixed by the President.

And the said tribe thus settled shall also pay into the national fund a sum of money, to be agreed on by the respective parties, not greater in proportion to the whole existing national fund and the probable proceeds of the lands herein ceded or authorized to be ceded or sold than their numbers bear to the whole number of Cherokees then residing in said country, and thence afterwards they shall enjoy all the rights of native Cherokees. But no Indians who have no tribal organizations, or who shall determine to abandon their tribal organizations, shall be permitted to settle east of the 96° of longitude without the consent of the Cherokee national council, or of a delegation duly appointed by it, being first obtained. And no Indians who have and determine to preserve the tribal organizations shall be permitted to settle, as herein provided, east of the 96° of longitude without such consent being first obtained, unless the President of the United States, after a full hearing of the objections offered by said council or delegation to such settlement, shall determine that the objections are insufficient, in which case he may authorize the settlement of such tribe east of the 96° of longitude.

Article 16

The United States may settle friendly Indians in any part of the Cherokee country west of 96°, to be taken in a compact form in quantity not exceeding one hundred and sixty acres for each member of each of said tribes thus to be settled; the boundaries of each of said districts to be distinctly marked, and the land conveyed in fee-simple to each of said tribes to be held in common or by their members in severalty as the United States may decide. Said lands thus disposed of to be paid for to the Cherokee Nation at such price as may be agreed on between the said parties in interest, subject to the approval of the President; and if they should not agree, then the price to be fixed by the President. The Cherokee Nation to retain the right of possession of and jurisdiction over all of said country west of 96° of longitude until thus sold and occupied, after which their jurisdiction and right of possession to terminate forever as to each of said districts thus sold and occupied.

Article 17

The Cherokee Nation hereby cedes, in trust to the United States, the tract of land in the State of Kansas which was sold to the Cherokees by the United States, under the provisions of the second article of the treaty of 1835; and also that strip of the land ceded to the nation by the fourth article of said treaty which is included in the State of Kansas, and the Cherokees consent that said lands may be included in the limits and jurisdiction of the said State.

The lands herein ceded shall be surveyed as the public lands of the United States are surveyed, under the direction of the Commissioner of the General Land-Office, and shall be appraised by two disinterested persons, one to be designated by the Cherokee national council and one by the Secretary of the Interior, and, in case of disagreement, by a third person, to be mutually selected by the aforesaid appraisers. The appraisement to be not less than an average of one dollar and a quarter per acre, exclusive of improvements. And the Secretary of the Interior shall, from time to time, as such surveys and appraisements are approved by him, after due advertisements for sealed bids, sell such lands to the highest bidders for cash, in parcels not exceeding one hundred and sixty acres, and at not less than the appraised value: *Provided,* That whenever there are improvements of the value of fifty dollars made on the lands not being mineral, and owned and personally occupied by any person for agricultural purposes at the date of the signing hereof, such person so owning, and in person residing on such improvements, shall, after due proof, made under such regulations as the Secretary of the Interior may prescribe, be entitled to buy, at the appraised value, the smallest quantity of land in legal subdivisions which will include his improvements, not exceeding in the aggregate one hundred and sixty acres; the expenses of survey and appraisement to be paid by the Secretary out of the proceeds of sale of said land: Provided, That nothing in this article shall prevent the Secretary of the Interior from selling the whole of said lands not occupied by actual settlers at the date of the ratification of this treaty, not exceeding one hundred and sixty acres to each person entitled to pre-emption under the pre-emption laws of the United States, in a body, to any responsible party, for cash, for a sum not less than one dollar per acre.

Article 18

That any lands owned by the Cherokees in the State of Arkansas and in States east of the Mississippi may be sold by the Cherokee Nation in such manner as their national council may prescribe, all such sales being first approved by the Secretary of the Interior.

Article 19

All Cherokees being heads of families residing at the date of the ratification of this treaty on any of the lands herein ceded, or authorized to be sold, and desiring to remove to the reserved country, shall be paid by the purchasers of said lands the value of such improvements, to be ascertained and appraised by the commissioners who appraise the lands, subject to the approval of the Secretary of the Interior; and if he shall elect to remain on the land now occupied by him, shall be entitled to receive a patent from the United States in fee-simple for three hundred and twenty acres of land to include his improvements, and thereupon he and his family shall cease to be members of the nation.

And the Secretary of the Interior shall also be authorized to pay the reasonable costs and expenses of the delegates of the southern Cherokees. The moneys to be paid under this article shall be paid out of the proceeds of the sales of the national lands in Kansas.

Article 20

Whenever the Cherokee national council shall request it, the Secretary of the Interior shall cause the country reserved for the Cherokees to be surveyed and allotted among them, at the expense of the United States.

Article 21

It being difficult to learn the precise boundary line between the Cherokee country and the States of Arkansas, Missouri, and Kansas, it is agreed that the United States shall, at its own expense, cause the same to be run as far west as the Arkansas, and marked by permanent and conspicuous monuments, by two commissioners, one of whom shall be designated by the Cherokee national council.

Article 22

The Cherokee national council, or any duly appointed delegation thereof, shall have the privilege to appoint an agent to examine the accounts of the nation with the Government of the United States at such time as they may see proper, and to continue or discharge such agent, and to appoint another, as may be thought best by such council or delegation; and such agent shall have free access to all accounts and books in the executive departments relating to the business of said Cherokee Nation, and an opportunity to examine the same in the presence of the officer having such books and papers in charge.

Article 23

All funds now due the nation, or that may hereafter accrue from the sale of their lands by the United States, as hereinbefore provided for, shall be invested in the United States registered stocks at their current value, and the interest on all said funds shall be paid semi-annually on the order of the Cherokee Nation, and shall be applied to the following purposes, to wit: Thirty-five per cent. shall be applied for the support of the common-schools of the nation and educational purposes; fifteen per cent. for the orphan fund, and fifty per cent. for general purposes, including reasonable salaries of district officers; and the

Secretary of the Interior, with the approval of the President of the United States, may pay out of the funds due the nation, on the order of the national council or a delegation duly authorized by it, such amount as he may deem necessary to meet outstanding obligations of the Cherokee Nation, caused by the suspension of the payment of their annuities, not to exceed the sum of one hundred and fifty thousand dollars.

Article 24

As a slight testimony for the useful and arduous services of the Rev. Evan Jones, for forty years a missionary in the Cherokee Nation, now a cripple, old and poor, it is agreed that the sum of three thousand dollars be paid to him, under the direction of the Secretary of the Interior, out of any Cherokee fund in or to come into his hands not otherwise appropriated.

Article 25

A large number of the Cherokees who served in the Army of the United States having died, leaving no heirs entitled to receive bounties and arrears of pay on account of such service, it is agreed that all bounties and arrears for service in the regiments of Indian United States volunteers which shall remain unclaimed by any person legally entitled to receive the same for two years from the ratification of this treaty, shall be paid as the national council may direct, to be applied to the foundation and support of an asylum for the education of orphan children, which asylum shall be under the control of the national council, or of such benevolent society as said council may designate, subject to the approval of the Secretary of the Interior.

Article 26

The United States guarantee to the people of the Cherokee Nation the quiet and peaceable possession of their country and protection against domestic feuds and insurrections, and against hostilities of other tribes. They shall also be protected against inter[r]uptions or intrusion from all unauthorized citizens of the United States who may attempt to settle on their lands or reside in their territory. In case of hostilities among the Indian tribes, the United States agree that the party or parties commencing the same shall, so far as practicable, make reparation for the damages done.

Article 27

The United States shall have the right to establish one or more military posts or stations in the Cherokee Nation, as may be deemed necessary for the proper protection of the citizens of the United States lawfully residing therein and the Cherokee and other citizens of the Indian country. But no sutler or other person connected therewith, either in or out of the military organization, shall be permitted to introduce any spirit[u]ous, vinous, or malt liquors into the Cherokee Nation, except the medical department proper, and by them only for strictly medical purposes. And all persons not in the military service of the United States, not citizens of the Cherokee Nation, are to be prohibited from coming into the Cherokee Nation, or remaining in the same, except as herein otherwise provided; and it is the duty of the United States Indian agent for the Cherokees to have such persons, not lawfully residing or sojourning therein, removed from the nation, as they now are, or hereafter may be, required by the Indian intercourse laws of the United States.

Article 28

The United States hereby agree to pay for provisions and clothing furnished the army under Appotholehala in the winter of 1861 and 1862, not to exceed the sum of ten thousand dollars, the accounts to be ascertained and settled by the Secretary of the Interior.

Article 29

The sum of ten thousand dollars or so much thereof as may be necessary to pay the expenses of the delegates and representatives of the Cherokees invited by the Government to visit Washington for the purposes of making this treaty, shall be paid by the United States on the ratification of this treaty.

Article 30

The United States agree to pay to the proper claimants all losses of property by missionaries or missionary societies, resulting from their being ordered or driven from the country by United States agents, and from their property being taken and occupied or destroyed by United States troops, not exceeding in the aggregate twenty thousand dollars, to be ascertained by the Secretary of the Interior.

Article 31

All provisions of treaties heretofore ratified and in force, and not inconsistent with the provisions of this treaty, are hereby re-affirmed and declared to be in full force; and nothin[g] herein shall be construed as an acknowledgment by the United States, or as a relinquishment by the Cherokee Nation of any claims or demands under the guarantees of former treaties, except as herein expressly provided.

In testimony whereof, the said commissioners on the part of the United States, and the said delegation on the part of the Cherokee Nation, have hereunto set their hands and seals at the city of Washington, this ninth [nineteenth] day of July, A.D. one thousand eight hundred and sixty-six.

D. N. Cooley, Commissioner of Indian Affairs.
Elijah Sells, Superintendent of Indian Affairs.
Smith Christie,
White Catcher,
James McDaniel,
S. H. Benge,
Danl. H. Ross,
J. B. Jones.

Delegates of the Cherokee Nation, appointed by Resolution of the National Council.

In presence of—

W. H. Watson,
J. W. Wright.

Signatures witnessed by the following-named persons, the following interlineations being made before signing: On page 1st the word "the" interlined, on page 11 the word "the" struck out, and to said page 11 sheet attached requiring publication of laws; and on page 34th the word "ceded" struck out and the words "neutral lands" inserted. Page 47½ added relating to expenses of treaty.

Thomas Ewing, Jr.
Wm. A. Phillips,
J. W. Wright.

Notes

Introduction

1 For one examination of this subject, see Johnson, *Black Masters*. Also see Schweninger, "Prosperous Blacks in the South." A provocative fictional work that sparked controversy on this topic is Jones, *The Known World*.

2 The interviews of African Indian freedpeople in Oklahoma conducted in the 1930s (during the Depression) by the Works Progress Administration (WPA) highlight the experiences of formerly enslaved African Indians living in Indian Territory. For interviews specifically with formerly enslaved people living in Oklahoma, see Rawick, *The American Slave*, vols. 7 and 12, and Baker and Baker, *The WPA Oklahoma Slave Narratives*. Volume 7 of Rawick's collection includes the interviews of seventy-five ex-slaves and/or children of ex-slaves. Of these interviewees, a total of fourteen self-identified as ex-slaves or children of ex-slaves of Indians in Indian Territory—six Cherokee, four Creek, two Choctaw, and two Chickasaw. Volume 12 of Rawick's collection includes the interviews of sixty-seven ex-slaves or children of ex-slaves. Of these interviewees, a total of thirty-four identified themselves as ex-slaves or children of ex-slaves of Indians in Indian Territory—sixteen Cherokee, nine Choctaw, eight Creek, and one Chickasaw. In addition to the Rawick series, the WPA-sponsored *Indian Pioneer History Collection* includes recollections of former African Indian, Indian, and European American residents of Indian Territory. Edited by Grant Foreman, this multivolume set is housed at the Oklahoma Historical Society and the University of Oklahoma Western History Collections. All references to volumes in this collection correspond with the copy at the Oklahoma Historical Society. Also see Minges, *Black Indian Slave Narratives*, and Minges, *Far More Terrible*.

Initially deposited in the Library of Congress, the WPA interviews of ex-slaves remained a relatively untapped source of information until Greenwood Press's publication of these interviews in the 1970s. The WPA conducted interviews with formerly enslaved people living in South Carolina, Texas, Alabama, Indiana, Oklahoma, Mississippi, Arkansas, Missouri, Georgia, North Carolina, Kansas, Kentucky, Maryland, Ohio, Virginia, Colorado, Tennessee, Florida, Minnesota, Missouri, Oregon, and Washington. In April 2001 the Library of Congress announced the release of the on-line collection, "Born in Slavery: Slave Narratives from the Federal Writers' Project, 1936–1938," part of the American Memory project. This collection includes more than 2,300 interviews, as well as 500 black-and-white photographs of formerly enslaved interviewees. Particularly insightful works on the uses and misuses of slave narratives, autobiographies, and oral interviews are Blassingame, "Using the Testimony of Ex-Slaves"; Cade, "Out of the Mouths of Ex-Slaves"; David Thomas Bailey, "A Divided Prism"; Escott, *Slavery Remembered*; C. Vann Woodward, "History from Slave Sources"; and Yetman, "Ex-Slave Interviews."

3   See, for example, Hawthorne, *Planting Rice and Harvesting Slaves*; Lovejoy, *Transformations in Slavery*; and John K. Thornton, *Africa and Africans*.

4   For an example of one of the landmark studies of Indian slavery in North America, see Lauber, *Indian Slavery*. Recent historical studies of Indian slavery analyzing the trade in Indian captives and slaves in various colonial regions include Barr, "A Diplomacy of Gender"; Brooks, *Captives and Cousins*; Gallay, *The Indian Slave Trade*; Newell, "The Drove of Adam's Degenerate Seed"; and Rushforth, "A Little Flesh We Offer You." Rushforth, for example, specifically underscores the diplomatic and symbolic elements of the exchange of Indian captives and slaves in New France between 1660 and 1710. From a geopolitical landscape different from Louisiana and the French Caribbean colonies, Indians offered captives to the French as an avenue for recognizing, sustaining, and stabilizing French-Indian alliances. By the late seventeenth century, Indian captives became an increasingly important element of French-Indian trading networks within the framework of Indian diplomacy.

5   Perdue, *Slavery*, 4. For the actual Cherokee letters for the word "slave," see Robinson, *Easy to Use Cherokee Dictionary*, 85.

6   di ge tsi na tla i is the plural (phonetic) form of a tsi na tla i. Robinson, *Easy to Use Cherokee Dictionary*, 85.

7   Perdue, *Slavery*, 12.

8   As Perdue proposes, "Cherokees never would have employed unfree la-

bor exclusively in the cultivation of the soil . . . nor would they have relied on *atsi nahsa'i* to supply game because in their indigenous culture
tasks affirmed sexual roles, social order, and cosmic balance." Perdue,
Slavery, 15.

9 Gallay, *The Indian Slave Trade*, 7–8.

10 Perdue, *Slavery*, 21–22. Echoing Perdue, Alan Gallay suggests that Indian
purchase and usage of European "goods largely filled existing functions
more efficiently. . . . European axes, pots and pans, guns, paint and
clothing made life easier but did not change its patterns." Gallay, *The
Indian Slave Trade*, 8. Rushforth also comments on a similar dynamic
related to captive exchanges and the Ottawa acquisition of French mus-
kets and kettles. Although Indians sought to acquire European guns, it is
important to point out that seventeenth-century guns were recognized by
European contemporaries as less accurate and effective than the bows
and arrows of southern Indians. See Rushforth, "A Little Flesh We Offer
You."

11 See Gallay, *The Indian Slave Trade*, and Rushforth, "A Little Flesh We Offer
You."

12 For one insightful discussion of the possible range of cultural exchanges
and contact experiences between Africans and Indians before and after
the sixteenth century, see Forbes, *Africans and Native Americans*, 6–64.

13 See, for example, Perdue, *Slavery*, 36.

14 Yarbrough, "Legislating Women's Sexuality," 387. Also see Yarbrough,
Race and the Cherokee Nation.

15 Though literal meanings of membership along bloodlines represented
one dimension of Cherokeeness, other symbolic and metaphoric connotations of Cherokee blood became signifiers of inclusion within Cherokee society. For an examination of the various metaphorical and literal
meanings of blood in Cherokee society in the eighteenth century, see
Sturm, *Blood Politics*, 27–51.

16 As Fay Yarbrough explains, "Cherokee women and European traders or
frontiersman sought each other to gain access to goods or territory and to
cement alliances. In a few instances these 'foreign' men would seek
formal adoption into the Nation and concomitant clan membership;
however, more often these men held the status not of clan members, but

of the husbands of clan members." Yarbrough, "Legislating Women's Sexuality," 387. See also Perdue, *"Mixed Blood" Indians*, 21. As "husbands of clan members," these men "held a liminal position not entirely within the clan system, but also not bereft of any clan protections. In the nineteenth century, the strength of the clan system waned, and the concept of legal citizenship substituted for clan in determining legitimate membership in the Cherokee Nation. American men who married Cherokee women could then seek legal rights in the Cherokee Nation without participating in the traditional ritual of adoption." Yarbrough, "Legislating Women's Sexuality," 387.

17　See Yarbrough, "Legislating Women's Sexuality," and Yarbrough, *Race in the Cherokee Nation*, for a discussion of this new law and its impact on the position and power of Cherokee women in Cherokee society.

18　Article 3, Section 4, of the New Echota Constitution of 1827 stated: "No person shall be eligible to a seat in the General Council, but a free Cherokee male citizen, who shall have attained to the age of twenty-five years. The descendants of Cherokee men by all free women, except the African race, whose parents may have been living together as man and wife, according to the customs and laws of this Nation, shall be entitled to all the rights and privileges of this Nation, as well as the posterity of Cherokee women by all free men. No person who is of negro or mulatto parentage, either by the father or mother side, shall be eligible to hold any office of profit, honor or trust under this Government." Cherokee Nation, *Laws of the Cherokee Nation adopted by the Council at Various Periods*, 120. Article 3, Section 5, of the Tahlequah Constitution of 1839 reiterated the same restrictions regarding positions in the Cherokee National Council. Cherokee Nation, *Constitution and Laws of the Cherokee Nation: Passed at Tahlequah, Cherokee Nation, 1839–1851*, 7. In addition, Article 3, Section 7, of the New Echota Constitution of 1827 stated: "All free male citizens (excepting negroes and descendants of white and Indian men by negro women who may have been set free) who shall have attained to the age of eighteen years, shall be equally entitled to vote at all public elections." Cherokee Nation, *Laws of the Cherokee Nation adopted by the Council at Various Periods*, 121. However, Article 3, Section 7, of the Tahlequah Constitution of 1839 stated: "All free male citizens, who shall have attained to the age of eighteen years shall be equally entitled to vote at all public elections." Cherokee Nation, *Constitution and Laws of the Cherokee Nation: Passed at Tahlequah, Cherokee Nation, 1839–1851*, 7.

19 Yarbrough, "Legislating Women's Sexuality," 389.

20 For a few references to occurrences of this kind of collusion and European American fears about it, see Gallay, *The Indian Slave Trade*, 94, 96, 170, 272–73, 290, 347–49.

21 For an excellent discussion of European American removal policies and the "invention of Indian Territory," see Ronda, "We Have a Country."

22 The treaty was signed by Chief John Jolly, Charles Hicks, Katchee of Cowee, John D. Chisholm, Roman Nose, White Man Killer, Going Snake, Sleeping Rabbit, Sour Mash, Big Half Breed, Young Davis, Beaver Carrier, and thirty-four other representatives of the Cherokee Nation who were planning on making the move to the west.

23 The chairman of the commission was Governor Montfort Stokes of North Carolina; the other members were Henry L. Ellsworth of Connecticut and Rev. John F. Schermerhorn of New York.

24 As Miles argues: "The men and women comprising this group might properly be called the Cherokee 'middle class,' measured not by exact formulations of wealth or position between the Cherokee elite and poor but by their geographical location in this middle region of Cherokee country where a particular kind of property-owning, slaveholding microculture was developing." Miles, *Ties That Bind*, 38.

25 Perdue, *Slavery*, 68.

26 For an analysis of the individual populations noted in the Cherokee Census of 1835, see Russell Thornton, *The Cherokees: A Population History*, 50–54.

27 Angie Debo, for instance, argues that there were 248 slaves and 19,554 Choctaws in the Choctaw Nation at this time. Debo, *The Rise and Fall of the Choctaw Republic*, 69.

28 See, for example, Littlefield, *Africans and Seminoles*, and Mulroy, *Freedom on the Border*.

29 See Doran, "Population Statistics," 496, 498, and 501.

30 Perdue, *Slavery*, 71.

31 Ibid., 99–102.

32 See Doran, "Population Statistics," 496, 498, and 501, for specific details regarding the estimated Indian population of the Five Tribes before removal in 1830, as well as the population of all residents in these nations in 1860, including Indians, whites, and African-descended slaves. In 1860 the Seminole Nation again refused to divulge the number of slaves. Of the 17,048 total residents of the Cherokee Nation, Doran's examination of the 1860 census data indicates that 13,821 (81 percent) were Indian, 2,511 were slaves (15 percent), and 716 were white (4 percent). Ibid., 501.

33 For example, see Abel, *The American Indian as Slaveholder*; Janet Halliburton, "Black Slavery"; Rudi Halliburton, *Red over Black*; Jeltz, "The Relations of Negroes"; Johnston, "Documentary Evidence"; Littlefield, *Africans and Creeks*; Littlefield, *Africans and Seminoles*; McLoughlin, "Red Indians, Black Slavery"; and Perdue, *Slavery*.

Chapter 1

1 Although linking certain acts of slave resistance to postremoval chaos in Indian Territory, Theda Perdue, in her seminal work on slavery in the Cherokee Nation, argued that "although Cherokee planters required hard work from their bondsmen, they probably treated their slaves much better on the average than did their white counterparts. . . . Thus relative leniency on the part of masters seems to have been characteristic of Cherokee slavery before and after removal." Perdue, *Slavery*, 98. In his dissertation, Michael Roethler also supported this hypothesis. He claimed that "the benign attitude thus demonstrated to the Negroes by the Cherokees leads one to conclude that slavery existed among the Cherokees in a mild form. . . . Surely, the slaves dreamed of freedom. Until that happy day would arrive, however, they remained content with their lot among the Cherokees." Roethler, "Negro Slavery," 129. The 1849 slave narrative of Henry Bibb also reinforces the notion of a "mild" form of slavery practiced by Indians. The brevity of Bibb's time in Indian Territory no doubt informed his particular experiences. Osofsky, *Puttin' on Ole Massa*, 141. Conversely, in the 1970s, Rudy Halliburton challenged these notions of benign slavery in his work *Red over Black*.

2 For an extended discussion of race and nineteenth-century laws of the Cherokee Nation, see Yarbrough, *Race and the Cherokee Nation*.

3　Though the Cherokee Nation created the New Echota Constitution in 1827 before removal, vehement altercations between parties of the Western Cherokees and the newly arrived Eastern Cherokees demanded a joint understanding of and agreement on the laws and policies of the Cherokee Nation in the new territory. On 23 August 1839, after a period of intense discussion and bloodshed, the Western Cherokees and Eastern Cherokees reached an agreement—"Act of Union between the Eastern and Western Cherokees." Two weeks after this agreement, on 6 September 1839, the reunited Eastern and Western Cherokees established a new Constitution of the Cherokee Nation—the Tahlequah Constitution. For the Act of Union and the Tahlequah Cherokee Constitution of 1839, see Cherokee Nation, *Constitution and Laws of the Cherokee Nation: Passed at Tahlequah, Cherokee Nation, 1839–1851*, 3–15.

4　Ibid., 19.

5　See Yarbrough, "Legislating Women's Sexuality," and Yarbrough, *Race and the Cherokee Nation*.

6　Cherokee Nation, *Constitution and Laws of the Cherokee Nation: Passed at Tahlequah, Cherokee Nation, 1839–1851*, 17–18. This act was amended twice. The first amendment was passed four years later; on 23 October 1843, the Cherokee National Council changed the language of the act to "any person charged with the offense of having *attempted or committed* a rape on any female." Ibid., 80 (emphasis added). The second amendment was passed two years later, on 17 October 1845; the act was "amended, so, that in case any Negro shall be convicted before the Courts of this Nation, of attempting by violence to commit a rape, he shall be punished with one hundred lashes." Ibid., 133. It is unclear why the punishment was reduced in the case of an attempted or committed rape against a woman by a man of African descent.

7　See Guy-Sheftall, "The Body Politic," and McLaurin, *Celia, a Slave*.

8　Cherokee Nation, *Constitution and Laws of the Cherokee Nation: Passed at Tahlequah, Cherokee Nation, 1839–1851*, 44.

9　As the Cherokee New Echota Constitution of 1827 stated in Article 1, Section 2: "The sovereignty and jurisdiction of this Government shall extend over the country within the boundaries above described, and the lands therein are, and shall remain, the common property of the Nation;

but the improvements made thereon, and in the possession of the citizens of the Nation, are the exclusive and indefeasible property of the citizens respectively who made; or may rightfully be in possession of them; Provided, that the citizens of the Nation, possessing exclusive and indefeasible right to their respective improvements, as expressed in this article, shall possess no right nor power to dispose of their improvements in any manner whatsoever to the United States, individual states, nor individual citizens thereof; and that whenever any such citizen or citizens shall remove with their effects out of the limits of this Nation, and become citizens of any other Government, all their rights and privileges as citizens of this Nation shall cease; Provided, nevertheless, That the Legislature shall have power to re-admit by law to all the rights of citizenship, any such person or persons, who may at any time desire to return to the Nation on their memorializing the General Council for such readmission. Moreover, the Legislature shall have power to adopt such laws and regulations, as its wisdom may deem expedient and proper, to prevent the citizens from monopolizing improvements with the view to speculation." Cherokee Nation, *Laws of the Cherokee Nation adopted by the Council at Various Periods*, 119. Article 1, Section 2, of the new Tahlequah Constitution of 1839 reiterated the same conditions regarding communal land ownership and improvements. Cherokee Nation, *Constitution and Laws of the Cherokee Nation: Passed at Tahlequah, Cherokee Nation, 1839–1851*, 5.

10   Cherokee Nation, *Constitution and Laws of the Cherokee Nation: Passed at Tahlequah, Cherokee Nation, 1839–1851*, 44.

11   Ibid., 53.

12   Ibid., 53–54.

13   Ibid., 55.

14   Ibid. The Cherokee National Council amended this act on 24 October 1848 to include specific references to the unlawful activities of whites (most likely missionaries) teaching slaves to read and write. This amended act stated, "if any white person, not a citizen of the Cherokee Nation, should be guilty of a violation of this act . . . [it would result in the] removal of such person or persons from the limits of the Cherokee Nation." Ibid., 173–74.

15 Theda Perdue describes this period as "post-removal chaos" in her book *Slavery and the Evolution of Cherokee Society, 1540–1866*. In chapter 5 she discusses the lawlessness and turmoil that existed in Indian Territory during the decade following removal. For another perspective on the chaotic postremoval period in Indian Territory, within the Seminole context, see Lancaster, *Removal Aftershock*. Lancaster's work examines the problems that the Seminoles confronted after removal to Indian Territory, such as ongoing disputes with the Creeks over land usage, limited provisions, smallpox epidemics, unfulfilled treaty promises with the U.S. government, false claims for slaves living among the Seminoles, and ongoing Creek domination. Lancaster's analysis revolves primarily around the interactions between the U.S. government, government agents, and the Seminoles. As a result, her work does not explore the Seminoles' efforts to attain and maintain their national identity outside of the limits of treaties and policies. In addition, Lancaster provides only brief references to enslaved African Seminoles among the Seminoles.

16 For the Act of Union and New Cherokee Constitution, see Cherokee Nation, *Constitution and Laws of the Cherokee Nation: Passed at Tahlequah, Cherokee Nation, 1839–1851*, 3–15.

17 Rawick, *American Slave*, 7:257.

18 Ibid., 259.

19 In order to disseminate information about the occurrences in the new land, the first issue of the *Cherokee Advocate* was printed in the new Cherokee capital of Tahlequah on 26 September 1844. This weekly newspaper's motto was "Our Rights, Our Country, Our Race." The *Cherokee Advocate* was not the first Cherokee newspaper to be published. The *Cherokee Phoenix* had been established in 1828 prior to removal to Indian Territory.

20 William Potter Ross was the eldest son of Scottish-born John Golden Ross (no blood relation to Chief John Ross) and Eliza Ross, sister of Chief John Ross. He was born on 20 August 1820 in Tennessee, in the Cherokee Nation. Educated initially in Tennessee and later at a preparatory school in New Jersey, W. P. Ross was able to attend Princeton University with the financial assistance of his uncle Chief John Ross. When he graduated from Princeton in 1842, he moved to his family's new home in Park Hill, Cherokee Nation. In October 1843, at the age of twenty-three,

W. P. Ross was elected clerk of the senate and the first editor of the *Cherokee Advocate*. He served in this capacity until 13 November 1848. During his tenure, he periodically transferred his editorial responsibilities to his brother, Daniel H. Ross, due to his participation in Cherokee delegations to Washington, D.C. In his lifetime, W. P. Ross served the Cherokee Nation in various political capacities, including senator to the National Council for the Tahlequah District and the Illinois District, secretary to his uncle Lewis Ross (Cherokee national treasurer in 1860), lieutenant colonel of the 1st Cherokee Regiment of Mounted Rifles, Field and Staff (part of the Confederate army) during the Civil War, and principal chief in 1866–67 and 1872–75. W. P. Ross died on 20 July 1891. For more information on William P. Ross and his work with the *Cherokee Advocate*, see Meserve, "Chief William Potter Ross," and Tattershall, " 'Our Rights, Our Country, Our Race.' "

21 *Cherokee Advocate*, 19 October 1844.

22 One episode concerned the arrest of two Cherokee women named Cheek for their participation in the murder of Martin Culsowhee near Fort Gibson. Another noted the trial of Wheeler Faught (nationality not identified) for his connection with the assassination of Ta-ka-to-ka in Going Snake District, Cherokee Nation. Additional stories documented the murder of Cherokee Samuel Martin by another Cherokee man named Squirrel and the stabbing of a woman (nationality not identified) in Delaware District, Cherokee Nation. Ibid.

23 *Cherokee Advocate*, 12 March 1846.

24 Although lighthorsemen were replaced with marshals, sheriffs, and constables in 1825 by the Cherokee National Council, in 1839 John Ross reinstated the employment of lighthorsemen due to the violent conditions of the postremoval period. For more information on the activities of lighthorsemen in the Cherokee Nation, before and after removal, as well as the development of law enforcement among the Five Tribes, particularly the Cherokees and the Choctaws, see Blackburn, "From Blood Revenge to the Lighthorsemen."

25 Although scholars of Cherokee history have examined the postremoval disorder, which included the feuds between members of the Ross Party and Treaty Party, the connection between this general state of turmoil in

the Cherokee Nation and resistance on the part of enslaved African Cherokees living in the Nation has not been thoroughly explored. Most scholars have overlooked this subject; historian Theda Perdue is an important exception. Perdue specifically commented on the connection between the chaos in the Cherokee Nation and runaways. Perdue, *Slavery*, 78–79.

26 *Cherokee Advocate*, 17 December 1846. In this article, entitled "Killed," editor William P. Ross expressed his concern about the rampant disorder in the Cherokee Nation as he described the events of this recapture. The first article stated that the runaway belonged to Cherokee Thomas Candy. However, a correction was noted in the next issue regarding the runaway killed. "The Negro killed near Mrs. Looney's belonged to Dennis Biggs— and not to Thomas Candy as was supposed." *Cherokee Advocate*, 24 December 1846.

27 *Cherokee Advocate*, 17 December 1846. This was not the only incident of resistance during recapture in the Cherokee Nation. In the process of being recaptured, a runaway belonging to Cherokee Dr. Robert Daniel Ross "resisted them with weapons which compelled them to shoot him." *Cherokee Advocate*, 3 August 1853.

28 *Cherokee Advocate*, 3 April 1848. For examples of violent confrontations in the southern United States between runaways and slave catchers, including overseers and slave owners, see the section "Violence in Defense of Freedom" in Franklin and Schweninger, *Runaway Slaves*, 83–86. Also see the section on "The Hunt" for a particularly striking description of a fatal confrontation between James C. Knox, a slave catcher from Baton Rouge Parish, Louisiana, and runaway Big Sandy. Ibid., 149–50.

29 *Cherokee Advocate*, 17 December 1846.

30 Osofsky, *Puttin' on Ole Massa*, 166. As John Hope Franklin and Loren Schweninger explained, "fear, anxiety, retaliation, frustration, anger, and hatred propelled slaves toward violence. The most prevalent 'crime' connected with runaways, however, was theft. . . . For slaves, stealing was not considered theft, merely appropriating their due." Franklin and Schweninger, *Runaway Slaves*, 79–80.

31 *Cherokee Advocate*, 17 December 1846.

32 Ibid.

33 Ibid. In his article, Ross articulated his concerns about not only enslaved

African Cherokees, but also the troubling presence of enslaved African Seminoles. Between 1838 and 1845, the ambivalent position of enslaved and free African Seminoles in the Seminole Nation, Indian Territory, resulted in a great deal of controversy within the Seminole Nation, as well as in the surrounding Cherokee and Creek nations. As local Cherokee feuding continued to create havoc in the Nation, many Cherokees believed that the presence and actions of outsiders, particularly enslaved and free African Seminoles, further jeopardized the chances for peace. The influence of recently freed African Seminoles also posed an incalculable threat to Cherokee control over their own enslaved people. See also *Cherokee Advocate*, 1 January 1849.

34 For an excellent description of truancy, absenteeism, and laying out, and the various reasons behind these strategies, see Franklin and Schweninger, *Runaway Slaves*, 97–109.

35 Theda Perdue points out that in the *Cherokee Phoenix*, established in 1828, "not one notice of an escaped slave belonging to a Cherokee appeared," whereas the *Cherokee Advocate* "frequently published advertisements for runaways." Perdue, *Slavery*, 79.

36 Before removal, Joseph Vann lived in Springplace, Georgia; after removal, he settled in Webbers Falls, Canadian District, Cherokee Nation. Today visitors can tour Joseph Vann's house in Georgia—a historic site administered by Georgia's State Parks and Historic Sites.

37 Cherokee freedwoman Lucinda Vann recalled one particularly lasting response to the death of Cherokee slave owner Joseph Vann. After the explosion of the *Lucy Walker*, she explained, "someone found an arm up in a tree on the bank of the river. They brought it home and my grandmother knew it was Joe's [Joseph Vann's]. She done his washing and knew the cuff of his sleeve. Everybody pretty near to crazy when they bring that arm home. A doctor put it in alcohol and they kept it a long time. Different friends would come and they'd show that arm. My mother saw it but the colored chillun couldn't. Master and missus never allowed chillun to meddle in the big folks' business. Don't know what they ever did with that arm. Lord, it was terrible." Rawick, *American Slave*, 12:349–50. Due to accounts of the mean steak of Joe Vann, one might expect that some of his

enslaved African Cherokees looked at his dismembered arm with a sense of contentment.

38 *Cherokee Advocate*, 16 November 1844. For various perspectives on the explosion of the *Lucy Walker*, see the interviews of Betty Robertson, Rawick, *American Slave*, 7:267, and Lucinda Vann, Rawick, *American Slave*, 12:349–50. Also see Grant Foreman, "Reminiscences of Mr. R. P. Vann."

39 *Cherokee Advocate*, 21 November 1844.

40 George Michael Murrell (1808–?), a European American man born in Lynchburg, Virginia, was a wealthy merchant and slaveholder who owned businesses in Park Hill and Tahlequah. In 1834 he married Minerva Ross (1818–55), daughter of Lewis and Fannie Holt Ross and niece of Cherokee Chief John Ross. See Moulton, *Papers*, 2:729, and Grant Foreman, *The Five Civilized Tribes*, 382, 402, and 406. In 1839 George M. Murrell relocated with his wife, Minerva Ross Murrell, during the forced removal of Cherokees to the West. Their plantation home in Park Hill, Indian Territory, was built around 1845. In the past several decades, the house has benefited from several renovation projects. The Murrell home, also referred to as "Hunter's Home," is the only surviving antebellum plantation building in the Cherokee Nation in Oklahoma. Free tours of the house continue to be conducted today.

41 Before removal Cherokee John Benge (1796?–1853) lived in Walker County, Georgia, and held property in Alabama. He was head of a Cherokee removal detachment, 1838–39. After removal he resettled in Skin Bayou (later Sequoyah) District, Cherokee Nation. See Moulton, *Papers*, 2:716; *Cherokee Advocate*, 17 August 1853; and Grant Foreman, *The Five Civilized Tribes*, 286 and 382.

42 *Cherokee Advocate*, 22 May 1845. The advertisement for Spencer also appeared in the following five weekly issues of the *Cherokee Advocate*.

43 Ibid.

44 For whites and blacks alike, there was often an "ignorance of geography, and blacks usually knew only what they had observed after being taken from one section to another or what they had been told by others." Franklin and Schweninger, *Runaway Slaves*, 109.

45 *Cherokee Advocate*, 23 October 1845. Peter Hildebrand (1782–1851) was a

prominent slave owner in the Cherokee Nation in Tennessee and later in Indian Territory. He was one of five children of German-born John Hilde-brand and Barbara Eaker. After Eaker died John Hildebrand married Cherokee Susannah Womancatcher in Tennessee; they had four children. John Hildebrand became a member of the Cherokee Nation due to his relationship with Cherokee Susannah Womancatcher. Peter Hildebrand married Cherokee Elizabeth Harlan (1793–1826) in Tennessee. Before removal, he lived in McMinn County, Tennessee. He was head of one of the Cherokee detachments in 1838–39. After removal, he settled in Dela-ware District, Cherokee Nation. For more information on Peter Hilde-brand, see Moulton, *Papers*, 2:725, and Starr, *History of the Cherokee Indians*.

46 *Cherokee Advocate*, 18 September 1848. The same advertisement for Harvey also appeared in the following three weekly issues of the *Cherokee Advocate*.

47 Franklin and Schweninger, *Runaway Slaves*, 59. Also see Henry Bibb's narrative for descriptions of his unsuccessful attempts to free his wife, Malinda, and child, Frances.

48 *Cherokee Advocate*, 3 September 1849. For another example of an enslaved person suspected of running away to see his wife, see the reward adver-tisement for George, who left his owner's residence on 15 April 1849 and "had a wife at Mr. N. B. Denenburg's near Evansville, and it is thought he has returned to that neighbourhood." *Cherokee Advocate*, 30 April 1849. The same advertisement for George also appeared in the following three weekly issues of the *Cherokee Advocate*. Also see Moses Perryman's notice for his runaway slave. *Cherokee Advocate*, 6 January 1852.

49 *Cherokee Advocate*, 3 September 1849. This advertisement also appeared in the following issues of the *Cherokee Advocate*: 10 September 1849; 17 Sep-tember 1849; 24 September 1849; 1 October 1849; 8 October 1849 (in English and Cherokee languages); 15 October 1849 (in English and Cher-okee languages); 22 October 1849 (in English and Cherokee languages); and 29 October 1849 (in English and Cherokee languages). The same reward ad reappeared (with the reward increased to fifty dollars) in the following issues of the *Cherokee Advocate*: 21 January 1850; 28 January 1850; 4 February 1850; 11 February 1850; 18 February 1850; 25 February 1850; 4 March 1850; 11 March 1850; 18 March 1850; 25 March 1850; 1 April 1850;

8 April 1850; 15 April 1850; and 22 April 1850. All advertisements for the fifty-dollar reward were in English only.

50   Franklin and Schweninger, *Runaway Slaves*, 25.

51   See *Cherokee Advocate*, 30 January 1845, 31 January 1848, and 16 July 1849.

52   *Cherokee Advocate*, 13 April 1848.

53   See *Cherokee Advocate*, 29 July 1847.

54   For examples of pregnant women and mothers running away with their children, see Franklin and Schweninger, *Runaway Slaves*, 63–65.

55   Rawick, *American Slave*, 7:267–68. Betty Robertson's father had worked aboard the *Lucy Walker* and died when that vessel exploded in 1844. Robertson also recalled how "Young Master" Joe Vann, son of Joseph Vann, "never whip his slaves, but if they don't mind good he sell them off sometimes. He sold one of my brothers and one sister because they kept running off." Ibid., 267.

56   Captain John Drew's recollection provides most of the details regarding the runaway attempt of the Cherokee and Creek slaves in November 1842. *Letters Received by the Office of Indian Affairs*, Statement of Captain John Drew, 3 January 1843, National Archives and Records Administration. For an excellent discussion of this runaway attempt, see Littlefield and Underhill, "Slave Revolt," 121. Also see Rudi Halliburton, *Red over Black*, 82.

57   Littlefield and Underhill, "Slave Revolt," 121–22. Halliburton argues that the number of runaways in this incident was significantly larger. He states, without citing any supporting evidence, that "some two hundred or more slaves belonging to Joseph Vann, Lewis Ross and other Cherokees in the Canadian District . . . were joined in the revolt by slaves from the Creek Nation." Rudi Halliburton, *Red over Black*, 82.

58   Statement of Captain John Drew, 3 January 1843. The runaways did not surrender to the group of Creeks and Cherokees; instead, they "entrenched themselves, and a battle ensued in which two of their numbers were killed, twelve were captured and the rest escaped. The pursuing parties returned home for reinforcements." Littlefield and Underhill, "Slave Revolt," 122.

59   Statement of Captain John Drew, 3 January 1843. A man named Chisholm captured the Choctaw runaways and turned them over to James Edwards,

Billy Wilson, and an unidentified Cherokee man, to be returned to their owners in the Choctaw Nation. While on route to the Choctaw Nation, the Cherokee man became separated from Edwards and Wilson.

60   Ibid.

61   See Cherokee Nation, *Constitution and Laws of the Cherokee Nation: Passed at Tahlequah, Cherokee Nation, 1839−1851*, 62−63. A copy of the claim submitted by Captain John Drew, dated 22 December 1842, for his expenses in recapturing the runaways of the attempted escape of 1842 is included in the John Drew Papers at the Thomas Gilcrease Museum in Tulsa, Oklahoma. The claim specifically states "claim of John Drew, captain of a company authorized to pursue certain runaway negroes." The claim is for the sum total of $351.80½. At the end of the claim is a note indicating that "the committee and council settled the foregoing claims of John Drew."

62   See Moulton, *Papers*, 2:721−22, and Carolyn Thomas Foreman, "Early History of Webbers Falls." During the Civil War, Captain Drew served as commander of the 1st Cherokee Regiment.

63   Statement of Captain John Drew, 3 January 1843.

64   Ibid.

65   Ibid.

66   Ibid. Also see Littlefield and Underhill, "Slave Revolt," 123.

67   Statement of Captain John Drew, 3 January 1843. Drew believed that Moses, one of Joseph Tally's slaves, had killed James Edwards, and John, one of William Mackey's slaves, had killed Billy Wilson.

68   In their excellent article on the escape of November 1842, Daniel F. Littlefield Jr. and Lonnie E. Underhill posit that the presence and influence of recently freed African Seminoles in the area could be construed as a contributing factor, as well as a partial explanation, for the laws restricting the movement of "free Negroes" in the Cherokee Nation. The impact of enslaved and free Seminoles on enslaved African Cherokees in the area is unknown; yet Littlefield and Underhill argue that the "likelihood is great that there was intercourse between them, especially before Cherokee legislation limited the movement of slaves." Littlefield and Underhill, "Slave Revolt," 126. Moreover, the "result of the easy relationship be-

tween Seminole slaves and masters, the large numbers of blacks to whom the titles were contested, and the great numbers who claimed to be free was a sizeable group of black people in a slave territory, who lived with little or no control on their activities, thereby setting an example, which slave owners in the surrounding regions feared." Ibid., 127.

69 *St. Louis Argus*, 23 July 1841. The *St. Louis Argus*, also known as the *Missouri Argus*, initially began as a weekly publication in 1835. From 1838 onward, the newspaper appeared on a daily basis, until its dissolution in 1841. Another *St. Louis Argus* was established in 1912. This newspaper is an African American newspaper, which still remains in existence today. The *St. Louis Argus* article is discussed in Rucker, "The Story of Slave Uprising." Also see also Carolyn Thomas Foreman, "Early History of Webbers Falls," 458–59.

70 *St. Louis Argus*, 23 July 1841.

71 Ibid. Although there is no further documentation of slave insurrections within the Cherokee Nation, the *Cherokee Advocate* included articles specifically regarding black insurrections in other countries. There are accounts of black insurrections in Martinique, Haiti, St. Croix, and Brazil. *Cherokee Advocate*, 24 July 1848, 31 July 1848, 21 August 1848, and 14 May 1849.

72 *Niles' National Register*, 7 August 1841.

73 *Niles' National Register*, 14 August 1841.

74 Cherokee Nation, *Constitution and Laws of the Cherokee Nation: Passed at Tahlequah, Cherokee Nation, 1839–1851*, 71. In his 1932 article about the slave uprising in 1841, Alvin Rucker attempted to connect it with the passage of this act. Rucker, "The Story of Slave Uprising."

75 Dale and Litton, *Cherokee Cavaliers*, 30. In this letter, dated 4 April 1846, H. L. Smith also mentioned several incidents in the Cherokee Nation of murder and stolen slaves.

76 Such revolts occurred in other parts of Indian Territory. Choctaw freedman Squire Hall recalled his mother's account of a slave uprising on the Hall plantation in the Choctaw Nation in 1860 or 1861. During this uprising, enslaved people murdered three of the four Hall sons. See Grant Foreman, *Indian Pioneer*, 92:78.

77 Rawick, *American Slave*, 12:187.

Chapter 2

1 For works dealing with slave resistance in the United States and the Caribbean, see Aptheker, *American Negro Slave Revolts*; Bracey, Meier, and Rudwick, *American Slavery*; Craton, *Testing the Chains*; Franklin and Schweninger, *Runaway Slaves*; Gaspar, *Bondmen and Rebels*; Gaspar and Geggus, *A Turbulent Time*; Geggus, *Slave Resistance*; Genovese, *From Rebellion to Revolution*; Okihiro, *In Resistance*; and Peter H. Wood, *Black Majority*.

2 Camp, *Closer to Freedom*.

3 As already stated, part of the reason for this void in Indian and African American historiography is that some scholars have argued that Indian slave owners were not as cruel as European American slave owners, especially when compared to those in the southeastern United States. Because of this reasoning, historians have not been compelled to pursue this topic.

4 Rawick, *American Slave*, 12:179. In February 1843, when Mary Lilley arrived with her husband, missionary John B. Lilley, at the Koweta Mission in the Creek Nation, she recalled having to deal with the troublesome nature of a particular hired slave. In her diary, she explained that she was not "accustomed to managing such servants as they had out there and the woman we had there was past managing an Indian raised Negress, just impossible to make her do anything only just what she pleased." Another woman, Miss Thompson "had tried her and in the end finished by giving her a whipping, a great big strapping black woman," but Mary Lilley stated that she "could not muster up courage to do that." This enslaved woman "belonged to Sanford Perriman," so Lilley "dismissed her and tried another one, she was an English speaking woman who did very well." (Mrs. John B.) Lilley, Diary of Mrs. John B. Lilley, 1842–57, 13–14.

5 Rawick, *American Slave*, 12:179–80.

6 Rawick, *American Slave*, 7:346.

7 Ibid., 346–47.

8 Doran, "Population Statistics of Nineteenth-Century Indian Territory," 501.

9 Baker and Baker, *The WPA Oklahoma Slave Narratives*, 465. Charlotte Johnson White's interview is one of the Oklahoma ex-slave interviews that was published for the first time in Baker and Baker's book.

10   Ibid.

11   Ibid. She had made her way into the Choctaw Nation. Skullyville is located in the northeast corner of the Choctaw Nation. After being recaptured, White was given "away to my Aunt Easter Johnson, but she was a mean woman—mean to everybody." Ibid.

12   Rawick, *American Slave*, 7:347.

13   Freedman Daniel Webster Burton also describes his Indian mistress-owner—a Chickasaw woman who was married to an Englishman. Rawick, *American Slave*, 12:82. For more on the position of European American women in the plantation complex, see Clinton, *The Plantation Mistress*, and Fox-Genovese, *Within the Plantation Household*.

14   See Perdue, *Cherokee Women*; Yarbrough, "Legislating Women's Sexuality"; and Yarbrough, *Race and the Cherokee Nation*.

15   Grant Foreman, *Indian Pioneer*, 27:335.

16   Ibid., 336.

17   Rawick, *American Slave*, 7:13.

18   Cherokee Nation, *Laws of the Cherokee Nation adopted by the Council at Various Periods*, 18.

19   Ibid., 139. Cherokee authorities punished horse thieves accordingly. For example, on 7 September 1848, "a Cherokee convicted of horse stealing was punished with one hundred stripes" in Saline District, Cherokee Nation. *Cherokee Advocate*, 11 September 1848.

20   There were also advertisements in the *Cherokee Advocate* for enslaved people who were initially assumed to be kidnapped but later simply returned on their own accord or were found. For example, in the 15 May 1848 issue of the *Cherokee Advocate*, an article stated: "We learn that a negro child, four or five years old, was kidnapped on last Wednesday evening from Mrs. Vann, mother of Joseph and David Vann, in Saline District." However, in the next issue on 22 May 1848, another article stated: "The negro child, belonging to Mrs. Vann, which was supposed to have been kidnapped, has been found. It had been absent four or five days when discovered in the woods, by a Cherokee."

21   *Cherokee Advocate*, 26 February 1846. The same advertisement also appeared in the following six weekly issues of the *Cherokee Advocate*. Many African Cherokee slaves in the Cherokee Nation understood and spoke

both English and Cherokee, which proved to be beneficial to enslaved people not only while in the Cherokee Nation but also while running away from their owners.

22 Franklin and Schweninger, Runaway Slaves, 273.

23 Cherokee Advocate, 26 March 1846.

24 Ibid.

25 Madison Gerring (commonly referred to as Mat Guering) and some of his associates, including Cherokee James Starr Jr., Samuel McDaniel, and James Coleston (identified as a "Cherokee man"), were often pursued by groups of Cherokees because of their criminal activities in the Nation, particularly murder and robbery. James Starr Sr. was a primary supporter of the Treaty Party and had been one of the signers of the Treaty of New Echota in 1835. As a result, he was one of the targets of the 1839 calculated assassination of treaty signers. However, unlike Elias Boudinot, Major Ridge, and John Ridge, the three treaty signers who had been assassinated, James Starr Sr. and Stand Watie had escaped the attempt on their lives. As a result of their support for their father and opposition to Chief John Ross and his party, the Starr men wreaked havoc on Ross supporters and sympathizers. Because of his bitterness toward the Starrs and the turmoil they created in the postremoval period, Chief John Ross issued a proclamation in 1845 that guaranteed rewards if these men were apprehended and delivered dead or alive to the "proper authorities" in the Cherokee Nation. The rewards ranged from $500 each for the apprehension of Ellis West or Samuel McDaniel to $1,000 each for the apprehension of Thomas Starr, Ellis Starr, or Ben Starr. For more information on each of the fugitives, see the reward notice appearing initially in the 16 January 1845 issue of the Cherokee Advocate.

The Cherokee Advocate often included articles on the criminal activities of Guering and others. In the 11 February 1847 issue of the Cherokee Advocate, three articles recounted the efforts to arrest these men on 6 February 1847. After a confrontation between the "banditti" and "a number of Cherokees, with an escort of Dragoons from Fort Gibson," members of the "banditti" escaped, though it was reported that some were seriously injured. One of the three articles noted that Samuel McDaniel, one of the "banditti" who was shot during the incident on 6 February, had been "killed by a company of twenty or thirty Cherokees" on 9 February.

26 *Cherokee Advocate*, 26 November 1846.

27 For details about the recovery, see *Cherokee Advocate*, 4 February 1847.

28 *Cherokee Advocate*, 19 November 1846.

29 Cherokee Nation, *Constitution and Laws of the Cherokee Nation: Passed at Tahlequah*, 71.

30 Ibid.

31 See, for example, Horton and Horton, *In Hope of Liberty*, and Schafer, *Becoming Free, Remaining Free*.

32 Free African Americans in the South "were forced to maintain constant vigilance against being thrust back into bondage. They remained cautious about traveling, circumspect in their dealings with whites, and sometimes even wary about their relationship with slaves." In the southern United States, the authorities often arrested and imprisoned free people of color, as some were erroneously deemed runaways. "Often illiterate, without papers, and at the mercy of whites, they found it difficult to prove that they were free men and women. In addition, the general assumption was that blacks were slaves until they could prove otherwise." Franklin and Schweninger, *Runaway Slaves*, 183–84.

33 *Cherokee Advocate*, 7 October 1847.

34 *Cherokee Advocate*, 11 November 1847.

35 Ibid.

36 Cherokee Nation, *Laws of the Cherokee Nation adopted by the Council at Various Periods*, 156. In her book, Tiya Miles evocatively relates the story of the multiracial family of Captain Shoe Boots, Doll, and their descendants. Miles, *Ties That Bind*. Theda Perdue briefly mentioned Captain Shoe Boots and his 1824 petition to the Cherokee National Council "to recognize the legitimacy and citizenship of his three children with a black slave." The National Council "granted the request on the condition that 'Capt. Shoe Boots cease begetting any more children by his said Slave *woman*.'" Perdue, *Slavery*, 84–85.

37 Franklin and Schweninger, *Runaway Slaves*, 193.

38 Miles, *Ties That Bind*, 177.

39 *Cherokee Advocate*, 19 February 1849. John T. Trezevant was mayor of South Memphis from January 1848 to January 1849. See *Memphis Daily Inquirer*, 4 January 1848, and Walk, *Memphis Executive and Legislative Government*, 27.

40 After John Brown returned to Tahlequah, Cherokee Nation, he attempted to investigate the situation further. Brown wrote Trezevant indicating "that a will made by the mistress of Pegy's [*sic*] mother, liberating her and her children, had been stolen—or lost—but that the witnesses to it, and the person who drew it, were all living." *Cherokee Advocate*, 19 February 1849.

41 Ibid.

42 Ibid.

43 Ibid.

44 Ibid.

45 Ibid. (emphasis added). A notice regarding the acquittal to which Vann referred appeared in the Cherokee newspaper. The notice stated that "the trial of Kah-lon-to-li-ta, in Canadian [District] last week, on the charge of having sold certain free negroes into slavery, resulted in his acquittal, as is alleged, through the refusal of one of the witnesses, to answer only such questions as he saw proper. The suit will probably be brought up in another form and against another party, and its actual merits be thus reached." *Cherokee Advocate*, 9 September 1847.

46 *Cherokee Advocate*, 19 February 1849 (emphasis added).

47 Ibid.

48 *Cherokee Advocate*, 1 October 1850.

49 In January 1848 an article in the Cherokee newspaper mentioned that "Calvin and Wm. Shores have been arrested in Arkansas, and taken to Van Buren for trial, for dealing in certain free negroes from this Nation. We know nothing about the case, but our impression is, that villainy has been practiced by others if not by them, in the way alleged—and if so, shall be glad to see justice done." *Cherokee Advocate*, 6 January 1848.

50 *Cherokee Advocate*, 1 October 1850. An article in the next issue of the *Cherokee Advocate* clarified exactly who purchased Peggy and Betsy. "In our remarks in reference to Peggy and Betsey, claiming to be Cherokees, and suing for the same in the State of Mississippi, we made a mistake, by representing Mr. Wair as the purchaser of Peggy and Betsey from the Shores'. It should

be L. P. C. Burford, purchaser of the Shores', and Mr. Wair acting Agent for the said Burford." *Cherokee Advocate*, 8 October 1850.

51 *Cherokee Advocate*, 1 October 1850.

52 Ibid.

53 Ratified on 18 September 1850, the Fugitive Slave Act of 1850 empowered and supported slave owners in their attempts to recapture runaways throughout the United States.

Chapter 3

1 For an excellent overview of the political and constitutional evolution of four of the southeastern Indian nations, see Champagne, *Social Order and Political Change*.

2 Sturm, *Blood Politics*, 55.

3 Ibid., 56.

4 Rawick, *American Slave*, 12:128. For one analysis of Choctaw slave owners in terms of their blood classification, see Jeltz, "The Relations of Negroes and Choctaw and Chickasaw Indians."

5 I use the term "mixed blood"; however, other terms have been proposed in order to critique notions of race, language, and meaning. Sharon P. Holland applies Gerald Vizenor's term "crossblood" instead of "mixed blood" in order to "make a point about language and terminology; to be a mixed blood African-American is to be counted among the thousands of African-Americans who have the *knowledge* of some European and/or Native ancestry, but to be a crossblood is to *identify* as such, to read the 'racial' categories on the U.S. census as bogus and to consistently cross the borders of ideological containment." Holland, "If You Know I Have a History," 335 (emphasis in original). Also see Vizenor, *Crossbloods*, vii.

6 For an extensive discussion of the emergence of "mixed bloods" in southeastern Indian nations in the colonial era, see Perdue, *"Mixed Blood" Indians*.

7 Hitchcock, *A Traveler in Indian Territory*, 187. Scholars have made similar observations regarding differences among Indian slave owners with whom enslaved African Indians interacted while living in Indian Territory. Kenneth W. Porter acknowledged that the institution of slavery "took various forms among the different tribes and with individual mem-

bers of the same tribe." Porter, "Relations between Negroes and Indians," 321. James Hugo Johnston even coined a phrase for a specific type
of Indian slaveholder. Instead of generalizing about the conditions of
enslavement created by Indian slaveholders, Johnston argued that one
cannot describe the harsh treatment of enslaved people as representative of the interactions between "the Negro and the American Indian."
Rather, "they are to be regarded as conditions existing between the Negro
and the Indian who had become, more correctly speaking a 'Southern-
white-slave-holding-Indian.' " Johnston, "Documentary Evidence," 36.

8   Rawick, *American Slave*, 12:315.

9   In their WPA interviews, African Indian freedpeople not only differentiated between "full bloods" and "mixed bloods" but also described the
differences they observed or perceived among masters of various nations.
Creek freedwoman Mary Grayson briefly compared people enslaved by
Creeks and those enslaved by whites: "I have had people who were slaves
of white folks back in the old states tell me that they had to work awfully
hard and their masters were cruel to them sometimes, but all the Negroes
I knew who belonged to Creeks always had plenty of clothes and lots to
eat and we all lived in good log cabins we built." Rawick, *American Slave*,
7:117. Like Grayson, Creek freedwomen Lucinda Davis and Nellie Johnson suggested that enslaved African Creeks were allowed more mobility
and worked with less restrictions than people enslaved by white, Cherokee, or Choctaw owners. Ibid., 55 and 157.

10 Rawick, *American Slave*, 12:293. Thomas ("Tom") Starr participated in
a range of criminal activities in the Cherokee Nation. Starr's associates included Mat Guering, James Starr Jr., Samuel McDaniel, and James
Coleston. In 1845 the reward for the apprehension of Thomas Starr was
$1,000. For more on Thomas Starr, see the reward notice appearing
initially in the *Cherokee Advocate*, 16 January 1845.

11 Rawick, *American Slave*, 12:293.

12 Ibid., 295.

13 Ibid., 293. Only a few interviewees actually participated in the forced
relocation of Indians to Indian Territory in the 1830s. In fact, those who
described this kind of migration from the United States to Indian Territory did so by recollecting what older relatives had related to them about

their experiences. See, for example, the WPA Oklahoma interviews of Jack
Campbell, Eliza Hardrick, Nellie Johnson, and Ned Thompson.

14 Regarding the complicated nature of sexual interactions between en-
slaved women and white masters, see Bush, *Slave Women in Caribbean
Society*; Hine and Wittenstein, "Female Slave Resistance"; and Jennifer L.
Morgan, *Laboring Women*.

15 Rawick, *American Slave*, 12:74.

16 The interviews of Choctaw freedwoman Peggy McKinney Brown and her
son Charley Brown also illustrate the generational differences of enslaved and free people in Indian Territory. Unlike comments made by his
mother, comments by Charley Moore Brown, who identified himself as a
"freedman citizen of the Choctaw Tribe, quarter blood Choctaw Indian
and three quarter negro," painted a positive portrait of the Choctaws with
whom he interacted in the post–Civil War era in the Choctaw Nation.
Ibid., 75. Although most of Charley Brown's comments are positive, his
personal memory of his interaction with Choctaws is interspersed with
other information he received from his father. By the time Charley Brown
was born, his father was a free man. Nevertheless, Charley Brown's
(re)telling of his father's story indicates the type of transfer of knowledge
that occurred between older generations and younger generations, and
how that knowledge was further incorporated into the memories and
stories of future generations.

17 In his interview, Cherokee freedman Morris Sheppard also referred to his
mother being "a Crossland negro before she come to belong to Master
Joe and marry my pappy, and I think she come wid old Mistress and
belong to her." Rawick, *American Slave*, 7:285. In Mary Grayson's interview she referred to herself as a "native." She explained that she was
"what we colored people call a 'native.' That means that I did not come
into the Indian country from somewhere in the Old South, after the War,
like so many negroes did, but I was born here in the Old Creek Nation,
and my master was a Creek Indian." Ibid., 115. In their WPA interviews,
formerly enslaved people explained two different connotations of the
term "crossland Negro." In the antebellum period, those born in Indian
Territory were "natives." "Crossland Negroes" were born in the East and
were initially owned by European Americans. After the Civil War, "cross-

land Negroes" were neither born nor raised in Indian Territory but migrated to the region in the final decades of the nineteenth century.

18 Rawick, *American Slave*, 12:234.

19 Ibid., 235.

20 Ibid. Though Nave stated his father's enslaver's name was Henry Nave in this part of the interview, at the end of the interview he referred to this owner as Daniel Nave. Cornelius Nave's description of his hair is particularly effective and telling as hair, especially hair length and texture, is often used as an indicator of racial classification.

21 Rawick, *American Slave*, 7:344.

22 Ibid., 347.

23 Ibid.

24 Though previously enslaved African Cherokees like Milton Starr, Sarah Wilson, and Cornelius Nave were raised among their Cherokee kin, other freedpeople recalled only a tenuous connection to their Indian relatives. See, for example, C. G. Samuel's comments about his mother being "half Creek Indian." Rawick, *American Slave*, 12:267. Some explicitly used the language of blood quantum in their description of their Indian connections. Creek freedman Richard Franklin declared that his mother, Thamore Franklin, "was one-fourth Creek Indian and was married to a negro slave, Fred Franklin, who was a slave of James Yargee of the Creek Nation." Franklin was very specific about his racial and ethnic composition. He stated, "I am one-eighth Creek Indian and seven-eights negro." Ibid., 132. The fact that Franklin highlighted his blood quantum in specific terms reveals not only his awareness of his "mixed blood" racial identity but also the increasing significance of blood quantum in relation to Indian membership requirements in the twentieth century. By declaring his blood quantum, he perhaps hoped to counter any external judgments that would claim his multiracial identity as imaginary or questionable in any way. Although not invoking blood quantum, Cherokee freedwoman Rachel Aldrich Ward highlighted her connection to a prominent Cherokee citizen. She explained that her father always stated "he was part Indian account of his mamma was a Cherokee Indian girl name Downing." Ward recognized the significance of the Downing name and proudly explained that her father's Downing connection made him "some kin to

Chief Downing who was a big man among the Cherokees after the Civil War when the Indians stop fighting amongst themselves." Ibid., 360. Indeed, Lewis Downing was elected principal chief of the Cherokee Nation after the Civil War. He served in this capacity until his death in 1872. Ward's interjection of this reference to Lewis Downing served as concrete evidence of her family's connection to a prominent Cherokee. Such an affiliation with a principal chief further authenticated her family's status within the Cherokee Nation. A few freedpeople, though neither born nor raised in Indian Territory, referred to their familial connections to Cherokees. See the interviews of Sam Jordan, ibid., 197; Mattie Logan, Rawick, *American Slave*, 7:187; and Sweetie Ivery Wagoner, Rawick, *American Slave*, 12:354.

25 Smith's testimony of his family's situation parallels the complicated status of "free Negroes" living in Indian Territory during the antebellum period. One of the most documented stories is that of the Beams family. For more information about this family, see Littlefield and Littlefield, "The Beams Family."

26 Rawick, *American Slave*, 12:281.

27 Ibid., 357. Although not stating the names of her father's parents, Walker mentioned that her "paternal grandparents took the name of their master Clem Rogers, as was the custom among the slaves." Ibid. Agnes Walker also indicated in her interview that Clem Rogers, "father of the famous Will Rogers . . . was a good friend of the family." Ibid., 358. Cherokee slave owner Clem (Clement Vann) Rogers was the father of humorist, actor, and social commentator Will Rogers (1879–1935). By incorporating this information about the Rogers family's slaveholding past, Walker highlights one dimension of the Rogers family that is often misrepresented or denied. For example, in Lary May's book, his examination of Will Rogers's Cherokee roots includes a brief discussion of Rogers's father Clem V. Rogers, whom he neglects to mention enslaved African Cherokees. Although May identifies Cherokees as slaveholding people, his description of them as such is inaccurate. He stated, "though many Cherokees grew rich off the exploitation of black labor, it was critical that they—unlike white southerners—continued the Native American slaveholding tradition that allowed slaves to buy their freedom and inter-

marry." Although a few Cherokee enslavers may have believed in such a tradition, this was clearly not a belief held by Cherokee slave owners in general. Lary May, *The Big Tomorrow*, 18–19. Will Rogers was born in Oolagah, Indian Territory, not far from Talala in what is currently Rogers County, Oklahoma, named for Clement Vann Rogers. Walker also correctly recalled Clem Vann Rogers's marriage to Mary Schrimsher. For more information on Clement Vann Rogers, see Love's biography of her grandfather, "Clement Vann Rogers," 389–99.

After the Civil War, Walker's maternal grandparents settled on her "grandmother's allotment of 80 acres in Rogers County, near Talala. Walker mentioned that her parents were buried on "Rabbs Creek, six miles west and one and one-half miles south of Talala." Talala was located in the Cooweescoowee District of the Cherokee Nation; it is currently located, as Walker indicated in her interview, in Rogers County, Oklahoma. Walker lived in her birthplace, Fort Gibson, for approximately two years, and then after the Civil War, she moved with her parents to Talala, where she "spent most of [her] life." In 1938, at the time of her interview, Walker still resided within the same general area; her home in Bartlesville, Oklahoma, was approximately twenty miles from Talala, Oklahoma. I have been unable to find any enrollment application or census card indicating Agnes Rogers Walker, or either of her parents, as enrolled Cherokee freedmen. Because Walker did not specifically state her maternal grandmother's name, I have been unable to check the Cherokee enrollment applications for her status or her Cherokee land allotment.

28 Rawick, *American Slave*, 12:351. Though generally stating that she was "part Indian," having been born and raised on Cherokee Jim Vann's plantation in the Cherokee Nation, Lucinda Vann was most likely "part Cherokee." The majority of slave owners in the Cherokee Nation cultivated small farms with only a few enslaved African Cherokees in such households, whereas a minority of slave owners had developed substantially larger plantations.

29 Ibid., 342.

30 Ibid., 344.

31 Perdue, *Slavery*, 58.

32 Rawick, *American Slave*, 12:344.

33 In his preface to *Black Indians*, William Loren Katz presented the particular point of view from which he examined the relationships between Indians, Africans, and African Americans compared to interactions between Europeans and Africans. "Europeans forcefully entered the African blood stream," he posited, "but Native Americans and Africans merged by choice, invitation, and love." Although there are cases where Indians, Africans, and African Americans indeed merged by "choice, invitation, and love," to place all African-Indian associations solely within the purview of a romanticized realm exemplifies some of the overly simplistic and problematic constructions of African-Indian relationships within the historical discourse. Katz's assertion fails to address the scope of interactions between enslaved African Indians and their Indian owners. Katz, *Black Indians*, 2.

Attempting to classify the multiracial and multicultural identities that often emerged primarily due to the range of historical interactions between Indians and people of African descent, Katz defined "Black Indians as people who have a dual ancestry or black people who have lived for some time with Native Americans." From Katz's definition African Americans who simply lived around Indians can be categorized as "Black Indians." In his work, Katz fails to point out explicitly which characteristics, life-styles, and worldviews may be utilized in defining "Black Indians." Although Katz's hypothesis is, at best, a gross generalization, his proposition elicits a number of questions. Exactly how and when do African Americans transform or become transformed into "Black Indians"? What sort of cultural process does this entail? Can we clearly differentiate between Indians and "Black Indians"? What are the cultural markers that can be used as defining signifiers of "Black Indians"? Does the term "Black Indians" reflect not only the hue of a people's skin color but also the substance of a people's sociocultural beliefs? Ibid., 7.

34 A. Irving Hallowell offered a potential framework for conceptualizing "Black Indians" in his discussion of what he called the "phenomenon of transculturalization." Hallowell defined transculturalization as "the process whereby individuals under a variety of circumstances are temporarily or permanently detached from one group, enter the web of social relations that constitute another society, and come under the influence of its cus-

toms, ideas, and values to a greater or lesser degree." Hallowell, "American Indians, White and Black," 523 (emphasis in original). The degree to which an individual undergoes transculturalization depends on a number of factors—"the age at which the process begins; the previous attitude toward the people of the second culture; length of residence; motivational factors; the nature of the roles played, and so on." Ibid. In the short section where Hallowell mentioned African Indian slaves of Indians, he remarked that "under these circumstances [enslavement] Negroes were assimilated to the same role in an Indian culture that they had played in white society. However there appears to have been a notable difference, for Negro slaves continued to run away from their white masters and offer themselves as slaves to the Indians. Negro freedmen, too, often chose to cast their lot with the Indians." Furthermore, Hallowell explained, "Indians intermarried with both slaves and freedmen. Thus like some whites there were Negroes who *became completely Indianized.* . . . Outside the South, the Indianization of Negroes occasionally occurred but it *did not involve slavery.*" Ibid., 522 (emphasis added). Hallowell describes enslaved African Indians as similarly placed compared to people enslaved by European Americans. Yet he intimates that the interactions between Indians and African Indians, free and enslaved, appeared different partially due to the frequency of intermarriage between African Americans and Indians. By so stating, Hallowell circumvents the complexity of the enslavement of African Indians in Indian nations; instead, he portrays a compressed reality that accentuates the traditional image of Indian nations as sites of refuge for enslaved people of African descent. Moreover, contrary to Hallowell's assessment, signs of acculturation or "Indianization" of enslaved African Indians occurred not only within the customary boundaries of the South but also further west in Indian Territory.

35 As Daniel Roche explained, "the historical study of clothes relates two levels of reality, that of dressing (*habillement*), which Roland Barthes identifies with speech in the Saussurian linguistic system, an individual act by which the individual adapts to himself what is proposed by the group, and that of costume or clothing (*vêtement*), seen from a sociological or historical standpoint as an element within a system which is formal,

normative and sanctioned by society." Roche, *The Culture of Clothing*, 45.
Also see Barthes, *The Fashion System*.

36 Roche, *The Culture of Clothing*, 43.

37 On the symbolic nature of Indian clothing, see Maurer, "Symbol and Identification"; Roediger, *Ceremonial Costumes*; Raczka, "Sacred Robes of the Blackfoot"; Shannon, "Dressing for Success"; Issenman, *Sinews of Survival*; and Sizemore, *Cherokee Dance*.

38 Maurer, "Symbol and Identification," 119.

39 Rawick, *American Slave*, 12:108–9.

40 Ibid., 113.

41 Ibid., 115.

42 Ibid.

43 In the end Clay benefited from his union with a Creek slave; he and his wife "got some of that Creek money and bought a house close to Honey Springs." Ibid., 115–16.

44 Galvin, *Through the Country of the Comanche*, 62 and 64.

45 As Timothy Shannon described, "Clothing exchanged in the Mohawk Valley [in the mid-eighteenth century] also challenged traditional cultural differences. Indians wore European clothing, but they did so in a distinctive way that contemporaries recognized as the 'Indian Fashion.' " Shannon, "Dressing for Success," 21. Both Europeans and Indians "recognized the peculiar type of costume known as the Indian fashion, but for entirely different reasons. Europeans distributed clothing in ways that allowed them to construct a visual sense of social difference and hierarchy among Indians. Indians incorporated this clothing into their dress for the decorative, ideological, and utilitarian value they attached to it. This blending of European goods with Indian custom enabled each side to interpret the clothing from its own perspective yet still use it as an agent of cultural exchange and mediation." Ibid., 25–26. In his work Shannon discussed the multiple ways Indians and Europeans wore Indian and manufactured European clothing to convey specific meanings, especially in particular trading and diplomatic scenarios.

46 Rawick, *American Slave*, 12:355. Cherokee Lucinda Hickey similarly described how "Cherokee men wore pants and coats made of buckskin and

were fringed. The pants were fringed down the outside of the leg and the coat was fringed around the bottom. They wore shirts made of homespun which were made loose like a sack. They called these their hunting shirts. The women wore dresses made of homespun which were made with tight fitting waists and real full skirts. These were made of the brightest colors." Grant Foreman, *Indian Pioneer*, 29:40.

47 Rawick, *American Slave*, 12:385–86.

48 Ibid., 385.

49 Ibid., 387.

50 Ibid., 311.

51 Although focusing on previously enslaved African Americans' memories of their experiences in the antebellum South, Helen Bradley Foster's work includes a few comments regarding clothing-related exchanges between African Americans and Indians. See Foster, *"New Raiments of Self,"* 238–39 and 261. Foster presents a brief discussion of tie dyeing in parts of Africa, as well as a comprehensive list of plant sources for dyeing clothes mentioned within ex-slave interviews. Ibid., 54–57 and 335–36. Also see White and White, *Stylin'*. For a critical socioeconomic analysis of Nigerian women indigo dyers from Abeokuta and the vital indigo dyeing industry in this region during the nineteenth century, see Byfield, *The Bluest Hands*.

52 As Theda Perdue explains, in traditionalist Cherokee homes "the only English-speaking person was frequently a bondsman. American Board missionaries reported in 1818 that all blacks in bondage to Cherokees spoke English." The missionaries thus "occasionally relied on bilingual slaves to translate their sermons. Furthermore, masters often turned to their slaves for aid in communicating with English-speaking visitors." Perdue, *Slavery*, 106. When an expedition to the Rocky Mountains in 1819 paused at Rocky Bayou, Arkansas, one of the visitors, Major Stephen H. Long, wrote in his journal: " 'Groves, our landlord, though unable to speak or understand our language, held some communication with us by means of signs, being occasionally assisted by a black girl, one of his slaves who interpreted the Cherokee language.' " Ibid. Listing the differences between Cherokee slavery and the institution in the southern states, Rudi Halliburton states, "slaves were used more extensively as

interpreters and business consultants, and many Cherokee slaves did not speak English." Halliburton, *Red over Black*, 143. In his work, Daniel F. Littlefield points out the extent of acculturation of enslaved African Indians in the Chickasaw Nation. By removal, "some families of blacks had been among the Chickasaws for generations. They knew no other language or culture. They had learned the Indian mode of agriculture and had adopted the Indians' diet, medicine and dress." Littlefield, *The Chickasaw Freedmen*, 25.

53 Creek freedman Ned Thompson mentioned that his grandfather, who survived the trek from Alabama to Indian Territory in the 1830s, had served as an interpreter from 1832 to 1866. Grant Foreman, *Indian Pioneer*, 112:179. In his journal documenting his 1845 expedition through Indian Territory, Lieutenant James W. Abert not only described the clothing worn by African Creeks in the Creek Nation, as previously mentioned, but also noted their ability to speak Indian languages. He related that they "are said to acquire the different Indian languages with great facility. . . . These people are supposed to be superior in intelligence to the Indians, who mostly have recourse to them in their intercourse with the whites." Galvin, *Through the Country of the Comanche Indians*, 64. Abert, like so many whites in various extensions of the British Empire around the world, viewed all who could speak in English as "superior in intelligence" to anyone who could not.

54 The work of Edward Sapir and Benjamin Whorf on language, and Indian languages in particular, explores the multiple meanings of language and the dynamic relationship between languages and worldviews—the Sapir-Whorf hypothesis of linguistic relativity. See Sapir, *Culture, Language and Personality*, and Whorf, *Language, Thought and Reality*.

55 Rawick, *American Slave*, 12:217.

56 Rawick, *American Slave*, 7:53.

57 A few African Indian freedpeople who were born in Indian Territory and learned Indian languages when they were young continued to remember specific Indian words several decades after emancipation. See the interview of Henry Henderson, Rawick, *American Slave*, 12:178.

58 The American Board of Commissioners for Foreign Missions (ABCFM) established its first mission, Brainerd Mission, among the Cherokees

in 1816, in Tennessee, under the direction of Cyrus Kingsbury. In 1818 Kingsbury instituted Mayhew Mission among the Choctaws in Alabama and Mississippi. He relocated with the Choctaws to Indian Territory and remained with them until his death in 1870. The first mission specifically created to work with the Western Cherokees was Dwight Mission, under the supervision of the ABCFM. It was originally launched in 1820 in Arkansas, by missionaries Cephas Washburn and Alfred Finney. As a result of the relocation of Western Cherokees to Indian Territory, in 1829 it was reestablished in Indian Territory, approximately thirty miles southeast of Fort Gibson. Named for Rev. Timothy Dwight (Yale College president and one of the organizers of the ABCFM), Dwight Mission, unlike many of the short-lived missions in Indian Territory, celebrated its 150th anniversary in Oklahoma in 1979. For more information, see West, *Missions and Missionaries*, 1–7. Also see Grant Foreman, "Dwight Mission."

59 Lockwood, Diary of Cassandra Sawyer Lockwood, 24–25.

60 As Daniel Littlefield Jr. explains, although the missionaries among the Chickasaws "discouraged lay preaching among the slaves, because 'of their ignorance, and for other reasons,' they encouraged them as leaders in prayer meetings." Missionaries "credited the increase in the number of full bloods attending their services to the efforts of a black slave who had 'been in the habit, for two or three years, of having a prayer-meeting in his hut every Wednesday evening.'" One night at the prayer meeting there were twenty-three Chickasaws among the fifty-five persons present. The prayer meetings were conducted by "Christian slaves" in the "Chickasaw language." As a result, Littlefield concluded, enslaved people "were used as instruments for extending a knowledge of the gospel to the Indians." Littlefield, *The Chickasaw Freedmen*, 9. Missionary G. Lee Phelps described how Creek John McIntosh often ridiculed the camp meetings of slaves early on; however, eventually he secretly "sought the council of an old negro slave, who led him to Him who 'came to seek and to save that which was lost.'" Foreman, *Indian Pioneer*, 8:216.

61 Rawick, *American Slave*, 7:266.

62 Ibid.

63 Rawick, *American Slave*, 12:249.

64 Ibid., 250–51.

65 See, for example, Farb and Armelagos, *Consuming Passions*; Brown and Mussell, *Ethnic and Regional Foodways*; and Counihan and Kaplan, *Food and Gender*.

66 I borrow this expression from Scapp and Seitz, *Eating Culture*.

67 Rawick, *American Slave*, 12:251.

68 Rawick, *American Slave*, 7:194 (emphasis added). Although Kiziah Love was enslaved by Frank Colbert, when she married Isom Love, enslaved by Sam Love (another "full blood Choctaw" living on a farm nearby), she took her husband's last name, thus Kiziah Love rather than Kiziah Colbert. Although born in the Cherokee Nation, near Tahlequah, Jane Battiest also remembered preparing food like the Choctaws after she had lived among the Choctaws for many years. In order to prepare one dish, "we beat our corn to make meal just like the Choctaws did, as there was no grist mills in the country. The only way to get bread was to beat the corn in the bowl made on one end of the block of wood. We made hominy as well as corn meal." Rawick, *American Slave*, 12:42. Cherokee E. F. Vann briefly mentioned how the Cherokees also used a mortar and pestle in preparing Cherokee dishes. Grant Foreman, *Indian Pioneer*, 95:59 and 63.

69 Polly Colbert's owners were Holmes Colbert and his wife, whom Colbert referred to as Miss Betsy (Love) Colbert. Colbert explained that her mother, Lisa, was enslaved by the Colbert family and her father, Tony, was owned by the Love family. In fact, when her master and mistress married, her parents were given to the newlyweds by their fathers as a wedding gift. Kiziah Love's interview also hints at the close connection between the Love family and Colbert family. Rawick, *American Slave*, 7:33–38.

Pashofa is a Chickasaw meal. A similar dish among the Choctaws is *ta fulla*. When prepared with meat, this Choctaw meal is called *tanchi lubona*.

70 Ibid., 34–35.

71 Ibid., 35. For detailed information on these instruments, as well as some Cherokee, Creek, Seminole, and Quapaw recipes for preparing corn-based dishes, see Muriel H. Wright, "American Indian Corn Dishes." Also see Hudson, "Choctaw Indian Dishes."

72 Rawick, *American Slave*, 12:123. Cole and other enslaved men in Indian Territory not only prepared game but also knew what was involved in

cooking game. "One way of preparing the dried meat for eating," he stated, "was to make a sort of hash. We put the meat in a mortar and beat it into small pieces. Then we boiled it in an iron pot. When it was done we poured grease over it, and it was good." Cole also described *ta fulla*, which was "made with hickory nuts and corn. First we dried the nuts. Then we beat them into a sort of mush in a mortar. We beat corn in a mortar, and sifted it. We mixed the corn and hickory nuts in a pot and boiled them." Ibid., 124. In addition to discussing his hunting experience in general, Choctaw freedman Daniel Webster Burton, born near Old Shawneetown in the Choctaw Nation, mentioned his participation in the fur trade economy in nineteenth-century Indian Territory. Like Jefferson Cole, he described the "abundance of game in this country at that time, such as deer, wild turkey, bear, wolves, panther and small game too numerous to mention." There was so much that "we never knew what it was to want for fresh wild meat of our own choice." Hunted animals provided not only meat to be eaten but also hides and fur to be sold. Burton proudly claimed that he had "sold as much as $90.00 worth of hides and furs to fur buyers at one time. We had everything we wanted. . . . I have tanned many a deer skin which could be used for coats and jackets and other purposes." Ibid., 83–84.

73 Ibid., 364. Born in 1846 in Indian Territory, Choctaw freedman Ed Butler indicated that "our mammies made all the medicine used from herbs gathered from the woods. We would take baskets into the woods and dig and gather herbs enough to last for months." Ibid., 88.

74 Ibid., 281. Creek freedman Jim Tomm described how "Indians used all kinds of barks, roots and herbs for medicine. That's why all us old negroes have got so many home remedies." Grant Foreman, *Indian Pioneer*, 112:303.

75 Grant Foreman, *Indian Pioneer*, 95:78.

76 Rawick, *American Slave*, 12:67–68.

77 Ibid., 68. "Cupping" is also a traditional Chinese medical treatment, most often used for pain resulting from the stagnation or obstruction of regular circulation. By applying heat or cutting the skin, cupping provides a way of curing certain conditions. The cupping process has been practiced in various parts of the world—from Eastern Europe to Central America.

78 Grant Foreman, *Indian Pioneer*, 24:498.

79 Ibid., 497.

80 See, for example, Fett, *Working Cures*.

81 Personal recollections from residents of Indian Territory often highlight women in this role. Ella Robinson, for example, described how "the old negro women always raised a few herbs for medicinal use." Grant Foreman, *Indian Pioneer*, 8:526.

82 Rawick, *American Slave*, 12:322.

83 Ibid., 92.

84 Ibid. The only information about the herbs and roots that Campbell disclosed was that "he always gathered his herbs and medicine in the Spring and in the Fall, and he is able to make many kinds of medicine." Ibid., 93.

85 As interviewer Bolinger pointed out, Campbell "in some instances as late as today, is called to see a sick Indian." Ibid., 92. The precious nature of this information makes sense with Campbell's admission that he still treated other persons even at the time of his interview. His knowledge about the herbs and roots still involved Indians, and perhaps African Indians, in his community and thus could not just be offered to Bolinger—a stranger to Campbell.

Chapter 4

1 Beginning in the early 1800s, the Moravians, Methodists, Baptists, and Presbyterians organized missions among the Cherokees, with a dual emphasis on Christianization and "civilization." The missionaries' presence served the needs of the Cherokee Nation in various ways, particularly in regard to the education of Cherokee youth. Missionary activity among the Cherokees began in 1800 with the establishment of a Moravian mission in Springplace, Georgia. The first mission established in Indian Territory was Protestant-associated Union Mission. Initially created in 1820 to serve the Osages, Union Mission eventually sought to minister as well to the Cherokees and the Creeks. In 1835, Union Mission was officially terminated. However, it continued to be used for housing and printing purposes. The American Board of Commissioners for Foreign Missions (ABCFM) established its first mission, Brainerd Mission, among the

Cherokees in 1816 in Tennessee. The first ABCFM mission working with the Western Cherokees was Dwight Mission, established in 1820 in Arkansas by missionaries Cephas Washburn and Alfred Finney. In 1829 Dwight Mission was reestablished in Indian Territory, approximately thirty miles southeast of Fort Gibson. For more information, see West, *Missions and Missionaries*, 1–7. Also see Grant Foreman, "Dwight Mission."

2   A number of missions and missionaries in Indian Territory became involved in controversies surrounding slavery in Indian nations. However, a few religious groups presented their positions in absolute terms. As Robert T. Lewit states, the American Baptist Missionary Union "took an inflexible stand against slavery. . . . On the other hand, the Southern Baptist Convention, the Methodist Episcopal Church South, and the Southern Presbyterian Board supported slavery. As a result, the problems which arose in the American Board's missions never had the opportunity to develop in these organizations." Lewit, "Indian Missions and Antislavery Sentiment," 41.

3   Although the specific question of slavery among the Cherokees and Choctaws emerged at the board's 1844 annual meeting, the issue of slavery in communities where ABCFM missionaries worked had been broached earlier by ABCFM missionaries in the Sandwich Islands (Hawaiian Islands). In 1837 three missionaries working in the Sandwich Islands, Rev. Jonathan S. Green, Rev. Peter Gulick, and Rev. H. R. Hitchcock, expressed their ardent concern for the ongoing existence of slavery in the Sandwich Islands and the need for the ABCFM's action in assisting with the abolition of slavery in this area. Rev. Green and Rev. Gulick wrote letters to the board directly. Rev. Hitchcock directed his letter to the antislavery newspaper, the *Emancipator*. To review the Sandwich Island missionaries' letters, see Whipple, *Relation*, 6–8. In response to these letters, and worried that abolitionism would undermine its mission work, the board adopted a resolution, the same year as the letters appeared, swiftly curtailing the printing of materials by ABCFM missionaries. Ibid., 9. Whipple's work presents a scathing critique of the inconsistencies in the Prudential Committee's demands on the ABCFM missionaries in the Cherokee and Choctaw nations, as well as on other missionaries in Hawaii, Asia, and Africa. In addition to these memorials, an ongoing correspondence occurred

between a few ABCFM missionaries and the board's secretaries on the issue of slavery. Rev. Cyrus Kingsbury, one of the most prominent ABCFM missionaries, voiced his opinions frequently to Secretary David Greene and Secretary Selah B. Treat, outlining the difficulty that would come from addressing this very issue. Rev. Kingsbury was particularly concerned about what he saw as the Choctaw Mission's dire need for hired slave labor. See, for example, the letter from Kingsbury to Greene, 27 December 1844, ABCFM, *Papers of the* ABCFM, microfilm, unit 6, series ABC 18.3.4, vol. 8 (Choctaw Mission, 1844–1859 Letters Ki–W), no. 8.

4   ABCFM, *Report at the Thirty-fifth Annual Meeting*, 66–69. The *Missionary Herald*, the official publication of the ABCFM, also included the annual reports and other relevant papers of the Prudential Committee and the ABCFM.

5   ABCFM, *Report at the Thirty-fifth Annual Meeting*, 66.

6   Ibid.

7   Ibid., 67.

8   Ibid., 69.

9   ABCFM, *Report at the Thirty-sixth Annual Meeting*, 54–63.

10 Initially the board selected Secretary David Greene for this trip as he was the board's corresponding secretary for the Indian missions. However, due to the grave state of his health, which even prevented him from attending the annual meeting in Buffalo, Greene requested that he be excused from this trip. Greene's situation resulted initially in a temporary delay of the trip. However, at the 1847 annual meeting, as a result of Greene's declining health, the board directed Secretary Selah B. Treat to replace Secretary Greene as corresponding secretary for the Indian missions. Treat served in this capacity from 1847 to 1876. The board's report of the annual meeting in 1848, held in Boston, included one of the more elaborate reports submitted by the Prudential Committee. This report, requested at the 1847 annual meeting, discussed the nature and extent of control of the board over ABCFM missionaries and mission churches, the existence and role of missionaries' "ecclesiastical liberty," and the board's responsibility for "the teaching of the missionaries, and for the character of the mission churches." ABCFM, *Report at the Thirty-ninth Annual Meeting*, 62–80. Also see Whipple, *Relation*, 59–82.

11 *Missionary Herald* 44, no. 10 (October 1848): 346.

12 Treat visited the ABCFM Cherokee Mission churches at Park Hill, Fairfield, Dwight, Mount Zion, and Honey Creek, as well as the ABCFM Choctaw Mission churches. For a list of the missionaries and other key employees associated with the Cherokee and Choctaw missions during that time, see *Missionary Herald* 44, no. 1 (January 1848): 12. The four primary European American ABCFM missionaries associated with the Cherokee Mission in Indian Territory were Worcester Willey, missionary at Dwight Mission; Elizur Butler, missionary and physician at Fairfield Mission; Samuel A. Worcester, missionary at Park Hill Mission; and Daniel S. Butrick, missionary at Mount Zion Mission. Dr. Elizur Butler and Reverend Samuel Austin Worcester served as missionaries among the Cherokees in Georgia before removal; they both were imprisoned in the summer of 1831 for their continued service to the Cherokees in opposition to the dictates of the State of Georgia. Dr. Elizur Butler arrived at the Fairfield Mission, Cherokee Nation, on 28 December 1839. Rev. Samuel A. Worcester relocated to the Cherokee Nation, Indian Territory, in May 1835. Worcester served initially at Dwight Mission and Union Mission briefly, before settling at Park Hill Mission in December 1836. As a result of his experience and expertise among the Cherokees, he supervised the other missions in the Cherokee Nation. Worcester was particularly successful in creating a printing press in the Cherokee Nation and published the Bible and other religious materials in the Cherokee language. Worcester died in the Cherokee Nation in April 1859. For more information about Dr. Elizur Butler and Rev. Samuel A. Worcester, see Bass, *Cherokee Messenger*.

13 The letter was written on behalf of Worcester Willey (Dwight Mission), Elizur Butler (Fairfield Mission), Samuel A. Worcester (Park Hill Mission), and Daniel S. Butrick (Mount Zion Mission). It is unclear whether the Cherokee preachers associated with these missions, like Stephen Foreman and John Huss, agreed with the sentiments of the letter.

14 *Missionary Herald* 44, no. 10 (October 1848): 352.

15 Ibid., 354.

16 Ibid. Indeed, at the beginning of their letter, the missionaries pointed out that Treat's visit with them in the Cherokee Nation "led to a conviction of

the propriety and expediency of expressing . . . some of our united views in relation to that difficult and delicate subject." The missionaries carefully explained their precarious position on this topic. "We are aware," they stated, "that we stand between two fires; in danger of displeasing, by what we may write, on the one hand, the people for whose good we labor, and on whose esteem and confidence our success must depend, and, on the other, the Christian community by whom we are sustained in our work. We do not say, in danger of displeasing the one or the other, but both at the same time, for opposite reasons." Nonetheless, they believed they "must ask the candor of all, and endeavor, frankly and kindly and meekly, to tell the truth." Ibid., 352 (emphasis in original). ABCFM missionaries working in the Choctaw Nation also wrote a separate letter to Secretary Treat, dated 31 March 1848, in response to their discussions with him on the subject of slavery in the Choctaw Nation. The eight people who cosigned the Choctaw Mission's letter to Treat were Cyrus Kingsbury, missionary at Pine Ridge Mission; Alfred Wright, missionary at Wheelock Mission; Cyrus Byington, missionary at Stockbridge Mission; Ebenezer Hotchkin, missionary at Good Water Mission; Charles C. Copeland, preacher at Norwalk Mission; David Breed Jr., steward at Pine Ridge Mission's Boarding School; Henry K. Copeland, steward at Wheelock Mission's Boarding School; and David H. Winship, steward at Stockbridge Mission's Boarding School. John C. Strong, missionary at Washita Mission, and Joshua Potter, preacher at Mount Pleasant Mission, did not sign this letter. Ibid., 355–58. The *Cherokee Advocate* also reprinted this letter from the Choctaw Mission to Treat in its 30 October 1848 issue.

17 For Treat's complete report, see *Missionary Herald* 44, no. 10 (October 1848): 346–52.

18 Ibid., 359. For the entire letter from Secretary Treat to the Choctaw Nation, see ibid., 358–62. The *Cherokee Advocate* reprinted the entire letter from Secretary Treat in its 30 October 1848 issue.

19 Letter from Cherokee Mission to Treat, 14 September 1848, ABCFM, *Papers of the ABCFM*, unit 6, series ABC 18.3.1, vol. 11 (Cherokees, 1822–1859, Documents, Reports, Letters), no. 75.

20 ABCFM, *Report at the Fifty-first Annual Meeting*, 137 and 145. Also see Whipple, *Relation*, 217–22. Although the Cherokee Mission had been discon-

tinued, the board explained that its connection with the missionaries continued. Indeed the closure of the Cherokee Mission did not translate into the termination of the "personal relations of the members of this mission to the Board, but leaves them at liberty to make such arrangements for the future as they shall severally judge proper; and the Committee will recognize their claim to such pecuniary aid, whenever they retire from their connection with the Board, as its rules, usages and means enable it to afford." ABCFM, *Report at the Fifty-first Annual Meeting*, 142.

21 *Missionary Herald* 44, no. 10 (October 1848): 352.

22 Ibid.

23 Grant Foreman, "Notes of a Missionary," 177.

24 Rawick, *American Slave*, 7:13.

25 Ibid., 287–88.

26 Ibid., 262.

27 For more on such spaces of secret, "invisible" slave spirituality, see Raboteau, *Slave Religion*.

28 Grant Foreman, "Notes of a Missionary," 178.

29 For example, Rev. Worcester Willey, ABCFM missionary at Dwight Mission, Cherokee Nation, for twenty years, remained at Dwight until he was forced to relocate to Fort Smith, Arkansas, and later to Fort Gibson, Cherokee Nation, to protect his family from Confederate forces. When the war ended, Willey returned to Andover, Massachusetts, where he died in 1899. Rev. Cyrus Kingsbury remained in the Choctaw Nation during the Civil War. He died in 1870 and was buried at Boggy Depot, Choctaw Nation. Although Rev. Samuel A. Worcester died in April 1859, he would probably have joined the number of missionaries who remained in Indian Territory during the Civil War.

30 Letter from John Ross to Lieutenant Colonel J. R. Kannady, 17 May 1861, Moulton, *Papers*, 2:468–69. For other examples of Chief John Ross's statements regarding the neutrality of the Cherokee Nation in the Civil War, see letter from John Ross to Henry M. Rector (governor of Arkansas), 22 February 1861, ibid., 464–65; John Ross's Proclamation to the People of the Cherokee Nation, 17 May 1861, ibid., 469–70; and letter from John Ross to Albert Pike, 1 July 1861, ibid., 476.

31 Letter from John Ross to Benjamin McCulloch, 17 June 1861, ibid., 474.

32 The Confederate victories early on in the war, especially at Wilson's Creek in Missouri on 10 August 1861, as well as Stand Watie's willingness to sign a strategic treaty with Albert Pike, forced Principal Chief Ross to join the Confederacy. The decision to form an alliance with the Confederacy was made formally at a general meeting of the Cherokees on 21 August 1861 at Tahlequah. See letter from John Ross, J. Vann, James Brown, John Drew, and William P. Ross to Brigadier General Benjamin McCulloch, 24 August 1861, ibid., 483. On 7 October 1861, Chief John Ross signed a treaty with Albert Pike confirming the Cherokees' alliance with the Confederacy. This treaty was ratified by the Cherokee National Council and the Confederate Congress. For a general overview of the treaty's main points, see Wardell, *A Political History*, 138–41.

33 Morris, Goins, and McReynolds, *Historical Atlas of Oklahoma*, 28. Jessie Randolph Moore highlighted nineteen battles in which Confederate Indian troops participated, including a few outside of Indian Territory. Moore, "The Five Great Indian Nations," 330–31. For an overview of Cherokee involvement in the Civil War, focusing on the efforts of Cherokee Stand Watie, see Hauptman, *Between Two Fires*, 41–61.

34 Grant Foreman, *Indian Pioneer*, 11:284–85. Also see Elizabeth Watts's entire interview, 277–97. In her recollection of the times, Elizabeth Watts referred to the Keetoowahs wearing crossed pins on their coats. Indeed, the Keetoowahs have often been regarded as the same organization as the "Pin Indians" or "Pins," who wore crossed pins on their shirts. Even though both groups were composed of Cherokees who espoused the continuance of traditional Cherokee ways, Janey E. Hendrix argues that they were two different organizations: "the Pins were a separate organization of activists that started among the militants of Goingsnake District, and while most of them were Keetoowahs it was not a requirement and there were many Keetoowahs who were not Pins." Hendrix, "Redbird Smith," 24. For an analysis of the religious, spiritual, and cultural foundation of the Keetoowah Society, see Minges, "The Keetoowah Society." For more information on the Keetoowahs, see Mooney, *Myths of the Cherokee*, 225, and McLoughlin, *The Cherokee Ghost Dance*, 467–68.

35 Adair, "The Indian Territory in 1878," 265. This issue of the *Chronicles of Oklahoma* reprinted William Penn Adair's speech in October 1878 at the fifth annual fair in Muskogee, Creek Nation, Indian Territory.

36 Slave narratives, written or dictated by enslaved people of African descent, represented one avenue for the expression of slaves' viewpoints in a public and international arena. Some narrators, like Frederick Douglass and Sojourner Truth, also articulated their thoughts in public antislavery meetings in the antebellum era.

37 James W. Duncan, "The Keetowah Society," 251.

38 "The Cherokee Question," Letter from Albert Pike to D. N. Cooley, 17 February 1866, 173.

39 Evan Jones worked with the Cherokees before removal and migrated with them to Indian Territory. Due to their beliefs, Evan and John Jones worked primarily with Cherokee conservatives or traditionalists who advocated the preservation of the Cherokees' traditional ways of life. Both men also assisted in the creation of the Keetoowah Society. U.S. Agent to the Cherokees George Butler removed John Jones from the Cherokee Nation in 1860, as a result of his relentless abolitionist views. During the Civil War, John Jones relocated to Kansas and continued his work among Cherokee Union supporters who had also temporarily moved to that area. After the termination of the Baptist mission in the Cherokee Nation at the outbreak of the war, Evan Jones joined his son in Kansas and reestablished his service to the Cherokee refugees in Kansas. For more information on Evan and John Jones, see McLoughlin, *Champions of the Cherokees*. Evan Jones, like Samuel A. Worcester, also worked on disseminating religious information in English and Cherokee to residents in the Cherokee Nation. Jones was instrumental in the publication of the *Cherokee Messenger*. See Routh, "Early Missionaries to the Cherokees," 461.

40 Founded in 1854 by George W. L. Bickley, the Knights of the Golden Circle supported the expansion of slavery not only in the United States, but also in Mexico, Central America, and the Caribbean. The "golden circle" represented the eventual inclusion of these areas as slave states or territories within the United States. For more on the Knights of the Golden Circle, see Crenshaw, "The Knights of the Golden Circle," 50.

41 The organizers of the Knights of the Golden Circle were previously asso-

ciated with the Ridge Party, including Stand Watie, William Penn Adair, James M. Bell (Stand Watie's brother-in-law), and E. C. (Elias Cornelius) Boudinot (son of executed Ridge Party leader Elias Boudinot).

42   As quoted in Rudi Halliburton, Red over Black, 119–20.

43   In addition, the Knights "assumed the offensive against the Ross adherents in order to protect their position in the Nation and to avoid, as it appeared to them, being crushed by Ross tyranny." Wardell, A Political History, 123. Also see letter from William Penn Adair to Stand Watie, 29 August 1861, regarding Ross's resolutions and the need to counter Ross's control over the Cherokee Nation, Cherokee Nation Papers, box 121, folder 4136, Western History Collections, University of Oklahoma, Norman. As Theda Perdue argues, "Watie's party effectively utilized southern proslavery rhetoric to mask the group's real motives [to dismantle Ross's control of the Cherokee Nation]. . . . The adoption of this rigid proslavery, antiabolition stance came easily to men who were in the main highly acculturated slaveholders." Perdue, Slavery, 130.

44   Rawick, American Slave, 7:288. For a description of these two groups and their actions specifically as it related to slaves, also see the interviews of Chaney Richardson, ibid., 257 and 259; Mary Grayson, ibid., 123; and Patsy Perryman, Rawick, American Slave, 12:252. In his interview, Creek freedman John Harrison also discussed the factionalism within the Creek Nation during the Civil War, ibid., 148–49.

45   Rawick, American Slave, 7:289.

46   Ibid., 288.

47   Born in the Cherokee Nation East, Georgia, in 1807, Cherokee Stephen Foreman served as assistant editor of the Cherokee newspaper, the Cherokee Phoenix, and later studied at Union Theological Seminary and Princeton Theological Seminary. Working closely with Rev. Samuel A. Worcester at the Park Hill Mission and Park Hill Mission Press, Rev. Stephen Foreman was instrumental in translating the Bible, hymnals, and other religious material from English to Cherokee. He preached at various sites throughout the Cherokee Nation during his lifetime. In addition to his religious work, Foreman also held several political positions in the Cherokee Nation, including superintendent of education, associate justice of the Supreme Court, and member of the Executive Council. Although he

worked with Rev. Samuel A. Worcester, Foreman's use of African Cherokee slaves in the development and success of his farm and other business
interests was not supported by Rev. Worcester. See McLoughlin, *The Cherokees and Christianity*, 84–85.

48 Stephen Foreman, Journal and Letters of Stephen Foreman, 36 (emphasis
in original).

49 Worcester Willey, Letters and Documents of the Worcester Willey Family
of the Cherokee Nation, 1864–75, Willey's undated report regarding the
condition of the Cherokee Nation during the Civil War, manuscript no.
M1034, chap. 2, 6, Western History Collections. Willey also poignantly
described the extent of the Cherokees' involvement in the Civil War and
the conditions of war in the Cherokee Nation. He believed "the Cherokees made greater sacrifices to keep their pledges & sustain the government of the United States, than any of her own citizens made, or perhaps
would have made in these circumstances. . . . Yet the war was not their
war—they fought & suffered for the United States, as they had promised
they would." In the end, the Cherokee Nation "was almost entirely deserted & laid waste, leaving us alone & unprotected, & in suspense night
and day, fearing what might come upon us at any moment." Ibid., 5.
Baptist missionary James Anderson Slover Sr. offers another vivid, first-
hand perspective about the devastating effects of the Civil War on the
Cherokee Nation. See Slover, Autobiography of James Anderson Slover,
Sr., folder no. 1260.46, chaps. 7–10, Western History Collections.

50 Stephen Foreman, Journal and Letters of Stephen Foreman, 33, Western
History Collections. Foreman related that another resident, Albert
Barnes, visiting from Dwight Mission, reported "every body around there
is alarmed, feeling that there was danger, and yet could not explain it. He
said the people could not understand the movements of the Pin party. It is
just as here. There is a stir here, or a scheme at work in the dark that few
can understand. I feel as if a heavy dark cloud hung over us." Ibid.

51 Ibid., 34.

52 Ibid., 34–35.

53 Hannah Worcester Hicks was the third daughter of ABCFM missionary Samuel A. Worcester and Ann Orr Worcester. Born in New Echota,
Georgia, in January 1834, she moved west with her family to Indian

Territory in April 1835. She assisted her father with various aspects of the Park Hill Mission Press, as well as tending to household duties of the mission itself. In January 1852 she married Cherokee Abijah Hicks, with whom she had five children. In her diary, Hannah Hicks wrote that her husband, Abijah Hicks, was mistakenly murdered by Pins in July 1862. Hannah Hicks remained in Indian Territory throughout the duration of the Civil War. In 1864 she married Assistant Surgeon Dwight Hitchcock at Fort Gibson. Hicks became a widow once again when Hitchcock died of cholera during an epidemic in the area in the summer of 1867. Hicks continued to live at Fort Gibson until her death in January 1917. Hannah Hicks, "The Diary of Hannah Hicks," 1–24.

54 Ibid., 22.

55 Ibid., 8–11, 14, and 17. In the summer of 1862, Hannah Worcester Hicks sheltered Stephen Foreman and his family from the Pins. In her diary, Hicks openly expressed that "it was a great relief to us all to have Mr. Foreman leave. He was so dreadfully bitter against all Yankee sympathisers. We had been obliged to believe that he was, in great part, the cause of many of our troubles. Yet when he was in trouble he ran right to us for help. When he was hiding for his life, from the 'Pins,' he staid in the garret here, two or three days & nights. I made him a bed there, and carried him his meals myself." Ibid., 20. Due to the ongoing harassment he experienced, Foreman eventually became a refugee in Texas until the war ended. What had begun as Foreman's loss of property ended with his displacement first from his home and later from the territory. After the war, Foreman returned to his home in Park Hill, Cherokee Nation, Indian Territory, and continued preaching until his death in 1881.

56 Ibid., 10 (emphasis in original).

57 Ibid., 11.

58 Ibid., 15.

59 Ibid.

60 Rawick, *American Slave*, 7:350–51. Shawneetown was located in the southeastern corner of the Choctaw Nation, approximately five miles north of the Red River.

61 Ibid., 351.

62 Rawick, *American Slave*, 12:287. Though a few reports of enslaved people's

successful crossings into Mexico exist, including the band of enslaved and free Seminoles led by Seminole Wild Cat in the 1840s, a comprehensive examination of specific Underground Railroad–related activities in antebellum Indian Territory remains to be written. See Tyler, "Fugitive Slaves in Mexico."

63 Rawick, *American Slave*, 12:361.

64 Grant Foreman, *Indian Pioneer*, 81:359–60.

65 Ibid., 7:415.

66 Ibid., 9:254.

67 Rawick, *American Slave*, 12:362.

68 Ibid. Creek freedwoman Lizzie Jackson recalled the devastation that occurred in the Creek Nation during the war. She stated that when the soldiers arrived at the plantations, "they burned the buildings, took what little food stuffs they could find and then sure enough we was hungry. Everybody almost starve to death. Some of the negroes did die with starvation. Everywhere was the same, not just on our place . . . There wasn't many of my own family left by that time. They was killed off with the guns and some died starved." Ibid., 187.

69 For a discussion of the southern path to freedom for South Carolina slaves during the eighteenth century, see Peter H. Wood, *Black Majority*, 259–60. For an examination of Mexico's significance as a refuge for fugitive slaves, see Tyler, "Fugitive Slaves in Mexico."

70 Rawick, *American Slave*, 12:351. Although Vann self-identified as "part Indian and part colored," she did not indicate in her interview her maternal or paternal racial and ethnic history.

71 For the involvement of African American troops in the Civil War, see Boyd, "The Use of Negro Troops"; Mays, *Black Americans*; Gooding, *On the Altar of Freedom*; Redkey, *A Grand Army of Black Men*; Cornish, *The Sable Arm*; Paradis, *Strike the Blow for Freedom*; and Trudeau, *Like Men of War*. Also see Tolson, *The Black Oklahomans*, 32–40.

72 Rawick, *American Slave*, 12:177.

73 Ibid., 225.

74 Ibid., 285.

75 Ibid.

76 Rampp, "Negro Troop Activity," 536 and 548.

77 For detailed descriptions of these battles, see Rampp, "Negro Troop Activity."

78 Report of Major General James G. Blunt to Major General John M. Schofield, 26 July 1863, U.S. War Department, *War of the Rebellion*, 448.

79 Ibid., 450–51. Colonel James M. Williams was actually the white commander of the 1st Kansas Colored Infantry Regiment; however, at the beginning of the Battle of Honey Springs, Colonel Williams was severely wounded. Once Lieutenant Colonel Bowles heard of Colonel Williams's injuries, he assumed command of the regiment.

80 Rampp, "Negro Troop Activity," 547. Alvin M. Josephy calls the Battle of Honey Springs "the biggest and most decisive of any fought in the Indian Territory." Josephy, *The Civil War in the American West*, 372.

81 Rampp, "Negro Troop Activity," 558. Also see Glatthaar, *Forged in Battle*, and Westwood, *Black Troops, White Commanders*.

82 After Chief John Ross was captured and removed from the Cherokee Nation by federal forces in July 1862, his position as principal chief of the Cherokee Nation was not officially filled. Although Joseph Vann had been elected assistant principal chief in 1859, he had sided with the Confederacy. As a result, the Union supporters of the Cherokee Nation remained without an executive officer within the Nation. Major Thomas Pegg, also captured by federal forces in July 1862, joined the federal effort and became an officer in the 2nd Indian Home Guard Regiment. Because he was elected president of the National Committee, he served as acting principal chief in John Ross's absence. See Wardell, *A Political History*, 171. For more information on Thomas Pegg's role as acting principal chief of the Cherokee Nation, see Litton, "The Principal Chiefs," 263.

83 "An Act Emancipating the Slaves in the Cherokee Nation," Cherokee Nation Papers, box 155, folder 6361.

84 These nations included the Cherokees, Creeks, Choctaws, Chickasaws, Seminoles, Shawnees, Delawares, Wichitas, Comanches, Osages, Senecas, and Quapaws. Abel, *The American Indian and the End of the Confederacy*, 188.

85 For daily reports of the Fort Smith council meeting, from 8 September to 21 September 1865, see U.S. Department of the Interior, *Annual Report of the Commissioner of Indian Affairs to the Secretary of the Interior for the Year 1865*,

315–53. For a thorough examination of the proceedings of the Fort Smith council, see Abel, *The American Indian and the End of the Confederacy*, 173–218. Also see Raleigh Archie Wilson, "Negro and Indian Relations," 79–109, and Saunt, "The Paradox of Freedom."

86 In fact, the Cherokees, Creeks, Chickasaws, Choctaws, and Seminoles all sent two delegations—one representing the Union-supporting faction and the other representing the Confederate faction—to Washington in 1866 to treat with the federal government. For more information on the activities of the two separate delegations from the Cherokee Nation, see Abel, *The American Indian and the End of the Confederacy*, 345–63, and Wardell, *A Political History*, 177–207. Also see Bailey, *Reconstruction in Indian Territory*, 55–81.

87 Kappler, *Indian Affairs*, 944. The 1866 treaties between each of the Five Tribes and the United States are reprinted in their entirety in Kappler's *Indian Affairs*: Treaty with the Seminoles, 910–15; Treaty with the Choctaws and Chickasaws, 918–31; Treaty with the Creeks, 931–37; and Treaty with the Cherokees, 942–50. The Treaty of 1866 between the United States and the Cherokee Nation also specified terms and conditions for granting a right-of-way to any company or corporation authorized by Congress to construct railroads through the Cherokee Nation; relocating other Indians within the Cherokee country; and establishing U.S. military posts or stations in the Cherokee Nation. Ibid., 942–50. Like the Cherokee Treaty of 1866, the Treaty of 1866 between the United States and the Creek Nation also included a time period during which freedpeople had to return to the Nation in order to claim Creek citizenship. The Cherokees gave their freedmen six months; the Creeks allowed their freedmen one year to return home. Ibid., 932.

Chapter 5

1 Rawick, *American Slave*, 12:234.
2 Ibid., 236.
3 Ibid., 139–40.
4 Ibid., 218–19.
5 Ibid., 252.

6   Rawick, *American Slave*, 7:351–52.

7   Ibid., 347.

8   Ibid., 352.

9   Ibid. Daniel Littlefield explained that "when the freedmen had begun to return to the Cherokee Nation, the federal troops had offered a source of refuge to them. Fort Gibson, located in the Illinois District of the Cherokee Nation, was the hub of activity, and most of the main routes of travel into the Nation ended there." Littlefield, *Cherokee Freedmen*, 28.

10 Even today, Four Mile Branch is still referred to as a "freedmen community."

11 Littlefield, *Cherokee Freedmen*, 49.

12 Although certainly not comprehensive, the incomplete returns of the Cherokee Nation Census of 1867 offer some indication of the districts in which Cherokee freedpeople resettled during the first years following the Civil War. The majority, 499 Cherokee freedpeople, were located in the Illinois District, 148 in the Saline District, 117 in the Sequoyah District (of whom 38 were noted as voters), 25 in the Canadian District (of whom 16 were noted as voters), and 13 in the Flint District (of whom 6 were noted as intruders-noncitizens of the Cherokee Nation). Cherokee Nation, Cherokee-Census (Tahlequah), Cherokee Census of 1867, Archives and Manuscripts Division, Oklahoma Historical Society, Oklahoma City. A more contemporary estimate of the Census of 1867 determined that there were probably between 2,000 and 2,500 Cherokee freedpeople. Littlefield, *Cherokee Freedmen*, 28. Also see Doran, "Population Statistics." Doran's article provides a critical examination of census information not only for the Cherokees but also for the Chickasaws, Choctaws, Creeks, and Seminoles. In 1867 the number of Cherokee citizens in the Cherokee Nation, Indian Territory, excluding Cherokee freedpeople, was estimated at 13,566. U.S. Department of the Interior, *Report on Indian Affairs by the Acting Commissioner for the Year 1867*, 21. This report also includes less precise population estimates for the population of other nations in Indian Territory for 1867: Choctaws—12,500; Chickasaws—4,500; Seminoles—2,000; and Creeks—14,300. By 1872, the estimated number of Cherokees in the Cherokee Nation, Indian Territory, excluding Cherokee freedpeople, had increased to 17,217. U.S. Department of the Interior, *Annual Report of the Commissioner of Indian Affairs to the Secretary of the Interior for the Year 1873*.

13 U.S. Department of the Interior, *Report on Indian Affairs by the Acting Commissioner for the Year 1867*, 22. In addition to the effects of the war, the summer of 1866 proved to be a particularly harsh one for the Creeks, when an onslaught of grasshoppers destroyed a great deal of their fruit and vegetable crops.

14 Ibid., 321.

15 Ibid., 319. This epidemic also severely affected the Seminole Nation. "As regards my own people, the Cherokees," William Penn Adair explained, after the Civil War "at least one-half of them had not animals or plows or farming instruments of any kind with which to cultivate the soil. These had to cultivate their patches with sharpened sticks and such animals and plows and hoes as their more fortunate neighbors could loan them, and I have known one solitary plow and horse to pass from house to house, over large settlements under loan for a whole season during the first two years that succeeded the war." Adair, "The Indian Territory in 1878," 265.

16 Wickett, *Contested Territory*, 104.

17 Ibid., 106. In the Creek Treaty of 1866 and the Cherokee Treaty of 1866, both nations agreed to adopt their freedpeople and grant them equal rights with native citizens of their respective nations. Though the Choctaw finally agreed to adopt their freedpeople, the Chickasaws refused to adopt formerly enslaved African Chickasaws into the Chickasaw Nation. For a thorough analysis of the story of Chickasaw freedpeople, see Littlefield, *Chickasaw Freedmen*. Once freedpeople began working their own land, Indian landowners utilized the labor of white farmers from the states to maintain their farms. Ibid., 106–9.

18 On 24 September 1839 the Cherokee National Council approved an act "regulating settlements on the public domain, and in regard to improvements." This act stated "that no person shall be permitted to settle or erect any improvement within one-fourth of a mile of the house, field, or other improvement of another citizen, without his, her, or their consent, under the penalty of forfeiting such improvement and labor for the benefit of the original settler." In addition, the act also stipulated that "all improvements, which may be left unoccupied by any person or persons, citizens of this Nation, and such person or persons remove to another

place, leaving no person or tenant on their former place for the term of two years, such place or improvements shall be considered abandoned, and revert to the Nation as common property; and any person or persons whatever, citizens of this Nation, may take possession of any such improvement so left, which shall thenceforward be considered their lawful property." Cherokee Nation, *Laws of the Cherokee Nation Passed during the Years 1839–1867*, 75–76.

19 Cherokee Nation, *Constitution and Laws of the Cherokee Nation Published by Authority of the National Council*, 25.

20 Ibid.

21 Excerpt from 1872 petition as quoted in Wickett, *Contested Territory*, 10.

22 For general information about the establishment and history of the Freedmen's Bureau, see Bentley, *A History of the Freedmen's Bureau*. For works focused on the Freedmen's Bureau's activities within specific states, see Abbott, *The Freedmen's Bureau in South Carolina*; White, *The Freedmen's Bureau in Louisiana*; Crouch, *The Freedmen's Bureau and Black Texans*; Richter, *Overreached on all Sides*; and Cimbala, *Under the Guardianship of the Nation*. Also see Oubre, *Forty Acres and a Mule*.

23 For information regarding the education of African Americans in the South during Reconstruction, see James D. Anderson, *The Education of Blacks in the South*; Morris, *Reading, 'Riting and Reconstruction*; and Butchart, *Northern Schools*. Also see Goodenow and White, *Education and the Rise of the New South*, particularly James D. Anderson's essay, "Ex-Slaves and the Rise of Universal Education in the New South, 1860–1880."

The Freedmen's Bureau provided a significant amount of funding toward the creation of a variety of schools for freedpeople, including day and night schools, technical schools, colleges, and universities. For example, Fisk University (originally Fisk School) in Nashville, Tennessee, was founded in January 1866. Sponsored in part by the American Missionary Association, it was named in honor of General Clinton B. Fisk of the Tennessee Freedmen's Bureau. The majority of funding for the establishment of Howard University in Washington, D.C., was provided by the Freedmen's Bureau. Oliver O. Howard, one of the founders of Howard University, was at the time of the university's creation serving as the commissioner of the Freedmen's Bureau.

24 See, for example, the interviews of Patsy Perryman, Rawick, *American Slave*, 12:251; Chaney Richardson, Rawick, *American Slave*, 7:262; Betty Robertson, Rawick, *American Slave*, 7:268; Morris Sheppard, Rawick, *American Slave*, 7:291; Johnson Thompson, Rawick, *American Slave*, 12:311; and Sarah Wilson, Rawick, *American Slave*, 7:351.

25 Littlefield, *Cherokee Freedmen*, 52.

26 In all these day schools "English studies are exclusively pursued, although they have primary studies in both English and Cherokee." U.S. Department of the Interior, *Annual Report of the Commissioner of Indian Affairs to the Secretary of the Interior for the Year 1876*, 61.

27 Littlefield, *Cherokee Freedmen*, 52. See Bailey, *Reconstruction in Indian Territory*, 182–83. Bailey provides a general overview of the reestablishment of social agencies in the Seminole, Creek, Choctaw, Chickasaw, and Cherokee nations. In addition, he also includes brief remarks specifically concerning the status of freedpeople in these nations. Also see Willson, "Freedmen in the Oklahoma Territory." For an analysis of the situation of Chickasaw and Choctaw freedpeople in the Reconstruction era, see Andrews, "Freedmen in Indian Territory."

28 The ten Cherokee schools for freedpeople were Tahlequah and Four Mile Branch schools in the Tahlequah District; Big Creek, Lightening Creek, and Goose Neck schools in the Cooweescoowee District; Moore school in the Delaware District; Vann's Valley school in the Saline District; Timbuctoo school in the Sequoyah District; and Land Town and Fort Gibson schools in the Illinois District. There were no schools for Cherokee freedpeople in the Going Snake District, Flint District, and Canadian District. U.S. Department of the Interior, *Annual Report of the Commissioner of Indian Affairs to the Secretary of the Interior for the Year 1887*, 109. From all indications in the census of 1867, there was a negligible freedmen population in Going Snake District, Flint District, and Canadian District in the post–Civil War period. Due to the small number of freedmen in these three districts, and by extension the number of school-age children in this population, there were no freedmen's schools established there during this time.

29 U.S. Department of the Interior, *Annual Report of the Commissioner of Indian Affairs to the Secretary of the Interior*, 1892, 254.

30 The Colored High School in Tahlequah opened under the leadership of Steward (also referred to as Superintendent) Nelson Lowrey, with an enrollment of approximately twenty-five students. For more information about the establishment of the high school for Cherokee freedmen, see Ballenger, "The Colored High School."

31 Even though only a limited number of schools were established for Cherokee freedpeople, at least the Cherokee Nation agreed to use the Nation's funds to provide teachers for the freedmen's schools and supplies for the children. This was not the case for all freedmen in the Five Tribes. A decade after the Civil War had ended, freedpeople of the Choctaw and Chickasaw nations were still not "allowed to attend their schools nor to receive any of the public funds for the support of schools among themselves." U.S. Congress, House, *Report of the Secretary of the Interior*, 44th Cong., 1st sess., H. Exec. Doc. 1, Pt. 5, 557. As a result of the Choctaw and Chickasaw nations' refusal to create schools for their freedpeople, the United States government established two schools for freedpeople within the Choctaw Nation. The Chickasaw Nation refused to create schools for its freedpeople. However, by 1892, the Choctaw Nation had established not only primary schools for its freedpeople, but also an academy (high school) for Choctaw freedpeople called the Tushka-luso Institute. In 1892 the Tushka-luso Institute enrolled thirty Choctaw freedpeople. U.S. Department of the Interior, *Annual Report of the Commissioner of Indian Affairs to the Secretary of the Interior, 1892*, 255. Creek freedpeople also recognized the importance of educating their children, and the Creek Nation responded more positively to the educational demands of its freedpeople. By 1876 the Creek Nation had established thirty-six schools with a combined attendance of 500 students. Of the thirty-six schools, six were specifically created for the children of Creek freedpeople. U.S. Department of the Interior, *Annual Report of the Commissioner of Indian Affairs to the Secretary of the Interior for the Year 1876*, 62.

32 *Cherokee Advocate*, 9 September 1876.

33 See Murray R. Wickett's discussion of the limited educational resources provided for freedpeople, particularly within the Cherokee and Choctaw nations. Although the Creeks, Seminoles, Cherokees, and Choctaws eventually provided some educational opportunities for their freedpeo-

ple, the Chickasaws never adopted their freedmen, and thus they never provided them access to any of their schools. Wickett, *Contested Territory*, 78–84.

34 *Cherokee Advocate*, 9 September 1876.

35 For more information about Cherokee freedmen's schools, see Littlefield's *Cherokee Freedmen*, 52–54. After the Civil War, Cherokee freedpeople, like African American freedpeople in the United States, depended on their local churches to provide spiritual development, social activities, and overall support, which cultivated a sense of hope in communities that were devastated by the aftermath of the Civil War.

36 Rawick, *American Slave*, 12:311.

37 In 1875 Joseph Brown, a resident of the Tahlequah District, became the first Cherokee freedman to be elected to the Cherokee National Council. Littlefield, *Cherokee Freedmen*, 64. Since publishing *Cherokee Freedmen*, Littlefield has discovered other African Cherokees engaged in public service in the Cherokee Nation. Other Cherokee freedmen who served in the Cherokee National Council include Stick Ross (1893), Ned Irons (1895), Frank Vann (1887), Samuel Stidham (1895), and Jerry Alberty (1889). Starr, *History of the Cherokee Indians*, 277–79.

38 Long before the significant land runs in the late nineteenth century in Oklahoma, the Cherokee Nation had been dealing with "intruders" of all races in Indian Territory. Though the legacy of intruders in the Cherokee Nation begins before removal east of the Mississippi, during Reconstruction intruders intensified their efforts to illegally lay claim to portions of land in the Cherokee Nation, Indian Territory. See Wickett, *Contested Territory*.

39 See Raleigh Archie Wilson, "Negro and Indian Relations," 126–53.

40 In the Reconstruction era, "Cherokees by blood" had been a label used in the Cherokee Nation to privilege Cherokees over adopted Shawnees and Delawares and adopted whites and freedmen.

41 Littlefield, *Cherokee Freedmen*, 119.

42 Ibid., 129.

43 Ibid., 129–30. Besides the various petitions submitted by groups of Cherokee freedpeople, in 1883 Isaac Rogers and Lewis D. Daniels were selected, at the Cooweescoowee District meeting, as delegates to present

the freedpeople's position and requests to Secretary Teller in Washington. Although the selection of Rogers and Daniels as freedmen delegates was later challenged by other groups of freedpeople, Rogers and Daniels did indeed meet with Secretary Teller in 1883 on behalf of Cherokee freedpeople. Even though this meeting did not affect the status of Cherokee freedpeople, Teller's hesitation during this time, regarding the disbursement of Cherokee funds, resulted in another delegation from the Cherokee Nation to Washington. This delegation was composed of Chief Bushyhead, R. M. Wolfe, and Robert B. Ross. Ibid., 130–31.

44 Ibid., 132. Freedpeople at this meeting on 6 December selected freedmen Moses Whitmire, Frank Ross, and Henry C. Hayden to represent their position in future negotiations with the United States government.

45 They elected freedmen William Thompson (Illinois District), William Brown (Canadian District), Berry Mayes (Tahlequah District), Jack Campbell (Sequoyah District), and Joseph Brown as additional representatives of the Cherokee freedmen delegation.

46 Littlefield, *Cherokee Freedmen*, 132–33. For a detailed account of the Cherokee freedpeople's organized response to the 1883 act passed by the Cherokee National Council, as well as to the U.S. government, see ibid., 119–41.

47 Ibid., 134. Using the Cherokee census of 1880, Atkins calculated the appropriate per capita share. Atkins estimated that the $300,000 appropriated by Congress divided among the 15,307 Cherokees by blood listed in the 1880 Census would be approximately $20 per capita. Since the Census of 1880 also listed 1,976 freedmen, 672 Delawares, and 503 Shawnees, the total number of excluded Cherokee citizens was 3,151. With the approximate figure of $20 per capita, Atkins estimated that the additional amount necessary to pay these 3,151 citizens was approximately $63,000. However, in the end Atkins proposed the figure of $75,000 in order to take into account any additional freedmen, Shawnee, or Delaware citizens.

48 Ibid., 135–37.

49 Ibid., 138–39.

50 Ibid., 148–50. For a comprehensive analysis of the creation of, and controversies surrounding, the Wallace Roll, see ibid., 148–59.

51 Ibid., 154–56. Commissioner Morgan also selected R. F. Thompson, a clerk in the Office of Indian Affairs, to verify the names on Wallace's lists.

52 Ibid., 156–59. Even after Wallace ended his work on these rolls in the summer of 1890, the rolls remained unfinished. Hired by the U.S. government to make payments to the Cherokee freedpeople on Wallace's rolls, Agent Leo Bennett began his work of distributing payments in January 1891. However, as Bennett began distributing payments, he discovered that a number of freedpeople recognized as citizens by the Cherokee Nation were not listed on Wallace's roll. In addition, there were still freedpeople listed on Wallace's doubtful roll who were indeed rightful citizens of the Cherokee Nation. In 1892 Bennett submitted his supplemental roll, of freedpeople he believed were entitled to payments, to Secretary of Interior John W. Noble. Even after Bennett completed this supplemental roll, freedmen continued to submit applications for review.

53 Ibid., 168. This per capita amount was significant due to the fact that the Cherokee National Council had distributed a third $300,000 to Cherokees by blood in November 1890. In addition, $6,640,000 had also been distributed to Cherokees by blood in May 1893, for partial payment from the U.S. government for the Cherokee Nation's sale of the Cherokee Strip. Because the Cherokee Nation had already distributed these funds to Cherokees by blood, the freedpeople would receive their payments from U.S. government funds.

54 Ibid., 171–73.

55 Because the Cherokee census of 1890 had enumerated 2,052 Cherokee freedmen, the Cherokees were particularly concerned with the significant increase in freedmen identified in the Wallace Roll. Ibid., 156.

56 National Records of the Cherokee Nation, Roll 81, Letter from Browning to Clifton, Kern, and Thompson, dated 20 February 1896, Archives and Manuscripts Division, Oklahoma Historical Society.

57 The court of claims also ruled that the six-month period stipulated in the Treaty of 1866 did not begin until the proclamation date of the treaty on 11 August 1866 and ended on 11 February 1867. Previously, the Cherokee Nation had used the date the treaty negotiations had concluded, 19 July 1866, as the beginning date of the six-month period.

58   The Cherokee Nation also appointed James M. Keys and W. W. Hastings as attorneys.

59   Littlefield, *Cherokee Freedmen*, 180–83.

60   Ibid., 181–82.

61   Ibid., 182–84.

62   Ibid., 184.

63   Ibid., 185–88. Although Hayden remained the site for the first disbursement of funds to the Cherokee freedmen, in March 1897 James G. Dickson moved from Hayden to Fort Gibson in an effort to avoid confrontations with bill collectors to whom the freedpeople allegedly owed money. However, due to controversy surrounding Dickson, he was relieved of his duty in May 1897 by Secretary of the Interior C. N. Bliss. Dickson was replaced by Agent Dew M. Wisdom of the Union Agency. Agent Wisdom began his work as paymaster in June 1897. He remained at Fort Gibson and completed the payments stipulated by the court of claims. Agent Wisdom then gave the rolls to Cherokee Nation treasurer D. W. Lipe.

64   Ibid., 185–86.

65   The charges of corruption were leveled not only at officials directly involved in the creation of this roll, particularly Robert H. Kern, but also at Cherokee officials including Cherokee Chief S. M. Mayes, E. C. Boudinot, Ed Campbell, and Cherokee attorney James M. Keys. There were also charges concerning attorney J. Milton Turner's actions, as well as allegations that some freedpeople had used paid witnesses to validate their claims of Cherokee citizenship. For an in-depth discussion and analysis of the persons involved in the alleged corruption surrounding the Kern-Clifton Roll and the charges directed against these individuals, see ibid., 186–213.

66   For information on the history and tactics of the Ku Klux Klan during the Reconstruction era, see Chalmers, *Hooded Americanism*; Horn, *Invisible Empire*; and Trealease, *White Terror*. The Ku Klux Klan emerged in Oklahoma in the decades following statehood, most notably in the 1920s. See Jessup, "Consorting with Blood and Violence."

67   For an analysis of some of the challenges and inequities African Cherokee freedmen faced following Reconstruction in the Cherokee Nation, see Katja May, *African Americans and Native Americans*. May offers a very limited

and cursory discussion of the experiences of, and interactions between, Cherokees and African Cherokee slaves and freedpeople between removal and the 1880s, especially the period between removal and the Civil War. Instead, the main focus of May's work is the period between the 1880s and 1920s. May's statistical analysis of random population samples from the 1900 and 1910 census records for the Creek and Cherokee nations provides information regarding the gender, age, marital patterns, frequency of interracial marriage, land usage, employment, and education of people of African descent (categorized as black Indians or black immigrants) and Indians (categorized as "mixed bloods" or "full bloods") in the Creek and Cherokee nations.

68 Rawick, *American Slave*, 7:288.

69 Scholarly works regarding the period of Reconstruction in the United States, as well as the development of postemancipation plantation societies in the Caribbean, have informed not only our understanding of slavery in the Americas, but also our interpretations of the meaning of freedom. See McGlynn and Drescher, *The Meaning of Freedom*. See also Foner, *Nothing But Freedom*; Foner, *Reconstruction*; Fraginals, Pons, and Engerman, *Between Slavery and Free Labor*; Richardson, *Abolition and Its Aftermath*; and Scott, "Exploring the Meaning of Freedom."

70 Information regarding this particular celebration was provided in an editorial article in the *Cherokee Advocate*, 9 September 1876.

71 Ibid.

Chapter 6

1 For an analysis of the destructive results of the Dawes Act on Indian sovereignty, see Debo, *And Still the Waters Run*.

2 The Dawes Commission initially included Henry Laurens Dawes (chairman of the commission), Meredith H. Kidd, and Archibald S. McKennon. Additional members of the Dawes Commission included Frank C. Armstrong, Tams Bixby, Thomas B. Needles, Clifton R. Breckenridge, and William E. Stanley. For a thorough examination of the creation and ramifications of the Dawes Commission within the Cherokee Nation, see Littlefield, *Cherokee Freedmen*, 214–48. Also see Carter, "Deciding Who Can Be Cherokee."

3   Congress specifically authorized the Dawes Commission to "hear and determine the application of all persons who may apply to them for citizenship" and "determine the right of such applicant to be admitted and enrolled." Carter, "Deciding Who Can be Cherokee," 178–79.

4   Littlefield, *Cherokee Freedmen*, 221. Under the Curtis Act, the Five Tribes were to make "agreements" with the U.S. government in order to allot their land into individual plots. The "agreements" stipulated that land allotments be given to individual citizens of the nations. Generally, each Indian citizen received between 160 and 320 acres and each freedman received 40 to 160 acres, depending on the dictates of the specific nation. See Debo, *And Still the Waters Run*, 31–60.

5   "Resolutions of the Freedmen Convention held at Fort Gibson, I. T., December 18, 1900," John Drew Papers, Thomas Gilcrease Museum, Tulsa, Oklahoma.

6   Carter, "Deciding Who Can Be Cherokee," 193. Carter concurred with Angie Debo's critical discussion of this issue. Debo stated that "the quantum of blood indicated by the rolls is somewhat misleading, partly because of the inaccuracies in a matter that at that time seemed unimportant, and partly because fullblood Indians of mixed tribal descent were classed as mixed bloods." Debo, *And Still the Waters Run*, 47.

7   For an excellent discussion of the ramifications of "blood politics" on Cherokee freedmen and their descendants, see Sturm, *Blood Politics*.

8   Even though one of the significant aspects of Article 4 of the Treaty of 1866 concerned the right of Cherokee freedpeople, recognized as such by the Cherokee Nation, to settle on land in the Nation, Cherokee freedpeople were not officially granted land allotments until they were enrolled as citizens of the Cherokee Nation by the Dawes Commission. Kappler, *Indian Treaties*, 1778–1883, 943. Though Chickasaw freedmen were never adopted into the Chickasaw Nation, they were enrolled by the Dawes Commission. See Littlefield, *The Chickasaw Freedmen*, for an examination of the Chickasaw Nation's refusal to adopt Chickasaw freedpeople within the Nation and the Chickasaw freedpeople's struggle to be recognized as members of the Chickasaw citizenry. Also see Willson, "Freedmen in Indian Territory."

9   U.S. Department of the Interior, *Reports of the Department of Interior for the*

Fiscal Year Ended June 30, 1907, 2:296. Also see U.S. Department of the Interior, *Reports of the Department of Interior for the Fiscal Year Ended June 30, 1908*, 2:195. In 1914 adjustments were made to the rolls by an act of Congress. As a result, there were 41,835 officially enrolled citizens of the Cherokee Nation, including 4,919 Cherokee freedmen. Littlefield, *Cherokee Freedmen*, 238.

10 U.S. Department of the Interior, *Reports of the Department of Interior for the Fiscal Year Ended June 30*, 1907, 2:305.

11 Documentation of land allotments to Cherokee freedpeople is located in the Land Allotment Records for the Cherokee Nation in the section on Cherokee freedmen. The original Land Allotment Records for Indian Territory are housed at the National Archives, Southwest Region, Fort Worth, Texas. The National Archives in Fort Worth, Texas, also houses the original Cherokee Freedmen Enrollment Applications and the Cherokee Freedmen Census Cards. The Cherokee Freedmen Enrollment Applications and the Cherokee Freedmen Census Cards are also available on microfilm at the National Archives, Southwest Region, and the Archives and Manuscripts Division, Oklahoma Historical Society, Oklahoma City.

12 Rawick, *American Slave*, 7:353. Sarah Wilson and her children were enrolled by the Dawes Commission. See Cherokee Freedmen Census Card Number 60 for Sarah Wilson and her five children (Lelia, Thomas, Bertha, Allie, and Robert). The enrollment application for Sarah Wilson and her children to the Dawes Commission was dated 3 April 1901. Their citizenship certificate was issued on 6 March 1905, National Archives, Southwest Region. Also see Land Allotment Record Numbers 182–87 for Sarah Wilson and her children.

13 Ibid., 269. Betty Robertson was enrolled as a Cherokee freedwoman by the Dawes Commission as Belle Roberson with her husband Calvin and their children. See Cherokee Freedmen Census Card Number 117 and Land Allotment Record Numbers 356–60 and 3076–77, for Calvin, Belle, Bertha, Watie, Amanda, Arthur Roberson, and Minnie Ivory, National Archives, Southwest Region.

14 Rawick, *American Slave*, 12:219.

15 Creek freedman John Harrison stated in his interview that his "folks who

were slaves were freed, and more too, the slaves became citizens of the tribe and became [sic] ownership in the land as much as the Creek themselves and also, we enjoyed a part of the tribal fund." Ibid., 151.

16 Ibid., 251–52.

17 I have been unable to find any enrollment card or application testimony stating that either Patsy Taylor Perryman or her sister was enrolled as a Cherokee freedwoman or received an allotment from the Cherokee Nation. However, Patsy Taylor Perryman's third husband, Randolph Perryman, was enrolled as a Creek freedman by the Dawes Commission. See Creek Freedmen Census Card Number 863 for Randolph Perryman, Dawes Commission, Creek Nation, Census Cards, National Archives, Southwest Region. At the time of the interview, Patsy Taylor Perryman was living in Muskogee, Oklahoma (previously part of the Creek Nation).

18 Rawick, *American Slave*, 12:320. I have been unable to find any census card or application testimony stating that Victoria Taylor Thompson was enrolled as a Cherokee freedwoman.

19 Rawick, *American Slave*, 7:290. Although Morris Sheppard stated he had received an allotment, his census card indicates that his enrollment application was rejected, and thus he should not have received an allotment. See Cherokee Freedmen Census Card Number FR 186 for Morris Sheppard, National Archives, Southwest Region. However, Morris Sheppard's wife, Nancy Hildebrand Sheppard, former slave of Joe Hildebrand, was enrolled as a Cherokee freedwoman. She and their children were enrolled by the Dawes Commission. See Cherokee Freedmen Census Card Number 186 for Nancy, Fannie, Emma, Annie, Thomas, and Claud Sheppard, National Archives, Southwest Region.

20 Rawick, *American Slave*, 7:292.

21 See Perdue, Barden, and Phillips, *Weevils in the Wheat*, 84 and 317. Also see Blassingame, *Slave Testimony*, 237–38 and 695–96. These examples from *Weevils in the Wheat* and *Slave Testimony* represent the extent to which notions of wildness or related characteristics linked to a "high-spirited" nature appear in interviews of ex-slaves, outside of Indian Territory, in regard to Indians. In a conversation with my colleague Alexander X. Byrd, he posited that formerly enslaved people related Africanness and Indian-

ness to wildness in the interviews from the southern states that he had reviewed. For example, Chaney Mack, a former slave from Mississippi, recalled her African father and Choctaw mother in her interview. Mack stated that "all of de other niggers wuz afraid of her [mother]." Rawick, *American Slave*, 9:1420. Mack remembered that "nobody fooled wid my mother. She'd grab a man by de collar, throw him down and set on him." Ibid., 1424. On St. Simons Island, one of the larger islands off the Georgia coast, former slave Ben Sullivan recalled "lots uh Africans, but al ub em ain tame. But I knowd some ub em wut is tame an I knowd one tame Indian." Georgia Writers' Project, *Drums and Shadows*, 179.

22   Rawick, *American Slave*, 12:211. Freedwoman Eliza Hardrick, former slave of Cherokee Lewis Ross, also mentioned how her father's decision to change their surname (from Ross to Hardrick) affected their ability to acquire land allotments in the Cherokee Nation. Ibid., 137.

23   Rawick, *American Slave*, 7:283.

24   Ibid.

25   Littlefield, *Cherokee Freedmen*, 231–32.

26   Debo, *And Still the Waters Run*, 179.

27   As Murray R. Wickett explains, "many illiterate and barely literate freedmen could not understand the legalese in which the contract was written and could not afford the cost of a lawyer to safeguard their interests." Wickett, *Contested Territory*, 63.

28   Debo, *And Still the Waters Run*, 130.

29   Hill, "The All-Negro Communities of Oklahoma," 256. For an interesting examination of the ways that African Americans used the biblical Exodus story to formulate notions of nation, peoplehood, and racial solidarity in the nineteenth century, see Glaude, *Exodus*.

30   Glen Schwendemann estimates that approximately 5,500 to 6,000 African Americans migrated to Kansas between March and July 1879 and between 300 and 500 of these migrants returned to their homes in the South. Schwendemann, "Negro Exodus to Kansas," 161. For another analysis of this migration, see Painter, *Exodusters*.

31   *American Citizen* (Baltimore), 26 July 1878.

32   Fleming, "Pap Singleton," 63–64. An article in the *Colored Patriot* claimed

that "between 1875 and 1880, Pap traveled back and forth repeatedly between Tennessee and Kansas, until he had conducted hither, according to statistics gathered from railroad and steamboat officials, 7,432 exodusters." *Colored Patriot* (Topeka, Kansas), 4 May 1882.

33 *Freeman* (Indianapolis, Indiana), 5 January 1889, as quoted in Gatewood, "Arkansas Negroes in the 1890s," 296.

34 Between 1870 and 1900, Arkansas's black population increased by 200 percent compared to a 161 percent increase for whites during the same period. However, after the passage of the Separate Coach Law of 1891 and incidents of racial violence in Arkansas, blacks looked to Oklahoma Territory with new dreams for a new homeland. Bogle, "On Our Way to the Promised Land," 163–64.

35 *American Citizen* (Topeka, Kansas), 1 March 1888.

36 *Advocate* (Leavenworth, Kansas), 12 October 1889.

37 For more information on the rise of the cattle industry and ranching in the Oklahoma District, see Collins, *Storm and Stampede on the Chisholm*; Skaggs, *Ranch and Range in Oklahoma*; Gard, *The Chisholm Trail*; Crisman, *Lost Trails of the Cimarron*; and Tennant, "The History of the Chisholm Trail." Tennant's article on the Chisholm Trail includes a detailed map of the cattle trail from River Station, Texas, through Indian Territory to Abilene, Kansas. Also see Thoburn and Holcomb, *A History of Oklahoma*, 141–75. The development and extension of railroads into Indian Territory after the Civil War only served to augment the growing demand for white settlement in Oklahoma. See Hofsommer, *Railroads in Oklahoma*. Also see Wardell, *A Political History*, 255–89, and Self, "The Building of the Railroads in the Cherokee Nation."

38 Although President Harrison issued this proclamation, the bill providing for the settlement of the Oklahoma District passed both houses of Congress on 2 March 1889 and was approved by President Grover Cleveland. See Dale and Wardell, *History of Oklahoma*, 244.

39 Although the first three land openings are frequently cited in books concerning Oklahoma settlement, they were not the only land openings in the territory. After the third run on 19 April 1892, the Cherokee Outlet opened on 16 September 1893, Kickapoo lands opened on 23 May 1895,

and lands of the Kiowa-Comanche and the Wichita-Caddo opened in 1901 by lottery. See Morris, Goins, and McReynolds, *Historical Atlas of Oklahoma*, map 48.

40   McReynolds, Marriott, and Faulconer, *Oklahoma*, 149–50.

41   Ibid., 157 (emphasis in original).

42   In order to coordinate a plan for black migration to Oklahoma Territory, in July 1890 Eagleson created the Oklahoma Immigration Organization, later becoming the Oklahoma Immigration Association. Based in Topeka, Kansas, with an auxiliary arm in Oklahoma, this organization was launched by Eagleson to establish emigration agents in major southern cities who would promote and support black settlement in Oklahoma Territory. For more information on W. L. Eagleson's organization and other similar emigration groups, see Littlefield and Underhill, "Black Dreams." Edward P. McCabe, a personal friend of Eagleson, also became a prominent advocate for black migration to Oklahoma. See Roberson, "Edward P. McCabe." McCabe actively encouraged black migration to Oklahoma Territory and directed his efforts to the promotion and creation of all-black towns in the territory.

43   In the 1890 U.S. census, the population of citizens categorized by county, race, and sex listed 1,643 "Colored" males and 1,365 "Colored" females in Oklahoma Territory. U.S. Department of the Interior, Census Office, *Compendium of the Eleventh Census, 1890: Population*, part 1, 639. However, there is a slight discrepancy in the figures. In the same census, the population of citizens grouped by county alone listed 2,973 total "Colored" citizens. Ibid., 503. For more information on McCabe's participation in the black migration to Oklahoma, including his role in the development of the all-black town of Langston, Oklahoma, see Roberson, "Edward P. McCabe"; Hill, "The All-Negro Communities of Oklahoma," 260–62; Littlefield and Underhill, "Black Dreams"; and Redkey, *Black Exodus*. The migration to Oklahoma proved fruitful for a number of African Americans. In the 1900 U.S. census, of the 13,225 African American farmers enumerated, 9,944 were landowners and 2,467 were sharecroppers in the Twin Territories—Oklahoma Territory and Indian Territory. In the same census, of the 94,775 white farmers in the Twin Territories, 43,675 were

landowners and 30,880 were sharecroppers. U.S. Bureau of the Census, *Negro Population of the United States*, 1790–1915, table 56.

44 In his article on all-black towns in Oklahoma, George O. Carney claimed that "twenty-eight communities and one colony were founded prior to statehood. Because a majority of blacks lived in Indian Territory, twenty-four were located there while the remaining four and the one colony were in Oklahoma Territory." Carney's article includes a map of the locations of these all-black towns. Carney, "Historic Resources of Oklahoma's All-Black Towns," 119.

As there were no restrictions placed on Indian freedpeople limiting the sale or leasing of their land, many sold a portion of their land to African American migrants for settlement and development of all-black towns. For more information on the development of all-black towns in Oklahoma, see Tolson, "A History of Langston, Oklahoma"; Tolson, "The Negro in Oklahoma Territory"; and Tolson, *Black Oklahomans*, 90–105.

Founded in 1859, Tullahassee, the oldest all-black town in the Twin Territories, was located within the limits of the Creek Nation, Indian Territory. A few Creek freedmen towns were established in the Creek Nation in 1869, including North Fork, Arkansas, and Canadian. Many of the all-black towns were founded in the Creek Nation after the turn of the century, including Boley, Taft, Grayson, and Vernon. Foreman and Gibson Station were the two primarily black towns in the Cherokee Nation. Lincoln City, established in 1889, was the first all-black town in Oklahoma Territory. Unlike Tullahassee, most of the all-black towns were created between the first run in 1889 and Oklahoma statehood in 1907.

45 Tolson, *Black Oklahomans*, 61.

46 In the spring of 1890, after the Democratic convention in Guthrie, Oklahoma Territory, masked homesteaders attacked African American settlers throughout the territory. In March 1890 Edward P. McCabe "became a victim when on one occasion he visited the Sac and Fox cession, near the Cimarron River, to observe black settlers and was fired on by three white men." Roberson, "Edward P. McCabe," 348. For an excellent analysis of racial stereotyping among Indian, African American, and European

American residents in the Twin Territories in the late nineteenth century, see Wickett, *Contested Territory*, 15–41.

47 Jimmie Lewis Franklin, *Journey toward Hope*, 18.

48 Ibid., 33.

49 Wickett, "The Fear of 'Negro Domination,'" 49. For a detailed account of the actions of the Oklahoma territorial legislatures of 1890, 1897, and 1901 regarding school segregation laws, including a personal account of the author's school experiences in 1892, see Balyeat, "Segregation in the Public Schools of Oklahoma Territory," 180–92. For a brief discussion of the segregation of schools in Oklahoma Territory, as well as African American resistance to it, see Wickett, *Contested Territory*, 85–90.

50 The *El Reno News* reported that the "Frisco now runs separate coaches into Oklahoma for white and Negro passengers. Each car has a sign showing which race it is provided for." *El Reno News* (El Reno, Oklahoma Territory), 4 July 1900.

51 *Indian Chieftain* (Vinita, Cherokee Nation, Indian Territory), 24 September 1896. The *El Reno News* also included this incident in an article entitled "Make the Negroes Leave." The article reported that "in the southern portion of Oklahoma Territory, whitecappers are running negroes out of the country. In the town of Norman, with a population of 2,000, not one Negro remains, and the inhabitants will not allow one to spend the night there." *El Reno News*, 24 September 1896. An article also appeared in the *Kingfisher Free Press* with the same information. *Kingfisher Free Press* (Kingfisher, Oklahoma Territory), 24 September 1896. The threat of expulsion and impending violence also occurred in the Oklahoma Territory towns of Shawnee, Blackwell, Lawton, and Norman. Antiblack harassment and expulsion also transpired within the Creek Nation, Indian Territory, in the towns of Sapulpa in 1901, Braggs in 1902, Holdenville in 1904, and Okmulgee in 1908. Katja May, *African Americans and Native Americans*, 245. In these cases, white residents initiated the actions by which black residents were threatened, abused, and in a few cases actually expelled from their homes. See Tolson, *The Black Oklahomans*, 67–68.

52 "What had happened to blacks as a journey toward hope," as Jimmie Lewis Franklin contends, "became more of a dark sojourn filled with uncertainty, with the potential of developing into an undemocratic and

racist nightmare." Franklin, *Journey toward Hope*, 31. The dream of Oklahoma as the "promised land" for African American migrants would quickly develop into the nightmare of racial violence in its various forms. The book *Without Sanctuary* includes evidence of one familiar example of racial violence in the new state of Oklahoma. The lynching of Laura Nelson and her son, L. W. Nelson, on 25 May 1911 in Okemah, Oklahoma (approximately twenty-five miles southwest of Okmulgee, Oklahoma, previously within the limits of the Creek Nation), clearly illustrates the fatal work of a lynch mob. See Allen et al., *Without Sanctuary*, 178–80 and pls. 37–38. The Tulsa Race Riot of 1921 also symbolized the ongoing resentment of a black (particularly successful) presence in Oklahoma.

53 Literacy and property requirements were often used to limit the black vote. However, in order to ensure that the voting rights of illiterate and/or non-property-owning whites would not be denied, some states passed a "grandfather clause" enabling whites to waive new voting requirements if they, or their fathers or grandfathers, were qualified to vote before 1 January 1867. See Franklin and Moss, *From Slavery to Freedom*, 235–37. In 1898, in the case of *Williams v. Mississippi*, the U.S. Supreme Court declared the poll tax and literacy requirements for voting were constitutional, thereby strengthening and endorsing black disenfranchisement.

54 Demonstrating its support of the movement for legal segregation, in 1896, the U.S. Supreme Court in *Plessy v. Ferguson* ruled Louisiana's railroad segregation law constitutional. Basing its decision on a "separate but equal" doctrine, the Court ruled that segregation was constitutional, as long as "equal" facilities and services were provided for African Americans.

55 See Maxwell, *The Sequoyah Constitutional Convention*.

56 The first plan, the "single or joint statehood" plan, proposed the joining of Indian Territory and Oklahoma Territory into one state. The second plan, the "double or separate statehood" plan, endorsed the creation of two separate states from the Twin Territories. The third plan, the "piecemeal absorption" plan, promoted statehood to Oklahoma Territory and the subsequent inclusion of Indian nations. The fourth plan recommended statehood for Oklahoma Territory, leaving Indian Territory under the control of the Five Tribes. See Gibson, *Oklahoma*, 192–93.

57 For information on the election of delegates and the Oklahoma constitutional convention, as well as brief biographical sketches on the delegates, see Clark, "Delegates to the Constitutional Convention"; Gibson, *Oklahoma: A History of Five Centuries*; and Ellis, *History of the Oklahoma Constitutional Convention*.

58 Murray also served as tribal attorney for the Chickasaw Nation. Gibson, *Oklahoma*, 196–97.

59 Excerpt from Murray's acceptance speech as quoted in Tolson, *The Black Oklahomans*, 137–38.

60 *Muskogee New-State Tribune* (Muskogee, Indian Territory), 13 December 1906, as quoted in Wickett, "The Fear of 'Negro Domination,'" 53.

61 For more information on the strategies and actions employed by African American residents of the Twin Territories against the passage of the new constitution and subsequent discriminatory amendments, see Tolson, *The Black Oklahomans*, and Wickett, "The Fear of 'Negro Domination,'" 54–56. Also see Wickett, *Contested Territory*, 194–95, 197, and 200.

62 They maintained this distinction even after Oklahoma statehood. Prominent African American statesman Booker T. Washington encountered this phenomenon during his visit to the Creek Nation in the fall of 1905. See Washington, "Boley: A Negro Town in the West." Also see Crockett, "Witness to History." For a discussion of the tension between Creek freedpeople and "state Negroes," also referred to as "watchina" by Creek freedpeople, see Sameth, "Creek Negroes."

63 Murray, *Contested Territory*, 31.

64 Wickett, "The Fear of 'Negro Domination,'" 56–57. As a result, "Article XXIII, Section 11 of the Constitution, entitled 'Definition of the Races,' noted that 'wherever in this Constitution and laws of this state, the word or words, 'colored,' 'colored race,' 'negro,' or 'negro race,' are used, the same shall be construed to mean or apply to all persons of African descent. The term 'white race' shall include all other persons." Ibid., 57.

65 Gibson, *Oklahoma*, 201.

66 Because this bill required the modification of 540 depots and the building of additional coaches for African Americans, this Jim Crow law did not go into effect until sixty days after it was approved. Tolson, *The Black Oklaho-*

mans, 147. For the entire "Coach Law," see Tolson, *The Black Oklahomans*, 278–80.

67 Ibid., 152.

Afterword

1 Du Bois, *The Souls of Black Folk*, 45.

2 *Riggs v. Ummerteskee.*

3 The form letter from Lela J. Ummerteskee (acting tribal registrar) to Bernice Riggs, regarding the status of her membership application, stated that the "Cherokee Nation can only certify the descendants of those Cherokee ancestors by blood who appear on the *Final Roll.*" *Riggs v. Ummerteskee,* letter from Lela J. Ummerteskee to Bernice Rogers Riggs, undated, document 3 (emphasis in original).

4 11 Cherokee Nation Code Annotated § 12 (1983).

5 Ibid.

6 *Riggs v. Ummerteskee,* appendix A, item 5.

7 Ibid., appendix A, item 6.

8 Ibid., appendix A, item 7.

9 Ibid., appendix A, item 10 (emphasis in original).

10 1975 Constitution of the Cherokee Nation of Oklahoma, 3.

11 Bernice Rogers Riggs's family members are listed on the Dawes Roll of Cherokee freedmen: Gabe Rogers (father), Joseph Rogers (paternal grandfather), and Sylva (Beck) Rogers (paternal grandmother), Census Card no. 236; and Malinda Bean (mother) and Louisa Bean (maternal grandmother), Census Card no. 286. Riggs's maternal grandfather, Joe Bean, is not listed as he was not a citizen of the Cherokee Nation. Riggs's paternal great-grandfather, Cherokee Will Rogers, is not listed on the Dawes Roll, as he died before these rolls were created.

In November 1998 I conducted separate interviews with Mrs. Bernice Riggs and with her European Cherokee attorney Kathy Carter-White in Tahlequah, Oklahoma. It was very clear from both of these interviews that achieving the goal of being officially recognized by the Cherokee Nation remains an important matter for many living descendants of Cherokee freedpeople.

Although the *Riggs* case received only limited notice, primarily in Oklahoma, the case of the Seminole freedmen garnered national attention. See William Glaberson, "Who Is a Seminole, and Who Gets to Decide?" *New York Times*, 29 January 2001. Also see a related article, "Mineral-Rights Money and Political Realities," in the same issue.

12 *Riggs v. Ummerteskee.*

13 Marilyn Vann, president of the association, has been engaged in specific lawsuits, involving the Cherokee Nation and the Bureau of Indian Affairs, concerning the rights of descendants of Cherokee freedpeople.

14 Press release for the Fourth Annual Conference on 3 June 2006.

15 Descendants of Freedmen of the Five Civilized Tribes, "Mission."

16 *Lucy Allen v. Cherokee Nation Tribal Council.*

17 Ibid. The three judges who ruled on the case were Justice Stacy L. Leeds (who filed the majority opinion of the court), Justice Darrell Dowty (who concurred with the decision), and Chief Justice Darell Matlock Jr. (who wrote the dissenting opinion).

18 *Lucy Allen v. Cherokee Nation Tribal Council, Opinion of the Court*, 13.

19 Ibid., 21.

20 Ibid., 22. As Justice Darrell Dowty reaffirmed in his concurring statement on the case, "*Riggs v Ummerteske must be reversed*" and "11 Cherokee Nation Code Annotated § 12 is unconstitutional because it imposes a more restrictive requirement on membership than does the plain language of the Constitution of 1975." Ibid., 23.

21 Due to the approval of the 2003 Cherokee Constitution in 2006, the Judicial Appeals Tribunal is now the Supreme Court of the Cherokee Nation.

22 Smith, "Citizen Views Fall on Both Sides of Freedmen Issue."

23 The current Cherokee Constitution was adopted by the delegates of the 1999 Constitutional Convention on 6 March 1999; approved for release by the 1999 Constitutional Convention Style Committee on 30 July 1999; approved for referendum by resolution passed by the Council of the Cherokee Nation on 15 May 2000; signed by Principal Chief Chad Smith on 24 May 2000; approved by vote of the citizens of the Cherokee Nation on 26 July 2003; certified by the Cherokee Nation Election Commission on 7 August 2003; and ruled effective and ordered implemented by the

Cherokee Nation Judicial Appeals Tribunal (now Cherokee Supreme Court) on 7 June 2006 in case no. JAT-05-04.

24 Cherokee Nation Election Commission, "Cherokee Special Election 2007 FAQS," Tahlequah, Oklahoma.

25 Cherokee Nation Election Commission, "Special Election Results-Official," Tahlequah, Oklahoma.

26 *Nash, et al. vs. Cherokee Nation Registrar*, "Temporary Order and Temporary Injunction."

27 Ibid.

28 Ibid.

29 Ibid.

30 Cherokee Nation, "Statement of Cherokee Nation Attorney General," 14 May 2007.

31 Ibid.

32 For national coverage of the Cherokee freedmen controversy, see the *New York Times* editorial on 8 June 2007 entitled "The Shame of the Cherokee Nation," as well as the responses to this editorial from Principal Chief Chad Smith, "Cherokees and Blacks" on 15 June 2007 and from Jon Velie, "Cherokee Freedmen" on 16 June 2007. Velie has been involved in a number of the recent cases regarding descendants of freedpeople of the Five Tribes. He is the lead counsel in another related case involving the rights of Cherokee freedpeople—*Marilyn Vann v. Kempthorne* in the District of Columbia District Court. See also Lee-St. John, "The Cherokee Nation's New Battle."

33 For the proposed bill, see Diane Watson, "HR 2824."

34 In addition, the majority of Cherokee voters also reaffirmed the removal of federal approval for any amendments to the Constitution of the Cherokee Nation.

35 The sociolegal construction of whiteness and blackness in the United States has been examined in a range of sociological, historical, and critical legal studies. See, for example, Davis, *Who Is Black?*, and López, *White by Law*.

36 Piper, "Passing for White, Passing for Black," 18–19 (emphasis in original).

37   For one discussion of the issue of blood quantum and "mixed bloods" in southern Indian nations, see Terry P. Wilson, "Blood Quantum," 108–25. Also see Strong and Van Winkle, "Indian Blood."

38   Limerick, *The Legacy of Conquest*, 338.

39   Vickers, *Native American Identities*, 164.

40   Ibid., 165–66.

41   Strong and Van Winkle, "Indian Blood," 552.

42   Ibid., 551.

Bibliography

Primary Sources

Manuscript Collections

Archives and Manuscripts Division, Oklahoma Historical Society, Oklahoma City.

Cherokee Nation. Cherokee-Census (Tahlequah), Cherokee Census of 1867.

Choctaw-Chickasaw Freedmen Census of 1885.

Grant Foreman, comp., *Indian Pioneer History Collection*. Oklahoma Historical Society Microfilm Publications, 1978–81.

National Records of the Cherokee Nation.

Oral History Program (Interviews).

Thomas Gilcrease Museum, Tulsa, Oklahoma.

John Drew Papers.

"Resolutions of the Freedmen Convention held at Fort Gibson, I.T., December 18, 1900." Gilcrease Broadside Collection No. MB-58.

National Archives, Southwest Region, Fort Worth, Texas.

Dawes Commission. Cherokee Nation.

Census Cards.

Enrollment Applications.

Land Allotment Records.

National Archives and Records Administration, Washington, D.C.

Letters Received by the Office of Indian Affairs. Washington, D.C.: National Archives Microfilm Publications, 1985.

Statement of Captain John Drew, 3 January 1843, M234, Roll 87, Cherokee folder 1843 S3322.

Northeastern State University, John Vaughan Library, Special Collections, Tahlequah, Oklahoma.

Letters of Andrew Nave.

Letters of Chief John Ross.

Bibliography

Western History Collections, University of Oklahoma, Norman.

Cherokee Nation Papers.

Stephen Foreman. Journal and Letters of Stephen Foreman. Box F-21. "A Private Journal Beginning January 1, 1862."

(Mrs. John B.) Lilley. Diary of Mrs. John B. Lilley, 1842–57. Lilley Collection. Minor Archives box L-5, folder no. 1152.05.

Cassandra Sawyer Lockwood. Diary of Cassandra Sawyer Lockwood. Roberta Robey Collection. Minor Archives R-33, folder no. 1235.33.

James Anderson Slover Sr. Autobiography of James Anderson Slover Sr. James Anderson Slover Collection, folder no. 1260.46.

Ruth Updegraff Collection. Declarations of sale of slaves in the Cherokee Nation in 1843 and 1853. Folder no. 1273.01.

Worcester Willey. Letters and Documents of the Worcester Willey Family of the Cherokee Nation, 1864–75. Pat Gomes Collection, box G-29, manuscript no. M1034.

Cherokee Nation Documents

11 Cherokee Nation Code Annotated § 12 (1983).

1975 Constitution of the Cherokee Nation of Oklahoma.

1999/2003 Constitution of the Cherokee Nation of Oklahoma.

Bernice Riggs, Petitioner v. Lela Ummerteskee. Acting Registrar of the Cherokee Nation, Respondent, case no. JAT-97-03.

Cherokee Nation. "Statement of Cherokee Nation Attorney General," 14 May 2007.

Cherokee Nation Election Commission. "Cherokee Special Election 2007 FAQS." Tahlequah, Oklahoma.

———. "Special Election Results-Official." Tahlequah, Oklahoma.

Lucy Allen, Petitioner v. Cherokee Nation Tribal Council, Lela Ummerteskee. Registrar of the Cherokee Nation and Registration Committee, Respondents, case no. JAT-04-09.

Raymond Nash, et al., Plaintiff, vs. Cherokee Nation Registrar, Defendant. "Temporary Order and Temporary Injunction," District Court of the Cherokee Nation, case nos. CV-07-40, CV-07-41, CV-07-42, CV-07-43, CV-07-44, CV-07-45, CV-07-46, CV-07-47, CV-07-48, CV-07-49, CV-07-50, CV-07-53, CV-07-56, CV-07-65, and CV-07-66.

Smith, Chad. "Citizen Views Fall on Both Sides of Freedmen Issue," 13 March 2006.

Newspapers

Advocate (Leavenworth, Kansas)

American Citizen (Baltimore)

American Citizen (Topeka, Kansas)

Cherokee Advocate (Tahlequah, Cherokee Nation, Indian Territory)

Chicago Tribune

Colored Patriot (Topeka, Kansas)

Colored Visitor (Logansport, Indiana)

El Reno News (El Reno, Canadian County, Oklahoma Territory)

Indian Chieftain (Vinita, Cherokee Nation, Indian Territory)

Kansas Herald (Topeka, Kansas)

Kingfisher Free Press (Kingfisher County, Oklahoma Territory)

Krebs Eagle (Krebs, Choctaw Nation, Indian Territory)

Memphis Daily Inquirer

Missionary Herald (Boston)

New York Times

Niles' National Register (Baltimore)

Oklahoma Guide (Logan County, Oklahoma Territory)

Stillwater Gazette (Stillwater, Oklahoma Territory)

St. Louis Argus

Published Primary Sources

Adair, William Penn. "The Indian Territory in 1878." *Chronicles of Oklahoma* 4, no. 3 (1926): 255–74.

American Board of Commissioners for Foreign Missions. *Papers of the American Board of Commissioners for Foreign Missions.* Woodbridge: Research Publications, 1985. Microfilm.

——. *Report of the American Board of Commissioners for Foreign Missions, Presented at the Thirty-fifth Annual Meeting.* Boston: Crocker and Brewster, 1844.

——. *Report of the American Board of Commissioners for Foreign Missions, Presented at the Thirty-sixth Annual Meeting.* Boston: Crocker and Brewster, 1845.

———. Report of the American Board of Commissioners for Foreign Missions, Presented at the Thirty-ninth Annual Meeting. Boston: T. R. Marvin, 1848.

———. Report of the American Board of Commissioners for Foreign Missions, Presented at the Fortieth Annual Meeting. Boston: T. R. Marvin, 1849.

———. Report of the American Board of Commissioners for Foreign Missions, Presented at the Forty-fifth Annual Meeting. Boston: T. R. Marvin, 1854.

———. Report of the American Board of Commissioners for Foreign Missions, Presented at the Fifty-first Annual Meeting. Boston: T. R. Marvin, 1860.

Baker, Lindsay T., and Julie P. Baker, eds. The WPA Oklahoma Slave Narratives. Norman: University of Oklahoma Press, 1996.

Blassingame, John W., ed. Slave Testimony: Two Centuries of Letters, Speeches, Interviews, and Autobiographies. Baton Rouge: Louisiana State University Press, 1977.

Cherokee Nation. Constitution and Laws of the Cherokee Nation: Passed at Tahlequah, Cherokee Nation, 1839–1851. Series 1, vol. 5 of The Constitutions and Laws of the American Indian Tribes. Wilmington: Scholarly Resources, 1973.

———. Constitution and Laws of the Cherokee Nation Published by Authority of the National Council. Vol. 7 of The Constitutions and Laws of the American Indian Tribes. Wilmington: Scholarly Resources, 1973.

———. Laws of the Cherokee Nation Adopted by the Council at Various Periods, Printed for the Benefit of the Nation. Series 1, vol. 5 of The Constitutions and Laws of the American Indian Tribes. Wilmington: Scholarly Resources, 1973.

———. Laws of the Cherokee Nation Passed during the Years 1839–1867. Series 1, vol. 6 of The Constitutions and Laws of the American Indian Tribes. Wilmington: Scholarly Resources, 1973.

"The Cherokee Question." Chronicles of Oklahoma 2, no. 2 (1924): 141–242.

Dann, Martin E., ed. and comp. The Black Press 1827–1890: The Quest for National Identity. New York: Capricorn Books, 1972.

Duncan, James W. "The Keetowah Society." Chronicles of Oklahoma 4, no. 3 (September 1926): 251–54.

Galvin, John, ed. Through the Country of the Comanche Indians in the Fall of the Year 1845: The Journal of a U.S. Army Expedition Led by Lieutenant James W. Abert of the Topographical Engineers. San Francisco: John Howell, 1970.

Georgia Writers' Project. Drums and Shadows: Survival Studies among the Georgia Coastal Negroes. Athens: University of Georgia Press, 1986.

Gooding, James Henry. *On the Altar of Freedom: A Black Soldier's Civil War Letters from the Front.* Edited by Virginia Matzke Adams. Amherst: University of Massachusetts Press, 1991.

Hicks, Hannah. "The Diary of Hannah Hicks." *American Scene* 13, no. 3 (1972): 1–24.

Hitchcock, Ethan Allen. *A Traveler in Indian Territory: The Journal of Ethan Allen Hitchcock, Late Major-General in the United States Army.* Edited by Grant Foreman. Foreword by Michael D. Green. Norman: University of Oklahoma Press, 1996.

Kappler, Charles J., comp. and ed. *Indian Affairs: Laws and Treaties.* Vol. 2. Washington, D.C.: Government Printing Office, 1904.

Moulton, Gary E., ed. *The Papers of Chief John Ross.* Vol. 1, 1807–1839. Norman: University of Oklahoma Press, 1985.

———. *The Papers of Chief John Ross.* Vol. 2, 1840–1866. Norman: University of Oklahoma Press, 1985.

Osofsky, Gilbert, ed. *Puttin' on Ole Massa: The Slave Narratives of Henry Bibb, William Wells Brown and Solomon Northup.* New York: Harper and Row, 1969.

Perdue, Charles L., Jr., Thomas E. Barden, and Robert K. Phillips, eds. *Weevils in the Wheat: Interviews with Virginia Ex-Slaves.* Bloomington: Indiana University Press, 1980.

Rawick, George P., ed. *Mississippi Narratives.* Vol. 9, pt. 4, suppl. series 1 of *The American Slave.* Westport: Greenwood Press, 1977.

———. *Oklahoma and Mississippi Narratives.* Vol. 7 of *The American Slave.* Westport: Greenwood Press, 1973.

———. *Oklahoma Narratives.* Vol. 12, suppl. series 1 of *The American Slave.* Westport: Greenwood Press, 1977.

Redkey, Edwin S., ed. *A Grand Army of Black Men: Letters from African-American Soldiers in the Union Army, 1861–1865.* Cambridge: Cambridge University Press, 1992.

Thoburn, Joseph B. "Letters of Cassandra Sawyer Lockwood: Dwight Mission, 1834." *Chronicles of Oklahoma* 33, no. 2 (Summer 1955): 202–37.

U.S. Bureau of the Census. *Negro Population of the United States, 1790–1915.* Washington, D.C.: Government Printing Office, 1915.

U.S. Congress. House. *Report of the Secretary of the Interior.* 44th Cong., 1st sess., H. Exec. Doc. 1, Pt. 5. Washington, D.C.: Government Printing Office, 1875.

Bibliography

——. *Report on Indians Taxed and Indians Not Taxed in the United States (except Alaska) at the Eleventh Census: 1890*. 52nd Cong., 1st sess., H. Mis. Doc. 340, Pt. 15. Washington, D.C.: Government Printing Office, 1894.

U.S. Department of the Interior. *Annual Report of the Commissioner of Indian Affairs to the Secretary of the Interior for the Year 1865*. Washington, D.C.: Government Printing Office, 1865.

——. *Annual Report of the Commissioner of Indian Affairs to the Secretary of the Interior for the Year 1873*. Washington, D.C.: Government Printing Office, 1873.

——. *Annual Report of the Commissioner of Indian Affairs to the Secretary of the Interior for the Year 1876*. Washington, D.C.: Government Printing Office, 1876.

——. *Annual Report of the Commissioner of Indian Affairs to the Secretary of the Interior for the Year 1887*. Washington, D.C.: Government Printing Office, 1887.

——. *Annual Report of the Commissioner of Indian Affairs to the Secretary of the Interior, 1892*. Washington, D.C.: Government Printing Office, 1892.

——. *Report on Indian Affairs by the Acting Commissioner for the Year 1867*. Washington, D.C.: Government Printing Office, 1868.

——. *Reports of the Department of Interior for the Fiscal Year Ended June 30, 1907*. Vol. 2. Washington, D.C.: Government Printing Office, 1907.

——. *Reports of the Department of Interior for the Fiscal Year Ended June 30, 1908*. Vol. 2. Washington, D.C.: Government Printing Office, 1908.

U.S. Department of the Interior. Census Office. *Compendium of the Eleventh Census, 1890: Population*. Part 1. Washington, D.C.: Government Printing Office, 1892.

U.S. War Department. *War of the Rebellion: A Compilation of the Official Records of the Union and Confederate Armies*. Series I, vol. 22, part 1. Washington, D.C.: Government Printing Office, 1888.

Whipple, Charles K. *Relation of the American Board of Commissioners for Foreign Missions to Slavery*. Boston: R. F. Wallcut, 1861.

Secondary Sources

Books

Abbott, Martin. *The Freedmen's Bureau in South Carolina, 1865–1872*. Chapel Hill: University of North Carolina Press, 1967.

Abel, Annie H. *The American Indian and the End of the Confederacy, 1863–1866.* Lincoln: University of Nebraska Press, 1992.

———. *The American Indian as Participant in the Civil War.* Lincoln: University of Nebraska Press, 1992.

———. *The American Indian as Slaveholder and Secessionist.* Lincoln: University of Nebraska Press, 1992.

Allen, James, Hilton Als, John Lewis, and Leon F. Litwack. *Without Sanctuary: Lynching Photography in America.* New Mexico: Twin Palms Publishers, 2000.

Anderson, James D. *The Education of Blacks in the South, 1860–1935.* Chapel Hill: University of North Carolina Press, 1988.

Anderson, William L. *Cherokee Removal: Before and After.* Athens: University of Georgia Press, 1991.

Aptheker, Herbert. *American Negro Slave Revolts.* New York: International Publishers, 1963.

Bailey, M. Thomas. *Reconstruction in Indian Territory: A Story of Avarice, Discrimination and Opportunism.* New York: Kennikat Press, 1972.

Barthes, Roland. *The Fashion System.* Translated by Matthew Ward and Richard Howard. Berkeley: University of California Press, 1990.

Bass, Althea. *Cherokee Messenger.* Norman: University of Oklahoma Press, 1936.

Beaver, R. Pierce. *Church, State and the American Indian: Two and a Half Centuries of Partnership in Missions between Protestant Churches and the Government.* St. Louis: Concordia Publishing House, 1966.

Beckles, Hilary McD. *Afro-Caribbean Women and Resistance to Slavery in Barbados.* London: Karnak House, 1988.

Bennett, Lerone, Jr. *The Shaping of Black America.* Chicago: Johnson Publishing, 1975.

Bentley, George R. *A History of the Freedmen's Bureau.* New York: Octagon Books, 1974.

Berkhofer, Robert F. *Salvation and the Savage: An Analysis of Protestant Missions and American Indian Response, 1787–1862.* Westport: Greenwood Press, 1977.

———. *The White Man's Indian: Images of the American Indian from Columbus to the Present.* New York: Random House, 1978.

Bibliography

Blackburn, Bob L. *Images of Oklahoma: A Pictorial History with Text.* Oklahoma City: Oklahoma Historical Society, 1984.

Blassingame, John W. *The Slave Community: Plantation Life in the Antebellum South.* New York: Oxford University Press, 1972.

Bolt, Christine. *American Indian Policy and American Reform: Case Studies of the Campaign to Assimilate the American Indians.* London: Allen & Unwin, 1987.

Boudinot, Elias. *Cherokee Editor, the Writings of Elias Boudinot.* Knoxville: University of Tennessee Press, 1983.

Bowden, Henry Warner. *American Indians and Christian Missions: Studies in Culture Conflict.* Chicago: University of Chicago Press, 1981.

Bracey, John H., Jr., August Meier, and Elliott Rudwick, eds. *American Slavery: The Question of Resistance.* Belmont: Wadsworth Publishing, 1971.

Brooks, James F. *Captives and Cousins: Slavery, Kinship, and Community in the Southwest Borderlands.* Chapel Hill: University of North Carolina Press for the Omohundro Institute of Early American History and Culture, 2002.

———, ed. *Confounding the Color Line: The Indian-Black Experience in North America.* Lincoln: University of Nebraska Press, 2002.

Brown, Linda Keller, and Kay Mussell, eds. *Ethnic and Regional Foodways in the United States: The Performance of Group Identity.* Knoxville: University of Tennessee Press, 1984.

Burton, Arthur T. *Black, Buckskin and Blue: African-American Scouts and Soldiers on the Western Frontier.* Austin: Eakin Press, 1999.

———. *Black, Red and Deadly: Black and Indian Gunfighters of the Indian Territory, 1870–1907.* Austin: Eakin Press, 1991.

Bush, Barbara. *Slave Women in Caribbean Society, 1650–1838.* Bloomington: Indiana University Press, 1990.

Butchart, Ronald E. *Northern Schools, Southern Blacks and Reconstruction: Freedmen's Education, 1862–1875.* Westport: Greenwood Press, 1980.

Byfield, Judith A. *The Bluest Hands: A Social and Economic History of Women Dyers in Abeokuta (Nigeria), 1890–1940.* Oxford: Heinemann, 2002.

Camp, Stephanie. *Closer to Freedom: Enslaved Women and Everyday Resistance in the Plantation South.* Chapel Hill: University of North Carolina Press, 2004.

Carter, Kent. *The Dawes Commission and the Allotment of the Five Civilized Tribes, 1893–1914.* Orem, Utah: Ancestry.com Incorporated, 1999.

Carter, Samuel. *Cherokee Sunset: A Nation Betrayed, a Narrative of Travail and Triumph, Persecution and Exile.* New York: Doubleday, 1976.

Chalmers, David M. *Hooded Americanism: The First Century of the Ku Klux Klan, 1865–1965.* Garden City, N.Y.: Doubleday, 1965.

Champagne, Duane. *Social Order and Political Change: Constitutional Governments among the Cherokee, the Choctaw, the Chickasaw and the Creek.* Stanford: Stanford University Press, 1992.

Cimbala, Paul A. *Under the Guardianship of the Nation: The Freedmen's Bureau and the Reconstruction of Georgia, 1865–1870.* Athens: University of Georgia Press, 1997.

Clifton, James A. *Being and Becoming Indian: Biographical Studies of North American Frontiers.* Chicago: Dorsey Press, 1989.

Clinton, Catherine. *The Plantation Mistress: Woman's World in the Old South.* New York: Pantheon, 1982.

Coleman, Michael C. *Presbyterian Missionary Attitudes toward American Indians, 1837–1893.* Jackson: University Press of Mississippi, 1985.

Collins, Hubert E. *Storm and Stampede on the Chisholm.* Lincoln: University of Nebraska Press, 1998. Originally published as *Warpath and Cattle Trail* in 1928.

Cornish, Dudley Taylor. *The Sable Arm: Black Troops in the Union Army, 1861–1865.* Lawrence: University Press of Kansas, 1987.

Counihan, Carole M., and Steven L. Kaplan. *Food and Gender: Identity and Power.* Australia: Harwood Academic Publishers, 1998.

Craton, Michael. *Testing the Chains: Resistance to Slavery in the British West Indies.* Ithaca: Cornell University Press, 1982.

Crisman, Harry E. *Lost Trails of the Cimarron.* Denver: Sage Books, 1961.

Crouch, Barry A. *The Freedmen's Bureau and Black Texans.* Austin: University of Texas Press, 1992.

Dale, Edward E., and Gaston Litton. *Cherokee Cavaliers: Forty Years of Cherokee History as Told in the Correspondence of the Ridge-Watie-Boudinot Family.* Norman: University of Oklahoma Press, 1939.

Dale, Edward E., and Morris L. Wardell. *History of Oklahoma.* New York: Prentice-Hall, 1950.

Davis, F. James. *Who Is Black?: One Nation's Definition.* 10th Anniversary edition. University Park: Pennsylvania State University Press, 2001.

Debo, Angie. *And Still the Waters Run: The Betrayal of the Five Civilized Tribes.* Princeton: Princeton University Press, 1991.

———. *The Rise and Fall of the Choctaw Republic.* Norman: University of Oklahoma Press, 1972.

Deloria, Philip J. *Playing Indian.* New Haven: Yale University Press, 1998.

Du Bois, W. E. B. *The Souls of Black Folk.* New York: New American Library, 1982.

Eaton, Rachel Caroline. *John Ross and the Cherokee Indians.* Chicago: University of Chicago Libraries, 1921.

Eggan, Fred. *The American Indian: Perspectives for the Study of Social Change.* Chicago: Aldine Publishing, 1966.

Ehle, John. *Trail of Tears: The Rise and Fall of the Cherokee Nation.* New York: Anchor Press, 1988.

Ellis, E. H. *History of the Oklahoma Constitutional Convention.* Muskogee: Economy Printing Company, 1923.

Escott, Paul David. *Slavery Remembered: A Record of Twentieth-Century Slave Narratives.* Chapel Hill: University of North Carolina Press, 1979.

Farb, Peter, and George Armelagos. *Consuming Passions: The Anthropology of Eating.* New York: Washington Square Press, 1983.

Fett, Sharla M. *Working Cures: Healing, Health, and Power on Southern Slave Plantations.* Chapel Hill: University of North Carolina Press, 2002.

Filler, Louis, and Allen Guttmann, eds. *The Removal of the Cherokee Nation: Manifest Destiny or National Dishonor?* Boston: D. C. Heath, 1962.

Foner, Eric. *Nothing But Freedom.* Baton Rouge: Louisiana State University Press, 1983.

———. *Reconstruction: America's Unfinished Revolution, 1863–1877.* New York: Harper and Row, 1988.

Forbes, Jack D. *Africans and Native Americans: The Language of Race and the Evolution of Red-Black Peoples.* Urbana: University of Illinois Press, 1993.

Foreman, Grant. *The Advancing Frontier.* Norman: University of Oklahoma Press, 1933.

———. *The Five Civilized Tribes.* Norman: University of Oklahoma Press, 1934.

Foster, Helen Bradley. *"New Raiments of Self": African American Clothing in the Antebellum South.* New York: Oxford, 1997.

Fox-Genovese, Elizabeth. *Within the Plantation Household: Black and White*

Women of the Old South. Chapel Hill: University of North Carolina Press, 1988.

Fraginals, Manuel Moreno, Frank Moya Pons, and Stanley Engerman, eds. *Between Slavery and Free Labor: The Spanish-Speaking Caribbean in the Nineteenth Century*. Baltimore: Johns Hopkins University Press, 1985.

Franklin, Jimmie Lewis. *The Blacks in Oklahoma*. Norman: University of Oklahoma Press, 1980.

———. *Journey toward Hope: A History of Blacks in Oklahoma*. Norman: University of Oklahoma Press, 1982.

Franklin, John Hope, and Alfred A. Moss Jr. *From Slavery to Freedom: A History of Negro Americans*. New York: Alfred A. Knopf, 1988.

Franklin, John Hope, and Loren Schweninger. *Runaway Slaves: Rebels on the Plantation*. New York: Oxford University Press, 1999.

Franks, Kenny A. *Stand Watie and the Agony of the Cherokee Nation*. Memphis: Memphis State University Press, 1979.

Gabriel, Ralph H. *Elias Boudinot, Cherokee and His America*. Norman: University of Oklahoma Press, 1941.

Gaines, W. Craig. *The Confederate Cherokees: John Drew's Regiment of Mounted Rifles*. Baton Rouge: Louisiana State University Press, 1989.

Gallay, Alan. *The Indian Slave Trade: The Rise of the English Empire in the American South*. New Haven: Yale University Press, 2002.

Gard, Wayne. *The Chisholm Trail*. Norman: University of Oklahoma Press, 1954.

Gaspar, David Barry. *Bondmen and Rebels: A Case Study of Master-Slave Relations in Antigua, with Implications for Colonial British America*. Baltimore: Johns Hopkins University Press, 1985.

Gaspar, David Barry, and David Patrick Geggus, eds. *A Turbulent Time: The French Revolution and the Greater Caribbean*. Bloomington: Indiana University Press, 1997.

Geggus, David Patrick. *Slave Resistance Studies and the Saint Domingue Slave Revolt*. Miami: Latin American and Caribbean Center of Florida International University, 1983.

Genovese, Eugene D. *From Rebellion to Revolution: Afro-American Slave Revolts in the Making of the Modern World*. Baton Rouge: Louisiana State University Press, 1979.

——. *Roll, Jordan, Roll: The World the Slaves Made.* New York: Vintage Books, 1974.

Gibson, Arrell M. *The Chickasaws.* Norman: University of Oklahoma, 1971.

——. *The History of Oklahoma.* Norman: University of Oklahoma Press, 1984.

——. *Oklahoma: A History of Five Centuries.* Norman: University of Oklahoma Press, 1981.

——. *The Oklahoma Story.* Norman: University of Oklahoma Press, 1978.

Glatthaar, Joseph T. *Forged in Battle: The Civil War Alliance of Black Soldiers and White Officers.* New York: Free Press, 1990.

Glaude, Eddie S., Jr. *Exodus!: Religion, Race and Nation in Early Nineteenth-Century Black America.* Chicago: University of Chicago Press, 2000.

Gonzalez, Nancie L. Solien. *Sojourners of the Caribbean: Ethnogenesis and Ethnohistory of the Garifuna.* Urbana: University of Illinois Press, 1988.

Goodenow, Ronald K., and Arthur O. White, eds. *Education and the Rise of the New South.* Boston: G. K. Hall, 1981.

Halliburton, Rudi, Jr. *Red over Black: Black Slavery among the Cherokee Indians.* Westport: Greenwood Press, 1977.

Harding, Vincent. *There Is a River: The Black Struggle for Freedom in America.* New York: Vintage Books, 1983.

Harmon, George Dewey. *Sixty Years of Indian Affairs: Political, Economic and Diplomatic, 1789–1850.* Chapel Hill: University of North Carolina Press, 1941.

Hauptman, Laurence M. *Between Two Fires: American Indians in the Civil War.* New York: Free Press, 1995.

Hawthorne, Walter. *Planting Rice and Harvesting Slaves: Transformations along the Guinea-Bissau Coast, 1400–1900.* Portsmouth, N.H.: Heinemann, 2003.

Hofsommer, Donovan L., ed. *Railroads in Oklahoma.* Oklahoma City: Oklahoma Historical Society, 1977.

Hoig, Stan. *The Oklahoma Land Rush of 1889.* Oklahoma City: Oklahoma Historical Society, 1989.

Horn, Stanley F. *Invisible Empire: The Story of the Ku Klux Klan, 1866–1871.* New York: Haskell House, 1968.

Horr, David Agee, ed. *Cherokee and Creek Indians.* New York: Garland Publishing, 1974.

Horton, James Oliver, and Lois E. Horton. *In Hope of Liberty: Culture, Community* and *Protest among Northern Free Blacks, 1700–1860.* New York: Oxford University Press, 1997.

Howard, Rosalyn. *Black Seminoles in the Bahamas.* Gainesville: University Press of Florida, 2002.

Issenman, Betty. *Sinews of Survival: The Living Legacy of Inuit Clothing.* Vancouver: UBC Press, 1997.

Johnson, Michael P. *Black Masters: A Free Family of Color in the Old South.* New York: W. W. Norton, 1984.

Jones, Edward P. *The Known World.* New York: Amistad, 2003.

Josephy, Alvin M., Jr. *The Civil War in the American West.* New York: Vintage, 1993.

Joyce, Davis D. *"An Oklahoma I Had Never Seen Before": Alternative Views of Oklahoma History.* Norman: University of Oklahoma Press, 1994.

Katz, William Loren. *Black Indians: A Hidden Heritage.* New York: Atheneum, 1985.

Kerns, Virginia. *Women and the Ancestors: Black Carib Kinship and Ritual.* Urbana: University of Illinois Press, 1997.

Kidwell, Clara Sue. *Choctaws and Missionaries in Mississippi, 1818–1918.* Norman: University of Oklahoma Press, 1995.

King, Duane H. *The Cherokee Indian Nation: A Troubled History.* Knoxville: University of Tennessee Press, 1979.

Lancaster, Jane F. *Removal Aftershock: The Seminoles' Struggles to Survive in the West, 1836–1866.* Knoxville: University of Tennessee Press, 1994.

Lauber, Almon W. *Indian Slavery in Colonial Times within the Present Limits of the United States.* Williamstown: Corner House, 1970.

Limerick, Patricia Nelson. *The Legacy of Conquest: The Unbroken Past of the American West.* New York: W. W. Norton, 1987.

Littlefield, Daniel F., Jr. *Africans and Creeks: From the Colonial Period to the Civil War.* Westport: Greenwood Press, 1979.

———. *Africans and Seminoles: From Removal to Emancipation.* Westport: Greenwood Press, 1977.

———. *The Cherokee Freedmen: From Emancipation to American Citizenship.* Westport: Greenwood Press, 1978.

———. *The Chickasaw Freedmen: A People without a Country.* Westport: Greenwood Press, 1980.

Bibliography

López, Ian F. Haney. *White by Law: The Legal Construction of Race*. New York: New York University Press, 1996.

Lovejoy, Paul E. *Transformations in Slavery: A History of Slavery in Africa*. 2nd ed. Cambridge: Cambridge University Press, 2000.

Malone, Henry Thompson. *Cherokees of the Old South: A People in Transition*. Athens: University of Georgia Press, 1956.

Mankiller, Wilma, and Michael Wallis. *Mankiller: A Chief and Her People*. New York: St. Martin's Press, 1993.

Marsden, George M. *The Evangelical Mind and the New School Presbyterian Experience: A Case Study of Thought and Theology in Nineteenth-Century America*. New Haven: Yale University Press, 1970.

Martin, Jack B., and Margaret McKane Mauldin. *A Dictionary of Creek/Muskogee, with Notes on the Florida and Oklahoma Seminole Dialects of Creek*. Lincoln: University of Nebraska Press, 2000.

Marty, Martin E. *Righteous Empire: The Protestant Experience in America*. New York: Dial, 1970.

Maxwell, Amos D. *The Sequoyah Constitutional Convention*. Boston: Meador Publishing, 1953.

May, Katja. *African Americans and Native Americans in the Creek and Cherokee Nations, 1830s to 1920s: Collision and Collusion*. New York: Garland Publishing, 1996.

May, Lary. *The Big Tomorrow: Hollywood and the Politics of the American Way*. Chicago: University of Chicago Press, 2000.

Mays, Joe H. *Black Americans and Their Contributions toward Union Victory in the American Civil War*. Lanham: University Press of America, 1984.

McCoy, Isaac. *History of Baptist Indian Missions: Embracing Remarks on the Former and Present Condition of the Aboriginal Tribes, Their Settlement within the Indian Territory, and Their Future Prospects*. Washington, D.C.: William M. Morrison, 1840.

McGlynn, Frank, and Seymour Drescher, eds. *The Meaning of Freedom: Economics, Politics and Culture after Slavery*. Pittsburgh: University of Pittsburgh Press, 1992.

McLaurin, Melton A. *Celia, a Slave*. New York: HarperCollins, 1999.

McLoughlin, William Gerald. *After the Trail of Tears: The Cherokees' Struggle for Sovereignty, 1839–1880*. Chapel Hill: University of North Carolina Press, 1993.

——. *Champions of the Cherokees: Evan and John B. Jones.* Princeton: Princeton University Press, 1990.

——. *The Cherokee Ghost Dance: Essays on the Southeastern Indians, 1789–1861.* Macon: Mercer University Press, 1984.

——. *Cherokee Renascence in the New Republic.* Princeton: Princeton University Press, 1986.

——. *The Cherokees and Christianity, 1794–1870: Essays on Acculturation and Cultural Persistence.* Athens: University of Georgia Press, 1994.

——. *Cherokees and Missionaries, 1789–1839.* New Haven: Yale University Press, 1984.

McReynolds, Edwin C. *Oklahoma: A History of the Sooner State.* Norman: University of Oklahoma Press, 1954.

McReynolds, Edwin C., Alice Marriott, and Estelle Faulconer. *Oklahoma: The Story of Its Past and Present.* Norman: University of Oklahoma Press, 1975.

Miles, Tiya. *Ties That Bind: The Story of an Afro-Cherokee Family in Slavery and Freedom.* Berkeley: University of California Press, 2005.

Minges, Patrick, ed. *Black Indian Slave Narratives.* Winston-Salem, N.C.: John F. Blair, 2004.

——. *Far More Terrible for Women: Personal Accounts of Women in Slavery.* Winston-Salem, N.C.: John F. Blair, 2006.

Mooney, James. *Myths of the Cherokee and Sacred Formulas of the Cherokees.* Nashville: Charles and Randy Elder, 1982.

Morgan, H. Wayne. *Oklahoma: A Bicentennial History.* New York: W. W. Norton, 1977.

Morgan, Jennifer L. *Laboring Women: Reproduction and Gender in New World Slavery.* Philadelphia: University of Pennsylvania Press, 2004.

Morris, John W., Charles R. Goins, and Edwin C. McReynolds. *Historical Atlas of Oklahoma.* Norman: University of Oklahoma Press, 1986.

Morris, Robert C. *Reading, 'Riting and Reconstruction: The Education of Freedmen in the South, 1861–1870.* Chicago: University of Chicago Press, 1981.

Moulton, Gary E. *John Ross, Cherokee Chief.* Athens: University of Georgia Press, 1978.

Mulroy, Kevin. *Freedom on the Border: The Seminole Maroons in Florida, the Indian Territory, Coahuila, and Texas.* Lubbock: Texas Tech University Press, 1993.

Bibliography

Nash, Gary B. *Red, White, and Black: The Peoples of Early America*. Englewood Cliffs: Prentice-Hall, 1982.

Newell, Margaret. *"The Drove of Adam's Degenerate Seed": Indian Slavery in New England*. Ithaca: Cornell University Press, forthcoming.

Okihiro, Gary Y., ed. *In Resistance: Studies in African, Caribbean and Afro-American History*. Amherst: University of Massachusetts Press, 1986.

Oubre, Claude F. *Forty Acres and a Mule: The Freedmen's Bureau and Black Land Ownership*. Baton Rouge: Louisiana State University Press, 1978.

Painter, Nell Irvin. *Exodusters: Black Migration to Kansas after Reconstruction*. New York: W. W. Norton, 1992.

Paradis, James M. *Strike the Blow for Freedom: The 6th United States Colored Infantry in the Civil War*. Shippensburg: White Mane Books, 1998.

Pearce, Roy Harvey. *Savagism and Civilization: A Study of the Indian and the American Mind*. Baltimore: Johns Hopkins University Press, 1964.

Perdue, Theda. *Cherokee Women: Gender and Culture Change, 1700–1835*. Lincoln: University of Nebraska Press, 1998.

——. *"Mixed Blood" Indians: Racial Construction in the Early South*. Athens: University of Georgia Press, 2003.

——. *Slavery and the Evolution of Cherokee Society, 1540–1866*. Knoxville: University of Tennessee Press, 1979.

Perdue, Theda, and Michael D. Green, eds. *The Cherokee Removal: A Brief History with Documents*. New York: St. Martin's Press, 1995.

Poole, Dewitt Clinton. *Among the Sioux of Dakota: Eighteen Months' Experience as an Indian Agent, 1869–1870*. St. Paul: Minnesota Historical Society Press, 1988.

Prucha, Francis Paul. *American Indian Policy in the Formative Years: The Indian Trade and Intercourse Acts of 1790–1834*. Cambridge, Mass.: Harvard University Press, 1962.

Raboteau, Albert J. *Slave Religion: The "Invisible Institution" in the Antebellum South*. New York: Oxford University Press, 1978.

Redkey, Edwin S. *Black Exodus: Black Nationalist and Back-to-Africa Movements, 1890–1910*. New Haven: Yale University Press, 1969.

Richardson, David, ed. *Abolition and Its Aftermath: The Historical Context, 1790–1916*. London: Frank Cass, 1985.

Richter, William. *Overreached on all Sides: The Freedmen's Bureau Administrators in Texas, 1865–1868*. College Station: Texas A&M University Press, 1991.

Rister, Carl C. *Baptist Missions among the American Indians*. Atlanta: Home Mission Board, Southern Baptist Convention, 1944.

Robinson, Prentice. *Easy to Use Cherokee Dictionary*. Tulsa: Cherokee Language and Culture, 1996.

Roche, Daniel. *The Culture of Clothing: Dress and Fashion in the "Ancien Regime."* Translated by Jean Birrell. New York: Cambridge University Press, 1996.

Roediger, Virginia More. *Ceremonial Costumes of the Pueblo Indians: Their Evolution, Fabrication and Significance in the Prayer Drama*. Berkeley: University of California Press, 1991.

Ronda, James. P., and James Axtell. *Indian Missions: A Critical Bibliography*. Bloomington: Indiana University Press, 1978.

Root, Maria P. P., ed. *Racially Mixed People in America*. Newbury Park: Sage Publications, 1992.

Sapir, Edward. *Culture, Language and Personality: Selected Essays*. Edited by David G. Mandelbaum. Berkeley: University of California Press, 1956. Originally published ca. 1949.

Scapp, Ron, and Brian Seitz, eds. *Eating Culture*. Albany: State University of New York Press, 1998.

Schafer, Judith Kelleher. *Becoming Free, Remaining Free: Manumission and Enslavement in New Orleans, 1846–1862*. Baton Rouge: Louisiana State University, 2003.

Seymour, Flora Warren. *Indian Agents of the Old Frontier*. New York: D. Appleton-Century, 1941.

Sheehan, Bernard W. *Seeds of Extinction: Jeffersonian Philanthropy and the American Indian*. Chapel Hill: University of North Carolina Press, 1973.

Sizemore, Donald. *Cherokee Dance: Ceremonial Dances and Dance Regalia*. Cherokee, N.C.: Cherokee Publications, 1999.

Skaggs, Jimmy M., ed. *Ranch and Range in Oklahoma*. Oklahoma City: Oklahoma Historical Society, 1978.

Sober, Nancy Hope. *The Intruders: The Illegal Residents of the Cherokee Nation, 1866–1907*. Ponca City: Cherokee Books, 1991.

Bibliography

Southwell, Kristina L., ed. *The Cherokee Nation Papers: Inventory and Index.*
Norman: Associates of the Western History Collections, 1996.

Spoehr, Alexander. *Changing Kinship Systems: A Study in the Acculturation of the
Creeks, Cherokee and Choctaw.* Anthropological Series, no. 33. Chicago: Field
Museum of Natural History, 1947.

Stampp, Kenneth M. *The Peculiar Institution: Slavery in the Antebellum South.* New
York: Alfred A. Knopf, 1956.

Starkey, Marion L. *The Cherokee Nation.* New York: Alfred A. Knopf, 1946.

Starr, Emmet. *History of the Cherokee Indians and Their Legends and Folk Lore.* New
York: Kraus Reprint, 1977.

Strickland, Rennard. *Fire and the Spirits: Cherokee Law from Clan to Court.*
Norman: University of Oklahoma Press, 1975.

———. *The Indians in Oklahoma.* Norman: University of Oklahoma Press, 1980.

Sturm, Circe. *Blood Politics: Race, Culture, and Identity in the Cherokee Nation of
Oklahoma.* Berkeley: University of California Press, 2002.

Teall, Kaye M. *Black History in Oklahoma: A Resource Book.* Oklahoma City:
Oklahoma City Public Schools, 1971.

Terrell, John Upton. *The Arrow and the Cross: A History of the American Indian and
the Missionaries.* Santa Barbara: Capra Press, 1979.

Thoburn, Joseph B. *A Standard History of Oklahoma.* Vol. 1. Chicago: American
Historical Society, 1916.

Thoburn, Joseph B., and Isaac M. Holcomb. *A History of Oklahoma.* San
Francisco: Doub, 1908.

Thoburn, Joseph B., and Muriel H. Wright, eds. *Oklahoma: A History of the State
and Its People.* Vol. 1. New York: Lewis Historical Publishing, 1929.

Thornton, John K. *Africa and Africans in the Making of the Atlantic World, 1400–
1680.* Cambridge: Cambridge University Press, 1992.

Thornton, Russell, with the assistance of C. Matthew Snipp and Nancy Breen.
The Cherokees: A Population History. Lincoln: University of Nebraska Press,
1990.

Tinker, George E. *Missionary Conquest: The Gospel and Native American Cultural
Genocide.* Minneapolis: Fortress Press, 1993.

Tolson, Arthur L. *The Black Oklahomans: A History, 1541–1972.* New Orleans:
Edwards Printing Company, 1974.

Trealease, Allen W. *White Terror: The Ku Klux Klan Conspiracy and Southern Reconstruction.* Baton Rouge: Louisiana State University Press, 1995.

Trudeau, Noah Andre. *Like Men of War: Black Troops in the Civil War, 1862–1865.* Boston: Little, Brown, 1998.

Vickers, Scott B. *Native American Identities: From Stereotype to Archetype in Art and Literature.* Albuquerque: University of New Mexico Press, 1998.

Vizenor, Gerald. *Crossbloods: Bone Courts, Bingo and Other Reports.* Minneapolis: University of Minnesota Press, 1990.

Walk, Joe. *Memphis Executive and Legislative Government.* Memphis: J. Walk, 1996.

Walker, Robert Sparks. *Torchlights to the Cherokees, the Brainerd Mission.* New York: Macmillan, 1931.

Walton-Raji, Angela Y. *Black Indian Genealogy Research: African American Ancestors among the Five Civilized Tribes.* Bowie: Heritage Books, 1993.

Wardell, Morris L. *A Political History of the Cherokee Nation, 1838–1907.* Norman: University of Oklahoma Press, 1938.

Washburn, Cephas. *Reminiscences of the Indians.* New York: Johnson Reprint Corporation, 1991.

West, C. W. "Dub." *Missions and Missionaries of Indian Territory.* Oklahoma: Muscogee Publishing, 1990.

Westwood, Howard C. *Black Troops, White Commanders, and Freedmen during the Civil War.* Carbondale: Southern Illinois University Press, 1992.

White, Howard A. *The Freedmen's Bureau in Louisiana.* Baton Rouge: Louisiana State University Press, 1970.

White, Shane, and Graham White. *Stylin': African American Expressive Culture from Its Beginnings to the Zoot Suit.* Ithaca: Cornell University Press, 1998.

Whorf, Benjamin. *Language, Thought and Reality: Selected Writings.* Edited and with an introduction by John B. Carroll. Cambridge: Technology Press of Massachusetts Institute of Technology, 1956.

Wickett, Murray R. *Contested Territory: Whites, Native Americans and African Americans in Oklahoma, 1865–1907.* Baton Rouge: Louisiana State University Press, 2000.

Wilkins, Thurman. *Cherokee Tragedy: The Ridge Family and the Decimation of a People.* Norman: University of Oklahoma Press, 1983. Originally published in 1970.

Bibliography

Wood, Peter H. *Black Majority: Negroes in Colonial South Carolina from 1670 through the Stono Rebellion*. New York: W. W. Norton, 1975.

Woodhouse, Samuel Washington. *A Naturalist in Indian Territory: The Journals of S. W. Woodhouse, 1849–1850*. Norman: University of Oklahoma Press, 1992.

Woodward, Grace Steele. *The Cherokees*. Norman: University of Oklahoma Press, 1963.

Wright, J. Leitch, Jr. *Creeks and Seminoles: Destruction and Regeneration of the Muscogulge People*. Lincoln: University of Nebraska Press, 1986.

———. *The Only Land They Knew: The Tragic Story of the American Indians in the Old South*. New York: Free Press, 1981.

Yarbrough, Fay. *Race and the Cherokee Nation: Sovereignty in the Nineteenth Century*. Philadelphia: University of Pennsylvania Press, 2007.

Articles

Andrew, John. "Educating the Heathen: The Foreign Mission School Controversy and American Ideals." *Journal of American Studies* 12 (1978): 331–42.

Andrews, Thomas F. "Freedmen in Indian Territory: A Post Civil War Dilemma." *Journal of the West* 4, no. 3 (July 1965): 367–76.

Axtell, James. "Some Thoughts on the Ethnohistory of Missions." *Ethnohistory* 29 (1982): 35–41.

Bailey, David Thomas. "A Divided Prism: Two Sources of Black Testimony on Slavery." *Journal of Southern History* 46, no. 3 (August 1980): 381–404.

Baird, W. David. "Are There 'Real' Indians in Oklahoma?: Historical Perceptions of the Five Civilized Tribes." *Chronicles of Oklahoma* 68, no. 1 (1990): 4–23.

Ballenger, T. L. "The Colored High School of the Cherokee Nation." *Chronicles of Oklahoma* 30, no. 4 (1952–53): 454–62.

Balyeat, Frank A. "Segregation in the Public Schools of Oklahoma Territory." *Chronicles of Oklahoma* 39, no. 2 (Summer 1961): 180–92.

Barr, Juliana. "A Diplomacy of Gender: Rituals of First Contact in the Land of the Tejas." *William and Mary Quarterly* 61, no. 3 (July 2004): 393–434.

Bateman, Rebecca B. "Africans and Indians: A Comparative Study of the Black Carib and Black Seminole." *Ethnohistory* 37, no. 1 (Winter 1990): 1–24.

Best, Frank J. "Recollections of April 22, 1889." *Chronicles of Oklahoma* 21, no. 1 (1943): 28–32.

Billington, Monroe. "Black Slavery in Indian Territory: The Ex-Slave Narratives." *Chronicles of Oklahoma* 60, no. 1 (1982): 56–65.

Blackburn, Bob L. "From Blood Revenge to the Lighthorsemen: Evolution of Law Enforcement Institutions among the Five Civilized Tribes to 1861." *American Indian Law Review* 8, no. 1 (1980): 49–63.

Blassingame, John W. "Using the Testimony of Ex-Slaves: Approaches and Problems." *Journal of Southern History* 41, no. 4 (November 1975): 473–92.

Bogle, Lori. "On Our Way to the Promised Land: Black Migration from Arkansas to Oklahoma, 1889–1893." *Chronicles of Oklahoma* 72, no. 2 (Summer 1994): 160–77.

Boyd, Joel D. "Creek Indian Agents, 1834–1874." *Chronicles of Oklahoma* 51, no. 1 (1973): 37–58.

Broemeling, Carol B. "Cherokee Indian Agents, 1830–1874." *Chronicles of Oklahoma* 50, no. 4 (1972–73): 437–57.

Brooks, James F., ed. Special issue. *American Indian Quarterly* 22, nos. 1–2 (Winter–Spring 1998): 123–258.

Brown, G. Gordon. "Missions and Cultural Diffusion." *American Journal of Sociology* 50 (1944): 214–19.

Brown, Thomas Elton. "Seminole Indian Agents, 1842–1874." *Chronicles of Oklahoma* 51, no. 1 (1973): 59–83.

Cade, John B. "Out of the Mouths of Ex-Slaves." *Journal of Negro History* 20, no. 1 (January 1935): 294–337.

Carney, George O. "Historic Resources of Oklahoma's All-Black Towns: A Preservation Profile." *Chronicles of Oklahoma* 69, no. 2 (Summer 1991): 116–33.

Carter, Kent. "Deciding Who Can Be Cherokee: Enrollment Records of the Dawes Commission." *Chronicles of Oklahoma* 69, no. 2 (Summer 1991): 174–205.

Chapman, Berlin B. "Freedmen and the Oklahoma Lands." *Southwestern Social Science Quarterly* 29, no. 2 (September 1948): 150–59.

Clark, Blue. "Delegates to the Constitutional Convention." *Chronicles of Oklahoma* 48, no. 4 (Winter 1970–71): 400–415.

Bibliography

Coleman, Louis. "Cyrus Byington: Missionary to the Choctaws." *Chronicles of Oklahoma* 62, no. 3 (1982): 360–87.

Craton, Michael. "From Caribs to Black Caribs: The Amerindian Roots of Servile Resistance in the Caribbean." In *In Resistance: Studies in African, Caribbean and Afro-American History*, edited by Gary Y. Okihiro, 96–116. Amherst: University of Massachusetts Press, 1986.

Crenshaw Ollinger. "The Knights of the Golden Circle: The Career of George Bickley." *American Historical Review* 47, no. 1 (October 1941): 23–50.

Crockett, Norman L. "Witness to History: Booker T. Washington Visits Boley." *Chronicles of Oklahoma* 67, no. 4 (Winter 1989–90): 382–91.

Crowe, Charles. "Indians and Blacks in White America." In *Four Centuries of Southern Indians*, edited by Charles M. Hudson, 148–69. Athens: University of Georgia Press, 1975.

Davis, J. B. "Slavery in the Cherokee Nation." *Chronicles of Oklahoma* 11 (1933): 1056–72.

Dilliard, Irving. "James Milton Turner: A Little Known Benefactor of His People." *Journal of Negro History* 19, no. 4 (October 1934): 372–411.

Doran, Michael F. "Population Statistics of Nineteenth-Century Indian Territory." *Chronicles of Oklahoma* 53, no. 4 (Winter 1975–76): 492–515.

Ellison, Mary. "Resistance to Oppression: Black Women's Response to Slavery in the United States." *Slavery and Abolition* 4 (1983): 56–63.

Fischer, LeRoy H. "The Civil War Era in Indian Territory." *Journal of the West* 12 (1973): 345–55.

Fleming, Walter L. "Pap Singleton, the Moses of the Colored Exodus." *American Journal of Sociology* 15, no. 1 (July 1909): 61–82.

Foreman, Carolyn Thomas. "Early History of Webbers Falls." *Chronicles of Oklahoma* 29 (1951–52): 444–83.

———. "John Gunter and His Family." *Alabama Historical Quarterly* 9 (Fall 1947): 412–51.

Foreman, Grant. "Dwight Mission." *Chronicles of Oklahoma* 12 (1934): 42–51.

———. "Notes of a Missionary among the Cherokees." *Chronicles of Oklahoma* 16, no. 2 (1938): 177–78.

———, ed. "Reminiscences of Mr. R. P. Vann, East of Webbers Falls, Oklahoma." *Chronicles of Oklahoma* 11 (1933): 838–44.

Fox-Genovese, Elizabeth. "Strategies and Forms of Resistance: Focus on

Slave Women in the United States." In *In Resistance: Studies in African, Caribbean and Afro-American History*, edited by Gary Y. Okihiro, 143–65. Amherst: University of Massachusetts Press, 1986.

Franks, Kenny A. "An Analysis of the Confederate Treaties with the Five Civilized Tribes." *Chronicles of Oklahoma* 50, no. 4 (1972–73): 458–78.

Gatewood, Willard B., Jr., ed. "Arkansas Negroes in the 1890s." *Arkansas Historical Quarterly* 33, no. 4 (Winter 1974): 293–325.

Gray, Linda C. "Taft: Town on the Black Frontier." *Chronicles of Oklahoma* 66, no. 4 (1988–89): 430–47.

Green, Rayna. "The Tribe Called Wannabee: Playing Indian in America and Europe." *Folklore* 99, no. 1 (1988): 30–55.

Grinde, Donald A., and Quintard Taylor. "Slaves, Freedmen, and Native Americans in Indian Territory (Oklahoma), 1865–1907." In *Peoples of Color in the American West*, edited by Sucheng Chan, Douglas Henry Daniels, Mario T. Garcia, and Terry P. Wilson, 288–300. Lexington: D. C. Heath, 1994.

Guy-Sheftall, Beverly. "The Body Politic: Black Female Sexuality and the Nineteenth-Century Euro-American Imagination." In *Skin Deep, Spirit Strong: The Black Female Body in American Culture*, edited by Kimberly Wallace-Sanders, 13–35. Ann Arbor: University of Michigan Press, 2002.

Halliburton, Janet. "Black Slavery in the Creek Nation." *Chronicles of Oklahoma* 56, no. 3 (Fall 1978): 298–314.

Halliburton, Rudi, Jr. "Black Slave Control in the Cherokee Nation." *Journal of Ethnic Studies* 3 (1975): 23–36.

———. "Origins of Black Slavery among the Cherokees." *Chronicles of Oklahoma* 52 (1974–75): 483–96.

Hallowell, A. Irving. "American Indians, White and Black: The Phenomenon of Transculturalization." *Current Anthropology* 4, no. 5 (December 1963): 519–31.

Helms, Mary W. "Negro or Indian?: The Changing Identity of a Frontier Population." In *Old Roots in New Lands: Historical and Anthropological Perspectives on Black Experiences in the Americas*, edited by Ann M. Pescatello, 157–72. Westport: Greenwood Press, 1977.

Hendrix, Janey E. "Redbird Smith and the Nighthawk Keetoowahs." *Journal of Cherokee Studies* 8 (Spring 1983): 22–39.

Hiemstra, William L. "Early Presbyterian Missions among the Choctaw and Chickasaw Indians in Mississippi." *Journal of Mississippi History* 10 (1948): 8–16.

Hill, Mozell C. "The All-Negro Communities of Oklahoma: The Natural History of a Social Movement." *Journal of Negro History* 31, no. 3 (July 1946): 254–68.

Hine, Darlene Clark, and Kate Wittenstein. "Female Slave Resistance: The Economics of Sex." In *The Black Woman Cross-Culturally*, edited by Filomina Chioma Steady, 289–99. Cambridge: Schenkman, 1981.

Holland, Sharon P. " 'If You Know I Have a History, You Will Respect Me': A Perspective on Afro-Native American Literature." *Callaloo* 17, no. 1 (Winter 1994): 334–50.

Hosmer, Brian C. "Rescued from Extinction?: The Civilizing Program in Indian Territory." *Chronicles of Oklahoma* 68, no. 2 (1990): 138–53.

Hudson, Peter J. "Choctaw Indian Dishes." In *A Choctaw Source Book*, edited by John H. Peterson Jr., 333–35. New York: Garland Publishing, 1985.

James, Parthena Louise. "Reconstruction in the Chickasaw Nation: The Freedman Problem." *Chronicles of Oklahoma* 45, no. 1 (1967): 44–57.

Jeltz, Wyatt F. "The Relations of Negroes and Choctaw and Chickasaw Indians." *Journal of Negro History* 33, no. 1 (January 1948): 24–37.

Jessup, Michael M. "Consorting with Blood and Violence: The Decline of the Oklahoma Ku Klux Klan." *Chronicles of Oklahoma* 78, no. 3 (Fall 2000): 296–315.

Johnston, James Hugo. "Documentary Evidence of the Relations of Negroes and Indians." *Journal of Negro History* 14, no. 1 (January 1929): 21–43.

Lewit, Robert T. "Indian Missions and Antislavery Sentiment: A Conflict of Evangelical and Humanitarian Ideals." *Mississippi Valley Historical Review* 50 (1963–64): 39–55.

Littlefield, Daniel F., Jr., and Mary Ann Littlefield. "The Beams Family: Free Blacks in Indian Territory." *Journal of Negro History* 61, no. 1 (1976): 16–35.

Littlefield, Daniel F., Jr., and Lonnie E. Underhill. "Black Dreams and 'Free' Homes: The Oklahoma Territory, 1891–1894." *Phylon* 34 (December 1973): 342–57.

———. "Negro Marshals in the Indian Territory." *Journal of Negro History* 56 (1971): 77–87.

——. "Slave 'Revolt' in the Cherokee Nation, 1842." *American Indian Quarterly* 3, no. 2 (Summer 1977): 121–31.

Litton, Gaston L. "The Principal Chiefs of the Cherokee Nation." *Chronicles of Oklahoma* 15, no. 3 (1937): 253–70.

Love, Paula McSpadden. "Clement Vann Rogers, 1839–1911." *Chronicles of Oklahoma* 48, no. 4 (Winter 1970–71): 389–99.

Maurer, Evan M. "Symbol and Identification in North American Indian Clothing." In *The Fabrics of Culture: The Anthropology of Clothing and Adornment*, edited by Justine M. Cordwell and Ronald A. Schwarz, 119–42. The Hague: Mouton, 1979.

McLoughlin, William Gerald. "Indian Slaveholders and Presbyterian Missionaries, 1837–1861." *Church History* 42 (1973): 535–51.

——. "Red Indians, Black Slavery and White Racism: America's Slaveholding Indians." *American Quarterly* 26, no. 4 (October 1974): 367–85.

McLoughlin, William Gerald, and Walter Conser. "Cherokees in Transition." *Journal of American History* 64, no. 3 (1977): 678–703.

Meserve, John Bartlett. "Chief William Potter Ross." *Chronicles of Oklahoma* 15, no. 1 (March 1937): 20–29.

Moore, Jessie Randolph. "The Five Great Indian Nations—Cherokee, Choctaw, Chickasaw, Seminole and Creek: The Part They Played in Behalf of the Confederacy in the War between the States." *Chronicles of Oklahoma* 29, no. 3 (1951): 324–36.

Morris, Cheryl H. "Choctaw and Chickasaw Indian Agents, 1831–1874." *Chronicles of Oklahoma* 50, no. 4 (1972–73): 415–36.

Murphy, Justin D. "Wheelock Female Seminary 1842–1861: The Acculturation and Christianization of Young Choctaw Women." *Chronicles of Oklahoma* 69, no. 1 (1991): 48–61.

Obitko, Mary Ellen. " 'Custodians of a House of Resistance': Black Women Respond to Slavery." In *Women and Men: The Consequences of Power*, edited by Dana V. Heller and Robin Ann Sheets, 256–69. Cincinnati: Office of Women's Studies, University of Cincinnati, 1977.

Perdue, Theda. "Cherokee Planters, Black Slaves and African Colonization." *Chronicles of Oklahoma* 60, no. 3 (Fall 1982): 322–31.

Piper, Adrian. "Passing for White, Passing for Black." *Transition: An International Review* 58 (1992): 4–32.

Poikal, George J. "Racist Assumptions of the Nineteenth Century Christian Missionary." *International Review of Missions* 59 (1970): 271–85.

Porter, Kenneth W. "Notes Supplementary to 'Relations between Negroes and Indians.' " *Journal of Negro History* 18, no. 3 (July 1933): 282–321.

——. "Relations between Negroes and Indians within the Present Limits of the United States." *Journal of Negro History* 17, no. 3 (July 1932): 287–367.

Raczka, Paul M. "Sacred Robes of the Blackfoot and Other Northern Plains Tribes." *American Indian Art Magazine* 17, no. 3 (1992): 66–73.

Rampp, Lary C. "Negro Troop Activity in Indian Territory, 1863–1865." *Chronicles of Oklahoma* 47 (1969): 531–59.

Records, Ralph H. "Recollections of April 19, 1892." *Chronicles of Oklahoma* 21, no. 1 (1943): 16–27.

Redfield, Robert, Ralph Linton, and Melville J. Herskovits. "A Memorandum for the Study of Acculturation." *American Anthropologist* 38 (1936): 149–52.

Roberson, Jere W. "Edward P. McCabe and the Langston Experiment." *Chronicles of Oklahoma* 51, no. 3 (Fall 1973): 343–55.

Ronda, James P. " 'We Have a Country': Race, Geography, and the Invention of Indian Territory." *Journal of the Early Republic* 19, no. 4 (Winter 1999): 739–55.

Routh, E. C. "Early Missionaries to the Cherokees." *Chronicles of Oklahoma* 15, no. 4 (1937): 449–65.

Rucker, Alvin. "The Story of Slave Uprising in Oklahoma: Drastic Laws Passed by Cherokees to 'Control' Negroes." *Daily Oklahoman*, 30 October 1932, sec. C.

Rushforth, Brett. " 'A Little Flesh We Offer You': The Origins of Indian Slavery in New France." *William and Mary Quarterly* 60, no. 4 (October 2003): 777–808.

Saunt, Claudio. "The Paradox of Freedom: Tribal Sovereignty and Emancipation during the Reconstruction of Indian Territory." *Journal of Southern History* 70, no. 1 (February 2004): 63–94.

Schweninger, Loren. "Prosperous Blacks in the South, 1790–1880." *American Historical Review* 95, no. 1 (February 1990): 31–56.

Scott, Rebecca J. "Exploring the Meaning of Freedom: Postemancipation Societies in Comparative Perspective." *Hispanic American Historical Review* 68 (1988): 407–28.

Searcy, Martha Condray. "The Introduction of African Slavery into the Creek Nation." *Georgia Historical Quarterly* 66 (1982): 21–32.

Self, Nancy Hope. "The Building of the Railroads in the Cherokee Nation." *Chronicles of Oklahoma* 49, no. 2 (Summer 1971): 180–205.

Shannon, Timothy J. "Dressing for Success on the Mohawk Frontier: Hendrick, William Johnson, and the Indian Fashion." *William and Mary Quarterly* 53, no. 1 (January 1996): 13–42.

Slater, Mary Ann. "The Controversial Birth of the Oklahoma Writers' Project." *Chronicles of Oklahoma* 68, no. 1 (1990): 72–89.

Spaulding, Arminto. "From the Natchez Trace to Oklahoma: Development of Christian Civilization among the Choctaws, 1800–1860." *Chronicles of Oklahoma* 45, no. 1 (1967): 2–24.

Strong, Pauline Turner, and Barrik Van Winkle. " 'Indian Blood': Reflections on the Reckoning and Refiguring of Native North American Identity." *Cultural Anthropology* 11, no. 4 (November 1996): 547–76.

Sturm, Circe. "Blood Politics, Racial Classification, and Cherokee National Identity: The Trials and Tribulations of the Cherokee Freedmen." *American Indian Quarterly* 22 (Winter–Spring 1998): 230–58.

Tattershall, Doug. " 'Our Rights, Our Country, Our Race': W. P. Ross and the *Cherokee Advocate*, 1844–1848." *Chronicles of Oklahoma* 70, no. 3 (Fall 1992): 326–37.

Tennant, H. S. "The History of the Chisholm Trail." *Chronicles of Oklahoma* 14, no. 1 (March 1936): 108–22.

Terborg-Penn, Rosalyn. "Black Women in Resistance: A Cross-Cultural Perspective." In *In Resistance: Studies in African, Caribbean and Afro-American History*, edited by Gary Y. Okihiro, 186–209. Amherst: University of Massachusetts Press, 1986.

Tyler, Ronnie C. "Fugitive Slaves in Mexico." *Journal of Negro History* 57, no. 1 (January 1972): 1–12.

Warren, Hanna R. "Reconstruction in the Cherokee Nation." *Chronicles of Oklahoma* 45 (1967–68): 180–89.

Washington, Booker T. "Boley: A Negro Town in the West." *Outlook* 88 (4 January 1908): 28–31.

Welsh, Carol H. "Struggle for Land." *Chronicles of Oklahoma* 72, no. 1 (1994): 36–51.

Bibliography

Welter, Barbara. "She Hath Done What She Could: Protestant Women's Missionary Careers in Nineteenth-Century America." *American Quarterly* 30 (1978): 624–38.

Wickett, Murray R. "The Fear of 'Negro Domination': The Rise of Segregation and Disfranchisement in Oklahoma." *Chronicles of Oklahoma* 78, no. 1 (Spring 2000): 44–65.

Williams, Nudie E. "They Fought for Votes: The White Politician and the Black Editor." *Chronicles of Oklahoma* 64, no. 1 (1986): 18–35.

Willis, William S. "Divide and Rule: Red, White, and Black in the Southeast." *Journal of Negro History* 48 (1963): 157–76.

Willson, Walt. "Freedmen in the Oklahoma Territory during Reconstruction." *Chronicles of Oklahoma* 49, no. 2 (Summer 1971): 230–44.

Wilson, Terry P. "Blood Quantum: Native American Mixed Bloods." In *Racially Mixed People in America*, edited by Maria P. P. Root, 108–25. Newbury Park: Sage Publications, 1992.

Winston, Sanford. "Indian Slavery in the Carolina Region." *Journal of Negro History* 19 (1934): 431–40.

Wood, Betty. "Some Aspects of Female Resistance to Chattel Slavery in Low Country Georgia, 1763–1815." *Historical Journal* 30 (1987): 603–22.

Woodward, C. Vann. "History from Slave Sources." *American Historical Review* 79, no. 2 (April 1974): 470–81.

Wright, Muriel H. "American Indian Corn Dishes." *Chronicles of Oklahoma* 36 (Summer 1958): 155–66.

Yarbrough, Fay. "Legislating Women's Sexuality: Cherokee Marriage Laws in the Nineteenth Century." *Journal of Social History* 38, no. 2 (Winter 2004): 385–406.

Yetman, Norman R. "Ex-Slave Interviews and the Historiography of Slavery." *American Quarterly* 36, no. 2 (Summer 1984): 181–210.

Dissertations and Theses

Boyd, Thomas J. "The Use of Negro Troops by Kansas during the Civil War." Master's thesis, Kansas State Teachers College, 1950.

Minges, Patrick Neal. "The Keetoowah Society and the Avocation of Religious Nationalism in the Cherokee Nation, 1855–1867." Ph.D. diss., Union Theological Seminary, 1999.

Morrison, James D. "Social History of the Choctaw, 1865–1907." Ph.D. diss., University of Oklahoma, 1951.

Roethler, Michael. "Negro Slavery among the Cherokee Indians, 1540–1866." Ph.D. diss., Fordham University, 1964.

Sameth, Sigmund. "Creek Negroes: A Study of Race Relations." Master's thesis, University of Oklahoma, 1940.

Schwendemann, Glen. "Negro Exodus to Kansas: First Phase, March–July, 1879." Master's thesis, University of Oklahoma, 1957.

Tolson, Arthur L. "A History of Langston, Oklahoma: 1890–1950." Master's thesis, Oklahoma State University, 1952.

———. "The Negro in Oklahoma Territory, 1889–1907: A Study of Racial Discrimination." Ph.D. diss., University of Oklahoma, 1966.

Wilson, Raleigh Archie. "Negro and Indian Relations in the Five Civilized Tribes from 1865 to 1907." Ph.D. diss., State University of Iowa, 1949.

Websites

"Born in Slavery: Slave Narratives from the Federal Writers' Project, 1936–1938." http://memory.loc.gov/aminem/snhtml/snhome.html.

Descendants of Freedmen of the Five Civilized Tribes. "Mission." http://www.freedmen5tribes.com/Mission.htm. 28 June 2006.

———. Press release for the Fourth Annual Conference on 3 June 2006. http://www.freedmen5tribes.com/Conference.htm. 20 May 2006.

Lee-St. John, Jeninne. "The Cherokee Nation's New Battle," *Time Magazine Online*, 21 June 2007. http://www.time.com/time/nation/article/0,8599,1635873,00.html. 23 June 2007.

Watson, Diane. "HR 2824." http://thomas.loc.gov/cgi-bin/query/z?c110:H.R.2824. 22 June 2007.

Index

Abert, James W., 93, 271 (n. 53)

Abolition debates, 126, 130, 133, 137, 139, 282 (n. 39)

Acculturation, 20, 21, 22, 90–92, 96, 98–99, 101–2, 109, 125. *See also* Belonging, sense of; Cultural identity

Adair, William Penn, 97, 135–36, 283 (n. 41), 290 (n. 15)

African American freedpeople: legalistic challenges of, 21; and Cherokee laws, 28, 48; and European American belief systems, 28; kidnapping of, 62, 66–67; status of, 64, 174, 187, 219, 259 (n. 32); education of, 162, 174, 176, 291 (n. 23); violence toward, 174–75, 185, 189, 191; Indians intermarrying with, 268 (n. 34)

African Americans: as slave owners, 3; cultural identity of, 22; Indian spaces as sites of refuge for, 52, 268 (n. 34); and "crossland Negroes," 82, 92, 94, 96, 99, 263–64 (n. 17); black separatism, 188–89, 192, 193; westward migration to Oklahoma Territory, 188–92, 194, 197, 303 (n. 34), 304 (n. 42), 305 (n. 44), 306–7 (n. 52); and black disenfranchisement cam-

paigns, 194, 197; and constitutional convention, 197; historical narratives of, 201–2; "two-ness" of, 202–3, 204. *See also* Enslaved blacks

African Cherokee freedpeople: and complexities of freedom, 20, 52, 71–72, 174–77; status of, 21, 64–65, 71–72, 73, 153–54, 165, 174, 175, 178, 199; and blood ties, 21, 87, 154, 159, 177, 181, 203, 210, 212, 264–65 (n. 24); citizenship of, 21, 154, 160–62, 164, 165–74, 176, 181–83, 199, 204, 206, 207, 208–16, 290 (n. 17), 294–95 (n. 43), 296 (nn. 52, 57); connection to Cherokee Nation, 21, 156–59, 162, 165, 176–77, 199, 202, 203, 205; and national identity, 21–22, 155; kidnapping of, 64, 66, 70–72, 73; and Indian identity, 73; connection to Indian Territory, 82, 155, 203; and herbal medicine, 107; on Civil War journeys, 145–46; searching for family members, 155, 159; return to Indian Territory, 155, 161–62, 204; resettlement patterns of, 158–59, 289 (n. 12); rebuilding after Civil War, 159–60; education of, 162–65,

343